MW01599598

SPLINTERED INNOCENCE: SURVIVAL

Harvest Meadow
Splintered Innocence: Survival

Published by Spines
ISBN: 979-8-89691-815-8

SPLINTERED INNOCENCE: SURVIVAL

Inspired by Real Events

HARVEST MEADOW

CONTENTS

❦ I ❦

A NEW BEGINNING

Lucas shifted uncomfortably on the bench outside the navy recruiter's office, the low hum of fluorescent lights accentuating the tension in the air. He clutched a worn photograph between his trembling fingers—a snapshot of himself as a child, grinning broadly next to a sister he barely remembered. It was the kind of picture that should have symbolized hope, but to Lucas, it felt like a reminder of everything he'd lost.

The recruiter finally emerged, clipboard under one arm, expression grim. "High blood pressure," he said without ceremony. "I'm sorry, son. You can't ship out."

In that instant, the navy's doors slammed shut. Lucas's chest tightened as the recruiter walked away, the hallway echoing with footsteps that only underscored his failure. He let out a ragged breath, half-wishing he could crumble to the floor and vanish. Another rejection, another testament to the gnawing doubt that he was never quite good enough.

He pulled the photo close, staring at his younger self—bright-eyed, naïve, certain that life held some promise. If only he'd known, Lucas thought bitterly. The dull ache behind his eyes warned him he was about to slip back into the old habit he loathed but couldn't resist: a quick high to drown out the guilt.

But what choice did he have? The tears that pricked at his vision reminded him that everything—his sense of worth, his ability to provide for Sophia, and the fleeting hope of a stable future—now rested on an unsteady foundation. With a heavy sigh, Lucas rose from the bench, the photograph still in hand, and stepped out into the glaring sun, bracing himself for the void that awaited him at home.

Lucas was a strikingly handsome man, standing at 5'10" with a lean, slender build that contradicted the toll substance abuse had taken on his body. Despite his outwardly appealing appearance, Lucas's life had been anything but glamorous, marked by an undercurrent of unhappiness and insecurity that few could ever guess just by looking at him. Raised in the comfort of privilege, he grew up with all the material wealth that should have afforded him security and contentment. Yet, it never filled the void within him. His early years were tainted by the absence of genuine emotional support, as his biological mother, an alcoholic, struggled to care for her children. Unable to properly raise them, she made the heart-wrenching decision to place some of her children into foster care, as she was unable to provide the care they needed.

Lucas was the fourth child in a family that had already been stretched thin. At the age of three, his parents, realizing they could not afford to care for all of their children, made the difficult decision to put two of them up for adoption. They chose the youngest two, reasoning that it would be easier for these children to adapt to new families than for the older ones. As a result, Lucas was separated from his older siblings and placed in the care of an adoption agency.

The agency paired Lucas and his elder sister, Anna, together, ensuring that the two would remain siblings despite the challenges of adoption. Their new family, eager to adopt, welcomed the pair with open arms, but it quickly became apparent that the dynamics within this new home would be far from ideal. Lucas's adoptive mother, determined to provide a life of comfort, showered him with affection, fulfilling every request and indulging his every whim. In contrast, Anna received a far more disciplined upbringing, with stricter rules and fewer freedoms. The difference in treatment did not go unnoticed, and it created an atmosphere of favoritism that was deeply felt by both siblings. Lucas, in particular, developed a sense of entitlement that created tension between him and his sister. The uneven distribution of love and attention left its mark on Lucas, who grew to believe he deserved more than what was being offered.

While Lucas appeared to thrive in his new home, a deep bitterness began to grow within him. His adoptive parents' proximity to his biological family was a constant reminder of the rejection he had endured. They lived close enough that Lucas attended school with his siblings from his birth family, a daily reminder of the life he had been forced to leave behind. The fact that his biological parents went on to have more children after Lucas was adopted only deepened his feelings of abandonment. He began to feel that there was something inherently wrong with him, something that made him unworthy of their love or care. His bitterness simmered beneath the surface, and by the time he reached high school, it manifested in his increasing drug use—a means of numbing the pain of his perceived inadequacies.

Lucas's descent into substance abuse was gradual but inevitable. His emotional struggles, compounded by a growing sense of alienation, drove him further into the arms of addiction. He began using drugs not only to escape the pain but also to fill the emptiness that lingered in his soul. At the same time, he demanded more and more from his adoptive mother, constantly testing her love and affection. His need for validation became insatiable, and his drug use spiraled out of control, escalating as his emotional turmoil deepened.

It was during this tumultuous period that Lucas met Sophia. From the moment their paths crossed, he felt an intense connection, a sense of hope that perhaps, just maybe, he had found the one person who could offer him the unconditional love he so desperately craved. Sophia, with her fiery red hair and striking beauty, seemed to embody everything Lucas had longed for. Despite her outward appearance, which suggested a fiery and passionate personality, Sophia was actually quiet and reserved, preferring solitude over social interaction. She felt misunderstood by those around her and harbored a deep sense of loneliness.

While Sophia loved her parents, she resented her siblings intensely, feeling that they stole the attention and affection that should have been hers. She yearned to escape, to break free from the family that had overshadowed her existence. In her mind, leaving her family behind and starting fresh with a new identity was the only way she could find peace. This deep-seated desire for escape would ultimately open the door for Lucas to enter her life.

Lucas, ever the charmer, quickly learned how to use his charisma to his advantage. Over the years, he had perfected the art of persuasion, knowing exactly what to say and how to act to gain the affection and loyalty of those around him. With Sophia, it was no different. He sensed her longing for freedom and recognized that he could be the means to that end. What he didn't know, however, was that Sophia's desire to leave her family was so strong that she would have agreed to anything that promised her an escape. When Lucas proposed, she accepted, and the young couple married quickly, their lives intertwining in a way neither could have predicted.

Within months of their marriage, Sophia found herself pregnant. The reality of impending parenthood hit Lucas hard, and for the first time in his life, he felt a sense of responsibility. He realized that he needed to provide for his new family, so he made the decision to join the Navy, hoping that it would offer him the structure and stability he had never known. This was the first time Lucas attempted to take real responsibility for those around him, and the weight of it took a physical and emotional toll on him.

Despite the anxiety and pressure, he passed the initial physical examination and was prepared to ship out. However, on the day of his final physical, he was disqualified due to high blood pressure, a devastating blow that deepened his feelings of inadequacy. The rejection left Lucas feeling more inferior than ever before. His sense of failure drove him further into the grip of addiction. Unable to find solace in anything else, he turned to drugs yet again to numb the pain.

Meanwhile, he found work as a janitor in the apartment complex where he and Sophia lived. This job served as a grim symbol of the instability that would define much of their life together. His transient employment, combined with drug use, ensured that they were constantly on the move, never truly settling into any real sense of security. And yet, for Lucas and Sophia, returning to their families was never an option. They had chosen to carve out their own path, uncertain though it was.

In the years that followed, their lives became a study in contradictions: two souls searching for something neither could name. They clung to each other, attempting to forge a future amid the wreckage of their pasts, even as addiction and the weight of responsibility pushed them further apart. Lucas and Sophia's story was not one of triumph but of survival—a fight to stay afloat in a world that never seemed to offer them the peace they sought.

❧ 2 ❧
CRISIS UNFOLDS

Sophia jolted awake, heart pounding, the sheets twisted around her legs. A searing pain tore through her lower abdomen, so sharp it stole her breath. For one delirious moment, she hoped it was just a cramp—a bad dream, maybe. But when she tried to shift her weight, the agony intensified, confirming that this was no nightmare.

"Lucas!" she choked out, her voice barely above a whisper as she fumbled for the lamp on the nightstand. "Something's wrong."

Sophia's pregnancy had been relatively smooth. Throughout the months, she had experienced no major complications, and everything seemed to be progressing as expected. The baby wasn't due for a few more weeks, and her doctor had assured her that she was on track for a healthy delivery. However, that calm was shattered in the early hours of the morning when she was jolted awake by an intense, sharp cramp. It was unlike anything she had felt before, and it sent waves of panic crashing over her. The cramp tightened in her lower abdomen, and for a moment, it felt as if her body itself was betraying her.

"Lucas, wake up! Something's wrong!" Her voice was steady but laced with an urgency that pierced the quiet night. She jabbed her elbow into his side, the force enough to stir him from his groggy slumber.

Lucas, who had stayed up far too late again, had barely found any rest. His eyes fluttered open, struggling to focus as the haze of sleep lingered, and his mind tried to catch up with the situation. The alcohol from the night before was still heavy on him, and his senses were dulled. He turned over too quickly and fell out of bed in the process, disoriented and clumsy. For a moment, he just sat there, his hands running through his disheveled hair as he tried to shake off the drunken stupor that still clung to him. At least he had the sense to fall asleep fully clothed, though finding his shoes now felt like an insurmountable task.

Sophia didn't wait for him. The cramp intensified, and she stood up slowly, clutching her stomach. Her legs felt weak, but she managed to stay on her feet, driven by a deep, visceral instinct. She moved to the dresser, searching for something to wear. Her trembling hands grazed over the fabric in the drawer before pulling out a simple summer dress—something easy and comfortable. It was the practical choice. Her heart was racing in her chest, and her thoughts were a whirlwind of fear. But as she stood up straight again, a small glimmer of relief washed over her—perhaps it wasn't as bad as she initially feared.

"The pain... it's starting to ease. Maybe it was nothing," she said, her voice quiet as she turned toward Lucas, who was still struggling to get his shoes on. His movements were erratic, and he kept wobbling and stumbling. He looked completely out of sorts.

"Lucas, are you drunk?" Sophia's voice cut through the fog in the room. The frustration and worry in her tone were unmistakable.

Lucas, barely able to keep his eyes open, muttered, "No, babe. I didn't drink tonight. I'm just... really tired." His words were sluggish; he didn't lie; he had only smoked pot tonight, but that didn't make it any easier to shake off the haze in which he found himself.

"Yeah, right," Sophia retorted, her impatience growing. The pain was subsiding, but her anxiety had only intensified. She needed to get to the hospital, and she needed Lucas to be coherent. "Let's just go back to bed."

Lucas, now managing to get one shoe on, muttered under his breath as he fell back onto the bed. "Geez, Sophia, I just got my shoe on. Whatever." His words were muffled by the pillow as he sprawled across the bed, taking up most of the space.

Sophia's frustration was noticeable, but there was no time for an argument. She sighed deeply, walking over to grab a pillow for herself. But as she turned back around, the sharp pain that had subsided earlier suddenly returned with a vengeance. It struck deep within her abdomen, and she gasped, doubling over. The scream that escaped her was loud and raw, echoing through the room in a desperate cry of pain.

Lucas shot up from the bed, his eyes snapping open in panic. "Sophia! What's wrong? Are you okay?"

But Sophia was already gripping her stomach, the pain becoming unbearable. "Get me my shoes," she managed to choke out, her voice strained, her body wracked with fear. But as the words left her mouth, she felt a sudden rush of fluid between her legs. It wasn't the simple discharge she had expected; it was blood. A lot of blood.

"Lucas! Now! I think I'm losing the baby!" The terror in her voice was unmistakable, and her eyes, wide with fear, locked onto his. For a moment, he froze, unable to process the enormity of what was happening. The sight of the blood, the fear in Sophia's eyes—it was as though the room itself was closing in on him.

Her frantic shout jolted him into motion. He rushed over to her, supporting her weight as she swayed unsteadily on her feet. "We need to go to the hospital. Now!" she cried, her panic palpable.

He helped her to the door, his mind a blur of chaotic thoughts. The only thing that mattered now was getting her the help she needed. She was barefoot, the blood from the floor staining her feet with every step she took. Once outside, Lucas remembered he had left the car keys inside. Panic surged through him as he sprinted back into the house. His hands fumbled in the dark, desperately searching for the keys. After what seemed like an eternity, he finally found them and ran back outside.

The engine of their old Chevette sputtered to life, and Lucas slammed his foot on the accelerator, pushing the car faster than he had ever driven before. His hands gripped the wheel with white knuckles, and the car swerved erratically as he sped down the street, narrowly avoiding obstacles. Sophia's cries only spurred him on, urging him to go faster.

"Hold on, Sophia!" he shouted, his voice barely audible over the screech of the tires as he rounded the corner.

Every bump in the road seemed to make the pain worse for Sophia. She winced with each turn, her body jostling in the seat, her breath coming in short, sharp gasps. The fear that had been steadily growing within her now overtook everything else. She could feel the weight of it—this terrifying uncertainty that made her question whether she would make it to the hospital in time.

Finally, they reached the emergency room. Lucas didn't bother with a proper parking space. He slammed the car to a halt right in front of the ER doors, throwing the car into park with almost reckless abandon. Without hesitation, he jumped out and ran to the passenger side, flinging the door open and rushing to Sophia's side.

"Help! Someone help!" he shouted as he helped Sophia out of the car. Her feet were covered in blood, and as she staggered toward the hospital doors, the bloody footprints she left behind seemed to symbolize the growing terror in Lucas's chest.

A nurse was quick to notice, rushing toward them with a wheelchair. "Please, follow me," she said calmly, though Lucas could see the urgency in her eyes.

A second nurse, more composed than Lucas felt, approached Sophia. "Hello, sweetie. I'm Emily. Can you tell me what happened?" she asked, her voice gentle and soothing, a stark contrast to the panic pulsing in Lucas's veins.

"She's bleeding! She's in pain!" Lucas practically shouted, his words tumbling out in frantic bursts.

Emily remained unfazed by his outburst, her attention fixed on Sophia. "How far along are you?" she asked, her tone calm and professional.

"Thirty-six weeks," Sophia whispered, the words barely escaping her lips.

Emily nodded, her expression softening. "And when did the pain start?"

"Just tonight. Everything had been fine until now," Sophia replied, her voice faltering.

"Don't worry," Emily said, offering a reassuring smile. "You're in the best place you can be."

With swift professionalism, Emily led Sophia into the emergency room, where a team of nurses and doctors quickly took over. They worked with a practiced efficiency that, while reassuring, only heightened Lucas's sense of helplessness. Sophia's vitals were taken, and a heart monitor was attached to her swollen belly. The steady rhythm of the baby's heartbeat offered a brief moment of relief to Lucas, though Sophia's anxiety remained palpable.

As Emily and another nurse continued to prepare for further examination, a doctor entered the room. Dr. Davis, a tall man with kind eyes, introduced himself. "Hello, I'm Dr. Davis. Let's take a look and see what's going on."

Sophia tried to explain what had happened, but the pain was intensifying, and she could barely keep her voice steady. Dr. Davis remained calm, his hands gentle as he touched her knees. "I'm going to take a look now," he said. "Is that okay?"

Sophia nodded, trying to focus on his calm presence as he lifted the blanket and continued his examination. A few minutes passed, and Sophia continued her recounting, but soon Dr. Davis closed her legs and turned to the nurse.

"Book an OR," he instructed, his voice firm.

Emily wasted no time. She quickly moved to unlock Sophia's bed and began wheeling it out of the room. "We need to move quickly. You'll be in good hands," she assured Sophia, though the urgency in her voice did nothing to calm Lucas.

"Wait! What's happening?" Lucas asked, his voice desperate.

"Sir, you should go to the waiting room. We'll take care of her," Dr. Davis said, his tone gentle but insistent. "Emily will show you where to go."

Lucas wanted to argue, to fight against the feeling of helplessness, but he could only watch as Sophia was wheeled away, the fear gnawing at him with each passing second. The doctor was right—there was nothing he could do now but wait.

❦ 3 ❦
ELIZABETH'S BIG DAY

"Today is going to be the best day ever," Elizabeth whispered to herself, swinging her legs off the bed. She was two and a half years old, and in her mind, that practically made her a grown-up. She hopped onto the floor, blinking away the last of her sleep. If she could just wake her parents, the day could begin. And what a day it would be—by nightfall, she would finally be a big sister.

The excitement buzzing in her small frame was more than her toddler heart could contain. For weeks, her parents had been preparing her, talking about the arrival of a baby sister. They explained how life would change, how she'd have to share her toys and help care for the baby. Elizabeth had taken all of it in with a sense of importance, feeling ready for this new chapter.

The morning sunlight filtered through her bedroom curtains, casting a golden glow on her small bed and scattered stuffed animals, illuminating all the things she was happy to share with her new baby sister. As Elizabeth stood there looking around the room, she imagined holding her baby sister for the first time. She told herself again, "Today is the best day ever."

Determined to prove just how grown-up she was, Elizabeth got herself dressed before her parents even stirred. Her mother, ever the planner, had laid out a blue dress, a pink pinafore, and white tights the night before, knowing Elizabeth liked to be independent. But Elizabeth, in her youthful determination to make her own choices, made a small adjustment. She pushed aside the pink shoes her mother had chosen and instead tugged on her bright yellow rain boots. They were her favorite, after all. Rain boots made her feel adventurous, like she could conquer anything.

Satisfied with her ensemble, Elizabeth padded out of her bedroom and into the hallway. Her heart raced with anticipation as she approached her parents' door. The brass knob felt cool in her hand as she turned it ever so carefully, cracking the door open just enough to peek inside. The room was dim, the curtains drawn, and her parents were still fast asleep. Elizabeth furrowed her brows. Didn't they know how important today was? How could they still be sleeping?

She pushed the door open a little wider and tiptoed to her mother's side of the bed. Her mother's long hair spilled over the pillow in soft waves, and her breathing was slow and steady. Elizabeth leaned close, her tiny hand gently patting her mother's arm. "Mommy, it's time to get up," she whispered, her voice sweet but insistent.

Her mother stirred slightly, murmured something unintelligible, and rolled over, brushing Elizabeth's hand away.

Undeterred, Elizabeth shifted her focus to her father. Circling the bed, she climbed onto her tiptoes and poked his cheek with one small finger. "Daddy, wake up," she said again, her voice a touch louder this time.

Lucas groaned but opened one eye, squinting at his daughter. A faint smile crossed his face as he pulled her onto his lap. "Shh," he said softly, his voice thick with sleep. His breath carried the unmistakable scent of whiskey and pot from the night before, but Elizabeth didn't notice. "Let Mommy sleep a little longer."

He stood, lifting Elizabeth in his arms, and carried her out of the room, closing the door gently behind them. As they entered the kitchen, he flipped on the light, making Elizabeth squint for a moment as her eyes adjusted. Lucas set her down on one of the chairs at the small kitchen table. "So," he began, his tone lighter now as he stretched and rubbed his stubbled chin, "what does my big girl want for breakfast? You can have anything you want today."

Elizabeth's face lit up with delight. She clapped her hands together, listing everything she could think of in rapid succession.

"Pancakes, cereal, donuts, chocolate milk, waffles, bacon, and ice cream!" she declared, her tiny voice bubbling with enthusiasm.

Lucas chuckled, reaching above the fridge for his "morning wake-me-up" bottle of whiskey. He unscrewed the cap and took a quick swig, his movements practiced and unthinking. "How about we start with pancakes and chocolate milk?" he suggested, setting the bottle aside. "I'm not sure your tiny tummy can hold all that food, kiddo."

Elizabeth nodded solemnly, as if the suggestion were a fair compromise. "Okay, Daddy," she agreed, swinging her legs back and forth under the table.

Then Elizabeth dragged a chair from the dining table to the kitchen counter, her tiny fingers gripping the wooden edges as she pulled it along the tiled floor with a determined expression. The chair's legs screeched against the floor, but Elizabeth didn't care. Today was a special day, and she wanted to help Daddy make breakfast. She climbed onto the chair with a little grunt and perched herself on her knees, leaning over the counter with wide eyes as she watched her father get to work.

Lucas, still slightly groggy but amused by his daughter's enthusiasm, turned on the stove and placed a skillet on the burner. The soft click-click of the ignition was followed by the whoosh of blue flames licking the bottom of the pan. He reached into the cabinets above the counter, retrieving a mixing bowl and a spoon. "Okay, Baby Girl, let's get started," he said, setting the items in front of Elizabeth. "Chef Elizabeth, reporting for duty."

Elizabeth giggled, covering her mouth with her hands. "I'm not a chef, Daddy. I'm just Elizabeth!"

"Well, just Elizabeth," Lucas replied with a wink, "I need you to help me make the best pancakes ever. Think you can handle it?"

"Yes!" Elizabeth shouted, her voice ringing with confidence.

Lucas grabbed a box of pancake mix from the pantry and set it beside her. From a nearby drawer, he pulled out a measuring cup, handing it to her with a look of mock seriousness. "Now, this is very important. Fill this cup all the way up, but don't spill a drop."

Elizabeth nodded solemnly. "I can do it," she promised, her tiny hands clutching the cup as though it were the most precious object in the world.

While Elizabeth carefully poured the pancake mix from the box,

Lucas turned to the refrigerator to grab milk and eggs. He cracked the fridge door open, its soft hum filling the quiet kitchen. As he reached for the milk carton, he glanced over his shoulder to check on Elizabeth. She was focused, her tongue peeking out of the corner of her mouth as she poured the mix into the measuring cup. A small cloud of white powder puffed into the air, landing on the counter—and a little on her dress—but she didn't notice.

When Lucas returned to her side, he chuckled at the sight of the flour-dusted countertop. "Good job, sweetie," he said, his tone warm. "You filled it up just right."

Elizabeth beamed. "I told you I could do it, Daddy."

"Now pour it into the bowl, okay?" Lucas held the bowl steady as Elizabeth tilted the cup. The pancake mix tumbled out in a soft cascade, leaving a faint trail on the rim of the bowl. Lucas added the milk and cracked two eggs, the sharp tap of the shells against the counter making Elizabeth jump slightly.

"Now comes the fun part," Lucas said, handing her the spoon. "Stir it all up!"

Elizabeth gripped the spoon tightly and began to stir with all her might. The batter swirled around the bowl, the sticky mix clinging to the sides as she mixed it with determined energy. Her little arm worked furiously until it began to ache. "Here, Daddy. I think it's ready now," she said, holding the spoon out to him with a satisfied smile.

Lucas took the bowl and gave the batter a few final, expert stirs. "Perfect," he declared. "You're a natural, kiddo."

Elizabeth giggled again, puffing up with pride as Lucas poured the first dollop of batter into the skillet. The batter sizzled on contact, filling the kitchen with the warm, comforting aroma of pancakes cooking. Elizabeth leaned forward in her chair, her eyes widening as she watched her father work. He flipped the pancakes with a quick flick of the wrist, creating perfect golden circles.

"Big ones and little ones," Elizabeth said, pointing to the varying sizes. "Daddy, can I have the littlest one?"

"Of course, Baby Girl. The littlest one is all yours," Lucas replied.

As the pancakes finished cooking, Lucas arranged them carefully on a plate, stacking them with the precision of an artist. Then he reached into the fridge for the chocolate syrup and a carton of milk, while Elizabeth returned to the table to receive her special pancakes. Elizabeth bounced on her chair as she watched him pour the milk into a small glass, adding a generous squirt of syrup and stirring it with a spoon.

"What are you making now, Daddy?" she asked, her voice full of curiosity.

"Chocolate milk," Lucas replied. "The perfect pairing for pancakes."

He set the glass aside and returned to the pancakes, drizzling the chocolate syrup over them in swirling patterns. Elizabeth gasped as he stepped back, revealing a teddy bear face made entirely of pancakes and syrup.

"It's a teddy bear!" she exclaimed, clapping her hands. "You made a pancake teddy bear!"

"Only the best for my Baby Girl," Lucas said with a grin. He placed the plate and glass in front of her, pulling out a chair to sit beside her at the table.

Elizabeth dug into her breakfast with gusto, taking big bites of pancake and washing them down with chocolate milk. Her feet swung back and forth beneath the table as she ate, her excitement bubbling over. "Daddy, this is the best breakfast ever!" she declared between bites. "When my baby sister gets here, can we make her a teddy bear pancake, too?"

"Of course we can," Lucas replied, resting his chin in his hand as he watched her eat. "But you'll have to teach her how to mix the batter, okay?"

"I will! I'll teach her everything," Elizabeth said proudly. "We're going to do so many fun things together."

Lucas smiled, his heart warming at her enthusiasm. "I bet you two are going to be the best sisters ever."

When Elizabeth finished her breakfast, Lucas picked her up and carried her toward the bedroom. "Mommy, it's time to get up," he said softly, rubbing Sophia's shoulder.

Sophia stirred, her eyes fluttering open. "I'm up," she murmured, stretching. "Let's do this."

While Sophia got dressed with Lucas's help, Elizabeth busied herself with the small suitcase her mother had packed the night before. She wrapped her arms around it and lifted it with a determined grunt. "I got it!" she announced proudly, her tiny frame wobbling under the weight.

Sophia smiled. "You're so strong, sweetie. Are you sure it's not too heavy?"

"Nope! I'm strong like Daddy," Elizabeth said, puffing out her chest.

When the family was ready, they climbed into the car and set off for the hospital. The drive took about half an hour, but for Elizabeth, it felt like no time at all. She chattered nonstop about all the things she would do with her baby sister, painting a vivid picture of their future together.

"First, we'll ride ponies together," she began, her hands gesturing excitedly. "Then we'll have tea parties with all my dolls. And I'll teach her how to tie her shoes and color in the lines!"

Lucas glanced at her through the rearview mirror, his lips curling into a smile. "She's lucky to have you as a big sister, Baby Girl."

Elizabeth grinned, her rain boots swinging back and forth. Today was already the best day ever, and she knew it was only going to get better.

When the couple arrived at the hospital, they were greeted by a cheerful woman at the front desk. She smiled warmly and brought out a wheelchair for Sophia, who sat down with a slight wince. Elizabeth, clutching her father's hand, could hardly contain her excitement.

"Are we going to see the baby now? Is it here? Is it my sister?" Elizabeth asked, her questions tumbling out in rapid succession.

Lucas laughed softly, ruffling her hair. "Not yet, Baby Girl. We'll settle Mommy in first. Then you'll meet the baby."

The lady escorted the family to the elevator, making small talk with Sophia about how exciting it must be to welcome another child. Sophia responded politely, but her focus remained on her family, her hand brushing against Lucas's arm every so often, as if drawing strength from him.

When they reached the third floor, the lady directed Lucas and Elizabeth to a waiting room filled with bright toys, picture books, and a small television playing cartoons. Elizabeth's eyes lit up at the sight, and she released her father's hand to run toward a tower of blocks.

"Take care of her," Sophia murmured as the lady wheeled her away.

Lucas nodded. "Always," he said with great confidence in her. "You'll do great."

For a while, Elizabeth entertained herself with the toys, her laughter filling the small room as she built towers and knocked them down. Lucas sat nearby, watching television absentmindedly but glancing up every so often to smile at his daughter.

"Look, Daddy!" Elizabeth called out, holding up a wobbly stack of blocks.

"That's amazing, sweetheart," he said, giving her a thumbs-up.

But as time dragged on, Elizabeth's excitement began to wane. She wandered back and forth between the toys and her father, occasionally tugging at his sleeve.

"Daddy, is it time yet? Can we see the baby?"

"Not yet, sweetie," Lucas replied, his voice tinged with weariness. He checked the time on his watch, wondering how much longer it would take. His body was starting to feel its lack of whiskey.

Elizabeth flopped onto the carpet with a dramatic sigh, then perked up when she noticed the cartoons on the TV. She crawled over and sat cross-legged in front of the screen, giggling at the antics of the animated characters.

Finally, after what felt like an eternity, a man in scrubs entered the waiting room.

"Lucas?" he asked, looking around.

"That's me," Lucas said, standing quickly.

"You can see them now," the man said with a smile.

Elizabeth jumped to her feet, her earlier boredom forgotten. "Yay! Let's go, Daddy!" She grabbed his hand and tugged him toward the door.

"Hold on, Baby Girl," Lucas said, chuckling as he allowed himself to be pulled along.

Elizabeth's chatter filled the hallway as they walked. "I'm going to show her my dolls, and we'll have tea parties, and I'll teach her how to color in the lines. She's going to love it!"

"I'm sure she will," Lucas replied, though his voice was distant as he was distracted by the thought of needing a drink.

When they entered the room, Sophia was lying in bed, cradling the baby in her arms. Her face was flushed but glowing, and she looked up with a tired yet radiant smile as her family entered.

Elizabeth ran to the bed, bouncing on her toes. "Can I see her? Daddy, pick me up!"

Lucas lifted Elizabeth into his arms and brought her closer. Together, they gazed at the tiny bundle wrapped snugly in a soft blue blanket.

Sophia's smile widened. "Meet your new baby brother," she said softly.

Elizabeth froze. Her smile faltered, replaced by confusion. "What?"

"Your baby brother," Sophia repeated gently.

Elizabeth's face scrunched up in frustration. "But... where's my sister? I wanted a sister!" She turned to Lucas, her voice growing louder. "Daddy, where's my sister? I don't want a brother!"

Sophia's expression softened, though a hint of exhaustion crept into her tone. "Elizabeth, I know you wanted a sister, but sometimes we don't get exactly what we expect. Brothers are wonderful too. You'll see."

Elizabeth wiggled out of Lucas's arms and stomped over to a chair in the corner. She climbed up, crossed her arms, and pouted, her bottom lip trembling.

Meanwhile, Lucas stood frozen. His gaze was fixed on the baby, and his breath was shallow.

"A boy?" he whispered, as if he hadn't fully processed the words. "I... I have a son?"

Sophia smiled proudly, tears glistening in her eyes. "Yes, Lucas. Meet your son."

She handed the baby to him, and Lucas took the tiny bundle with a reverence that made the room go still. He stared at the baby's delicate features—his tiny nose, his tiny fingers—and something shifted in his expression. Pride, awe, and something deeper flashed across his face.

Elizabeth watched her father, her confusion deepening. "Daddy, are brothers good?" she asked hesitantly.

"Yes, of course they are," Sophia answered quickly.

But Elizabeth wasn't satisfied. "Daddy," she repeated, louder this time, "are brothers good?"

Lucas didn't respond. He was too engrossed in the baby, his hand gently cradling the infant's head.

"Daddy!" Elizabeth's voice grew more insistent. She jumped off the chair and tugged on his sleeve. "Are brothers good?"

"Elizabeth, please," Sophia said, her tone edged with warning.

Lucas finally glanced at Elizabeth, his expression distant. "Quiet, Elizabeth. Don't wake him."

The harshness in his tone startled her. She stepped back, her lip trembling.

"But—" she began, her voice wavering.

"Enough!" Lucas snapped, his voice sharp and commanding.

Elizabeth froze, her wide eyes brimming with tears. She backed away, retreating to the corner where she curled into herself.

Sophia watched the scene unfold, her expression shifting from concern to something deeper—something wary.

"Lucas," she said softly, her voice probing.

He didn't respond. He sat down in the chair by the bed, cradling the baby as if the rest of the world had fallen away.

Elizabeth sniffled quietly, her small frame trembling. She glanced at her mother, who gave her a reassuring smile, but it did little to soothe her confusion and hurt.

After a long, tense silence, Lucas finally spoke, his voice filled with pride. "We will call him Oliver."

Sophia nodded, but her eyes lingered on Elizabeth, who remained curled up in the corner. The family was together, yet the distance between them had never felt so vast.

🦋 4 🦋
FRACTURED MORNINGS

In spite of the new son, Lucas couldn't seem to escape his downward spiral. Drugs and alcohol still called to him, louder than the quiet pleas of his wife or the unspoken needs of his children. The arrival of Oliver, a son he'd once imagined would change everything, had barely scratched the surface of his resolve to do better. No matter how wild the nights got or how deep the hangovers ran, Lucas still prided himself on one thing: paying the bills. But beyond that, the cracks in his sense of responsibility were beginning to show with the haze of drugs and alcohol dampening his desires to to do better.

This particular morning started no differently than most for the weary household.

The alarm clock bellowed into the silence of the room, a piercing sound that jolted Lucas from the shallow haze of sleep. He groaned, fumbling to silence it before it could wake Sophia. Despite his quick reaction, Sophia stirred, her eyes opening reluctantly. Her thoughts immediately turned to the children—Elizabeth would be awake soon, and Oliver would need his bottle. Though her body ached for a few more moments of rest, her mind wouldn't allow it. She forced herself up, adjusting the thin robe wrapped around her as she prepared for another day of navigating the chaos.

Lucas remained in bed, a hand clutching his forehead. His skull felt like it was caught in a vise, a familiar but unwelcome sensation.

He knew he'd overdone it last night. He always overdid it. He reached for the bottle of aspirin on his nightstand, shaking three into his hand before tossing them back dry. The taste of chalk lingered on his tongue as he lay back, trying to will away the headache.

Moments later, Sophia reappeared in the doorway, holding a small glass of whiskey. She didn't say a word as she handed it to him, her face devoid of the tenderness that used to soften her gaze when she looked at him. Lucas took it without protest, downing the drink in a single swig. The alcohol spread through him like a warm balm, dulling the edges of his hangover but leaving the exhaustion intact.

"You're not going to get out of bed, are you?" Sophia asked flatly.

"Give me a minute," Lucas muttered, not even opening his eyes.

Sophia didn't wait for an answer. She turned and left, heading to the kitchen to start her morning. Her steps were heavy, her mind preoccupied with the thought of the groceries she'd bought yesterday. She'd carefully planned every meal for the week, stretching their limited funds to make it work. It wasn't until she opened the fridge and saw the empty shelves that her stomach sank.

"No," she whispered to herself, opening the pantry in frantic hope. But it was the same there—bare. The new loaf of bread was gone, along with the cereal, the eggs, and the milk.

Sophia's heart pounded as her mind raced. She knew exactly what had happened. Lucas's friends, those leeches he couldn't seem to cut loose, had raided their kitchen during their late-night party session. Rage boiled in her chest as she stormed back to the bedroom.

Lucas was still lying in bed when she threw the door open. "Lucas," she snapped.

"What now?" he groaned, opening one eye lazily.

"Your buddies ate all the groceries I bought yesterday!" she yelled.

"So?" Lucas replied, his tone as indifferent as ever.

"So?" Sophia repeated, her voice rising. "So, I spent every last dollar we had on that food! What are we supposed to eat for the rest of the week?"

"Well, that wasn't too smart, was it?" Lucas retorted, finally sitting up.

Sophia's face twisted with disbelief. "Are you kidding me right now? You let your friends eat everything we had, and it's my fault?"

The argument escalated quickly, their voices growing louder with each exchange. From the next room, Elizabeth stirred awake, blinking in confusion as she listened to the muffled shouting. She stayed in bed, her small hands clutching her blanket. She had learned long ago not to interrupt when her parents were fighting, no matter how bad it made her feel.

But the sound of her baby brother stirring pulled her attention away. She sat up, her resolve strengthening. If her parents were too busy to take care of Oliver, she would.

Elizabeth climbed out of bed and retrieved a clean diaper, an outfit, and the wipes from the dresser. She carried them to the crib, setting them down neatly before climbing in beside Oliver. He squirmed, letting out soft coos, but Elizabeth spoke to him in a soothing voice. "It's okay, baby brother," she said, carefully unbuttoning his onesie.

In the master bedroom, Sophia's patience was wearing thin. "You need to get out of bed and help," she said, her voice trembling with anger.

"I need to sleep," Lucas replied, closing his eyes again.

Sophia stared at him for a moment, her chest rising and falling as she fought the urge to scream. Instead, she turned and left, slamming the door behind her. She walked briskly to the children's room, her anger dissipating slightly as she heard Elizabeth's soft giggles.

When she opened the door, she froze. There was Elizabeth, sitting in the crib with Oliver, who was now clean and dressed. Tears pricked at Sophia's eyes as guilt washed over her. Elizabeth shouldn't have to shoulder this responsibility; she was just a child.

"What are you doing in there, Elizabeth?" Sophia asked gently.

Elizabeth looked up, her face beaming with pride. "I changed him, Mommy. He was wet."

Sophia's heart ached. She walked over and lifted Elizabeth out of the crib, placing her on the floor. "Thank you, sweetheart. You're such a good big sister," she said, her voice thick with emotion.

She picked up Oliver and took both children to the kitchen, determined to figure out breakfast. "Are you hungry?" she asked Elizabeth.

"Yes!" Elizabeth said enthusiastically, her face lighting up.

Sophia forced a smile as she opened the pantry again, searching for anything she might have missed. But there was nothing. She turned to the fridge, where a single jar of jelly sat on the shelf.

"Mayonnaise sandwiches, Mommy?" Elizabeth asked quietly, her voice small.

"No, my sweet. There's no bread left," Sophia replied. She grabbed the jar of jelly and set it on the counter. "Guess it's jelly for breakfast!"

Elizabeth clapped her hands. "Yay, jelly!"

Sophia spooned the jelly into a bowl and handed it to Elizabeth with a small spoon. Elizabeth dug in happily, while Sophia prepared a bottle for Oliver. As Elizabeth ate, oblivious to the heaviness in the air, Sophia stared at the empty pantry, her mind racing with worry.

In the background, she heard the front door slam. Lucas had left, likely heading to work or wherever his friends were waiting for him. Sophia's hands clenched into fists as she swallowed her anger.

She couldn't keep doing this, not like this. Something had to change. For her children's sake, if not for her own.

✿ 5 ✿

DANGEROUS CROSSROADS

Lucas left the apartment feeling lighter, despite the rough start to the morning. The short walk to the front office was a blessing on days like this. It gave him just enough time to collect his thoughts and shake off the lingering effects of last night's escapades. He rubbed his temple, his headache dulling but still present, though it was a small price to pay for the kind of night he'd had. A faint grin spread across his face as he replayed the memories. The laughter, the music, the haze of smoke, and—most thrilling of all—Clarissa.

Clarissa, with her quick wit and easy charm, had been the highlight of his night. She wasn't like Sophia, who had grown weary and serious over the years, burdened by the demands of their family and Lucas's increasingly unpredictable behavior. No, Clarissa was lighthearted, uninhibited, and always ready to indulge in a little mischief. It was dangerous, of course, but that danger was part of what made it so exhilarating.

Lucas reached the back of the front office just as Clarissa was stepping out of her car. She had her bag slung over one shoulder, her hair tied back in a loose ponytail, and a casual confidence in her stride that caught his attention immediately. She glanced up and saw him, and a flicker of hesitation crossed her face before it softened into a small smile. Lucas raised his hand in a casual wave, motioning her over.

"Morning," he called, his voice low enough to ensure that no one else would hear.

"Morning," she replied, her tone neutral, but her eyes gave away a trace of amusement. "You're here early."

"Couldn't sleep in," Lucas said with a shrug. "Too much on my mind."

Clarissa arched an eyebrow but didn't press him further. Instead, she followed him as he unlocked the tool shed, glancing around to make sure no one was watching. Once inside, the air between them shifted. The shed was small and dimly lit, its shelves lined with tools and supplies, but the atmosphere felt charged.

Lucas leaned against the workbench, crossing his arms as he looked at her. "So," he began, a teasing edge in his voice, "about last night..."

Clarissa stepped closer, tilting her head with a smirk. "What about it?" she asked, her voice light but inviting.

"You seemed to be enjoying yourself," Lucas said, his grin widening. "I didn't expect you to stick around as long as you did."

Clarissa laughed softly, a sound that seemed to fill the small space. "Let's just say I was having too much fun to leave early," she replied. Her tone was playful, but there was an unspoken understanding in her words—a recognition of the line they had crossed and the risks they were taking.

Lucas took a step toward her, closing the distance between them. His hand brushed against hers, and for a moment, they stood in silence, the weight of their choices hanging in the air. He knew he should stop—knew he was already walking a fine line with Sophia, who was at home juggling their kids and the chaos he often left in his wake. But here, with Clarissa, none of that seemed to matter.

She met his gaze, her eyes filled with a mixture of curiosity and daring. "You're playing a dangerous game," she murmured, her voice barely above a whisper.

"Maybe," Lucas admitted, his voice low. "But isn't that what makes it exciting?"

Clarissa's lips curved into a sly smile. "You're impossible," she said, shaking her head. But she didn't step away.

The moment stretched, tension crackling between them like electricity. Then, as if by some unspoken agreement, Lucas leaned in, and their lips met in a kiss that was both impulsive and deliberate. It wasn't just about passion—it was an escape, a way for Lucas to momentarily forget the weight of his responsibilities and the growing distance between him and Sophia.

Clarissa pulled back slightly, her expression softening as she looked up at him. "You should get to work," she said, her voice tinged with both amusement and seriousness.

Lucas hesitated, the spell momentarily broken. He nodded, stepped back, and ran a hand through his hair. "Yeah, you're right," he said, his tone quieter now. "I've got things to do."

Clarissa adjusted her blouse and gave him a final look before slipping out of the shed. Lucas watched her leave, a mix of adrenaline and guilt swirling in his chest. For a brief moment, he considered the life he was leading and the choices he was making. But the thought passed quickly, replaced by the familiar sense of justification to which he clung whenever doubt crept in.

Lucas stepped out of the shed, the late-morning sun blinding him for a moment. He paused, inhaling the lingering smell of Clarissa's perfume on his shirt—a subtle reminder of how close they had just been. Despite the flicker of guilt thrumming at the back of his mind, a stronger wave of anticipation coursed through him.

He wanted to see her again. Soon.

Sophia's disappointed face flashed across his thoughts, but he shoved it aside. He'd do the bare minimum to keep the peace at home—pay the bills, maintain appearances—and then lose himself in moments like this, where everything felt electric and free.

Clarissa.

The name alone made his pulse jump. Yes, they were flirting with fire, but for once, he wasn't afraid of getting burned.

❧ 6 ❧
BREAKDOWN AND SACRIFICE

Payday came again, and Sophia was determined to make it count. With a sense of purpose, she grabbed her shopping list and loaded the kids into the Chevette. This time, she had a plan. After the chaos of the last shopping trip, Sophia vowed never to let Lucas and his friends raid the pantry to the point where her children had to scrape by on scraps.

The grocery store was bustling, but Sophia moved through the aisles with efficiency, Elizabeth trotting beside her and little Oliver cooing softly from his seat in the cart. She scanned the shelves, filling the cart with essentials—cereal, canned vegetables, and pasta. But this time, she was thinking ahead. Near the baking aisle, she grabbed a box of just-add-water pancake mix. Next came a jar of peanut butter and a loaf of bread—simple, non-perishable staples that wouldn't spoil quickly.

As Elizabeth tried to reach for a box of cookies, Sophia knelt beside her. "Not this time, sweetie," she said gently, brushing a strand of hair from her daughter's face. "We need to make sure there's enough food for everyone."

"But I really like cookies," Elizabeth pouted, her big eyes pleading.

"I know, honey. Maybe next time."

Inwardly, Sophia felt a pang of guilt. Elizabeth deserved a treat, but Sophia's primary concern was ensuring her children didn't go hungry. These items—the pancake mix, peanut butter, and bread—would be hidden in the back of the kids' closet, where Lucas would never think to look. She smiled to herself, feeling a small but comforting sense of control over the situation.

When they reached the checkout counter, Sophia carefully counted out the cash, making sure not to overspend. As they left the store, Elizabeth helped carry the bags to the car, proudly holding the loaf of bread while Sophia juggled the rest with Oliver balanced on her hip.

The Chevette groaned as Sophia started the engine, its familiar rattling noise filling the car. She sighed, knowing the vehicle wasn't in the best shape, but it had been holding up well enough to get them where they needed to go. They set off toward home, Sophia humming softly along with the radio to keep the kids entertained.

As they drove, Elizabeth chattered excitedly about what they could make with the groceries. "We can have pancakes tomorrow, right, Mommy?" she asked.

"Yes, baby," Sophia replied with a smile, glancing at her daughter in the rearview mirror. "Maybe pancakes with peanut butter. Doesn't that sound good?"

"Yummy!" Elizabeth exclaimed, clapping her hands.

The drive was peaceful at first, the warm afternoon sun shining through the car windows. But as they approached a busy intersection, Sophia felt a sudden jolt. The Chevette began to shudder, and the engine let out a sputtering cough.

"No, no, no," Sophia muttered, her hands gripping the steering wheel tightly. The car slowed, despite her pressing the gas pedal, and within moments, the engine died entirely. The Chevette coasted to a stop on the shoulder of the road, leaving them stranded.

"Mommy, what's wrong?" Elizabeth asked, her voice tinged with worry.

"The car stopped working, sweetheart," Sophia said, forcing a calm tone. "But it's okay. We'll figure it out."

Sophia sat for a moment, trying to process what had just happened. She turned the key in the ignition again, but the engine refused to start. She could feel the heat rising in the car as the sun bore down on them, and she knew they couldn't sit there for long.

Taking a deep breath, she glanced around and spotted a gas

station a short distance away, its payphone standing near the entrance. "Alright, kids," she said, putting on a brave face. "We're going to walk over to that gas station and see if we can get some help."

She grabbed the diaper bag and hoisted Oliver onto her hip, while Elizabeth clung to her free hand. Together, they crossed the grassy divider and walked along the shoulder of the road toward the gas station, the bags of groceries resting in the back of the car. Despite the heat and the unexpected setback, Sophia felt a small glimmer of hope. She could get through this—she had to.

She fumbled with the coins, dropping one in her haste. "Stay close to me," she told Elizabeth as she bent down to pick it up. Once she had all the coins in place, she dialed the number for Lucas's workplace, her heart pounding as she waited for someone to answer.

"Sundance Apartments," came a familiar female voice.

Sophia hesitated for a moment, then cleared her throat. "Hi, this is Sophia, Lucas's wife. I've broken down, and I need him to come pick us up."

"Oh, hi, Sophia," Clarissa replied smoothly. "I'm sorry, but Lucas isn't here right now. Can I give him a message?"

Sophia's shoulders sagged. "Please tell him I'm two blocks west of the Safeway on Hickory Street. We're stranded, and it's really hot."

"Of course," Clarissa said, her tone saccharine. "I'll let him know as soon as he gets back."

"Thank you," Sophia said, though the knot in her stomach told her not to trust Clarissa.

She hung up and turned back to Elizabeth, who was sitting on the ground at her feet, looking tired and flushed. "Let's head back to the car and wait for Daddy," she said, forcing a smile.

The walk back was even harder, the heat sapping what little energy she had left. When they reached the car, Sophia opened all the doors to let in some air and sat on the edge of the passenger's seat, bouncing Oliver on her knee while Elizabeth leaned against her side.

Minutes turned into an hour. The groceries were wilting, and so was Sophia's patience. She kept glancing at the road, hoping to see one of Lucas's buddies' cars or even a tow truck. But the only vehicle that eventually pulled up was Clarissa's, with Lucas sitting in the passenger seat, looking sheepish.

Sophia's relief at seeing him was overshadowed by her irritation. "What took you so long?" she demanded as he stepped out of the car.

Lucas scratched the back of his head. "I, uh, didn't get the message right away." He kept the image of Clarissa's initial message fresh in his mind.

Clarissa stayed in the driver's seat, her lips curving into a faint smirk as she watched the family reunion.

Lucas tried to start the Chevette, but it was clear the car was beyond saving. After a long wait for the tow truck and an even longer ride to the auto shop, the mechanic confirmed what Sophia had already feared: the car was dead, and fixing it would cost more than it was worth.

Grateful that Clarissa waited, they all went back to the apartment complex. As the young family walked back to their apartment that evening, carrying the groceries and the kids, Sophia's mind raced with plans. They needed a car, but more than that, they needed stability. And if Lucas wasn't going to step up, she would have to figure out how to carry the weight alone.

❧ 7 ❧
THE PRICE OF DREAMS

The following weekend, Sophia, Lucas, and Clarissa set out for the dealership with a sense of urgency and, in Sophia's case, a twinge of apprehension. Alice's generous offer to cosign for a car was a lifeline, but it came with a weight of responsibility that Sophia didn't take lightly. The Chevette had been unreliable for months, but at least it was paid for. The idea of adding a car payment to their already tight budget filled her with anxiety.

They arrived at the dealership mid-morning, the lot gleaming under the bright sunlight. Rows of cars stretched before them, each one polished to perfection, with colorful price tags and balloons swaying in the breeze. Salesmen hovered like vultures, ready to pounce at the first sign of interest.

Sophia adjusted Oliver on her hip, keeping Elizabeth close by her side as they stepped onto the lot. Clarissa, ever the joker, let out a low whistle. "Look at all these beauties. Lucas, are you ready to trade up from the old tin can?"

Lucas grinned, already scanning the lot. "Oh, I'm more than ready. Let's find something with some style."

Sophia sighed, already anticipating the battle that lay ahead. "We need something practical, Lucas: affordable and reliable, not flashy."

Lucas waved her off. "Don't worry, I'll find something that works for everyone."

The salesman assigned to them was a middle-aged man named Carl, with a receding hairline and an eager smile. "Good morning, folks! Looking for something special today?"

"Something that runs," Sophia muttered under her breath, though Carl didn't seem to hear.

"We're looking for a family car," Lucas said, stepping forward and shaking Carl's hand. "Something spacious, dependable... and a little fun."

Carl's eyes lit up. "Oh, I've got just the thing. Follow me."

The first car Carl showed them was a used sedan, modest but clean, with low mileage and decent gas efficiency. Sophia leaned in, inspecting the interior and asking about maintenance records, while Lucas hung back, clearly unimpressed.

"It's a good, solid car," Carl said, directing his pitch to Sophia. "Perfect for a young family like yours."

"It's boring," Lucas cut in, crossing his arms. "We're not shopping for a car to retire in."

Sophia glared at him. "We're shopping for a car that won't break down in the middle of the road."

Clarissa, sensing the tension, chuckled nervously. "Let's keep looking, huh? There are plenty of cars out here to choose from."

Carl led them to a small SUV next, pointing out its spacious trunk and sturdy design. Elizabeth climbed inside, giggling as she explored the backseat, but Lucas was already distracted by a flashier vehicle parked a few rows down.

"Now, this one's a beauty," Carl said, gesturing to the SUV. "Safety features, great mileage, and room for the kids. What do you think?"

Sophia was about to respond when she realized Lucas was no longer paying attention. "Where did he—"

"There," Clarissa said, nodding toward the back of the lot.

Sophia turned and saw Lucas standing next to a van, its chrome accents gleaming in the sun. She sighed, her stomach sinking. "Of course."

By the time she reached him, Lucas was already enamored. "Look at this, Sophia. It's perfect."

The van was oversized and flashy, with tinted windows and plush interior seating. The back featured a fold-out bed and built-in storage compartments, clearly designed for someone prioritizing comfort over practicality.

"We can take road trips in this," Lucas said, opening the door and climbing inside. "Think of the possibilities. The kids would love it." "We could go see your parents," he added charmingly.

Sophia folded her arms, skeptical. "And what about the gas mileage? The cost of repairs? This isn't practical, Lucas."

"It's a van," he argued, gesturing to the spacious interior. "How is it not practical?"

Carl, sensing Lucas's enthusiasm, jumped in. "This is a great choice for a family: lots of space, and it's built to last."

Sophia caught the way Carl avoided mentioning the price and crossed her arms tighter. "I don't know..."

Clarissa climbed into the passenger seat, laughing as she leaned back in the cushioned seat. "Well, it sure is comfortable. You could live in this thing."

Lucas laughed. "Exactly! It's like a house on wheels. It can be my pimpmobile."

Sophia's patience was wearing thin. "We're not looking for a house on wheels, Lucas. We need something reliable and affordable."

But Lucas wasn't listening. He was too busy imagining himself behind the wheel, already referring to the van as "his."

"I'll take it," Lucas said suddenly, turning to Carl.

"What?" Sophia exclaimed, her voice rising. "Lucas, we haven't even—"

Carl stepped in smoothly. "Why don't we head inside and talk numbers? I'll make sure you get a good deal."

Lucas followed Carl toward the office without hesitation, leaving Sophia standing by the van, fuming. Clarissa slid out of the passenger seat and joined her, leaning casually against the side of the van.

"Looks like he's made up his mind," Clarissa said with a shrug.

Sophia shook her head, exasperated. "This is ridiculous."

Clarissa tilted her head, studying Sophia. "You know, it's not a bad van. And Lucas seems excited. Maybe that's worth something."

Sophia sighed. "We need a car that works for the family, not one that feeds his ego."

For a moment, the two women stood in silence. Then Clarissa

said, "You're a good wife, Sophia. Better than most. He's lucky to have you."

Sophia wasn't sure how to respond. "I'm just trying to do what's best for my kids."

Clarissa nodded. "I get that. And for what it's worth, if you ever need help, you know where to find me."

When Lucas finally emerged from the office, grinning ear to ear, Sophia knew it was a done deal. The van was theirs.

As they drove off the lot, Lucas couldn't contain his excitement, while Sophia sat quietly in the passenger seat, her hands clasped tightly in her lap. She wanted to be happy, but all she could feel was unease. This van was supposed to be a fresh start, a step forward— but to her, it felt like yet another weight added to an already heavy load.

8

A WEB OF SHADOWS

The days following the acquisition of the van brought with them a shifting tide within the family dynamic. Sophia remained cautiously optimistic about the change, even though doubts lingered in the recesses of her mind. She wanted to believe that the vehicle marked a new chapter of reliability and stability for their family, but deep down, the sinking feeling in her gut about Lucas's "pimpmobile" comment refused to subside.

Lucas, on the other hand, seemed invigorated by the purchase, though not in a way that reassured Sophia. He treated the van not as a tool for family life but as a symbol of his own indulgence. He bragged about its spacious interior to anyone who would listen and spent hours polishing it to a mirror shine, as if its pristine condition would reflect his status. But Sophia couldn't help noticing that Lucas never invited her along when he decided to "take it out for a spin."

Clarissa had also taken a keen interest in the van. The vehicle's novelty gave her the perfect excuse to spend more time around Lucas, offering unsolicited advice on keeping it in top shape or dropping hints about possible upgrades they could make. She often lingered by the driver's side door, running her fingers along the chrome trim, her comments peppered with a familiarity that bordered on flirtation.

"Lucas, you really lucked out with this beauty," Clarissa said one afternoon, leaning against the van as Lucas fiddled under the hood. "I can see why you're so attached to it already. I mean, this thing screams personality."

Lucas glanced at her, a sly smirk tugging at the corner of his lips. "Yeah, well, a man's gotta have his castle on wheels, right? And this one's got everything I need."

Clarissa tilted her head, her eyes narrowing slightly as she crossed her arms. "Everything, huh? You sure you don't mean 'everyone' you need?"

Lucas chuckled, his laugh low and unhurried. "Careful now, Clarissa. People might think you're flirting."

"And what if I am?" she teased back, her voice light, but her gaze unwavering.

Sophia's stomach twisted the moment she saw Clarissa leaning against the van, chatting with Lucas.

It wasn't just Clarissa's presence—it was the casual way Lucas smiled at her, as if he'd forgotten whom he was supposed to come home to.

The days since buying that van had unraveled their fragile peace, and Sophia's patience was wearing dangerously thin.

Inside, Elizabeth toddled around the living room, babbling to her baby brother. Sophia tore her eyes away from the window and tried to focus on her children, but the knot in her stomach tightened. She wanted to trust Lucas, to give him the benefit of the doubt, but his behavior left her with too many unanswered questions.

Later that evening, after the kids had been put to bed, Sophia decided to confront Lucas. He was lounging on the couch, a whiskey in hand, flipping aimlessly through television channels.

"Lucas, can we talk?"

He didn't look up; his attention was fixed on the screen. "What's up?"

"It's about Clarissa," she said, hesitating.

Lucas finally turned his head, raising an eyebrow. "What about her?"

"I've noticed... she's been around a lot lately. Always hanging around the van, talking to you. It just feels—"

"Feels like what, Sophia?" Lucas cut her off, his tone sharper now. "She's our friend. Shouldn't you be glad she's helping out?"

"I am," Sophia said quickly, trying to keep her voice steady. "But it's more than that. The way she looks at you, the way you talk to her... I just don't want anything—"

Lucas threw his whiskey glass towards Sophia, and the sound of it hitting the wall echoed through the small apartment. Sophia ducked so the glass wouldn't hit her in the face. Lucas proceeded without hesitation or regard. "Don't start with this crap, Sophia. Clarissa's a friend. End of story. Stop trying to make something out of nothing."

Sophia recoiled slightly, the force of his reaction catching her off guard. She wanted to push back, to demand answers, but the weight of his anger silenced her. Then, as she looked at the wall, it would have hit her in the face. Her heart skipped a beat.

"Fine," she muttered, turning away and heading for the bedroom.

Lucas sighed, rubbing a hand over his face. He knew Sophia wasn't wrong to be suspicious, but he also knew how close to the edge he was walking. Clarissa's flirtations were becoming harder to ignore, and a small part of him enjoyed the attention. But he couldn't afford to cross that line boldly in public—not yet.

9

CLARISSA'S GROWING BOLDNESS

The following week, Clarissa's visits became even more frequent. She found excuses to stop by, whether it was to drop off something trivial or to suggest taking the van out for a test drive. Sophia grew increasingly wary, her anxiety simmering just beneath the surface.

One evening, Clarissa arrived unannounced, a mischievous grin on her face. "Hey, Lucas, you up for a ride? I've been dying to see what this van can really do on the open road."

Lucas hesitated, glancing toward the kitchen where Sophia was preparing dinner. "I don't think now's a good time, Clarissa."

"Come on," she urged, her tone playful but insistent. "Just a quick spin. I won't tell Sophia."

Lucas sighed, grabbing the keys off the counter. "Fine. We'll make it quick."

The two of them climbed into the van and pulled out of the parking lot, leaving Sophia to watch helplessly from the window.

As they drove, Clarissa leaned back in her seat, her legs crossed provocatively. "You know, Lucas, this van suits you. It's got character, just like you."

"Clarissa," Lucas said, his tone cautious, "we've got to keep this professional in front of Sophia. I don't want to lose my son."

"Oh, please," she said, rolling her eyes. "She is so mousey that she wouldn't dare leave you."

Lucas tightened his grip on the steering wheel, his jaw clenched. He couldn't deny that Clarissa's boldness was intoxicating.

"Clarissa, stop," he said firmly. "You need to rein it in when she is around. I am serious."

For the first time, Clarissa seemed taken aback. She fell silent, the weight of his rejection settling heavily in the air. But as they drove back to the apartment, a glint of determination returned to her eyes. Clarissa wasn't one to give up easily, and she vowed to find another way to get closer to Lucas. The following week, Clarissa's visits became even more frequent.

10

SOPHIA'S UNEASY MIND

The days passed with a heavy sense of unease that Sophia couldn't shake. On the surface, life seemed to carry on as normal—Lucas went to work, Clarissa continued to drop by with her usual exuberance, and the kids provided constant, if chaotic, distraction. But underneath the routine, something felt profoundly off.

Sophia began to notice small things that fed into her growing suspicions. Clarissa's visits had become almost a daily occurrence, and while they were often cloaked in seemingly innocent excuses—a forgotten sweater, an offer to babysit, or an invitation to hang out— Sophia couldn't ignore how Clarissa's demeanor changed around Lucas.

It was in the way Clarissa laughed a little too loudly at his jokes, leaning in closer than necessary. It was in the way her hand would linger on his arm for just a second longer than it should. It was in the way Lucas, though outwardly indifferent, never pushed her away.

Sophia didn't have concrete proof, but her instincts screamed at her that something was brewing just out of sight. It didn't help that Lucas had become more distant lately, brushing off her attempts to connect with him.

"Where are you going?" Sophia asked one evening as Lucas grabbed the keys to the van.

"Just out for a bit," he replied, avoiding her gaze.

"For what?"

Lucas sighed, clearly irritated. "I need to clear my head, okay? I'll be back in an hour."

Sophia bit back the urge to argue. She watched him leave, the door clicking shut behind him, and felt a wave of helplessness wash over her. She hated the feeling of being left in the dark, of not knowing where Lucas had gone or what he was doing.

Her thoughts immediately turned to Clarissa. Had she called him? Were they meeting somewhere? The possibility twisted Sophia's stomach into knots.

A DISCOVERY

Sophia's resolve hardened over the next few days. She couldn't bear the gnawing suspicion any longer—the endless doubt that kept her awake at night, replaying every odd moment and every offhand comment. If Lucas was hiding something, she intended to find out.

Steeling herself, Sophia began her quiet investigation. Whenever Lucas peeled off his clothes and tossed them aside, she discreetly patted down the pockets of his jeans. She memorized the mileage on the van's odometer each time he left, noting any difference upon his return. Sometimes, when he disappeared into the bathroom, she would check his jacket for signs of lipstick or lingering perfume. A tiny voice warned her that Lucas would be furious if he caught her snooping, but her need for answers outweighed the fear of his anger —at least for now.

One afternoon, Lucas had just come home from one of his unexplained outings, the kids were busy in the living room, and Sophia saw her chance. She grabbed the van keys and slipped outside, telling herself she would "tidy up" the vehicle. It felt like a flimsy pretense, yet her heart pounded with a mix of guilt and determination as she opened the driver's door. She wasn't sure what she was even looking for—just...something.

At first, nothing stood out except the faint smell of stale fast food and a stray soda cup in the cupholder. Then, as she leaned over to gather a crumpled receipt from the passenger floor mat, she caught it: a delicate, floral perfume drifting up from the seatbelt. It wasn't hers. The realization hit like a punch in the gut.

Her breath caught, and she sank into the driver's seat, fingers gripping the wheel as she tried to steady herself. A swirl of thoughts —anger, betrayal, vindication—warred inside her. "It's such a small thing," she told herself, but she couldn't deny how her pulse hammered. It was the final push that made all her suspicions feel real, no longer just paranoid musings. For a moment, she recalled the times Clarissa had lingered around the van and how Lucas's outings had grown more frequent. A sense of dread pooled in her stomach, and she felt almost dizzy, as though the air in the van had grown thick and claustrophobic.

That night, as Lucas lay snoring beside her, Sophia stared blankly at the ceiling, hugging the knowledge of what she'd found like a burden she couldn't set down. She considered confronting him on the spot—shaking him awake, demanding an explanation. But the mental image of his anger, the sting of being labeled "irrational" or "paranoid," made her heart pound with fear. Lucas's temper had been unpredictable lately. Besides, if he realized she had been snooping around, he'd likely turn the blame on her. What if he found out I've been tracking mileage and searching his pockets?" she thought, shuddering at the potential blowup.

Instead, she decided to do something she rarely did: reach out for help. After all, Alice had always been the practical one in the family—someone who'd offered support in the past, whether or not Sophia had been willing to accept it. While her siblings could be meddlesome, Alice had a knack for cutting through nonsense and giving it to you straight. "If anyone can help me see this clearly, it's her," Sophia reasoned.

A plan took shape in her mind. She'd call Alice tomorrow, under the guise of a casual catch-up. Then she'd muster the courage to share what she'd found—every detail, including that faint perfume and her creeping fear that Clarissa was more than just a friend. A small sliver of relief accompanied the idea, warming her chest momentarily. She wouldn't be alone in this investigation; maybe Alice could confirm her instincts or talk her down if she were reading too much into it.

As she closed her eyes, Sophia exhaled slowly, Lucas's steady snores rattling in her ears. In the darkness, the scent of that unfamiliar perfume still seemed to cling to her senses—a subtle, damning reminder that her world might be on the brink of unraveling. She held onto Alice's name like a lifeline, determined to shed light on the shadows creeping into her marriage.

12

A CONVERSATION WITH ALICE

Sophia lingered in the kitchen, the midday light casting a warm glow across the counters. Both kids had finally drifted off for their nap, granting her a brief, precious silence. Her heart pounded with uncertainty as she picked up the phone, her finger hovering over the keypad longer than it should. "What if Alice thinks I'm being paranoid?" she wondered. But she couldn't bottle up her fears any longer.

With a steadying breath, she dialed her sister's number. Each ring felt like a countdown.

"Hello?" came Alice's voice.

"Alice..." Sophia's throat constricted. "It's me. I—I need help."

Her sister's tone softened. "Sophia, what's going on? You sound upset."

A shiver ran through Sophia as she glanced at the hallway, listening for any sign of Lucas, though she knew he was out. Quietly, she poured out everything that had been eating away at her: Clarissa's near-constant visits, Lucas's distant demeanor, that maddening floral perfume in the van. As she spoke, her voice wavered, frustration mingling with guilt for violating Lucas's privacy and fear for what might happen if she confronted him.

Alice let her speak without interruption, offering the occasional gentle hum of acknowledgment.

"So," Sophia finished, her words tumbling out in a desperate rush, "I'm terrified I'm reading too much into this, but every instinct tells me something's wrong. He's pulling away, and Clarissa acts like... like he belongs to her somehow. I don't know what to do."

"Have you asked him point-blank?" Alice said, her tone calm and measured. "Have you told him you found the perfume and that you're worried about Clarissa?"

Sophia swallowed. The idea of directly accusing Lucas made her chest tighten. Images of his anger flared in her mind—harsh words, broken trust, or worse. "I tried hinting, but he shuts down," she admitted. "And the last time I pressed him, he got so defensive. I just can't stand the thought of another blowup."

Alice sighed. "Then do something else. Sophia, you deserve the truth, one way or another. If Lucas won't give it to you, you have to find it yourself."

"What... what are you suggesting?"

A beat of silence. "Look," Alice said, her voice lowering as if to ensure no one overheard. "Take the kids to a sitter, tell Lucas you're going out for the afternoon. Then watch the apartment from a distance. Or if he drives the van somewhere, find out where. That way, if Clarissa's meeting him or there's something else going on—"

Sophia's heart pounded so loudly that she could scarcely hear her sister's next words. Spying on Lucas? It feels deceitful. Wrong. But the more Alice explained, the more plausible it sounded.

"You really think I should do that?" Sophia whispered, leaning against the counter. Her palms were damp, and her mind was spinning with possible outcomes. What if I see him with Clarissa? she thought, the mental image sending a wave of sickness through her. Or worse, what if Lucas realizes I'm following him? She could almost picture his furious disbelief, the accusations that she was the untrustworthy one.

Alice's tone turned gentle again. "Sophia, you can't let fear paralyze you. If you find nothing, you'll have peace of mind. If you find... something—well, at least you'll know. No more guessing or lying awake at night."

Sophia squeezed her eyes shut, tears threatening at the corners. She was right. The torment of not knowing was shredding her. "Okay," she said finally, her voice trembling. "I'll do it. Just once, to see what's really happening."

"I'm sorry it's come to this," Alice said softly. "But I'm here for you, no matter what you find."

Sophia nodded, though Alice couldn't see her. "Thank you," she managed. The line went silent for a moment before they said their goodbyes.

Hanging up, Sophia stared at the phone in front of her. "What am I getting myself into?" The rational part of her whispered, "If Lucas discovered her spy plan, their marriage could implode faster than it already was." She swallowed hard. But each day spent in the dark felt like slow torture—maybe risking Lucas's wrath was the only way to reclaim her own sanity.

A soft cry from the kids' room cut through her anxiety. Sophia brushed away the stray tears clinging to her eyelashes. She inhaled, steadying herself. Tomorrow, she'd set Alice's plan into motion. For now, she'd wrap her arms around her children, keep her composure, and try not to let the weight of secrets crush her.

She left the kitchen, each footstep echoing her resolve. If answers lay beyond the safe confines of her routine, she would step into the unknown—no matter the price.

13

A SHATTERED REVELATION

A few days later, Sophia finally set her plan into motion. She told Lucas she'd be out that evening, dropping the children off next door under the guise of going to a movie with a friend. He barely acknowledged her, preoccupied with his own unspoken agenda. Her heart pounded the moment he pulled out of the parking lot in the van. This was her chance.

Once the coast was clear, Sophia rushed back inside and turned off every light, drawing the curtains across each window except for a small slit in the living room. She crouched there, hardly breathing, scanning the parking lot for any sign of his return. Minutes ticked by like hours, her nerves stretching taut. "I know he's up to something," she told herself, clinging to the memory of the perfume and the distance in his eyes.

Eventually, headlights cut across the dark lot. The van eased into a parking space farther down the building—far enough that he must've assumed she wouldn't notice. Sophia stiffened. "It's happening." Her breath caught in her throat as she watched the van's silhouette, waiting for Lucas to emerge. But he didn't. Tension clawed at her mind. Could Clarissa be in there with him? she wondered, remembering how she'd prepared for that possibility. A twisted part of her almost expected it—yet feared it.

When the van started rocking, a surge of adrenaline shot through her. "This is real," her thoughts screamed. "I'm about to catch them in the act." Fueled by anger and heartbreak, she flung the front door open, not bothering to hide. Her legs felt shaky as she sprinted across the parking lot, but fury drove her forward. He's humiliating me in our own home... how dare he...

The van's windows were fogged, faint murmurs escaping into the humid night air. Sophia's chest rose and fell in quick, shallow breaths as she grabbed for the back doors. In that split second, she braced herself to see Clarissa's face—that infuriating smirk, she imagined. She yanked the door open with more force than she realized.

Inside, Lucas turned at once, his eyes wild with shock, his shirt halfway off. Sophia's gaze darted around, searching for Clarissa's familiar blonde hair and her bold expression. Instead, she locked eyes with a stranger—a dark-haired woman she had never seen before. Confusion slammed into her chest. This isn't Clarissa... so how many women has he brought here?

Her body felt numb. Lucas was shouting something, but the roar of her pulse swallowed his words. Sophia's eyes stayed glued to that unknown woman, wide-eyed and frantic, scrambling to cover herself. "He's not just with Clarissa—he's with anyone willing to cross that line." The realization cut deeper than any single affair. Her world spun on its axis, heartbreak lancing through her lungs.

"Sophia, what the hell?" Lucas barked, fumbling to pull on his pants. Anger and embarrassment churned in his expression. She could almost see him trying to figure out whom to blame first.

"You—" she tried to speak, her voice choking on the accusation. "How could you—why are you—who is she?" The questions knotted in her throat, refusing to emerge as coherent words.

Before she could unleash her fury, a sharp ache ripped through her lower abdomen. She gasped, one hand flying instinctively to her stomach. The dull cramp turned piercing in seconds, and a hot flush spread between her legs. Confusion and terror blurred her rage into a dizzying swirl. "No... not now, please..."

She glanced down. Blood stained her jeans, droplets hitting the asphalt. Her breath stuttered; panic flared. "What is happening?" The shock paralyzed her for an instant.

Lucas's angry glare dissolved into alarm the moment he saw the red staining her pants. "Sophia!" he yelled, his tone shifting abruptly. "What is that? Are you—"

She lifted her gaze, tears flooding her vision. The ache in her abdomen doubled, and she bent forward, her hand braced on the van's frame. The unknown woman huddled in the corner, hastily pulling on her blouse, her eyes flicking between Sophia and Lucas as though she were unsure whether to flee or to help.

Sophia's fury and heartbreak gave way to raw fear. "This can't be happening now, not in the middle of this nightmare." She tried to speak, but the pain stole her words. Lucas scrambled out of the van, nearly tripping as he reached for her shoulder.

"Sophia—look at me," he demanded, his voice breaking. "Are you hurt? Jesus..."

Her heart hammered, sweat beading at her temple. Anger still flared in the back of her mind—anger at Lucas, at the stranger behind him, at the entire situation. Yet the terror of her own body failing overwhelmed everything else. She could barely stand upright, a dizzy haze consuming her.

The woman, sensing the gravity, slipped out of the van and darted away, footsteps echoing across the dark lot. Lucas hardly noticed her departure, one arm around Sophia, his eyes wide with alarm. Sophia pressed a hand to her abdomen, lips quivering.

"Lucas..." she managed, her voice trembling. "I—I need help."

His nod was frantic, half-panicked. "Okay... okay," he stammered. "I'm calling an ambulance. Right now."

Sophia's vision wavered, the lot spinning, as she clung to Lucas for support. She wanted to lash out, scream at him for his betrayal, but pain claimed all her strength. In the end, she could only gasp for breath, her tears mingling with the night's humid air, aware that her entire world had just shattered in more ways than one.

❊ 14 ❊
THE EMERGENCY

Lucas paced the length of the waiting room, each footstep echoing off bright white tiles. The buzz of fluorescent lights stung his eyes, and the sharp tang of disinfectant clung to the back of his throat. Every so often, he'd glance at a clock on the wall, its ticking second hand feeling like a slow, mocking taunt. He couldn't remember the last time he felt so utterly powerless.

The image of Sophia collapsing, blood staining her jeans, replayed in his mind, each replay striking him with fresh shame. "How did I let everything come to this?" He silently cursed himself for every selfish choice that had led him here—to this moment, in a sterile hospital corridor, not knowing if his wife would be okay.

He dropped into one of the rigid plastic chairs, pressing his palms against his forehead. He wanted to believe that staying here, anxious and restless, could somehow redeem him. "Maybe if I'm here, it'll prove I still care. That I'm not completely lost." But the stench of whiskey still lingered in his memory, mingling with the guilt that coiled tighter around his chest.

A sudden beep of a medical monitor from down the hall cut through the low hum of conversation, making him jump. "Calm down," he told himself, but calm felt impossible. Every fiber of his body was clenched in dread.

Finally, after what felt like an eternity, a doctor in pale blue scrubs approached, scanning the room with purposeful steps. Lucas sprang to his feet so quickly that the chair nearly toppled over.

"Mr. Marino?" the doctor asked, glancing at his clipboard. He offered a tight nod, his voice gentle but direct. "I'm Dr. Allen."

"That's me," Lucas replied, his throat nearly closing around the words. His heart hammered. "Is Sophia... is she okay? What happened?"

Dr. Allen's gaze softened. "Your wife experienced a miscarriage," he said, choosing his words carefully. "It appears it was early in the pregnancy—she might not have known she was expecting at all."

Lucas's stomach lurched, a cold wave of shock washing over him. He hadn't even known. He squeezed his eyes shut for a moment, fighting the sting of tears. *She was pregnant... and I was off doing—* He couldn't finish the thought.

The doctor continued, "She's stable. We're monitoring her vitals, but she'll need time to recover, physically and emotionally. These situations can be very difficult."

Lucas swallowed hard, forcing himself to focus on the here and now. "Can—can I see her?"

"Of course," Dr. Allen said, offering a small, reassuring nod. "They're getting her settled in a room. A nurse will come to get you in a minute."

As the doctor walked away, the overhead speakers crackled with a page for another patient. Lucas slumped back into the chair, exhaling shakily. She was pregnant. They were going to have another kid, and he never even knew. The realization stabbed at his heart. He couldn't help but think about Elizabeth and baby Oliver—how it felt to hold them for the first time, the promise of being better for them, and how he'd squandered that promise in late nights and secret encounters.

He studied the floor, dappled with faint scuff marks. The surrounding white noise of monitors, footsteps, and distant chatter seemed to blur. "Do I tell her the truth now? About the nights out, the stupidity, the women...?" The idea tore at him. He imagined Sophia's face, pale in a hospital bed, her eyes holding a mix of betrayal and heartbreak. Yet, a small voice inside whispered that maybe this was the line he'd finally crossed, the moment that demanded he keep his mouth shut if there was any hope of salvaging their marriage.

As he tried to piece together his next move, a nurse approached, softly calling his name. Lucas stood, wiping damp palms on his jeans. His gaze lingered on the corridor that would lead him to Sophia's room. "Whatever I do now... it has to be a believable lie."

Walking through that corridor, the smell of antiseptic grew stronger, almost suffocating. Every beep of a heart monitor behind closed doors made him flinch, imagining Sophia lying among tubes and wires. He could almost see her quiet, tear-stricken face. He prayed she'd be stable enough to talk, to let him hold her hand. Maybe she wouldn't want him near her at all.

But I have to try, he thought, fingers curling into fists. I have to be the husband she deserves—or at least start now. The single flicker of determination in his chest warred with the heavy boulder of guilt. He wondered if Sophia would let him make amends or if the line between them had snapped for good.

As he approached the door to Sophia's room, each step felt like a final step onto a battlefield. The next few minutes would shape everything—her recovery, the future of their family, maybe even the direction of his own life. With a raw breath, he paused at the threshold, bracing himself. "Please be okay... please let me fix this."

Then, steeling himself, he gently pushed the door open, the fluorescent light spilling into the dim hallway behind him.

15

THE WEIGHT OF BETRAYAL

Sophia flinched as the back door slammed, rattling the thin walls of their apartment. It had been a week since she'd found Lucas tangled with another woman in the van—one week of bruising silence and a suffocating sense that nothing would ever be the same.

She bustled around the kitchen, mechanically washing dishes while her thoughts replayed that night on a loop. "Why would he do this? Why am I still here?" Each question felt heavier than the last. She glanced at the cracked clock above the sink—only noon, yet the air was thick with dread, as if an entire day's worth of conflict had already passed.

In the living room, Elizabeth, not even four years old, peeked around the corner. She clutched a stuffed bunny against her chest, her wide eyes reflecting an unspoken fear. Sophia managed a tight smile, her heart twisting at the realization that Elizabeth, though too young to grasp the full meaning of betrayal, sensed the tension poisoning the house.

"Mommy, is Daddy mad?" Elizabeth asked quietly. She twirled one of her pigtails, her lip trembling with confusion. "He won't talk to me."

Sophia swallowed the lump in her throat. "He's just... tired, baby," she said softly, praying the half-truth would keep Elizabeth's worries at bay. But she could see Elizabeth's hesitation, her arms hugging the bunny tighter as if even that small comfort might slip away.

As she dried a plate, Sophia's hands shook, her thoughts drifting to the moment she'd flung open the van door. That image was seared into her memory—Lucas's shock, the stranger's startled face. A burning ache flared in her chest whenever she recalled how easily he'd shattered her trust. Yet beneath the anger lay an inexplicable thread of love, stubbornly refusing to fade. "Why can't I just hate him?" she wondered bitterly.

From the hallway, Lucas trudged into the living room, ignoring Sophia's presence. He moved toward the couch with a forced casualness, as if hoping to appear normal. She watched his every step, noticing the slump of his shoulders and the guilt etched into his brow. Elizabeth ran up to him, hugging his leg, but he only ruffled her hair and muttered something about needing a nap. The child's hopeful expression flickered with disappointment as he gently pried her away and headed to the bedroom.

He can't even look me in the eye, Sophia thought, a fresh wave of hurt pulsing through her. She set the plate aside, forcing herself to breathe. The week had been an endless parade of stony silence and clipped conversations. They hadn't so much as touched on the topic of the van incident. That raw wound kept festering, fueling an unspoken war between them.

An hour later, while Sophia helped Elizabeth build a tower of blocks, the phone rang. Lucas, who was returning from the bedroom, froze in the hallway. Sophia locked eyes with him, and for an instant, it looked like she might speak—her mouth opened, tension brimming. "Ask him. Demand to know if he's meeting that woman again." The words trembled on her tongue, but the phone's shrill ring sliced through the moment.

Lucas hesitated, then stepped forward to answer it. Sophia released a breath she didn't realize she had been holding. The blocks tumbled in Elizabeth's hands, scattering across the floor.

"Who is it?" Sophia ventured softly when Lucas hung up. She could taste the confrontation forming at the back of her throat.

He slammed the handset down, his eyes avoiding hers. "Work," he lied, his voice rough. He turned away, muttering about picking up extra hours—anything to sidestep a real conversation.

Sophia's jaw tightened. She nearly stood, compelled to chase him down and force the words out—"Stop lying, talk to me, give me something." But Elizabeth tugged at her sleeve, eyes large, needing her mother's reassurance more than she needed a fight right now. The confrontation died on Sophia's lips, leaving her heart pounding with frustration.

Elizabeth blinked up at her mother, her tower of blocks forgotten. "Mommy, why's Daddy so mad?" she asked, her voice barely above a whisper. Sophia swallowed hard, tears threatening. She sees everything, Sophia realized. Even if she can't name it, she feels it.

She scooped Elizabeth into her arms, pressing a gentle kiss to her forehead. "Daddy's going through some stuff," she whispered, hugging the toddler close. "But you did nothing wrong, sweet girl. I promise."

Elizabeth nodded against her shoulder, but Sophia felt the tremor of worry in the child's small frame. The quiet heartbreak in that embrace stung worse than any angry words might have.

Late that night, Sophia lay awake on the sofa—a deliberate choice to avoid sharing a bed with Lucas. The stale hush of the apartment weighed on her, unrelenting. "I can't live like this forever. One of us has to break this silence." She stared at the ceiling, tears hot in her eyes. "Tomorrow," she resolved, "I have to do something —call him out or call it quits. For Elizabeth, for me..."

She clenched her fists, summoning courage she didn't fully believe she possessed. The sense of an imminent confrontation hung thick in the air, a silent storm about to break. And in the final hush of the night, with Elizabeth's quiet breathing in the next room, Sophia made a vow to face the morning ready for whatever might unfold.

16

A MOMENT OF CONFRONTATION

Late evening had cast deep shadows across the tiny kitchen. Sophia sat at the worn table, arms folded against her chest. A single overhead bulb buzzed, illuminating the sink piled with dishes and the battered walls that had witnessed too many secrets. She stared at her untouched mug of tea, the tendrils of steam long gone cold.

She was so lost in thought that she didn't notice Lucas enter until he cleared his throat. She looked up, startled, her eyes heavy with exhaustion and hurt. The faint smell of dish soap mingled with the lingering tang of stale tea, and Sophia's pulse quickened at the sight of him—still handsome, still calm, as if he had no reason to be ashamed.

"Hey," he said softly, stepping into the glow of the overhead light. A hint of a smile teased the corner of his mouth, disarmingly warm. "Mind if I sit?"

Sophia's jaw tightened. "It depends on whether you've come to actually talk or just pretend that nothing is wrong."

Lucas let out a small, charming laugh and pulled out a chair, sliding in fluidly. "I get it, Sophia," he said, his voice low and smooth. "You're angry. You have every right to be. But I need you to hear me out." He paused, offering her a gaze that was equal parts regretful and persuasive, as though promising the world. "I can't lose you, okay? I can't lose us."

She swallowed hard, her grip on the mug tightening. "You

should've thought of that before—" Her words shook with anger, but also with that undercurrent of lingering love she hated acknowledging.

"I know, I know," he interjected, lifting both palms in a calming gesture. "I messed up, big time. And I promise you, from the bottom of my heart, I'm going to fix this." His tone dripped with sincerity. "I'll be better. No more secrets. No more late nights. Whatever you need, I'll do it. You deserve that much."

Sophia's stomach twisted. For a second, she almost believed him. Lucas had that knack—an irresistible magnetism that once charmed her into thinking he could be everything she needed. Yet now, the memory of seeing him with another woman cut through her reluctance like a knife. "Words," she said bitterly, dropping her gaze to her lap. "Just words, Lucas."

Inside, Lucas noted her wariness, but a swell of confidence rose in him. "I can convince her," he thought, buoyed by his own ability to spin a heartfelt speech. If he could just pour on the right mix of gentleness and earnestness, maybe they'd move past all this drama. Regret flickered in his mind, but not for the act itself. He only regretted the fallout, the messy aftermath that threatened the comfort of home. "I'll promise whatever it takes," he decided. "And I'll make it sound real."

"Look at me." He slid his hand across the table, palm up, inviting her touch. "I'm not proud of how I acted. But, Sophia, it never meant I didn't love you. Sometimes... a man just gets lost," he said, mustering a wistful sadness. "I swear, though, I'm done with that life. Let me prove it to you."

She eyed his outstretched hand. The anger in her chest warred with something else—hope, maybe, or just the simple longing not to feel so alone. But the memory of the van's door yanked open, revealing a stranger in her place, wouldn't let her give in so easily. "What if it's too late?" she whispered. "What if I can't just pretend you didn't shatter everything?"

He leaned forward, lowering his voice to a near whisper, a note of desperate vulnerability edging his tone. "Then I'll pick up every broken piece and glue it together myself if I have to. I don't want to lose this family. We can move, start fresh. I'll cut ties with old habits, break from all that. You, me, the kids—somewhere new, where these walls don't echo with mistakes."

The warmth in his eyes sparkled with what appeared to be honesty. Inside, though, Lucas felt a subtle rush of triumph. Yes, keep going, his mind told him. She's listening. A flicker of guilt at manipulating her threatened to rise, but he shoved it down quickly. He'd say whatever was needed to keep the home stable—and the consequences of his affair behind him.

Sophia exhaled shakily, tears threatening. She pressed trembling fingers to her forehead. "I want to believe you," she said, her voice barely above a hush. "I want to believe that we can fix us. But you have no idea how badly this hurts, how scared I am that you'll just do it again."

He reached across, daring to lay his hand gently over hers. "I get it," he murmured. "I do. But I promise, I won't do that to you again. I can't. I won't." The vow spilled from his lips effortlessly, a polished script he believed would soothe her.

She locked onto his gaze, searching for any flicker of sincerity beneath the practiced charm. Her chest felt impossibly tight, torn between the longing to forgive and the fear of further betrayal. "We'll see," she managed. "Maybe if you show me, day by day, that you've changed..." The words caught in her throat, trailing off into uncertainty.

Lucas squeezed her fingers, letting out a relieved breath. "Got her," he thought privately, a swirl of anticipation stirring in his chest. "Thank you," he said, wearing relief like a triumphant mask. "Thank you for giving me a chance."

Her eyes shimmered with tears she refused to let fall. "A chance is all I can offer. Don't waste it."

"I won't," he promised immediately, nodding. "We'll start over. Move to that new place we talked about. I'll be the husband you deserve."

He withdrew his hand gently, noticing the tension still strung tight in her posture. She said nothing more, just stared at the table. The heavy silence returned, but this time it pulsed with the possibility of cautious reconciliation.

Behind his seemingly earnest gaze, Lucas felt that now-familiar swirl of half-relief, half-restlessness. "I'll do my best... or at least enough to keep Sophia calm," he reasoned, ignoring the faint tug of memory that said he'd done something profoundly wrong. Besides, it's not like I plan on repeating that exact mistake...

At last, he stood, carefully pushing the chair back. "I'll let you rest," he said, his voice soft. "We can talk more in the morning."

She didn't reply, only nodded once, her expression unreadable. As he turned away, the corners of his mouth almost twitched into a satisfied smile. "Things will be fine," he assured himself, crossing the threshold. "As long as I keep up the right words."

Sophia remained at the table long after he'd left, tears burning hot behind her eyes, a single thread of hope entwined with a deep, unyielding caution—unaware that Lucas, though seemingly repentant, still carried no real regret for the path that had led them here.

17

A SECOND SUNRISE

The move to Arizona wasn't the clean slate Sophia had imagined—it was more like a blank page stained by smudges she couldn't erase. The dry desert air carried a sense of change, but with every box unpacked and every cautious glance exchanged, Sophia couldn't help but wonder: Could this place really offer a fresh start, or was it just a new backdrop for the same old heartbreak?

Arizona felt like stepping into another world. The air was dry and warm, carrying the faint scent of dust and mesquite. It wrapped around Sophia like a reminder that she was far from everything familiar—both a comfort and a quiet ache. The pale blue sky stretched endlessly overhead, vast and uncaring, and the quiet of the neighborhood settled uneasily over the family.

Sophia stood in the living room of their new house, surrounded by half-unpacked boxes. The children darted between them, laughing as Elizabeth pretended one of the empty boxes was a racecar. Oliver toddled after her, his giggles filling the air, but even their joy felt muted. The house was smaller than their old one, with thin walls and sun-faded curtains that barely kept the light out. But it was close to her parents' home, and that mattered most to Sophia now.

Sophia's mother, Margaret, had been by earlier, dropping off a casserole and helping her fold laundry. "You're doing great, sweetheart," Margaret had said, her tone kind but laced with that familiar hint of worry. "I know it's hard, but you're strong. You'll figure it out."

Sophia had smiled and nodded, but her thoughts churned. Was she strong? Or just desperate? The move was supposed to be a fresh start, but so far, it felt more like a holding pattern—a fragile attempt to keep the cracks in her marriage from shattering completely. She wanted to believe Arizona could fix something, anything, but the doubt gnawed at her.

Lucas, for his part, had thrown himself into unpacking and job hunting. At least, that's what he said. Sophia couldn't shake the feeling that his efforts were more about avoiding her than about building a new life. She watched him now as he wrestled with the instructions for assembling a bookshelf, his jaw tight and his movements stiff. He swore under his breath as a wooden plank slipped from his grasp.

"Need help?" Sophia asked from the doorway.

Lucas looked up, his expression unreadable. "I've got it," he said shortly, turning back to the task.

Sophia sighed, retreating to the kitchen, where the counters were cluttered with grocery bags and utensils. She opened the fridge, only to close it again, unable to focus. Her parents meant well, dropping by with meals and supplies, but their presence only deepened Lucas's discomfort. He avoided Margaret and Henry as much as possible, his easy charm evaporating in their judgmental silence.

Elizabeth ran into the kitchen, her face flushed from playing. "Mommy, is Daddy mad at us?" she asked, her voice small.

Sophia's heart twisted. She crouched down, brushing a strand of hair from her daughter's face. "No, sweetie. Daddy's just... tired. Moving is hard, even for grown-ups."

Elizabeth frowned. "Do you think he likes it here?"

Sophia forced a smile. "I think he's trying to like it. That's what matters."

Elizabeth didn't seem convinced, but she nodded, her attention quickly drawn to the pantry, where she began rummaging for a snack. Sophia straightened and returned to her work, but Elizabeth's words lingered. Did Lucas like it here? Did he even want to try?

That night, after the kids were asleep, Sophia sat on the front porch with a cup of tea. The air was cool now, the desert quiet broken only by the occasional rustle of wind through the sparse trees. She stared at the faint outlines of her parents' house next door, wondering if they were watching, if they were silently waiting for her to admit defeat and move in with them.

The screen door creaked open, and Lucas stepped out. He hesitated before sitting beside her on the porch steps. For a long moment, neither of them spoke.

"Nice night," Lucas said finally, his voice low.

Sophia glanced at him, her gaze flat. "Yeah."

Lucas rubbed the back of his neck, his movements awkward. "I, uh... I've been thinking."

Sophia arched an eyebrow but didn't reply, waiting.

"I know things have been rough," Lucas continued, his tone growing smoother, more practiced. "But I want to make it work, Sophia. I want us to be... better."

Sophia's fingers tightened around her mug. "And what does 'better' mean to you, Lucas?"

Lucas turned to her, his brown eyes shining in the moonlight. "It means starting over. Here. With you and the kids. It means finding a job, being a better husband, a better dad."

Sophia searched his face, looking for cracks in his confidence, but he held her gaze with that same easy charm he'd always had. For a moment, she wanted to believe him. She wanted to believe that he could change and that they could find their way back to each other.

But then she thought of the van, the other woman, and the lies he had told. The weight of it pressed down on her chest, making it hard to breathe.

"Words are easy, Lucas," she said quietly. "It's the follow-through that's hard."

"I know," he said quickly, leaning toward her. "And I'll prove it to you. I swear, Sophia. I'll get a job. I'll take care of things. I'll make you proud."

His words were smooth, almost rehearsed, and Sophia couldn't tell if they came from his heart or his desperation. Maybe both. She wanted to ask if he even regretted what he had done, but the words stuck in her throat. She wasn't sure she could handle the answer.

"We'll see," she said finally, her voice heavy with exhaustion.

Lucas smiled, as if he had won some small victory. He reached out to touch her hand, but she pulled away, retreating into the house.

As Sophia climbed into bed, the sound of Lucas's footsteps lingered on the porch. She stared at the ceiling, her mind racing with doubt. She wanted to believe in second chances, in fresh starts, but deep down, she feared that Arizona would only bring more of the same.

Outside, the wind stirred the dust, whispering through the quiet streets. Somewhere in the distance, a coyote howled—a haunting reminder that some things never change.

18

THE TURNING POINT

A thin haze of smoke hovered in the kitchen, clinging to the corners where the early morning light struggled to reach. The smell of scorched pancake batter hung in the air, a bittersweet reminder of Lucas's latest attempt at mending fences. Sophia stood by the sink, arms folded, watching him flip yet another batch. The heat of the Arizona summer radiated through the window, intensifying the heaviness in the room.

"Breakfast," Lucas said quietly, turning to place a plate on the table.

Sophia eyed the pancakes—charred around the edges, pale in the center. "I'm not really hungry," she muttered, her gaze drifting to the floor.

She hated how his small gestures made her waver, even for a second. A pang of guilt tugged at her for rejecting him, but the anger she still harbored burned hotter. In the next room, the kids' laughter clashed with the tense silence in the kitchen, their carefree voices a stark contrast to the turmoil clawing at Sophia's chest.

That evening, they headed to Sophia's parents' house. The oppressive heat had only intensified, and by the time they arrived, beads of sweat dotted her forehead. Her mother, Margaret, ushered them inside, where the air conditioning offered some relief. A feast of roast chicken and mashed potatoes filled the dining room with savory aromas, and for a split second, Sophia wished she could vanish into the warmth and familiarity without Lucas shadowing her every move.

Her children squealed with delight upon seeing their grandparents, their small bodies hugging Margaret and Henry's legs, oblivious to the tension trailing their parents like ghosts.

They ate in near silence, utensils clinking against plates as the grandfather clock ticked ominously in the hallway. Sophia forced herself to swallow bits of chicken, each bite tasting dry, emphasizing her mother's culinary skill. When dinner ended, Margaret gently guided Sophia to the back porch, away from the murmuring voices in the living room.

"How are you holding up?" Margaret asked, the concern in her eyes as tangible as the cool night breeze.

Sophia inhaled sharply, wishing the darkness could swallow her whole. "I don't know," she admitted. "It's like... every time he does something nice, I want to believe it. But all I feel is this knot in my stomach. I can't shake the memory of him letting me down. Over and over."

Margaret's hand found Sophia's shoulder, the familiar warmth of a mother's reassurance. "Trust isn't built overnight, honey. And it's not your job to make this easy for him. You're allowed to be angry and to be unsure."

A sting of tears blurred Sophia's vision, but she refused to let them fall. She didn't want to cry, not now, not in front of her mother, and definitely not because of Lucas.

In the living room, Lucas stood by the dusty mantle, his posture rigid. Henry's gaze bore into him.

"You've got a lot to prove," Henry said gruffly, folding his arms. "Sophia deserves better than what you've given her so far."

Lucas lowered his eyes. "I know," he mumbled. "I'm... I'm trying to do better."

Henry's voice remained even, though his jaw tightened. "Then show her. Words don't fix anything. She needs more."

A sharp silence followed, broken only by the hum of the ceiling fan and the distant giggle of a child. Lucas swallowed hard, feeling the weight of Henry's disappointment pressing down on him.

Over the next few weeks, Lucas did make changes—or tried to. He landed a job at the local glass shop in Williams, the scent of cut glass and industrial cleaning solution clinging to his clothes when he arrived home. He started coming home earlier, helping the kids with their homework, and volunteering to cook more often—though the results were usually overcooked or undersalted. Sophia watched each gesture with a wary eye, her heart torn between longing and resentment.

The Arizona sun bore down relentlessly, reflecting off the pavement like a mirror. Sometimes, Sophia would step outside just to feel the dry heat slam into her lungs, hoping it could melt the ice she felt inside. But each time she crossed paths with Lucas—his tentative smile, his cautious greetings—she felt the familiar ache in her chest, a pulsing reminder of betrayals past.

They began attending counseling at a squat adobe building on the outskirts of town, where the reception area smelled faintly of peppermint tea and the waiting-room clock ticked so loudly it invaded Sophia's every thought. On their first visit, she sat rigidly in a mint-green chair, arms clamped around herself, as though any moment she might bolt from the room. Lucas's leg bounced nervously beside her, his gaze fixed on the scuffed tile floor.

The counselor, a middle-aged woman named Denise, led them into a cramped office decorated with potted succulents. She motioned for them to sit on the small loveseat, the stiff fabric scratchy against Sophia's thighs.

"So, Sophia," Denise began softly, "what brings you here today?"

Sophia hesitated, the words trapped in her throat. She heard the soft whir of the overhead fan and smelled lavender air freshener. Finally, she forced her voice out. "I'm here because I... I don't trust him anymore."

Lucas exhaled, turning toward Sophia. "I know I messed up," he said, his voice trembling slightly. "But I'm trying—"

Denise held up a hand gently. "Let's focus on Sophia's feelings first. Sophia, can you tell Lucas why you're finding it difficult to trust him?"

Sophia felt the shame crawl up her neck, flushing her cheeks. "Because he says one thing and does another. He disappears when it matters. He just... leaves me alone with everything."

Lucas swallowed. "I'm sorry," he whispered.

Sophia's eyes stung, but anger flared up in her chest. "It's easy to say you're sorry. But how many times have you said that before?"

Denise spoke quietly, "Lucas, how does it feel to hear that?"

His fingers curled around the edge of the loveseat cushion. "Terrible. I hate knowing I've caused her this much pain. But I can't erase the past. All I can do is try to be better."

Sophia's voice turned hollow. "And I'm supposed to just wait around and see if you finally get it right?"

The room felt stifling; even the potted cacti seemed to droop under the tension. Denise nodded, unflinching. "These are the hard conversations that need to happen. Sophia, it's important that you allow yourself to feel this anger. Lucas, it's important that you truly hear her."

That first session ended with Sophia feeling raw, her heart pounding like a trapped animal's. She walked out into the blazing sun, sweat dotting her upper lip. Lucas hovered at her side, unsure whether to reach for her hand or keep his distance. She never gave him the chance; she hurried to the car, the door slamming shut with a heavy thud.

More sessions followed, each leaving them both emotionally drained. Sophia's doubts only grew more persistent, whispering that no matter what Lucas did, she could never fully forget. She struggled to articulate her pain, sometimes choking on her words until she tasted salt on her lips. Lucas would sit there, silent tears occasionally escaping him, but it wasn't enough to soothe her.

At home, the children's chatter provided a fragile curtain of normalcy. Sophia found pockets of time when she'd step outside to the porch, the rough wooden planks warm beneath her feet. She'd watch the sun dip below the stucco houses, painting the sky in oranges and purples. A gentle wind would rustle the sparse shrubs in their yard, offering a momentary lull in the chaos. But even in the quiet, her mind swirled with unspoken fears:

What if he hurts me again? What if I can never trust him? Will this ever feel like home?

One night, after a particularly tense counseling session, they sat in the car together. The air smelled of dusty earth and the faint exhaust of passing vehicles. Neither spoke for a long time. Finally, Lucas reached out, resting a shaky hand on Sophia's shoulder. She glanced at him—saw the desperation, the regret etched into his features—but her chest remained tight.

"I'm not giving up," Lucas whispered. "Not on us."

Sophia stared ahead through the windshield, the parking lot

lights harsh and sterile in the darkness. "You might not, but I don't know if I have anything left to give."

She gripped the steering wheel until her knuckles turned white, tears burning in the corners of her eyes. Her body felt too heavy to move, as though the weight of her doubts pinned her to the seat.

The next few days blurred into a routine of work, counseling appointments, and stifling summer heat. Lucas stuck to his newfound responsibilities—making the kids' lunches, fixing minor things around the house, and showing up for dinner on time. Sophia noticed all of it, yet her heart remained locked behind the memory of every promise Lucas had broken.

Each night, as she lay in bed, she'd hear him breathing beside her, the mattress sagging under his weight. She thought about how, once, that sound had soothed her—the steady in-and-out of the person she'd chosen to spend her life with. Now it felt like a reminder that the same body, the same breath, had walked away when she needed him most.

No matter how hard she tried, she couldn't see the future with anything but dread. The desert wind rattled the windows, and she wondered if the storms outside would ever rival the one still raging within her.

Despite the counseling, despite Lucas's earnest attempts, Sophia couldn't shake the sense that something between them was irrevocably broken. And as she curled into herself on the bed, listening to Lucas's quiet snores, her tears finally came—silent, relentless, and soaked with uncertainty.

For now, doubt was the only emotion she trusted, and she worried it might never leave.

❧ 19 ❧
BREAKING POINT

A blistering Arizona sun beat down on the small house as Sophia stood at the kitchen sink, hands trembling slightly as she rinsed off the breakfast dishes. Through the dusty windowpane, she could see her children playing in the yard—a swirl of laughter and innocence amid the red-brown earth. The sight should have comforted her, but all she felt was a hollow ache.

They had moved here for a fresh start. Yet, in the past few weeks, the tension she had hoped to escape had returned with a vengeance, creeping into every corner of their lives. Sophia's shoulders tightened as she recalled the night before: Lucas stumbling in after midnight, reeking of whiskey, his words slurred and defensive.

She wanted to scream at him then, but she'd swallowed her anger, too weary to argue. Now, as the heat pressed down on her chest, it was all bubbling to the surface. The overhead fan did little to break the thick, suffocating air.

Lucas walked into the kitchen, letting the screen door slap shut behind him. Dust drifted off his boots, settling into the cracks of the worn linoleum. Without a glance at Sophia, he yanked open the fridge and pulled out a bottle of whiskey, pouring it into a glass as though it were routine.

Sophia's voice came out harsher than she intended. "Nice of you to join us."

He froze, the glass halfway to his lips. "What's that supposed to mean?"

"It means," Sophia said, turning off the faucet with a sharp twist, "that you're never around. The kids barely see you, and when you are here, you act like you resent every second."

Lucas's jaw set, and he lowered the glass. "I work hard, Sophia. I'm busting my ass in the shop every day, trying to keep this family afloat. All you do is nag me."

A bitter laugh escaped her, and she dropped the dishcloth onto the counter with a wet slap. "Don't you dare act like you're some hero. You're the one who dug this hole. You think I don't notice you sneaking out at night—or wonder if you're—"

"Don't start," he barked, his voice rising, eyes flashing with anger. "I'm not doing this with you right now."

"Oh, you're not doing this? Then what are you doing, Lucas?" Sophia demanded, stepping closer. She could smell the whiskey on his breath, stinging her nostrils. "Because it sure as hell isn't anything that looks like fixing our marriage."

He threw back the rest of his drink, slamming the glass on the counter with a dull thud. "You think it's easy for me? I'm under so much pressure—maybe if you didn't ride me every second—"

"I have every reason to be on your back!" Sophia's hands trembled with rage. "You've given me no reason to trust you. You can't just disappear and come back drunk, acting like it's normal—"

Lucas's voice thundered, echoing off the cramped kitchen walls. "Shut up, Sophia!"

And then it happened. In the split second that followed, his hand came up—fingers curled and tense—and struck Sophia across the face. The sound ricocheted in the silence that fell, bouncing off the dingy walls like a gunshot.

The force staggered Sophia; she stumbled, one hand flying to her stinging cheek. For a heartbeat, it felt as if time had stopped. Her breathing turned shallow, her ears rang, and she became hyperaware of the heat pressing in, the faint hum of the fridge, and the distant giggles of her children filtering in from outside.

Lucas's eyes went wide, as though he couldn't quite believe what he had just done. His hand hovered in the air, trembling, before dropping limply to his side. "Sophia... I didn't—"

"Don't," she breathed, her voice like broken glass. She backed away, her heart pounding like a frightened animal's. She found herself glancing nervously at his raised arm, now lowered, but the terror didn't subside. Something vital had shattered in that moment, and she could feel it in every cell of her body. "Stay away from me."

Lucas reached for her. "I'm sorry. God, Sophia, I'm so sorry."

She flinched at his movement, raw fear flaring in her chest. The sight of it hit him like a punch: his own wife recoiling from him, eyes wide with shock and something close to dread.

"Don't you dare come near me," she hissed through tears. Her voice wavered, but she forced steel into it. "You have no idea what you've just done."

A few minutes later, Sophia managed to gather the children, her voice quivering as she coaxed them inside. "We're going next door, okay? To Grandma and Grandpa's."

Confusion flickered in their eyes, but they sensed her urgency and didn't protest. They followed her across the narrow strip of desert lawn that separated the two houses. As they approached the older, single-story home, she felt her heart hammering against her ribs.

Margaret and Henry were already on their porch, alarmed by the raised voices they had heard. Seeing Sophia's reddened cheek and tear-streaked eyes, they hurried forward. The prickly desert sun still beat down, but their presence lent a fragile sense of safety.

"What happened?" Margaret asked, her voice quivering as she took in her daughter's appearance.

Sophia's throat tightened. "I... I just need to stay here tonight," she managed. "Just—give me some space, please."

Margaret wrapped Sophia in a hug that smelled of lavender lotion and comforting familiarity. The tension in Sophia's body refused to melt away, but the warmth of her mother's arms allowed her a moment's breath. Henry stood near them, his face dark with fury, and ushered the children inside.

That evening, after the children were settled in the spare bedroom, Sophia found herself in the living room of her parents' house, sinking into a worn floral couch. A dull ache still throbbed along her cheekbone, and she fought the urge to press a cold compress against it—somehow, the pain felt like a necessary reminder.

Henry walked in with careful, measured steps, pausing by the front window that offered a clear view of Sophia's house next door. He saw no sign of Lucas. He turned to Sophia, seating himself across from her. He was silent for a long moment, taking in the stiff set of her shoulders and the tears she struggled to keep at bay.

Finally, he spoke. "Did Lucas do that to you?"

Sophia swallowed, staring at her hands curled in her lap. She gave a small nod. Her father's knuckles went white as he gripped the arm of the chair.

"Where is he now?"

She shrugged, feeling a wave of bitterness. "Probably still there, drinking himself into oblivion."

Henry pressed his lips into a thin line. "Damn it, Sophia. I... I never wanted this for you." His voice was thick with anger, but there was heartbreak there, too. "If he tries to come over here, I'm sending him packing. Do you understand? I don't care if he's sorry. I'm not letting him near you until you decide what to do."

Sophia let out a shuddering breath. A part of her wanted to say she'd never see Lucas again. Another part wanted to break down and sob because, despite everything, she still loved him—once upon a time, he had been the one she needed by her side. Now, she wasn't even sure who he was.

"I don't know what I'm going to do, Dad," she whispered. "I'm scared. And I'm so angry at him—at myself—for letting it get this far."

Henry's expression softened. "We'll figure it out. But you're safe here."

Meanwhile, next door in the dimly lit living room, Lucas sat alone. The overhead fan creaked, stirring the stale air. He stared at his hand, recalling the moment it had lashed out as if it belonged to someone else. His stomach twisted with guilt, and the whiskey he poured only deepened the sickening feeling.

He replayed the slap over and over: the shock on Sophia's face, the horror in his own heart. He wanted to numb it, but no amount of alcohol could erase the truth—he had hurt her in a way that words could never undo.

At some point, he stumbled to the couch, burying his face in his hands. Sleep came, but it offered no peace—only nightmares.

When Sophia woke in her parents' home the next morning, the desert sun was already blazing through the windows. She could feel a tightness in her neck from sleeping on the couch, and the dull pain in her cheek reminded her that this wasn't just a nightmare.

She was getting the kids ready for breakfast when the front door rattled. Sophia's heart seized. She peered out the window to see Lucas standing on the porch, shoulders slumped and eyes bloodshot.

Henry stepped forward, blocking Lucas's view of Sophia. "What are you doing here?" he demanded, his voice low and guarded.

"I need to talk to Sophia," Lucas said, his voice hoarse. "Please."

Henry looked to Sophia for guidance, his protective stance never wavering. Sophia swallowed hard. Finally, she gave a tiny nod and turned toward the back door. "Meet me out back," she called, her voice tremulous.

Sophia sat on a weathered wooden bench beneath the shade of a mesquite tree in her parents' yard. From this vantage point, she could see her own house next door, the windows still and silent. The faint smell of dust and warm pavement drifted in the air, underscoring how close their worlds still were—despite feeling miles apart.

Lucas approached, head bowed. She noticed the dark circles under his eyes and the unsteady way he held himself, like a man drowning in regrets. He stopped several feet away, as if sensing her fear.

"What do you want, Lucas?" Her tone was flat; her arms were crossed over her chest in a protective stance.

He stood there, fiddling with his hands. "I came to apologize," he began, his voice trembling. "I know I can never take back what I did, but I needed you to know how sorry I am."

She let out a slow breath, remembering the snap of his palm against her cheek, the shock and terror that followed. She hated how her body tensed at his every move, as though still expecting violence. "Do you even understand what you did, Lucas? Hitting me —" She shook her head, pain twisting her features. "I don't know if I can ever trust you again."

His eyes filled with tears. "I know. I'm not making excuses. I've been a terrible husband. I've let anger and stress—and booze—take control. I wouldn't blame you if you never wanted to speak to me again. But please, Sophia... I want to do whatever it takes to change. For you, for the kids."

She studied him, her heart a storm of hurt, anger, and an unsteady flicker of something like hope. "If you're serious about changing," she said slowly, "then prove it. Go to counseling. Alone. I can't even consider letting you back into our lives until you face your own demons first."

He nodded, tears trailing down his cheeks. "I swear, I'll do it."

A few days later, Sophia found herself in the now-familiar waiting room: the peppermint-scented air freshener, the stiff beige chairs, the low hum of the air conditioner. She hadn't planned to join Lucas at this session—he was supposed to start going alone—but after some urging from their counselor, Denise, she agreed to sit in on part of it.

Lucas walked in with hesitant steps. Sophia's cheek was healing, but the emotional bruise still throbbed. She could barely look at him without recalling the moment his hand had connected with her face.

Inside Denise's office, dim lamplight contrasted with the fluorescent overhead. Sophia perched on one end of the loveseat, and Lucas on the other, as though a gulf separated them.

Denise glanced between them. "Sophia, Lucas has told me a bit about what happened. First, I want to acknowledge how difficult it is to come here after such a traumatic event."

Sophia's arms stayed folded, her shoulders rigid. "I'm here because I need to know if this is just another promise he won't keep."

Lucas's voice was unsteady. "It's not empty this time. I feel sick about what I did—"

Denise raised a hand gently. "Lucas, let's name it. You hit your wife in anger. That isn't something words alone can fix. Can you share what you feel when you think about that moment?"

He swallowed hard, tears gathering in his eyes. "I feel disgusted —at myself. I never thought I'd be that kind of man. But I was. And I—" His voice cracked. "I'm scared of myself now."

Sophia trembled, recalling the jolt of pain, the rush of disbelief. She looked down, blinking back tears. "I'm scared of you, too," she admitted, her voice catching. "I never thought I'd say that, but I am."

Denise let the silence hold for a moment, the hum of the AC filling the space. Finally, she spoke gently. "Lucas, do you understand how much work it will take to rebuild Sophia's sense of safety?"

He nodded slowly, tears slipping down his cheeks. "I do. I'll do anything: anger management classes, more individual counseling—whatever it takes."

Sophia's lips thinned. Part of her wanted to believe him. Another part whispered that believing was dangerous. She managed, "I'm not promising anything, but I'll keep coming to these sessions... if you keep doing the work."

Lucas looked up, relief and sorrow etched into his expression. "I will. I promise."

From then on, Sophia chose to stay at her parents' house for the time being. She went about daily life in a subdued haze—preparing simple meals in her mother's kitchen, watching the kids play under the mesquite tree, and reading them bedtime stories with a strained but gentle voice. Each night, she lay awake, the faint desert wind rustling outside, replaying the slap in her mind.

A few times, she caught herself peering out the window toward her own house next door, half-expecting Lucas to appear. Even the sight of those familiar walls was enough to send a shiver down her spine.

One morning, as she stepped onto the porch, Henry joined her, placing a steady hand on her shoulder. The thin layer of dust on the wooden planks floated up at their feet, glinting in the harsh sun. "You know you can stay as long as you need," he said, his voice gruff with emotion. "If he tries to come around and you're not ready, I'll make sure he knows he's not welcome."

Sophia nodded, her eyes stinging with tears she no longer tried to hide. "Thank you, Dad," she whispered.

Despite the turmoil, the Arizona sun kept rising over the desert each morning—hot, unapologetic, and unchanging. The air smelled of dust and dry sage, and the landscape glowed with a harsh beauty that mirrored her own situation: even in a barren place, life found a way to persist.

Lucas began regular counseling and anger management sessions. Sophia, still bruised inside and out, balanced her fear with a glimmer of possibility—if he truly changed. But the wound on her trust was deep, and she wasn't sure it would ever heal completely.

For now, they lived apart, only a patch of yard separating their two houses, though it felt like an unbridgeable distance. Each time she recalled the slap, a fresh wave of heartache and caution washed over her. She wasn't ready to share a home with him again—not yet. Perhaps not ever.

But in the stifling Arizona heat, amid the dusty roads and endless skies, Sophia found a fragile resolve: to protect herself, to protect her children, and to demand more from Lucas than just promises. The desert wind still howled at night—a lonely, mournful sound—but as she lay in bed in her parents' spare room, she told herself that no matter how dark things seemed, she owed it to herself—and to her kids—to keep going.

And so she did.

20

ELIZABETH'S PERSPECTIVE

Elizabeth sat on the soft, squishy carpet in Grandma and Grandpa's extra room. All her stuffed friends were around her—Mr. Fuzzy, Princess Bunny, and Spot the Puppy. She liked to have pretend tea parties with them, but today she just held Mr. Fuzzy tight. She didn't feel like pouring pretend tea or singing silly songs.

She heard grown-up voices down the hall. Mommy was talking softly with Grandma. Daddy wasn't there. He hadn't come to Grandma and Grandpa's house after that big fight.

Elizabeth scrunched her face, trying not to think about it. But she still saw it in her head: Daddy yelling, then a loud slap, and Mommy crying. It made her tummy hurt to remember. She wished she could make that memory go away.

Elizabeth wondered if she was brave enough to be okay again. And what if Daddy got angry once more? Could she keep Mommy safe?

It happened back at their own house. Elizabeth was coloring in her room when she heard Mommy's loud voice. It sounded scared. Daddy's voice was angry. She got up to see, peeking from behind the door. Then Daddy shouted, and there was a big smack sound.

Elizabeth felt her heart thump-thump-thump so fast it hurt. Mommy cried, so Elizabeth ran outside. She ran until she couldn't see the house anymore. She kept thinking maybe Mommy and

Daddy were mad because of her. She heard Daddy say "kids" and "trouble" and other words she didn't understand. Maybe if she were a better girl, Daddy wouldn't be so mad.

Mommy took Elizabeth and her brother to Grandma and Grandpa's house that night. Elizabeth kept looking at Mommy's sad face, feeling heavy in her chest. Grandpa paced around a lot, looking at the door as if he were waiting for someone.

Now, Elizabeth looked at her stuffed animals in a circle. She touched Spot the Puppy's ear. "Is it my fault Daddy got mad?" she whispered, but the puppy's brown eyes didn't answer.

A gentle knock on the door made her jump. Grandma peeked in, smiling with kind eyes. "Hello, sweetheart," she said. "Can I sit with you?"

Elizabeth nodded. Grandma kneeled down on the carpet next to her and put a warm hand on Elizabeth's back. "Mommy says you haven't been talking much," Grandma said. "Are you feeling okay?"

Elizabeth shrugged. "I'm scared," she said, hugging Mr. Fuzzy. "Daddy was really mad. He said words about me and Oliver."

Grandma hugged her close. "Oh, honey," she whispered. "Daddy's upset about grown-up things. It's not because of you."

Elizabeth's eyes got wet. She sniffed. "But... he said 'kids' when he was yelling. I heard him."

Grandma shook her head. "That still doesn't make it your fault," she said gently. "Sometimes, grown-ups get angry and make mistakes."

Elizabeth clung to Grandma's sweater. She wanted to believe her, but part of her still felt a big, yucky feeling inside. "I want everything to be nice again," she whispered.

That evening, Elizabeth went to the living room. Mommy was there with Grandpa, talking in quiet voices. She thought maybe they were talking about Daddy, but she wasn't sure. The TV was on low, showing a funny cartoon, but Elizabeth wasn't laughing. She kept thinking about how Daddy used to pick her up high and make her laugh. Could he still be the same Daddy if he hurt Mommy?

Mommy came over and sat next to her. "How are you, baby?" Mommy asked, smoothing Elizabeth's hair.

Elizabeth didn't look up right away. "Are we going home?" she asked in a small voice.

Mommy's face went sad. "Not tonight," she said, reaching for Elizabeth's hand. "Daddy needs time to think. But we're safe here with Grandma and Grandpa."

Elizabeth wanted to feel better, but her heart was still squeezing. She missed Daddy, the happy Daddy who played with her and told silly jokes. Now she wasn't sure who Daddy was. Daddy seemed to be changing a lot since Oliver joined the family.

At bedtime, Elizabeth lay in a big bed with scratchy sheets that smelled like Grandpa's old closet. She cuddled Mr. Fuzzy, the glow of the hallway light shining under the door. She heard Grandma and Grandpa talking somewhere, and Mommy's voice, too.

She closed her eyes, but the loud slap noise popped into her head. What if I said something to Daddy? Would that have stopped him? Did I do something bad? Tears dripped down her cheeks, and she squeezed Mr. Fuzzy even tighter. Grandma told her it wasn't her fault, but it still felt like her fault in her chest.

"I'm a good girl," she whispered to the dark room. "Right?" Mr. Fuzzy didn't answer.

She breathed in and out, trying to calm down. Finally, she reminded herself of what Grandma said: "Daddy's problems are grown-up things." She repeated it over and over until she became a little sleepy.

When morning came, bright sun peeked through the flower-patterned curtains. Elizabeth opened her eyes and looked around, feeling a little lost. Then she remembered: she was at Grandma and Grandpa's house, not home.

Mommy was already in the kitchen with Grandpa and Grandma, making breakfast. Grandpa set out a plate with scrambled eggs for Elizabeth. She climbed onto a chair, staring at the yellow fluff. She wasn't sure she was hungry.

Mommy touched Elizabeth's shoulder. "Did you sleep okay, my sweet girl?"

Elizabeth shrugged. "I guess," she said softly. She poked at the eggs. Then she saw the bruise on Mommy's cheek again, partly covered by makeup. She looked away, her tummy twisting.

Elizabeth knew she was safe here, but she still wondered if Daddy's anger would come back. And if it did, how could a little girl stay brave in a big, scary world?

She took a shaky bite of her eggs, repeating in her head, "I'm a good girl; it's not my fault." Even though she wasn't sure she believed it yet, she held on to that thought—because for now, it was all she could do.

21

NEW BEGINNINGS

As Sophia closed the door of their old life behind her, she couldn't shake the sensation that everything ahead—rolling hills, endless sky, and the weight of her past—would collide on this sprawling ranch, testing not just her family's resolve but also her own hope for a fresh start.

The morning sun glinted off the moving trucks, each rumble echoing along the dirt road. Sophia stood on the porch of their old house for the last time, her heart caught between excitement and a nagging flicker of anxiety. She watched Lucas tighten the rope around the final boxes in their van, sweat darkening the back of his T-shirt.

They were leaving behind cramped houses and prying neighbors for something much bigger. Her parents, Henry and Margaret, had bought a 720-acre ranch that felt more dreamlike than real. Dotted with wildflowers and overshadowed by distant mountains, this land sprawled so far that Sophia couldn't see where it ended. Here, Sophia's family and extended relatives would each find their own corner, yet still remain connected.

Sophia let her gaze roam over the small town behind them. Privacy had been a luxury there, and she yearned for open skies and cleaner air. But living so close to her parents and younger siblings again stirred up old uncertainties. She inhaled the dry breeze, reminding herself of how far she and Lucas had come in the past year.

Inside, the house buzzed with last-minute packing. Four-year-old Elizabeth knelt on the floor, carefully placing her toys in a box. She paused to hug Mr. Fuzzy—her beloved stuffed bunny—before tucking him in.

"Mommy, I'm helping!" Elizabeth called, beaming.

Sophia offered a tired but warm smile. "You're the best helper. I don't know what I'd do without you."

Before Elizabeth could bask in the praise for too long, her almost-two-year-old brother, Oliver, waddled over and yanked Mr. Fuzzy out of the box. "Mine!" he declared, clutching the bunny with sticky hands.

"Hey!" Elizabeth squealed, trying to retrieve her bunny. "No, Oliver, that's mine!"

Sophia peered in from the kitchen, where she was now wrapping dishes in yellowed newspaper. "Elizabeth, let him hold it for a minute. You'll get it back."

Elizabeth let out an exasperated sigh but relented, stomping her foot softly. "He takes everything, Mommy," she grumbled.

"You're handling it well. Being a big sister can be tough," Sophia said kindly, smoothing the hair from Elizabeth's eyes. Elizabeth's frown softened under her mom's praise, and she returned to her packing with renewed determination, though she kept one wary eye on Oliver.

Lucas appeared at the doorway, arms dusted with dirt. "That's the last of the furniture loaded," he said, wiping sweat off his forehead. He flashed Sophia a small, proud grin.

She let her gaze linger on him. Their journey over the past year had been messy—Lucas still drank and smoked pot occasionally, but he'd curbed his worst habits. There were fewer broken promises and no more late-night disappearances. For the first time in a long time, they felt like partners.

"Thanks," Sophia replied, her voice carrying a note of gratitude she couldn't quite hide. She rose from her makeshift seat on a box. "I'll help you tie off the tarp."

He shrugged. "I've got it. You should probably sit for a second. You've been at this all morning."

She shook her head. "We're almost out of here. Let's finish strong."

Soon, the family van was loaded, and the kids were strapped into their car seats. Elizabeth hugged Mr. Fuzzy so tightly he looked about to burst a seam, while Oliver babbled happily about the "big twuck" ahead. Sophia climbed into the passenger seat, securing her own seatbelt. She glanced over at Lucas, who turned the key in the ignition.

"Are you ready?" he asked, a shadow of nerves beneath his hopeful smile.

She forced herself to breathe out the tension. "As ready as I'll ever be."

The drive to the ranch was only thirty minutes but felt like venturing into a new world. Asphalt bled into gravel, the horizon opening into golden hills under a wide, bright sky. Elizabeth pressed her face to the window, eyes wide at the sight of open fields. Oliver kicked his legs, squealing whenever they hit a bump in the road.

When they finally reached the ranch, Sophia's breath caught. Rolling grasslands, groves of trees, distant mountains: it was breathtaking and daunting all at once. She sensed in her bones how monumental this move was—not just physically, but emotionally, too.

They parked near their new single-wide mobile home on the western 40 acres, which was nestled among the trees with a new gravel drive. Beyond her home, her parents' single-wide occupied the lower 40 acres, on the other side of the small woods that separated the homes, providing perfect privacy and proximity. The rest of the land remained open for livestock and future family projects.

"Welcome home!" Margaret called, hurrying over to hug Sophia. "We set up a space for you guys to drop your boxes. We'll help you get settled."

Sophia's younger sisters, Isabelle and Evelyn, bounded over from the porch. Isabelle, thirteen, exuded energy like a firecracker; she hopped from one foot to the other, her curly hair bouncing with every step. Evelyn, twelve, hovered just behind her, fingers twisting in her shirt hem. She gave Sophia a small wave, her cheeks tinged pink—shyness had always been Evelyn's armor.

Sophia released Margaret and turned to her sisters. "Thanks for the welcome committee," she teased, offering Isabelle a fist bump. "I see you're as bouncy as ever."

Isabelle grinned, her eyes sparkling. "Are you kidding? I've been counting down the days for you to get here. We've got so much room to run around, and Dad said I can learn to ride the horses once they arrive!"

Evelyn shifted from foot to foot. "I... I'm happy you're here, Sophia," she said quietly. She stole a glance at Elizabeth, who was hiding behind Sophia's leg. "Hi, Elizabeth."

Elizabeth peeked up, hugging Mr. Fuzzy to her chest. "Hi," she mumbled.

Isabelle's attention snapped to Oliver, who was attempting to climb out of the van on his own. "Hey, let me help you, little guy!" she said, rushing over to scoop him up. "He's so chubby," she giggled.

Evelyn offered a shy smile as she helped Elizabeth unbuckle. "We can play in the meadow," she told Elizabeth. "It's really pretty, and we have a swing by the oak tree now."

Not long after, Julian—Sophia's youngest sibling at eleven— wandered over, hands tucked in his pockets. He was quiet by nature, preferring to observe more than speak. He gave Sophia a small nod of greeting, then said in a low voice, "I can help unload if you want."

"That'd be awesome," Sophia said, ruffling his hair. He didn't protest; he just offered a faint smile and headed toward the trucks, quietly getting to work hauling lighter boxes.

Meanwhile, Lucas and Henry unloaded the heavier furniture, exchanging the occasional grunt of effort. From the corner of her eye, Sophia noticed Elizabeth and Oliver trailing Isabelle and Evelyn, but soon the children started drifting back underfoot. The novelty of the big space seemed overwhelming—especially since Sophia and Lucas still had so much to unpack.

Sensing the chaos, Sophia asked her sisters for a favor. "Hey, Isabelle, Evelyn—could you take the kids to the back room for a bit? There's an air mattress in that big box over there. I figured they could bounce on it... safely."

Isabelle snapped a salute. "You got it, sis!" She grabbed Evelyn by the arm and practically dragged her toward the boxes. Evelyn shot Sophia a timid smile—helping made her happy, but she often let Isabelle take the lead.

For a good stretch of time, Sophia and Lucas enjoyed relative peace, carting boxes into the modest living space. Outside, a soft breeze ruffled the grass, carrying the scent of wildflowers. Now and then, Sophia peeked through a window, marveling at the sheer expanse of land. "We really did it," she thought. "We're actually here."

But the calm broke with a sudden thump and a chorus of panicked cries from down the hall. Sophia froze, exchanging a wide-eyed look with Lucas. She dropped the box in her arms and sprinted toward the sound.

In the spare room, chaos reigned. The air mattress was indeed blown up—and the kids, plus Isabelle and Evelyn, had invented a game of jumping as high as they could, launching each other into the air. Oliver, still just a toddler, had been caught in the fray. He tumbled off the mattress with a plop, tears streaking his cheeks.

Sophia's heart hammered. "Isabelle! Evelyn! Are you kidding me?" she snapped, scooping up her wailing son. She bounced him gently, checking his limbs for injury.

Isabelle, face flushed, held up her hands. "We were only playing, Sophia. Nobody meant to hurt Oliver."

Evelyn clasped her hands in front of her chest, tears in her eyes. "I'm so sorry," she whispered, her voice barely audible. "I told them to be careful."

Elizabeth stood nearby, Mr. Fuzzy clutched tight, clearly torn between excitement and fear. "Mommy... Oliver flew so high," she said, her eyes wide.

"It's okay, baby," Sophia murmured, calming Elizabeth with a stroke of her hair. Then she shot a stern look at her siblings. "You can't be throwing around a toddler, for crying out loud. If something serious happened—"

Isabelle lowered her gaze. "We're sorry. We'll stop."

Lucas peeked in from behind Sophia, relief crossing his face when he saw Oliver was mostly fine. "Let's find a safer activity," he suggested.

Julian appeared in the doorway, quiet as ever, his voice almost a mumble. "The chicks arrived at the main house... maybe we can show them to Elizabeth and Oliver?" He shrugged, one hand fiddling with the hem of his T-shirt. "It'd be calmer."

Sophia took a moment to let her pulse settle. "That's actually a good idea. Take them along the trail—no wandering off, got it?" She leveled a look at Isabelle, who flashed a sheepish grin, and Evelyn, who stared at her sneakers.

"We'll be good, promise," Isabelle said quickly, her usual spark returning. Evelyn just nodded, her lips pressed tight.

With that, Isabelle grabbed Elizabeth's hand and led her out the door, Evelyn following with Oliver carefully perched on her hip. Julian trotted behind, casting Sophia and Lucas an apologetic glance before disappearing into the sunlight. Their chatter and laughter faded as they headed toward the main house, the lure of baby chicks too tempting for toddler tears to last.

Sophia sank against the doorframe, exhaling a long breath. "I guess that's our new normal—herding kids and siblings all day."

Lucas reached out, lightly rubbing her back. "Hey, we did choose a family ranch. At least they'll all grow up around each other, right?"

She mustered a wry smile. "Sure. Built-in babysitters, though I might need to set some ground rules."

Lucas hefted a box of kitchenware, glancing outside to see the bright expanse of land. "You, me, and 720 acres. We'll figure it out."

Sophia looked at him, a mix of trepidation and warmth swirling in her chest. "We always figure it out," she said quietly, trying to reassure both him and herself.

From somewhere beyond the window, the breeze carried the distant sound of children's laughter—and beyond that, the promise of wide, open space. Despite her nervous heart, Sophia felt a gentle rise of hope. They were all here—together, messy, imperfect, but united by a chance at something better: a place to grow and heal.

No matter how uncertain the path ahead, Sophia knew this ranch pulsed with possibilities—and even if they stumbled, she intended to stand strong for the family she loved.

22

CREEKSIDE TEA PARTY

No one noticed Elizabeth slip away at first. Amid the chatter about baby chicks and the sunlit path through the woods, her little footsteps veered off course—and by the time anyone realized she was gone, the peaceful ranch felt dangerously vast.

Elizabeth walked at the back of the group, humming softly as she followed her aunts—Isabelle and Evelyn—and her uncle, Julian. The four of them had decided to head from Sophia and Lucas's trailer on the west 40 acres toward the main trailer—where the new baby chicks were kept. Sophia was Elizabeth's mother, but also Isabelle and Evelyn's older sister, having stayed behind at the trailer to finish some chores.

Isabelle led the way, her hair bouncing with each energetic step, while Julian stayed near the middle, quiet and watchful. Evelyn lingered close to Elizabeth, shy but protective, holding the little girl's hand. Elizabeth giggled at the springy grass underfoot, reveling in the adventure.

They'd barely made it halfway when Isabelle called Evelyn over to help navigate a tricky patch of uneven ground. Evelyn hesitated before letting go of Elizabeth's hand to check the footing with Isabelle. By the time she turned around, Elizabeth was still a few steps behind—apparently safe. "Just keep an eye on her," Evelyn told herself, feeling the weight of responsibility.

In those few moments, though, Elizabeth heard the soft gurgle of a creek. Without a word, she slipped off the path, Yeller—Grandma Margaret's loyal dog—following behind, his keen eyes on the little girl.

The water sparkled under a canopy of shifting light. Elizabeth's eyes shone with delight. "Oh, it's so pretty," she whispered, stepping carefully toward the creek's mossy bank.

Kneeling on the soft ground, she set out smooth stones for an impromptu tea party. One "cup" for herself, another for Yeller, who watched contentedly. She felt no fear—only a child's wonder at the magic of flowing water and sun-dappled woods.

"One for me," she said, miming pouring water into a stone "cup," "and one for you, Yeller." She dipped her hand into the creek, letting cool droplets slide off her fingers.

Unaware of Elizabeth's quiet exit, Isabelle, Evelyn, Julian—and a fussy Oliver in Isabelle's arms—continued on until they reached the main trailer. Isabelle glanced over her shoulder, expecting Elizabeth to be right behind them, but saw only the empty trail.

"Where's Elizabeth?" Isabelle blurted, her eyes darting around.

Evelyn's stomach twisted. "She was just... oh no..." Her voice trembled. "I let go of her hand for a second when you asked me to help."

Julian's face tightened. "Maybe she got turned around in the woods?"

Isabelle's earlier confidence faded. "We have to get back to Sophia and Lucas—tell them Elizabeth's missing. Hurry!"

They retraced their steps through the grassy paths linking the main trailer to the west 40 acres. The ranch's expanse suddenly felt daunting, with open fields rolling out in every direction. Isabelle held Oliver close, his cries punctuating their anxious footsteps.

Once they reached Sophia and Lucas's trailer, they found Margaret and Henry there, helping Sophia organize boxes. Lucas was hauling supplies from the truck. The moment Margaret saw her younger daughters' worried expressions, her heart lurched.

"What's wrong?" she demanded, setting aside a box.

"Elizabeth... she wandered off somewhere between here and the main trailer," Isabelle explained, breathless. "We thought she was right behind us."

Evelyn's eyes brimmed with tears. "I'm so sorry, Sophia," she choked out. "I—I only let go of her hand for a second."

Sophia's face went pale. "Gone? When did you last see her?" she asked, her voice tight with panic.

"Not long," Julian cut in, glancing at his watch, "maybe fifteen minutes. But we need to move. She could be anywhere."

Henry placed a hand on Margaret's arm, tension apparent in his posture. "We'll split up. I'll check around the north side, Lucas can go south. Sophia, you and the kids head back through the woods. Margaret and I will meet you halfway."

Sophia exhaled shakily. "Okay. Let's go—now."

They dispersed quickly. Lucas jogged off to explore a southward path, while Henry followed the tree line north. Sophia and Margaret led Isabelle, Evelyn, and Julian back into the woods. Sophia's heart pounded with every step, her eyes scanning for any sign of her daughter. The thought of Elizabeth lost out here made her stomach twist.

Margaret hurried beside Sophia, keeping calm for her family's sake. But inside, her mind raced with "What if...?" She refused to let the thought finish.

Isabelle called out steadily, "Elizabeth! Elizabeth!" Her usually chipper tone shook with worry.

Evelyn, wracked with guilt, peered into every cluster of bushes. "Elizabeth!" she cried, her voice cracking. "I'm so sorry... answer me, please!"

Julian trudged in silence, scanning every shadow. The forest felt eerily quiet, broken only by its calls and the rustle of leaves.

At last, Margaret paused, hearing a soft giggle over the gentle babble of a creek. Relief flooded her senses. She beckoned Sophia and the others forward, pressing a finger to her lips to keep them quiet. Pushing aside a cluster of ferns, Margaret spotted a small figure on a mossy bank.

Elizabeth, kneeling at the water's edge, had stones spread out like tiny teacups. Yeller sat loyally beside her. The creek's soothing murmur underscored the child's calm, oblivious to everyone's panic.

Margaret nearly collapsed with relief. "Elizabeth!" she called, her voice brimming with both exasperation and joy. She stumbled down the short slope, falling to her knees by her granddaughter. "Oh, honey—we've been so worried."

Elizabeth looked up, surprise flickering in her bright eyes.

"Grandma?" she said sweetly, as if expecting no less. "I'm having tea with Yeller."

Margaret let out a shaky laugh, pressing a trembling hand to Elizabeth's cheek. "You gave us such a scare," she breathed. "This ranch is huge, sweetheart—you can't just wander off alone."

Evelyn hurried up behind her mother, eyes wet. "Elizabeth," she gasped, "I'm so sorry... I let go of you."

Elizabeth blinked as if puzzled by the drama. "It's okay, Aunt Evelyn," she answered gently, patting Evelyn's hand. "I had Yeller. I wasn't scared."

Sophia arrived next, her heart hammering. She scooped Elizabeth into her arms, hugging her fiercely. "You cannot run off like that," Sophia said, her voice breaking. "Do you know how worried we were?"

Elizabeth nodded against Sophia's shoulder. "I won't do it again," she promised, though she cast a longing glance at her half-finished 'tea party.' Yeller thumped his tail, oblivious to the tension.

Moments later, Henry and Lucas came bounding through the trees, alarm etched on their faces. They spotted Elizabeth safe in Sophia's arms, and a collective sigh of relief rippled through the group. Henry stroked Yeller's head. "Good dog," he murmured, his voice unsteady.

Lucas ruffled Elizabeth's hair, relief and residual fear in his eyes. "Don't ever do that again, kiddo," he said, his words tight with emotion.

Isabelle let out a shaky laugh. "Thank goodness," she breathed, pressing a hand to her chest.

Evelyn wiped her tears, her cheeks still flushed. "I'm so sorry," she repeated, her voice trembling. "I'll never take my eyes off her again, Sophia, I swear."

Margaret stood, helping Elizabeth gather her little collection of stones. "We're just glad she's okay," she said softly, eyeing each of her children. "We all need to be more careful. The ranch is beautiful, but it can be dangerous if we're not cautious."

Sophia nodded, hugging Elizabeth close. "Thank you, Mom. I— I don't know what I would have done..." Her words trailed off, the raw terror of the last several minutes still coursing through her veins.

Henry guided them gently back toward the trail. "Let's head to the trailer. We can talk about the rules to keep everyone safe."

And so they walked, the sun breaking through the canopy above, the crisis behind them but the lesson lingering. Elizabeth clung to Sophia, yawning as the adrenaline faded, while Margaret and Evelyn exchanged looks of relief and guilt. They would hold onto that little hand much more firmly next time—no matter how difficult the path might be.

In the hush following their frantic search, the family made their way back to the west 40, each step a reminder of the balance between wonder and caution on their sprawling ranch. Elizabeth had found magic by the creek; they'd all found a renewed sense of just how precious—and fragile— their safety was.

✵ 23 ✵
STOLEN INNOCENCE

Something about the house felt off tonight—like a single thread pulled too tight, ready to snap at any moment.

It was a quiet evening at Margaret and Henry's house—the sort of night when the hum of the television in the living room melded with the soft creak of floorboards. A warm lamp glow covered the kitchen, where Elizabeth and Oliver sat at the small table, wolfing down homemade biscuits slathered in jam. The savory aroma of a stew simmering on the stove lent the place its usual comfort.

"Alright, kids," Margaret said, wiping her hands on a dish towel. "Dinner won't be ready for a while, so why don't you go on and play in Julian's room?"

"Yes, Grandma," Elizabeth replied politely. At four years old, she carried herself with a maturity beyond her years—often guiding two-year-old Oliver as though she were a seasoned caretaker. True to form, Oliver copied her manners, sliding off the chair to toddle beside his sister.

Margaret ushered them down the narrow hallway. "Keep it quiet. Grandpa's working," she added in a hushed tone, bestowing them with a gentle smile before returning to the stew pot, humming a soft tune.

Usually, Margaret and Henry's home was a haven for Elizabeth and Oliver—a place steeped in familiar scents, cozy quilts, and unconditional love. But tonight, Elizabeth sensed a subtle shift in the air, though she couldn't name what was different.

She pushed open the door to Julian's room with a faint creak. A single low-watt bulb cast weak light, its flicker stretching uncertain shadows across the walls. Elizabeth paused, letting her eyes adjust to the dimness.

"It's dark," she said softly.

"I can see," Oliver replied, gripping her hand. The two stepped cautiously inside.

Julian—twelve years old—was perched cross-legged on his bed, fiddling with a small figurine that Elizabeth recognized all too well: her favorite figurine. He didn't greet them; he merely shifted his gaze briefly to acknowledge their arrival.

With a shrug, Elizabeth guided Oliver to a pile of wooden blocks on the floor. "Let's build a tower," she suggested, her voice gentle.

"Okay!" Oliver plopped down with enthusiasm, handing blocks to his sister as she stacked them. The hush in the room was broken only by their quiet murmurs and the occasional clack of blocks. Overhead, the bulb flickered, casting the walls into wavering silhouettes.

From the corner of her eye, Elizabeth tracked Julian's restless movements. He kept glancing at the door, fiddling with the figurine in a way that seemed more nervous than casual. His posture and the tightness in his jaw set off a small alarm inside Elizabeth, though she didn't understand why. She tried to focus on stacking the last block—a teetering piece that Oliver clapped for when it didn't fall.

"You want to play, Julian?" Oliver asked innocently, craning his neck to see their uncle.

Julian exhaled, sounding both bored and tense. "Maybe," he muttered, placing the figurine down with an uneasy carefulness. Something in his tone made Elizabeth's stomach flutter.

Just then, the door eased open a crack. Margaret's voice drifted in, warm and curious. "Everything all right in here?" she asked gently. She peeked in, her eyes flicking from Julian to Elizabeth and Oliver.

Julian jerked upright, mustering a half-smile. "We're fine."

Elizabeth cleared her throat. "We're making towers," she said, forcing a bright note. She wished Margaret would linger, but her grandmother only nodded and smiled.

"Good job staying quiet," Margaret commended them, then quietly closed the door. The instant her presence vanished, a chill seemed to settle back into the space, like a draft sneaking under the door.

Oliver nudged Elizabeth to build a second tower. She obliged, carefully balancing each piece, but the knot in her stomach tightened. She caught Julian watching them with an intensity that made the hairs on her arms prickle. The light overhead flickered again, and a brief darkness cloaked the room before returning to its faint glow.

Julian rose from the bed, pushing past scattered toys on the floor. He paced near them, every step eliciting a subtle floorboard squeak. Elizabeth felt the tension coil in her chest. "Why do I feel afraid?" she wondered, pressing closer to Oliver.

"Want help or something?" she asked, her voice wavering. She hated how small she sounded, but anxiety was crawling through her.

Julian didn't immediately respond. His gaze flicked to the door, then back to Elizabeth. "We'll see," he said, and that unsettling smirk curved his lips again. It wasn't reassuring—if anything, it unnerved her more.

"Look, Julian!" Oliver said, oblivious to the tension. "We're making it really tall!"

Julian eyed the tower, seemingly bored. "Sure," he muttered.

Outside, they heard the faint clatter of pots and pans—Margaret busy preparing dinner. Elizabeth wished her grandmother would suddenly step in, or that Grandpa would take a break and shuffle down the hall. Maybe I should call them, she thought, but the notion felt both silly and urgent. He's just Julian... right?

The bulb flickered again, sending a jagged wave of shadow across Julian's face. He bent closer, eyes locked on Elizabeth. "We could do something different," he said quietly, in a tone so soft it made her skin prickle.

Elizabeth carefully put down a block, her heart hammering. "Different how?" she managed. She glanced at Oliver, who kept stacking. She squeezed her brother's small hand protectively, feeling that something was very wrong.

A floorboard groaned in the hallway. Elizabeth's pulse soared, hoping Margaret or Henry might open the door. But no one came. Silence stretched, broken only by the flicker of the light and the steady drip of tension Elizabeth couldn't name but felt deep in her bones.

She forced a shaky smile. "We could build another tower," she suggested, trying to sound confident for Oliver's sake. "You could show us a new way to stack them."

Julian didn't move, didn't answer. He merely stood there, his shadow covering the blocks. Oliver glanced up, a question forming on his lips, but Elizabeth tugged him closer, afraid of what she might see in Julian's eyes.

Time seemed to slow as Julian took another step toward them. The toy blocks scattered slightly under his feet. In the background, Elizabeth caught the comforting hum of Margaret's singing from the kitchen—so close, yet impossibly distant.

She swallowed, feeling that unnamed danger coil tighter. "I don't know how to call for help," her mind screamed. "I can't even say what's wrong." But she knew something was off—deeply, disturbingly off.

Julian's gaze settled on her, his face unreadable. Oliver blinked, utterly oblivious, still clutching a wooden block. Elizabeth's heart thundered, bracing for a threat she couldn't define.

Then, when Julian reached Elizabeth, he grabbed her and forced her onto her hands and knees. He then pulled up her dress and pulled down her panties in spite of her fighting him. "Oliver, come here. Let me teach you how to..."

✺ 24 ✺
A SECRET TOO HEAVY

Elizabeth had never realized how quickly sunlight could turn into shadows—until she learned a secret she didn't know how to keep.

Elizabeth sat cross-legged on the thin rug in her room, her small fingers idly tracing over a loose thread. The late-afternoon sun angled through the window, painting the walls in warm gold. Just outside, the ranch stirred with its usual hum: Lucas tinkering with a stubborn tractor, distant dogs barking, and faint radio tunes from the kitchen. Normally, these comforting sounds soothed her. But now, they felt far away, muffled by the heavy secret lodged in her chest.

A single tear escaped as she clutched the fraying edge of her blanket. She tried to bury the memory of what Julian had done, but it kept surfacing at the worst moments—like a heavy stone pressing on her heart. She swallowed hard, lifting her gaze to the corner where her favorite doll lay forgotten. Once, that doll had been her confidante; now, Elizabeth felt as though no toy, no game could shield her from the confusion and hurt swirling inside.

From outside, a door slammed, making Elizabeth flinch. "Daddy again," she thought. She listened for any sign of her mother—perhaps a shout, or maybe the clink of dishes. The only sound that floated back to her was a muffled, frustrated sigh. Elizabeth exhaled shakily and turned back to her doll, her heart aching at how different everything felt.

Since that day with Julian, a part of her felt missing. She used to laugh with Oliver—her little brother's giggles were once a treasure. Now, her happiness seemed so distant. She sensed that if she listened too closely, she might start crying and never stop.

A subtle knock rattled her bedroom door. Elizabeth's pulse spiked, but it was only her mother's footsteps passing by, not actually coming in. Elizabeth caught a glimpse of Sophia's weary shadow stretching beneath the door, heard a soft sigh, then retreating footsteps. The brief moment made Elizabeth's chest tighten: "Maybe she'll come check on me," she hoped. But Sophia's footsteps faded.

Elizabeth scooted closer to the window, letting the sun's warmth fall on her. She tried to focus on the comforting smell of the ranch —a blend of hay, engine oil, and fresh bread from the kitchen. Normally, she'd bask in that homeliness. But she couldn't shake the echo of Sophia's sigh.

Lately, Elizabeth noticed every little sign that her mom was hurting again. Lucas's loud voice, the smoky smell that clung to his clothes, the nights he'd disappear and come back looking hollow-eyed—Elizabeth saw how all of it weighed on Sophia. She saw the slump in her mom's shoulders when no one was watching, the way her smiles never quite reached her eyes. And Elizabeth couldn't bear the thought of adding more to that burden.

"Maybe tomorrow," Elizabeth whispered, rubbing the tears from her cheeks. "I can't tell her now—she has enough worries."

But the idea of not telling churned her stomach. She worried that if Julian hurt her once, maybe he could hurt Oliver next. She glanced across the rug, where Oliver had curled up with a worn toy truck, dozing in the golden light. He looked so peaceful, so innocent. She cringed at the idea of him losing that innocence to the same terror she felt.

Then she twisted the blanket between her fingers, forming a quiet plan in her head. "I could draw a picture," she thought. "Or maybe wait until bedtime, when Mommy tucks me in, and tell her." The plan was hazy—Elizabeth wasn't sure how to find the words to explain what Julian had done, but the idea of telling her mother in a soft, safe moment felt a little more manageable.

Her eyes flicked toward the hallway again, half-hoping Sophia might appear. "If I leave a note under her pillow, maybe she'll read it when she's not so sad." The childlike notion warmed her briefly—like a glimmer of hope in the darkness. Still, doubt gnawed at her, warning that the truth might shatter what little comfort her mother had left.

She drew her knees to her chest, hugging them tight. Another soft noise from the kitchen drifted in—clinking dishes. Her mother was cleaning again; Elizabeth knew Sophia always scrubbed the counters and floors whenever she was upset.

"Am I a bad daughter if I keep this a secret?" Elizabeth wondered. A lump rose in her throat at the memory of Julian's unsettling grin, the confusion that had paralyzed her, and the hollow feeling lingering in her chest ever since. "I can't let it happen again—not to me, and definitely not to Oliver."

Yet she was certain that telling Sophia would bring tears, anger, and more door slamming. She imagined Lucas's voice roaring, the way it sometimes did when he'd been drinking too much or smoking the stuff that clouded his eyes. Then, in her mind's eye, she saw Sophia at the kitchen table, face in her hands, shoulders shaking. The thought of causing that pain made Elizabeth's eyes sting with new tears.

Blinking away tears, she slid over to where Oliver lay down, tucking the blanket around both of them. His warm, rhythmic breathing soothed her nerves just enough to form a resolve—tenuous but real.

"I'll tell her soon," she promised herself, slipping an arm around Oliver's shoulders as if shielding him from the world. Maybe tomorrow night... or the next day. When Mom's smiling again, even just a little. She wanted Sophia's eyes to have that spark of strength before Elizabeth shattered her illusions.

For now, she would keep the secret locked inside, carrying its suffocating weight alone. But she forced herself to believe it wouldn't be forever.

Restless, she rose to her feet and approached the window, pressing her forehead against the glass. The sun was dipping lower, spilling orange hues across the horizon. Shadows lengthened over the ranch, hints of purple and red blooming in the sky. A faint breeze rattled the glass, as if whispering a warning about the coming dusk.

She noticed Lucas trudging back toward the house, cursing at the engine's sputter. The door slammed again, making Elizabeth flinch. She clutched the windowsill, her knuckles white with tension. "Soon," she repeated in her head, hearing the ghost of her own voice.

Finally, Elizabeth turned back to Oliver, lying down beside him again. She wrapped the blanket around them both, wanting him to feel safe and warm— even if she couldn't feel that safety herself. She silently prayed that someday telling the truth would fix what felt so broken. But even as she prayed, a part of her wasn't sure.

For now, all she could do was stay close to Oliver and keep her promise: "I'll tell Mom... just not today." And in the quiet hush of the evening, as the last rays of sunlight slipped away, Elizabeth squeezed her eyes shut, holding onto a faint, flickering hope that maybe, just maybe, tomorrow would bring the courage she needed.

25

STANDING UP

From the day they first arrived, Elizabeth thought the ranch might give her family a fresh start—but as old habits returned, she realized some people would never let go of the past.

Life on the ranch had settled into a predictable rhythm— morning chores, midday meals, and late afternoons tending to animals or tinkering with machinery. But to Lucas, that rhythm felt more like a cage. Days bled together, each chore feeling more tedious than the last. Before long, he started inviting his old work buddies over again, seeking relief in the shape of familiar faces and rowdy nights.

At first, Lucas only indulged in the occasional joint—just enough to "take the edge off." But as the monotony pressed on, he found himself diving headfirst into his old vices. The whiskey, which he'd never truly quit, became a near-constant presence in his hand; the pot, once occasional, slipped back into a nightly ritual. He told himself it was only temporary—that once the ranch got going, he'd need less of an escape. But the haze of smoke and liquor said otherwise.

It was one of those warm afternoons when the sun hung low over the western acres, painting the fields in golden light. Inside the modest living room, Lucas sank into a sagging couch, a film of sweat on his brow. A joint smoldered between his fingers, whiskey close at hand. He exhaled slowly, his eyes half-lidded from the potent combination.

Oliver, now three and endlessly curious, toddled in with the purposeful steps of a child who adored his father. He clambered onto the couch beside Lucas, his bright eyes flicking between the bottle and the thin stream of smoke curling toward the ceiling.

"Daddy, whatcha doin'?" the boy asked, his voice piping.

Lucas gave a lazy grin, inhaling another drag. "Just relaxin', buddy. Why don't you go find your sister, huh?"

But Oliver clung to Lucas's arm, determined not to leave. "No, I wanna stay wif you," he insisted.

Lucas let out a slow chuckle that ended in a whiskey-scented sigh. "Suit yourself."

Oliver's gaze settled on the lit joint. "You 'mokin'?" he asked, his head tilted in that earnest way only toddlers possess.

A mischievous glint sparked in Lucas's glazed eyes. "Sure am, little man. Wanna try?"

He leaned in and deliberately blew a cloud of smoke toward Oliver's face. The child coughed, eyes watering, too confused to protest.

"Now go play," Lucas said with a dismissive wave, leaning back into the couch.

Unseen in the doorway, Elizabeth watched the exchange with a growing knot of anger and dread in her stomach. Five and a half now, she stood taller, wore her hair a bit longer, but carried a wariness beyond her years. Ever since what had happened with Julian, she had learned to observe adults carefully, cataloging their moods and habits as a form of self-preservation.

Her father's reckless grin and Oliver's stifled cough lit a spark of indignation in her. She stepped forward into the room, her voice trembling but resolute. "I'm telling Mom."

Lucas turned, blinking in the smoky light. His bloodshot eyes narrowed. "Oh, shut up," he slurred. "She won't believe you."

Elizabeth's heart pounded, but she forced herself to stand firm. She felt the tremor in her fingers at her sides—she hated that fear.

Lucas let out a low, mean laugh and took a swig of whiskey. "Go back to your room before I spank you," he said, each word steeped in liquor and threat.

For a moment, Elizabeth considered the possible outcomes: her father's anger, the sting of his hand, the chaos it might stir. Yet the memory of Oliver choking on secondhand smoke fueled her sense of injustice. The old Elizabeth might have run. Instead, she met Lucas's gaze with a flicker of defiance.

She didn't speak again—words felt useless against his glazed eyes. Instead, she turned on her heel and left, her small shoulders set in a determined line.

As she slipped down the hallway, she heard Lucas's ragged chuckle behind her, followed by the hiss of the couch's worn cushions as he shifted. The smell of burned pot still clung to the air, stinging her nostrils.

Once in her room, she closed the door gently, not wanting to draw further ire. She leaned against it, her breath coming in uneven waves. "He's hurting Oliver, and he thinks nobody will believe me." The thought circled in her mind, making her chest tighten.

She glanced at the toys scattered across her floor—an unfinished puzzle, a couple of crayons. They felt irrelevant. She hadn't played much lately; not since the day she lost her simple faith in family. She sank down onto her bed, the mattress springs creaking under her weight.

Her eyes stung, but she blinked back tears. She refused to cry—crying never changed anything. "I'll protect Oliver somehow." The vow floated silently between her heartbeat and her anger. If no one else would step in, she'd find a way. She didn't yet know how, but she promised herself she would try.

From the living room came a faint clatter—possibly Lucas fumbling with the whiskey bottle. The sound crawled under her skin, igniting the same cold resolve she had felt earlier. At five years old, she already carried too many burdens. But she refused to let Oliver bear them, too.

She listened intently for more noises: a slammed door, a sharp remark. Nothing yet. Lucas's muffled voice muttered something unintelligible, then faded into low curses. Elizabeth let out a slow exhale, relief and frustration intertwining. She wondered if her father might crash on the couch, oblivious to the fear he caused.

Reaching for her worn blanket, she pulled it over her knees, wishing she could wrap Oliver in that same protective layer. Maybe later she'd find him in the small bedroom they shared, read him a story, or distract him with a game—anything to keep him safe from the swirling haze in the living room.

In the hush of her own space, Elizabeth pressed a hand to her chest. She could feel her heart's steady thump, echoing her private resolve: "I won't let him hurt Oliver." The vow felt too big for a five-year-old, but she clung to it anyway.

26

ELIZABETH'S BURDEN

Elizabeth realized too late that a house could feel both wide open and suffocating all at once—especially when the secrets inside it kept growing.

The days at the ranch dragged on, each one heavier than the last. Outside, the sun rose faithfully every morning, splashing the fields with soft gold. But for Elizabeth, now six, the brilliance of dawn no longer brought hope. She often ended her evenings on the porch steps, knees drawn to her chest, watching a sky streaked with breathtaking color. Once, she would have gasped at the sunsets. Now, they barely stirred her.

It wasn't the ranch she disliked. On the contrary, she had been excited to move here—looking forward to the trees, the creek, the endless sky. She remembered how her parents had spoken of more space, a chance to breathe after the cramped house they had left behind. But any sense of freedom had been slowly eroded by the tension within these wide-open spaces.

Her dad's laughter had changed, becoming sharp and mocking when his "buddies" came over, and hollow when they weren't around. Strangers with hard eyes and loud voices now roamed their home, sometimes helping around the ranch but just as often leaving behind bottles, smoke, and an unsettling hum of chaos. They smelled strange—sweet, acrid, or bitter—and she hated when they patted her head or mumbled words she didn't understand.

Lucas didn't seem to notice her discomfort, or if he did, he brushed it aside like a gnat. He was too busy complaining about chores, nursing a whiskey, or disappearing into the haze of smoke that made his eyes seem far away. A part of her missed the dad who used to spin her around until she was dizzy with laughter.

She'd seen him blow smoke into Oliver's face. Oliver. The brother who could barely form complete sentences yet was forced to breathe in the harsh sting of whatever Dad puffed from those pungent, hand-rolled sticks. Remembering how Oliver coughed made Elizabeth's stomach churn even now. She'd wanted to speak up—scream, even—but fear and the knowledge that Mom was already so burdened had silenced her.

These days, Mom floated through the house like a worn-out ghost, her eyes rimmed red. She'd push out halfhearted smiles, always accompanied by, "Go play, sweetheart. You don't need to worry about grown-up stuff." Elizabeth couldn't decide if it was the swirling smoke that stung Mom's eyes or her own sadness.

But Elizabeth did worry—about Lucas's substance use, about the new men in the house, about the persistent memory that felt like a stone lodged in her chest.

Julian's face had appeared more and more frequently, walking up the driveway as if he belonged there. Dad mostly ignored him unless they were talking about repairs or chores. Mom, on the other hand, often lit up with relief. "I'm so glad Julian can help us," she'd say, or "Thank goodness Julian is here; he's good with the kids."

But Elizabeth felt anything but relief. Her body tensed every time she glimpsed him. She'd linger in a corner or press herself behind a doorway, her heart pounding at the sound of his footsteps. "He took something from me," she thought, her fingertips going cold at the memory. "And no one even notices."

Sometimes, Lucas would offer Julian a beer before stomping out to the barn, leaving Julian alone inside. Each time, Elizabeth felt a wave of dread, as though the walls were closing in on her.

She'd considered telling Mom about Julian—she even rehearsed the words late at night. But each time, the idea of Mom's disappointment or anger, or worse, her disbelief, made Elizabeth feel queasy. After all, Lucas dismissed her fears out of hand. What if Mom did the same? Or what if it just pushed Mom deeper into her own sorrow?

Elizabeth often found herself trembling, her stomach in knots, whenever Julian came near. In the mornings, she'd wake with her pulse racing, as if bracing for another day of heaviness. Sometimes she would catch a glimpse of herself in the mirror—a thin-faced six-year-old with eyes far too guarded—and wonder if that was what "being strong" looked like.

Her father had once told her, "You gotta be tough out here," but he never explained how or why. Maybe "tough" meant swallowing secrets for the sake of everyone else.

One afternoon, Elizabeth sat on the porch steps, cuddling Oliver on her lap while he rolled a toy car up and down her arm. The sunlight felt warm, and for a fleeting moment, she closed her eyes and let his babbling ease her. She inhaled, imagining it could fill the emptiness inside her.

"I'll keep you safe," she whispered into Oliver's soft hair, the words barely audible even to herself. She wrapped her arms around him, pressing her cheek to his. He looked up, trusting and unknowing, and the ache in her chest deepened. He has no idea how bad things can get.

A breeze drifted by, carrying distant laughter and the smell of hay. She savored the simple normalcy of the moment—until she saw a figure emerging from between the houses.

Elizabeth's gaze sharpened. Julian was walking up from the woods, hands in his pockets, a casual grin on his face as if he had just finished some chore. Her heart pounded, and sweat slicked her palms. "Calm down. Breathe." She tightened her hold on Oliver without meaning to.

"Elizabeth, can you take Oliver outside to play?" Mom's weary voice rang out from the kitchen window. "Let Julian help you keep an eye on him."

Elizabeth swallowed, her throat dry. She glanced at Mom's silhouette, wanting to shout, "No, please don't make me go with him," but she couldn't find the words. Her heart thudded as Julian approached, raising a hand in greeting.

"Let's go to the creek," he suggested lightly, that strange smile tugging at the corners of his mouth.

For a moment, Elizabeth froze, her feet rooted to the porch. She considered grabbing Oliver and darting inside—but she pictured Mom's exhausted eyes and Dad's dismissive sneer. The ranch suddenly felt very empty.

"C'mon," Julian insisted, a tone of playful persuasion in his voice. Oliver tugged at Elizabeth's shirt, oblivious to her fear. "Creek!" he repeated, excitement brightening his face. He pulled free of her grasp and toddled down the steps.

Elizabeth's heart fluttered with dread, but she followed him, her body tense. "Don't show fear," she told herself, recalling how Lucas sometimes mocked her tears. "Be strong. It's what they all keep saying."

Each step toward the woods felt heavier than the last. Her chest grew tight, her palms damp. The creek had once been a place of laughter and adventure, but now it loomed like a silent threat. With Oliver's hand in hers, she trudged behind Julian, the afternoon sun casting elongated shadows across the ground.

Glancing back at the house, Elizabeth spotted Sophia at the kitchen window again, caught in a moment of half-wave. Sophia turned away, disappearing back into her chores, leaving Elizabeth alone with Oliver and Julian. The stone inside her chest felt bigger than ever.

She tried to breathe through the panic, telling herself, "I can do this. I'll watch Oliver. I won't let him out of my sight." But deep down, she wondered how much longer she could pretend to be strong when every day chipped away a bit more of who she used to be.

As they slipped under the canopy of trees, the air cooled, and the sound of running water beckoned. In that hush, Elizabeth felt the secret in her heart pressing harder, growing heavier with each step—reminding her that silence might keep Mommy from more sadness, but it was also strangling Elizabeth's own fragile sense of safety.

Then it happened, "Elizabeth, lay down on this rock here," Julian ordered.

27

LUCAS'S DESCENT INTO
DARKNESS

No matter how wide the ranch spread under the open sky, the shadows closing in on Lucas's family felt too dark to outrun.

In the beginning, the ranch overflowed with hope—new land, new dreams, new promises. But over the course of a few months, the signs of Lucas's deeper slide into addiction began to harden. He had always favored whiskey, yet what started as nightly drinks turned into all-day companions. His once-occasional visitors now drifted in at odd hours, bringing a restless energy that crackled through the house like a faulty wire.

Sophia tried to keep busy with chores, cooking, and homeschooling the children. She told herself that if she maintained order, maybe Lucas would remember the man he used to be. Meanwhile, Elizabeth and Oliver often huddled in their shared room, playing quietly to avoid the strangers who moved in and out of the living space, reeking of smoke and guarded laughter.

One afternoon, a new face arrived—a gaunt man with hollow eyes and a tight grin. Elizabeth watched him from a distance, uneasy at the way he whispered in Lucas's ear, then disappeared into the back room. Later that night, the house filled with a tension more suffocating than marijuana smoke. For Sophia, the truth crept in when she noticed Lucas's arm tied off with a belt and small foil packets scattered on the counter.

Heroin entered the household silently, but its impact was

immediate. Lucas's mood vacillated between a drowsy calm and sudden, fierce anger. Occasionally, he tried to rationalize it—"It's just to take the edge off," he'd mutter, or "I work hard; I deserve some relief." But those half-hearted excuses didn't match the fear in Sophia's eyes or the confusion etched on Elizabeth's face.

Lucas's temper became a daily storm, rolling in without warning. A misplaced tool or a child's question could trigger a rage that rattled the windows. One sweltering afternoon, he erupted when he heard small footsteps pounding on the hall floor.

"Elizabeth, stop running around the house!" he roared, his voice echoing through the living room.

Elizabeth froze in the doorway, Oliver trailing behind her. "I wasn't running, Dad," she whispered, hugging her stuffed rabbit.

Lucas's glare locked on her. "Don't argue with me!" he snapped, his eyes wild.

Elizabeth backed away, her heart pounding. She took Oliver's hand and slipped into their bedroom, shutting the door carefully behind them. Inside, she held her breath, waiting to see if Lucas would follow. When he didn't, she sank to the floor, pulling Oliver close. "We'll just stay here," she said in a tremulous voice. "It's safer."

The next few weeks blurred as Sophia tried in vain to reach her husband. She pleaded with him at night when his eyelids drooped, a needle nearby. "Lucas, please," she murmured, gripping his arm. "We can't live like this. The kids need you."

He hardly met her gaze. "You don't understand," he mumbled. "Just leave me alone." Sometimes he'd nod off mid-sentence; other times, he'd lash out, yelling until Sophia left the room, tears stinging her eyes. She sought refuge in the kitchen, where she'd bury her face in her hands and let silent sobs wrack her shoulders.

Henry and Margaret tried to help, offering dinners at their trailer. Elizabeth and Oliver welcomed the reprieve—an evening without shouting, a table without strangers. But Sophia felt guilty leaning on them so heavily. Her dream of building a proud legacy on the ranch seemed to be crumbling beneath Lucas's addiction.

For Elizabeth, Lucas's unpredictable moods were a constant source of dread. She'd see his sallow skin, his shaking hands, and wonder why he didn't care about playing with her and Oliver like before. Late one night, thirst drove her from her bed, and she tiptoed through the house to fetch water. Peeking into the living room, she gasped at the sight of Lucas and a friend hunched over, a needle glinting in the lamplight.

"Go back to bed, Elizabeth," Lucas said flatly when he spotted her.

She ran, heart pounding, the image burning in her mind. Under her blanket, she squeezed her eyes shut, trying to block out the needle, the vacant stare in Lucas's eyes. She didn't know what to call that small tube, didn't understand the belt tied around his arm, but she felt the palpable wrongness seeping into her home.

Heroin coiled around Lucas's life, dragging the entire family into its deadly undertow. The once-welcoming house felt like a battlefield where every footstep risked waking a dragon. Mom tried to put on a brave face, but Elizabeth saw the worry lines deepen on her forehead and how her hands shook sometimes when she thought no one was watching.

Elizabeth, once a bright spark of energy, grew quieter and more careful. Whenever someone knocked at the door, she braced herself. Strangers with pinched faces wandered in, exchanging hushed words with Lucas. Oliver, sensing the tension, often clung to Elizabeth, his small arms around her waist.

"Why does Daddy yell so much?" he asked one day, his eyes brimming with confusion.

Elizabeth swallowed, brushing hair from his forehead. "I don't know," she said, her voice hushed. "But it's not your fault, okay?"

Oliver nodded, but his downcast gaze told her he didn't really believe it. She wished she could whisk him away to a place where Daddy was still gentle, where Mommy still smiled.

Night after night, Sophia wrestled with the decision looming in her mind—Should I leave with the kids? Once the house fell silent, she often found herself at the kitchen table, arms folded, staring at the blank wall. Sometimes she'd think of how easy it would be to pack a few bags and rush Elizabeth and Oliver over to her parents' place for good. But the love she'd once shared with Lucas lingered, a stubborn hope that the man she married might still be in there somewhere.

One evening, she couldn't hold it in. "Lucas," she pleaded, tears pooling in her eyes, "I'm taking the kids if you don't stop this. We can't stay here—this is killing you, killing us."

He sneered, eyes glassy. "You won't leave," he said softly. "You need me too much." Then he sank onto the couch, belt already in hand.

Sophia stormed out, pressing a hand to her mouth to stifle her sobs. Elizabeth peered around the corner, her heart hammering at the cruelty in Lucas's words.

That night, a fierce argument erupted between Lucas and Sophia—louder and more explosive than usual. The walls seemed to tremble with every shouted accusation. Lucas slammed the door so violently that a crack formed in the living room window. Sophia stumbled back, her face pale, tears falling openly now.

In her bedroom, Elizabeth held Oliver against her, his small body shaking in fear. She could hear Lucas's furious roars and Sophia's desperate pleas. A final crash echoed—something shattering on the floor. Then, sudden silence.

Minutes ticked by like hours. At last, Elizabeth heard Sophia's ragged breathing and footsteps retreating into the kitchen. Dad's voice, slurred and spiteful, cursed a few more times before his heavy tread stomped to the bedroom.

Elizabeth exhaled slowly, hot tears slipping down her cheeks. She glanced at Oliver, who was trembling in her arms. The weight of it all—the shouting, the needles, the strangers—crushed her chest. Yet she gently stroked Oliver's hair, whispering comfort she didn't feel.

"I'll keep you safe," she said, her voice quavering but determined.

Deep down, she wasn't sure how. But as the hush settled back over the ranch, she clenched her fists around that promise. If no one else could shield her brother from the darkness consuming Lucas, then she would find a way—because in the middle of this chaotic, heroin-fueled storm, all they had left was each other.

※ 28 ※
A DANGEROUS ESCALATION

Sophia once believed the stillness in the house might finally bring peace, but in truth, it was only the hush before the cruelest storm.

The house felt different now, and not in a good way. Where once Lucas's friends came and went—filling the home with raucous laughter, clinking bottles, and clouds of smoke—there was now a tense, unsettling quiet. At first, Sophia welcomed the silence, imagining it a chance for rest. Yet deep down, she sensed a darker truth: the friends weren't staying away because they had outgrown the chaos, but because Lucas had crossed a line so grave that they wanted no part of it.

Heroin was that line.

Lucas, oblivious to this unspoken boundary, sank deeper into his addiction with every passing day. The quiet hours he spent locked away, or the restless nights he wandered the house with glassy eyes, all pointed to something far more destructive than his old vices of whiskey and pot. Sophia saw the track marks creeping up his arm, the jittery hands he tried to hide under the table, and the harsh mood swings that frightened Elizabeth and Oliver. She had tried to talk to him, to beg and reason, but he was too far gone to hear her pleas.

Before the children woke one morning, Sophia stood in the kitchen, aimlessly wiping down already clean countertops. She couldn't sleep—hadn't slept well for weeks—because each night ended with Lucas either disappearing or passing out somewhere. A thousand times, she'd glanced out the window, hoping to see him return to the man she once loved. But each time, she was met with the same cold dread.

She recalled a conversation with her mother just a few days ago, whispered while the children played outside. "I think he's using something worse than pot, Mom," she had confessed, her voice cracking.

Margaret had gently squeezed her hand. "Sophia, I'm worried. You can't fix this on your own."

Sophia had only nodded, tears threatening. She hadn't told Margaret how often she thought about leaving, how she felt she was teetering on the edge of a final decision. But she knew, in her heart, that the time was drawing near.

Late one night, when the children were sound asleep, Lucas sat alone in the dim living room, phone clutched in trembling hands. Sophia watched from the kitchen doorway, her breath caught in her throat. She overheard him speaking in hushed, frantic tones:

"I need something stronger. The usual isn't working."

Her stomach tightened into a knot. After he hung up, he barely acknowledged her as he stumbled toward the bathroom, muttering about "taking a shower." The hush that followed felt heavier than any drunken gathering. Sophia stood rooted to the spot, fear prickling at the back of her neck.

Within an hour, a faint rap on the front door cut the stillness. Sophia peered around the corner just in time to see a shadowy figure slip inside—a man she'd never seen before, calm and clinical, carrying a small bag. Lucas led him to the bathroom, shutting the door softly behind them.

Sophia hovered in the hallway, torn between intervening and protecting herself from what she might see. A dull thud and low voices filtered through the door. Her chest tightened. "God, please let him be safe," she thought, though she dreaded what "safe" meant in a house with heroin. Eventually, the faint click of the latch signaled the dealer's exit, and Sophia ducked out of sight, her heart hammering.

She heard the front door open, then shut quietly. The hush of night returned, eerily calm. She left Lucas to his own devices as she went to bed.

Before dawn, Elizabeth woke with an odd sense of unease. She tiptoed down the hallway, the floor cold under her bare feet. A thin light, the earliest gray of morning, seeped through the windows. As she passed the bathroom, she noticed the door was ajar.

Pushing it open, she froze, her breath catching in her throat. Lucas lay sprawled on the tile, pants around his ankles. A frayed belt still cinched his arm, a needle dangling precariously from his skin. The sour smell of vomit and sweat hit her first. The linoleum was cold and slick under her toes as she stepped closer, trembling.

"Daddy?" she whispered, her voice quivering. She reached out with shaking hands. "Daddy, wake up! Please, please don't die!"

Her cries echoed in the cramped space. Lucas's face was slack, his skin chalky, and there was no response except for a faint wheeze. Panic surged through Elizabeth, and she screamed his name, tears cutting hot trails down her cheeks.

Sophia jerked awake to the sound of Elizabeth's frantic screams. Heart pounding, she raced down the hallway. The sight that met her in the bathroom nearly knocked the air from her lungs: Elizabeth kneeling over Lucas's limp body, tears streaming down her small face.

"Mommy, he won't wake up!" Elizabeth sobbed, her voice raw. "Please help him!"

Swallowing back a wave of nausea, Sophia dropped to her knees and pressed trembling fingers to Lucas's neck. She found a sluggish pulse—life, but barely. Relief warred with anger inside her. "How could you do this to us?" she wanted to scream.

Tears burned at the back of her eyes, but she refused to fall apart. She scooped Elizabeth into her arms, pulling her away from Lucas's unconscious form. "It's okay, baby," she murmured, her voice edged with shaking determination. "We have to go."

Sophia grabbed Oliver from his bed, then wrapped him in a blanket, despite his sleepy protests. Elizabeth clung to her mother's shirt, eyes darting back toward the bathroom, her face etched with horror. Sophia's throat tightened at the thought of leaving Lucas in that condition, but she also knew that staying wouldn't save him—not when he refused to save himself.

They slipped out into the dawn light, the woods swallowing them as they took the narrow path to Henry and Margaret's place.

Twigs snapped underfoot. A cool wind rustled the branches overhead. The hush felt alive with the secrets they were carrying.

"Is Daddy going to die?" Elizabeth asked, her voice small and trembling.

Sophia knelt, swallowing her own terror as she looked into her daughter's wide eyes. "He's alive," she said. "And I pray he finds help. But we can't make him do it. Right now, we need to be safe."

Elizabeth nodded, tears shimmering. She reached for Oliver's hand, tightening her grip as they walked. Behind them, the ranch house receded into the trees—still and silent, with Lucas unconscious on the bathroom floor.

When they arrived at the lower 40 acres, Margaret answered the door, alarm etched into every line of her face. One glance at Sophia, arms full of two frightened children, told her everything she needed to know.

"I can't go back," Sophia said, her voice cracking, tears threatening. "He was... I found him with a needle. Elizabeth saw it all."

Margaret drew them inside, hugging Sophia fiercely, then ushering the children to the table where bowls of cereal would be welcomed. "You did the right thing," she whispered. "We'll figure it out. But you've got to keep them safe."

Back at the West 40, Lucas remained motionless on the bathroom floor, the dawn sunlight creeping across the tiles.

For Elizabeth, the image of her father slumped and nearly lifeless would remain seared in her mind. She learned a hard lesson that morning: sometimes, no matter how deeply you love someone, you can't save them from themselves. All you can do is walk away and pray that one day they'll find their way back.

❧ 29 ❧
ROCKY BOTTOM

Each frantic compression on Lucas's chest pounded out one truth: he was closer to death than ever—and it might already be too late to save the family he'd left behind.

Lucas's chest heaved under the paramedic's determined thrusts, pain bursting through the fog of near death. Each gasp felt like shards slicing his lungs, the world a kaleidoscope of red and blue lights. Voices around him blurred, urgent but unintelligible—until one cut through.

"Stay with us!" barked a paramedic, sweat glistening on his temple.

Lucas groaned weakly, his limbs numb and his thoughts tangled. A sour wave of nausea rose in him as the paramedics hoisted him onto a gurney. The overhead lights seared his retinas, intensifying his headache. "Where the hell am I?" The acrid smell of antiseptic, the weight of the needle in his arm—he pieced together the grim puzzle. He knew exactly what this was: an overdose.

A burst of anger tore through him, clarifying briefly: Sophia. She must have called. She had ruined the sweetest high he'd ever tasted. "Fucking bitch" was the first coherent thought that sliced through his mind, fueled by rage that overshadowed the shame creeping at the edges.

A paramedic leaned in. "Sir, can you hear me? Do you know where you are?"

Lucas ignored him, scanning the bathroom he'd nearly died in: the belt on the floor, the whiskey bottle uncapped, his pants half-off. Shame tangled with fury. Then he saw two silent police officers, arms folded at the door. His heart lurched in dread, but he forced his face to remain blank.

The paramedics steadied the gurney. An officer stepped forward. "Time to go."

"What the—? What's happening?" Lucas croaked, trying to sit up. A paramedic pressed him back down, strapping him securely.

"You're being detained," the officer said flatly. "Possession of a controlled substance. Child endangerment. Public endangerment."

The words cracked over Lucas like a whip. "Child endangerment." "Elizabeth." A jolt of cold shame twisted his gut as he imagined her frightened face, but it vanished beneath a swell of bitterness. Sophia must be behind this. She's always been out to ruin me. He clenched his jaw, letting the handcuffs bite into his wrists without flinching.

Inside the ambulance, the monitors beeped and the sirens wailed. Lucas's head pounded, his body trembling—whether from withdrawal or shock, he wasn't sure. One paramedic wiped sweat off his brow, muttering, "You're lucky you came back."

Lucas stared at the ceiling, bright fluorescent lights merciless on his weary eyes. Lucky? He felt only betrayal, humiliation, and anger. The high he'd pursued for months had finally peaked—and Sophia had ripped it away. The hatred churned inside him, along with a dark prophecy: "She'll take the kids and walk away, too. Everyone else already did." He refused to see his own hand in that abandonment, blaming the world for his downfall.

Only an hour earlier, Sophia had made the 911 call, her voice trembling as she found Lucas sprawled unconscious. Now she sat in her parents' kitchen, a cup of tea shaking between her palms. Elizabeth and Oliver hovered at the table, eyes darting between their mother and grandparents.

Margaret's voice was gentle but urgent. "You did the right thing, Sophia."

Sophia nodded stiffly. She wished she could feel relief, but the image of Lucas, lifeless on the floor, wouldn't leave her mind. And worse—Elizabeth had found him first. That small voice screaming,

"Don't die on me, Daddy!" echoed in her thoughts, threatening to tear her apart.

"I don't know what to do anymore," she whispered, her voice taut with exhaustion. "He's not the man I married. He's... gone."

Margaret reached across the table, taking Sophia's hand. "Think about the kids. They need stability."

Sophia cast a glance at Elizabeth, whose gaze was fixed on her lap, her face pale and set. "What has she seen already? How many times have I tried to shield her?" Guilt clawed at Sophia's chest. She had tried so hard to keep their family together, but now all she could do was minimize the damage.

At the hospital, Lucas lay on a narrow bed under harsh fluorescent lights, cuffed to the railing. His anger simmered at every needle prick and every officious question from nurses and doctors. He tuned them out, focusing on one thought: "Sophia betrayed me."

When the doctor finally cleared him for discharge the next day, two officers stepped in, reading him his rights. They guided him out of the hospital on shaky legs, cuffs biting into his wrists. He forced himself to walk tall, ignoring the weakness radiating through his body.

The squad car door slammed behind him. The city's neon glow streaked past the windows as the car pulled away. Lucas stared at the blur, feeling no remorse, no guilt. Only a pulsing rage, tinted with a darkness he refused to acknowledge as fear. Yet deep in his chest, a flicker of terror whispered, "What if I've gone too far this time?"

As they headed away from the hospital, Lucas closed his eyes, swallowing hard. For the first time in years, he was stone-cold sober, and it felt like hell. His mind buzzed with images of Elizabeth's frightened face, Sophia's tearful eyes, and the paramedics and cops invading his home.

He clenched his fists, letting the anger mask the faint tremor in his heart. "She'll pay for this," he promised himself, bitter and unrepentant. But no matter how fiercely he seethed, the small voice of fear lingered: You lost them. They're gone.

At Sophia's parents' house, Elizabeth and Oliver huddled close. Sophia closed her eyes, her heart heavy with what she had done— and heavier still with what she might do next. But one truth pulsed through her weary mind: "He's alive, and they're safe. For now, that has to be enough."

30

FINDING STRENGTH IN
SURVIVAL

Sophia's hand trembled on the phone, and she realized for the first time just how far she'd fallen—that the only lifeline left might be the woman she suspected had once betrayed her.

Sophia sat in the dim kitchen of her trailer, staring at the tattered phone book. The kids were asleep in the living room, curled together under a single worn blanket. Outside, the moon cast pale light across the yard, exposing the old rusted truck and the overgrown weeds that had once been part of a dream ranch. Now it all felt like a trap—a reminder of how far Lucas's addiction had dragged them down.

Her mother, Margaret, had urged her to stay as long as needed, but Sophia knew she couldn't remain there forever. Each day she looked around, seeing the haunted expressions on her children's faces, and felt an urgent need to do something. With Lucas in jail for the overdose and subsequent charges, the ranch had become a symbol of heartbreak. Sophia needed to escape, if only for a while.

And so, in her desperation, she reached for Clarissa's number—a name that still stirred uneasy questions. But she dialed anyway, forcing her voice to be steady.

The phone rang twice before Clarissa answered, her tone familiar yet laced with surprise. "Hello?"

Sophia's throat tightened. "Clarissa... it's Sophia." She swallowed hard, her voice cracking. "I—I need help."

A pause hung in the air, giving Sophia time to regret this call. But then Clarissa replied softly, "Sophia? Are you okay? Tell me what's going on."

Sophia took a shaky breath. "No, I'm not. Lucas is in jail, and I... I can't stay here. I don't know where to go. I need somewhere safe for me and—" Her words choked off, shame flushing her cheeks.

Clarissa didn't miss a beat. "You can stay with me. Bring who you need. Space is limited, but we'll figure it out."

Sophia closed her eyes, relief and wariness warring inside her. Maybe she was doing this out of guilt, she thought, recalling old suspicions about Lucas and Clarissa. But desperation overshadowed any lingering doubt. "Thank you," she whispered.

After the call ended, Sophia paced the small living room, gathering Oliver's clothes into a battered suitcase. Her chest tightened with every fold of a shirt, every zip of a compartment. Across the room, Elizabeth perched on the couch, hugging a ragged stuffed bunny. Sophia's gaze slid to her daughter, who was watching silently, too used to adult turmoil to interrupt.

"Elizabeth," Sophia began, her throat raw, "you'll stay here with Grandma and Grandpa for a while. I'm... I'm taking Oliver with me. Until I can get a job, I can't afford two kids."

Elizabeth's eyes widened, panic flickering. "But I want to come with you, Mommy." Her voice trembled on the last word, fear evident.

Sophia forced a smile she didn't feel. "Grandma and Grandpa will take good care of you," she said quickly, avoiding Elizabeth's gaze. "They'll keep you safe. Julian's here, too, so... you'll have someone to play with."

Elizabeth's stomach lurched at the mention of Julian. What if he tries something?

The memory of Elizabeth's unease around Julian gnawed at Sophia. She shoved the worry down, telling herself it was temporary, that she would come back for Elizabeth soon.

"Mommy, please—" Elizabeth's plea cracked Sophia's heart, but she bit her lip, zipping the suitcase.

"I can't do this right now," Sophia snapped, hating how harsh she sounded. Immediately, she knelt beside Elizabeth, kissing her forehead. "I promise I'll come back for you soon. I love you."

Elizabeth's eyes brimmed with tears as Sophia lifted Oliver into her arms. The little boy, too young to grasp the situation, yawned sleepily. He glanced at his sister and then buried his face in Sophia's shoulder.

The front door creaked open, letting in a sliver of moonlight. Sophia stepped over the threshold, Oliver's small head lolling against her neck. Elizabeth bolted off the couch, half-reaching for her mother, but Sophia was already gone. The door closed with a click, leaving Elizabeth alone in a hush punctuated by Grandpa's soft voice telling her it would all be okay. Then he followed Sophia so he could drive her to Clarissa's apartment.

From the corner of her eye, Elizabeth saw Julian lowering his comic book. He shot her a smirk that made her skin crawl. "Looks like it's just you and me, kid." His tone dripped with false warmth.

Elizabeth swallowed hard, hugging her bunny tighter. She glanced at the window, where the truck's engine rumbled to life outside. She willed her mother to turn around, to change her mind. But the sound faded into the distance, and Elizabeth felt a cold pit open in her stomach.

The drive to Clarissa's apartment was fraught with doubt. Sophia rubbed her hands tightly, her mind awash in regrets. "Am I terrible for leaving Elizabeth? What if Julian... no, I can't think about that. I'm doing this so I can provide for us." In the backseat, Oliver fiddled with an old toy, occasionally mumbling about Daddy. Sophia fought a surge of grief, whispering, "Not now, baby. We can't see Daddy right now."

Clarissa was waiting in the parking lot, arms open wide. She wrapped Sophia in a hug, her voice quiet with concern. "You're safe here. One step at a time, okay?"

Despite the lingering suspicions about Clarissa's past relationship with Lucas, Sophia found relief in her warmth. She was the only one who offered her a place, the only person who stepped up, Sophia reminded herself. If Clarissa had ulterior motives, Sophia didn't have the luxury to question them now. Survival came first.

Moving in proved both comforting and tense. By day, Clarissa helped Sophia apply for jobs—showing her how to budget, prepare for interviews, and cook on a shoestring budget. Sophia felt awkward, but a spark of hope glimmered in learning new skills. "Maybe I can do this," she thought.

Yet at night, doubts crept in. She recalled rumors of Clarissa and

Lucas's "friendship." She sometimes found herself staring at Clarissa across the table, wondering if she had once been among the betrayals. But each time, she shook off the suspicion. Clarissa was here now, offering help when no one else could.

Over the following weeks, Sophia secured a part-time job at a local diner. It wasn't glamorous, but it brought in enough to cover basic expenses and put a few dollars aside. Oliver struggled with the change, throwing tantrums and crying for his father at night. Sophia consoled him, her voice gentle even while her own fears gnawed at her heart. "I'm here, sweet boy," she murmured, holding him close in the cramped living room. "Mommy's not leaving."

Privately, Sophia wrestled with her guilt over Elizabeth. Each day that passed without picking her up felt like an unspoken betrayal. She tried calling her parents, checking in, but hearing Elizabeth's small voice on the other end always ended in tears—for both of them. "Soon," she promised every time she hung up.

Though life with Clarissa was a patchwork of gratitude and tension, Sophia felt a new strength igniting. "I left." The words echoed in her mind whenever she doubted herself. "I did what I had to do, and I'll get Elizabeth back soon."

One evening, after Oliver was asleep, Sophia sat in Clarissa's tiny kitchen, nursing a cup of tea. Her eyes drifted to the phone on the counter—her lifeline to the rest of her fractured world. "Tomorrow, I'll start looking for a second job," she decided, her heart pounding at the thought. She rubbed her palms on her jeans, forging a mental plan: save enough for a small place, gather the courage to reclaim Elizabeth.

The next day, she rose at dawn, quietly leaving the apartment for her diner shift. In the mirror, she caught her reflection—tired, worn, but determined. "I've made it this far," she thought. "I can make it further."

And with that small surge of conviction, Sophia believed—for the first time in a long time—that escape from Lucas's shadow was possible, that the future might hold more than survival. It could hold a second chance for her, for Oliver, and eventually, when she was stable enough, for Elizabeth too. The long road ahead still terrified her, but she would walk it step by uncertain step, clinging to the hope that this time she wouldn't be walking alone.

31

FRACTURED PATHS

The day Lucas stepped out of jail, Sophia felt an invisible clock reset—counting down to yet another heartbreak or maybe, at last, a genuine new beginning.

Lucas stood beyond the chain-link fence of the county jail, an overnight bag at his feet. It felt strange—too bright, too loud—after weeks behind bars. A guard shoved release paperwork at him with a curt nod. Lucas offered a small, tight smile in response. Though good behavior had earned him early freedom, he still grappled with whether he actually deserved it.

Still, once outside, he inhaled the autumn air, letting the crisp chill anchor him. "I'll fix things this time," he promised himself, gripping the papers. "I'll get Sophia back. I'll get my family back." He found his way to a bus stop, each minute of that half-hour ride into town flipping an anxious churn in his stomach. When he finally stepped off downtown, late sunlight burnished the streets. "Where to start?" he thought, steeling his nerves.

Across town, Sophia ended another demanding shift at Brian and Bethany's bustling diner—a tidy place known for homemade pies and warm, small-town service. After leaving the chaos of the ranch and all that came with Lucas, Sophia had needed a stable job. Brian, a genial man with a broad smile, and Bethany, his more reserved yet supportive wife, had offered her that chance.

Finishing up the last of the lunch crowd's dishes, Sophia dried her hands on an apron while Bethany checked off receipts behind the counter. "You handled that rush flawlessly, Sophia," Bethany noted, glancing up with a smile. "We're lucky we found you."

Sophia returned the smile, grateful warmth sliding through her. "I'm the lucky one, believe me. Thanks for letting me learn on the job."

Brian, who'd been tallying the till, chimed in, "You're a natural. We couldn't run this place half as smoothly without your hustle."

Sophia felt a slight flush at the praise but simply nodded, setting aside a tray she had just wiped. In moments like these, she felt useful—like she was shedding the ghosts of her past life.

It was nearing closing time when the diner door swung open, the little bell overhead jangling. Sophia's heart briefly lurched, expecting another late customer. Instead, her gaze locked with Lucas's. He stood in the doorway, hesitant, scanning the room until his eyes found hers. She felt her stomach twist: He's out.

Brian and Bethany exchanged puzzled glances but remained discreet, retreating near the kitchen to allow them privacy. Sophia placed her cleaning rag aside and approached slowly.

"You... you're out," she managed, her voice subdued.

Lucas nodded, his throat bobbing as he swallowed. "Got released early," he said, shifting on his feet. "Could we talk outside, please?"

Tension wired through Sophia's limbs. She exhaled and glanced at Bethany, giving a short wave of acknowledgment, then followed Lucas onto the sidewalk. The late afternoon sun cast long shadows, a crisp breeze stirring the diner's sign overhead.

Lucas rubbed the back of his neck, his eyes flicking from a passing car to Sophia's guarded stance. "I know I messed up. But jail... it forced me to see how bad I'd let things get. I'm clean now, Sophia. I—" He paused. "I want to fix us. I miss the kids. I miss you."

Sophia folded her arms, recalling every broken promise he'd delivered back at the ranch. "You didn't call."

He winced. "I wanted to see you face-to-face. I'm not using anymore, and... a really nice couple, Mark and Lacy, gave me a shot at their glass company. I'm learning the trade and working real hours. It's a chance for me to stay straight."

The mention of Mark and Lacy—the owners of the glass

business—caught Sophia off guard. So he's working again. She pressed her lips together. "Lucas, you can't expect me to believe you've magically changed," she murmured. "It's not that simple."

His eyes flickered with anxiety. "I get that. But let me at least see the kids. Let me try to be the father they deserve."

Memories threatened to swamp Sophia: Elizabeth's anxious eyes, Oliver's small hand in hers, the day she'd left the ranch for good. She forced herself to stay calm. "I can't decide right here," she finally said. "I'll talk to you more, but... I'm not promising anything."

Relief momentarily lit Lucas's face. "That's all I'm asking," he said quietly. "Thank you."

That night, after Sophia arranged a sitter for Oliver at her apartment complex, she met Lucas at a local café. She found him slouched in a booth, his posture uncertain. She slid into the seat across from him, tension pulsing in her temple.

He spoke of his time in jail, how being locked up forced him to re-evaluate everything: the overdose, losing Sophia, and nearly losing himself. She stirred her tea, cautious, yet a flicker of old affection tugged at her heart.

Lucas reached out, brushing her wrist with calloused fingers. "I want to be in your life," he said, his voice hushed. "I love you."

She inhaled shakily. "Words aren't enough anymore, Lucas. I need proof." Yet, deep down, she couldn't ignore a spark of hope— maybe, just maybe, he'd truly turned a corner.

But as they talked, Clarissa was leaving a message at the front desk of Lucas's hotel: "Need you tonight, babe." She secretly hoped Sophia would be there when he read the note, even though she knew he was resolute about keeping this side arrangement hidden until Sophia's guard was down.

Over the next few days, Lucas showed up at Sophia's modest apartment, meeting Elizabeth (who had come from the ranch for a short visit) and Oliver. He tried to act fatherly again, making small talk about Elizabeth's art and lifting Oliver into the air for giggles. Sophia's cautious exterior began to crack, just enough to consider letting him back in.

Then, on a crisp morning, Sophia stepped out to retrieve the mail. She found Lucas loitering by his car, with Clarissa standing nearby, their hushed words spilling into the air. She heard him say, "I can't wait to see you again, babe. Tonight's still good?"

He stiffened, realizing Sophia stood behind him. Her stomach twisted at the guilt etched on his face. "Babe?" she asked, her voice low.

Lucas swallowed. "It's not how it looks."

A rush of anger scalded Sophia's cheeks. "Behind my back again? All this talk of family while you're sneaking around with her?" She stared him down, tears burning at the corners of her eyes. "No more, Lucas. We're done."

He stuttered an apology, but she turned away, letting the mail slip from her hands. "He'll never change."

That evening, Sophia stuffed her few essentials into an old suitcase. She couldn't stay in the same place she'd briefly imagined Clarissa sharing with Lucas. Tapping gently on Elizabeth's makeshift bedroom, she found the girl hugging a pillow in silence.

"I'm sending you back to Grandma and Grandpa's ranch," Sophia began, each syllable tasting bitter. "I... I can't provide for both you and Oliver here."

Elizabeth's lip trembled. "I just got here," she whispered. "You don't want me?"

Sophia's heart wrenched. "It's not that. I promise. I need a cheaper place, more shifts. Once I'm stable, I'll get you home again." She forced a shaky kiss to Elizabeth's forehead. "I love you, baby."

Elizabeth nodded, tears slipping down her cheeks. Sophia swallowed her own tears, hoisting Oliver into her arms and vowing, "I'll bring her back soon."

By dawn, Sophia had arranged a ride to a tiny apartment across town—another move, another forced separation. Watching the ranch fade from view, she clung to the shaky reassurance that Elizabeth would be safe with Margaret and Henry.

Within a week, rumors reached Sophia that Lucas had moved in with Clarissa and was already talking marriage. The news left her numb, a strange sense of inevitability souring in her gut. When a mutual friend called to confirm they'd tied the knot at City Hall, Sophia's only response was a heavy sigh. They weren't even divorced yet. What was Lucas doing?

So that's that, she thought, her head resting against the tiled wall of the diner's kitchen on a break. "He's Clarissa's problem now." Sophia filed for divorce promptly the next day.

Determined to push forward, Sophia poured herself into her job at Brian and Bethany's diner. She arrived early to help prep, stayed late to restock, and took extra shifts whenever possible. Brian praised her diligence, while Bethany offered encouraging words each day.

One late afternoon, after she'd finished serving a round of customers, Bethany caught Sophia at the counter. "You've been wonderful for business," she remarked, smiling. "We'd love for you to add a few more hours a week if you're interested."

Sophia's chest warmed with cautious optimism. "I'd appreciate that. Thanks so much."

She realized that every bit of overtime, every tip saved, brought her closer to independence. Some nights, she came home to her cramped apartment, only to fall into bed next to Oliver, exhausted but oddly proud: "I'm doing this on my own terms."

Days bled into weeks. Sophia heard sporadic updates: Lucas was settling into Mark and Lacy's glass shop, learning the ropes. He and Clarissa shared a place, newlyweds in a rush of ill-advised romance. "Good riddance," Sophia mused, though a twinge of sorrow lingered over the fractured family.

Alone in her apartment one evening, she stared at a photo of Elizabeth and Oliver, tears pricking. Elizabeth... She dialed the ranch, listening anxiously until Margaret picked up, reassuring her that Elizabeth was doing fine, though she missed her mother terribly. Sophia promised to visit soon—once she secured more stability.

When she hung up, she breathed in the hush around her. "I'm lonely. Truly lonely for the first time since I met Lucas." The admission stung but also brought relief. She had no illusions left to chase, no betrayals to anticipate.

Standing on her worn balcony, she gazed at the city lights, her mind churning with thoughts of a future shaped by her own will, not Lucas's chaos. Slowly, she felt her spine straighten, a faint smile brushing her lips. This separation felt real—and for all its heartbreak, it also felt like the first day of a new life. Two months later, the divorce was final.

32

LEFT BEHIND

Elizabeth could still see the dust settling from her mother's car as a sudden hush descended on the ranch—a hush that felt colder than any nightfall ever had.

Elizabeth stood on the creaking porch of her grandparents' trailer, the evening sun casting her shadow long across the worn planks. A swirl of dust hung in the air where the truck had disappeared moments ago, the echo of its engine fading into an oppressive silence. She clutched her stuffed bunny by one ear, her heart pounding so loudly that she wondered if anyone else could hear it.

Why didn't she take me, too? Did I do something wrong? The questions throbbed in her mind, each one tangling with the knot in her stomach. She wanted to call out to her mother—"Come back!" —but the words wouldn't come, lodged in her throat alongside a surge of tears she fought to hold back. She had decided a long time ago that crying didn't fix things; it just left her feeling emptier.

Finally, the truck's rumble vanished entirely, leaving only the soft rustle of distant pasture grass. The tall shapes of her grandparents' ranch buildings loomed in the fading sunlight, the hollow quiet swallowing up her last glimmer of hope that her mother might return. Behind her, the door to the trailer creaked open, and Elizabeth tensed.

Julian stepped onto the porch, arms crossed in a too-casual pose.

His smirk made Elizabeth's skin prickle; it was the same half-smile that always left her feeling small and cornered. The boards under his feet groaned, a reminder that the safest places in her world were suddenly very fragile.

"Guess you're stuck with me now," he said lightly, but Elizabeth heard the undercurrent that made her pulse race. Her cheeks felt hot, and her chest tightened.

She pressed closer to the porch railing, gripping her bunny so tightly her knuckles turned white. She refused to look at Julian, fear gluing her feet to the spot. "Don't say anything. Don't say anything. Don't make him mad." The logic spun through her mind—childlike but firm. If I stay quiet, maybe he'll just go away.

A beat later, her grandmother's voice cut through from inside, sharp and protective: "Leave her alone, Julian." The tension in the air softened, just enough for Elizabeth to release a shaky breath. She heard Julian mutter something under his breath as he retreated inside.

Elizabeth glanced toward the trailer door, relief trickling through her that Grandma had intervened—even if it felt fleeting. At least someone sees me. But her grandparents were old, tired from years of ranch work and life's toll, and they didn't seem to grasp how uneasy Julian made her. She turned back to the silent road, her heart heavy with longing.

The wind picked up a little, making the dry leaves skitter across the yard. She eased herself onto the porch step, her legs wobbly from the emotional storm swirling in her mind. The setting sun bathed everything in an orange glow, but the warmth felt hollow compared to the icy dread creeping over her.

"Mommy, please come back," she wanted to whisper, but she was too afraid the words would shatter her fragile resolve. Instead, a single tear slid down her cheek, and she wiped it away quickly before anyone—especially Julian—could see.

Her thoughts spiraled: "Maybe Mommy left me because I'm too big to carry. Maybe it's because I didn't help enough. Maybe she's mad I didn't want Julian to watch me..." Each idea stabbed deeper into her chest. She tried recalling the last time her mom looked at her with a real smile, but all she remembered was tension, hurried packing, and the sighs that said, "I can't do this right now."

Her bunny—threadbare and missing an ear—was the only thing

that felt steady. Stroking its matted fur, she made a silent vow: "I'll be quiet. I'll be quiet. I'll stay out of Julian's way. I'll protect myself." Even though she was only six, she sensed that no one else would do it for her.

Inside the trailer, she heard muffled conversation from her grandparents. It should have been reassuring, but it wasn't. She felt excluded from their easy banter, aware they probably believed she was safer here with Julian than out in the world. They don't know him like I do, she thought, goosebumps crawling up her arms.

The sun dipped below the horizon, painting the yard in purples and blues. A few early stars twinkled overhead, but their faint glow only made the vast ranch look lonelier. The gentle neigh of a distant horse and the clank of a windmill brought fleeting comfort— reminders that she wasn't the only living thing out here. Yet, it all felt too big, too quiet for a child left behind by her mother and brother.

Elizabeth pressed her back against the porch railing, letting the hush settle over her. This place was supposed to be home, she mused, remembering her mother's excitement about the ranch and how it was meant to be a haven for their family. Now, it felt more like a cage.

Her stomach growled, a subtle reminder of a missed dinner, but she wasn't eager to go inside—where Julian might be. She stared at the open road once more, half-expecting to see headlights cresting the horizon, her mother changing her mind. The road remained empty.

At that moment, Grandma's voice carried through the screen door, abrupt and unfeeling: "I'm putting your things in Julian's room. You'll be staying in there."

Elizabeth's insides twisted. "Julian's room?" She inhaled sharply, her gaze snapping to the door. Her feet nearly turned to stone. She could practically feel her heart racing in her chest, hammering against her ribs. Why do I have to stay in his room? Panic swelled. She imagined trying to sleep with Julian in the next bed, or maybe he'd be in and out... She didn't know which was worse.

Behind the door, Julian chuckled low, and Elizabeth's breath caught. She forced herself not to cry. "No one else is going to fix this for me," she reminded herself, her chest tight. She wrapped her arms protectively around her bunny, wishing she could vanish into the twilight.

Elizabeth rose unsteadily, knees wobbling, stepping off the porch. She hovered at the edge of the yard, dust swirling around her feet, before finally turning toward the trailer. Her grandmother's silhouette stood in the doorway, arms folded with a kind of weary impatience. She doesn't understand... Elizabeth thought, pulse thrumming.

But her mother was gone; Oliver was gone. She had no choice but to endure. Summoning a fragile courage, she stepped closer.

Stay quiet. Stay safe. That was the promise she clung to—her only armor in a world that felt too big and too dangerous for a six-year-old girl left behind by the one person she believed would protect her. And as she neared the trailer door, heart hammering, she prayed that somehow her mother would keep her promise to return—before it was too late.

33

A FRAGILE ESCAPE

Elizabeth woke with a flutter in her stomach—not from fear this time, but from the tiny spark of hope that, for a few hours at least, she could breathe free of the ranch's shadows.

Elizabeth's heart thumped faster than usual as she slipped out of bed, the dawn light casting soft shapes on the trailer walls. Today was her first day of kindergarten. She'd never felt so eager to leave the ranch behind—even if just for a morning. School meant no Julian lurking, no suffocating silence when her grandparents turned a blind eye. It meant a fleeting refuge where she could be a little girl without the weight of fear dragging her down.

She tugged on her favorite yellow dress, the one her mother bought months ago—before everything shifted. She'd learned early to change in the small bathroom, locking the flimsy door behind her to ward off Julian's prying stares. As she pulled the dress over her head, she felt her heart pounding in her ears. "Stay calm," she told herself. "Just a few more minutes, and you'll be on the bus, far away from him."

Entering the kitchen, she gulped cereal, every spoonful a dash of haste. Her grandmother scolded, "You'll choke, Elizabeth," but Elizabeth ignored the worry in her tone. She just wanted to finish before Julian's footsteps appeared. The mere thought of his gaze twisted her stomach into knots.

Sure enough, the moment she was dreading arrived: Julian's

arrival. Elizabeth swallowed another spoonful, willing her hands not to shake. The trailer felt too still, the hush too oppressive. The click of her spoon against the bowl sounded loud in her own ears, and she wiped a bead of sweat from her forehead with the back of her hand.

Finally done, she darted to the living room, finding Grandpa tending the fireplace. He stoked the flames until they roared softly, the orange glow dancing on the paneled walls. When he finished, he slumped into his recliner, and that was the cue for the "game."

Elizabeth stood by the fire, letting the heat chase away the morning chill on her back. She giggled, darted away, and leaped onto Grandpa's lap, pressing her warm back against his chest.

"Hot as a fire poker!" Grandpa teased, pretending to squirm. The tension in Elizabeth's chest loosened just a bit. Isabelle and Evelyn joined in, each warming their backs before "burning" Grandpa in turn. For a bright moment, laughter filled the living room, and Elizabeth's smile came naturally. She almost forgot about Julian and the ache in her chest.

But after a few minutes, she heard a faint shift in the hallway—Julian's door, maybe. Her giggle halted abruptly. She slid off Grandpa's lap, her pulse quickening, fear pricking at her arms like tiny pins. The game died away as her aunts headed for the kitchen. Elizabeth hung back, her stomach flipping with dread. She had heard Julian's veiled threats and caught a glimpse of his mocking grin the night before. She remembered him leaning close, voice dripping malice she couldn't fully decipher: "Keep quiet, kid." The memory tightened her throat.

Thankfully, Grandma called out, "Time to load up!" At that moment, Elizabeth felt relief rush through her veins. If she could just get to the truck, she could avoid Julian's presence altogether. She grabbed her backpack, scurrying behind Isabelle and Evelyn. Her grandparents ushered them outside, the ranch air crisp against Elizabeth's cheeks.

Climbing into the truck cab, she wedged herself between her aunts. Grandpa started the engine, and the vehicle rattled over the dirt road. Elizabeth gripped the bench seat, exhaling as the ranch buildings blurred into the distance. Her mind conjured images of a classroom full of bright posters, children drawing pictures, and a teacher's welcoming smile. Just a few hours of peace...

The highway emerged ahead, and Elizabeth spotted the

gleaming yellow school bus parked at the turnoff, waiting. Her heart soared—this was the first real taste of freedom she had experienced in a long while.

When they stopped, Grandpa patted Elizabeth's shoulder, and Grandma fussed over her hair, smoothing down stray strands. "You'll do great," her grandmother said, forcing a bright smile. Elizabeth nodded, the knot in her stomach easing slightly. At least they care enough to make sure I am dressed right... she thought, though her chest tightened, remembering how little they did about Julian.

She boarded the bus, stepping gingerly up the steps. Her aunts and uncle, who were the only others on the bus, filled the air with laughter and singing. She found the noise surprisingly comforting— no tension, no lurking threat. She slid into a seat, clutching her small backpack in her lap.

As the bus lurched forward, she glanced through the window at Grandpa's truck. In the back of her mind, she wondered if she should tell them what happened, if they would take her out of Julian's room if they knew. She refused to think about it any further, refusing to let that fear follow her onto the bus.

The ranch shrank behind her, the fields and driveway melting into a dusty horizon. For a few hours, at least, she wouldn't have to worry about him or be told she must stay in his room. The clatter of the bus engine felt like a heartbeat guiding her to a safer place.

Elizabeth's pulse steadied as she peered at the rolling scenery. Maybe her teacher would be kind; maybe she'd make a friend. Even the simple idea of crayons and storytime felt like a magical escape from the hush of secrets at home. She let out a breath she hadn't realized she was holding, relishing the chance to just be a little girl.

She knew, of course, that by afternoon the bus would bring her back, and Julian's shadow would still hang over the ranch. But in this fragile span of morning and midday, she could live without that weight on her shoulders.

Pressing her forehead to the window, she allowed a tentative smile. "Today, at least, I can feel normal. The road stretched ahead, and she let that glimmer of hope guide her—if only for a few hours —away from the darkness she called home."

❧ 34 ❧
A SANCTUARY OF SUNLIGHT

In the soft glow of dawn, Elizabeth clutched her backpack like a secret promise—that for a few hours, she could leave behind the shadows of her home and step into a world painted in bright colors and hope.

Elizabeth's heart pounded as the school bus came to a halt in front of the large brick building. The engine's low rumble and the gentle squeak of the bus doors opened a portal to another world—a world that promised safety, laughter, and the chance to simply be a little girl. As she stepped off the bus, a cool morning breeze brushed against her cheeks, and the air smelled faintly of fresh-cut grass and possibility.

For a brief moment, Elizabeth hesitated at the curb, gripping the straps of her small backpack so tightly that her knuckles turned white. Today was her first day of kindergarten—a day that meant more than learning the alphabet; it was her escape. At school, she could forget the constant dread that haunted the ranch, the memories of looming figures and the oppressive weight of unspoken threats. Here, among the vibrant chatter of children and the promise of crayons and laughter, she might feel normal again.

Elizabeth's eyes widened as she took in the scene: clusters of children with cartoon-adorned lunchboxes darted toward the school doors, their voices bubbling with excitement. A flurry of cheerful shouts filled the air as friends reunited, and the sound of running footsteps punctuated the crisp morning. Determined, Elizabeth tucked a stray strand of hair behind her ear and followed the flow of new friends inside, her heart both anxious and hopeful.

Inside the classroom, bright posters splashed across the walls declared messages like "You Can Do It!" and "Every Day Is a New Adventure!" Shelves overflowed with books, puzzles, and art supplies. The room exuded the comforting aroma of crayons, glue, and fresh paper—a stark contrast to the stale tension of home. Mrs. Andersen, with kindly crinkled eyes and a warm smile, greeted Elizabeth at the door.

"Good morning, Elizabeth! We're so happy to have you here," Mrs. Andersen said, crouching to meet her eye to eye.

Elizabeth managed a shy smile. "Hello," she replied, her voice soft yet filled with tentative excitement.

"Your cubby is right over there," Mrs. Andersen continued, pointing to a neat row of wooden compartments. Elizabeth found her name printed neatly on one tag, and a small burst of pride flared within her. In that moment, she felt seen and safe.

The morning unfolded in a whirlwind of activities. Elizabeth was paired with a boy named Liam to build a tower of blocks. Though she was initially hesitant, Liam's friendly chatter—"This will be the tallest tower ever!"—brought her out of her shell, and soon, her fingers danced nimbly as she added block after block. Each time the tower wobbled, her heart fluttered, but when it finally stood tall, a genuine smile lit her face.

During art time, Elizabeth devoted herself to drawing a radiant sun, carefully blending yellows and oranges until the rays seemed to shimmer with light. Mrs. Andersen's gentle praise—"Beautiful, Elizabeth! Your sun is so bright"—made her cheeks flush with warmth and pride, if only for a little while.

At recess, Elizabeth's initial uncertainty melted away when a friendly girl with bright red hair introduced herself as Emily. "Come swing with me!" Emily chirped. Nervously, Elizabeth accepted the hand extended to her, and together they ran to the swings. As Elizabeth soared higher with each pump of her legs, the cool wind tangled in her hair, and the world below shrank away, leaving her with a fleeting sense of freedom and joy.

Lunch was a boisterous affair in a cafeteria flooded with natural light from large windows. Amid the chatter and clatter, Elizabeth found solace in the colorful environment. Yet, as she laughed with new friends and traded stories about pets and silly games, a small, persistent worry nagged at the back of her mind—what if the safety of school was only temporary? Every so often, she caught herself glancing toward the bus door, half-expecting to see Julian's familiar, ominous figure lurking in the shadows. Even so, she forced herself to focus on the playful banter around her, clinging to the laughter that made her feel momentarily whole.

As the final bell rang, a pang of disappointment tugged at Elizabeth's heart. She wasn't ready for the day to end; she had tasted a slice of normalcy that she desperately needed. But as the bus rumbled to a stop at the usual pull-off, the bright yellow vehicle stood as a symbol of her temporary sanctuary. She climbed aboard, her small backpack clutched tightly against her, and for a fleeting moment, she let her guard down—she allowed herself to dream of a life filled with light.

The bus ride back was markedly different from the bus ride to school. The landscape of the ranch loomed ahead, darkening as it approached; the familiar silhouette of the old buildings and dusty roads filled her with dread. She sensed the weight of her home waiting for her, the memory of Julian's presence—a threat she refused to fully confront—lingering like a shadow across her mind.

When the bus finally came to a stop, Elizabeth stepped off slowly. She hesitated at the edge of the driveway, her heart heavy with the realization that the safety of school would soon vanish. In that moment, she clenched her eyes shut and forced a deep breath, trying to hold onto the bright memories of the day—the playful giggles, the sunny classroom, and the sound of Emily's laughter on the swings.

As she walked toward the house, her steps grew reluctant. She kept her head down, avoiding the thought of looking back at the ranch, where the darkness threatened to reclaim her. Instead, she whispered to herself, "Just make it to tomorrow," a quiet mantra that promised a return to the brief hours of normalcy she so cherished.

For now, Elizabeth would treasure the day's light and hope,

knowing that tomorrow might bring more than just fleeting safety —it might be the start of a new beginning. But as the bus faded into the distance, the ranch and its haunting shadows remained, a reminder that even a sanctuary of sunlight could be as fragile as a dream.

35

A BRIEF RESPITE

In the suffocating darkness of the night, when every creak of the old house whispered secrets of despair, Elizabeth's small heart pounded with an uncertain promise—that maybe, just maybe, tomorrow might offer her a fleeting escape.

The night seemed to stretch on forever. Outside, the wind whispered through barren trees, and inside, the old house groaned and creaked as though burdened with sorrow. Elizabeth lay awake in her narrow bed, every sound magnified in the oppressive silence. At first, she had hoped the night might lull her into peaceful sleep, but a faint, deliberate rustle in the room soon shattered that hope.

Her small fingers gripped the rough edge of her thin sheet like a lifeline. The fabric offered little comfort against the chill that seeped through the walls. With each shallow, rapid breath, she felt as if the walls were slowly closing in on her, shrinking her tiny world. Desperate to disappear, she curled into the smallest corner of her bed, willing herself to be invisible. But the relentless sound would not be ignored.

In a single, frozen moment, a chilling realization struck her: Julian was awake.

A sudden shudder raced up her arms as memories flashed— Julian's cold, unsettling stare and a whisper from the previous night that still made her skin crawl. Elizabeth's mind raced, and in a frantic bid to distract herself, she focused on the shifting patterns of shadows that danced along the wall. They swirled and merged, momentarily masking the terror pounding in her chest.

"Don't cry," she whispered to herself in a trembling mantra, clinging desperately to the thought that silence might shield her from the night's terror. Yet even as she repeated these words, soft tears began to fall, silently etching tracks down her cheeks.

In the depths of this oppressive darkness, one thought shimmered—a fragile memory of school. "School is tomorrow," she reminded herself. Once, the bright colors of posters, the joyful chatter of classmates, and the familiar scent of crayons and glue had offered her sanctuary—a place where she could just be Elizabeth, a little girl without the heavy burden of fear. Now, even that hope felt uncertain, as if it might be nothing more than a brief, borrowed relief.

Elizabeth's senses were sharply attuned to every detail in the room. She felt the cool draft sneaking in through the open window, the worn sheet's smooth texture around her trembling body, and even the slight, almost imperceptible sound of her own heartbeat thundering in her ears. Every creak of the floor, every whisper of the wind, deepened her loneliness—but also steeled her resolve with a quiet, desperate promise: "Tomorrow, I'll be free. I'll be safe."

As the minutes dragged by, the oppressive silence was intermittently broken by the house's settling groans—a sound that was both strangely comforting and profoundly terrifying. Gradually, the tension in her body began to ebb; the relentless noise blended into a soft, lulling hum that slowly coaxed her toward fitful sleep.

In her dreams, Elizabeth found herself on a swing, soaring high above a world that stretched out in a vast, endless blue. The wind ruffled her hair as she laughed—a momentary escape where the weight of the night and the memories of Julian's menace were forgotten. Yet even in that blissful illusion, a dark edge lingered at the periphery, a reminder that such freedom was as fragile as a whispered promise.

When the soft, pale glow of dawn finally seeped through the window's cracks, Elizabeth slowly stirred. Faint tracks of dried tears marked her cheeks, and her stuffed bunny lay clutched tightly in her arms. But the anticipated relief was tinged with uncertainty. In that quiet moment, as the first light pushed back the shadows, Elizabeth couldn't help but wonder: "Will tomorrow truly bring safety, or will the darkness follow me even into the bright, bustling world of school?"

With a trembling voice, she whispered into the stillness, "Just make it to tomorrow." The words were more a hesitant plea than a confident vow—a promise as delicate as the light of dawn itself. For now, Elizabeth was caught in the limbo between despair and the faint possibility of escape, her fragile hope a quiet, unresolved promise in a night that seemed to stretch on forever.

36

A DAY OF REST

Elizabeth awoke to a heavy, foggy morning. Instead of the usual anticipation for school, her body ached, and her head throbbed as if the night's darkness had seeped into her bones. She lay still in bed, the thin blanket slipping from her small frame, her eyes fluttering open to a room that felt colder and lonelier than ever.

She tried to call out, but her voice came out as a barely audible whisper. "Grandma..." she murmured, clutching her stuffed bunny close as if it could provide the warmth she desperately needed.

In the kitchen, the soft hum of the refrigerator and the occasional clatter of a dish were the only sounds breaking the silence. Elizabeth's grandmother, Margaret, appeared in the doorway with a concerned expression, her eyes crinkling with worry. "Elizabeth, sweetheart, you don't look so good," she said gently. "Let's check you out."

After a quick touch on her forehead, Margaret sighed. "You've got a fever, baby. I'm afraid you won't be able to go to school today." The words, though meant to be caring, felt like a final blow to Elizabeth's hopes. School was her sanctuary—a place of bright colors, friendly voices, and a promise of escape from the shadows of the ranch. Now, the thought of missing that haven filled her with a quiet dread.

Elizabeth's small face fell as she listened. "But... I wanted to go to school," she whispered, her voice trembling. She stared at the ceiling, the worn fabric of her blanket rubbing against her arms, and felt as if the day ahead would only drag her deeper into loneliness.

Later that morning, as she sat at the kitchen table with a cup of cool ginger tea and a bowl of cereal, she overheard a conversation between her grandparents. Through the thin walls of the trailer, Margaret was softly talking with her grandfather, Henry.

"They're all off to school," Henry said, his tone laced with quiet resignation. "Seems like I'm the only one left here with little Elizabeth."

Margaret shook her head. "It's a pity, but perhaps it means that today we can have some peace for you."

Elizabeth's heart sank at the realization. The familiar rumble of the school bus and the excited chatter of her classmates would be absent today. Instead, she was to spend the day alone at the ranch— a thought that both saddened and unsettled her.

By mid-morning, however, the quiet of the trailer began to shift. Her grandmother, ever attentive, made her way to Elizabeth's room with a gentle knock. "Come on, darling," Margaret urged kindly, "I've got something for you." Elizabeth's eyes, still heavy with drowsiness, brightened slightly as she followed her grandmother down the hall.

In the living room, Henry was setting up a cozy arrangement on the worn couch—a cluster of blankets and pillows forming a makeshift fort. "I thought we could watch some of your favorite movies today," he said in a low, soothing voice. The soft glow of the television flickered, casting gentle light across the room, and the scent of popcorn and warm ginger tea began to fill the space.

Margaret settled beside Elizabeth, gently brushing stray hair from her face. "You don't have to worry about school today," she murmured. "We're here with you. Let's just take it easy."

Elizabeth nodded, though her eyes still held a trace of longing for the bright classroom she had once cherished.

As the day unfolded, the initial dread of missing school slowly softened. Elizabeth lay on the couch, snuggled among the blankets, while Henry and Margaret attended to her every need. They brought her a new book to read, one filled with colorful pictures and simple stories. Margaret prepared a small snack, whispering, "Eat slowly, sweetheart, and rest your little body." Henry occasionally ruffled her hair or offered a gentle smile that made her feel less alone.

At one point, Elizabeth's best friend from school, Emily, was mentioned in a whispered conversation between the grandparents, a reminder that the world outside still held laughter and light. Although Elizabeth missed the daily sanctuary of her classroom, she began to realize that this unexpected day of rest held its own quiet comforts. The soft murmur of the television, the warmth of the blankets, and the kind, attentive care of her grandparents provided a different kind of safety—one that was gentle and unassuming.

Elizabeth's thoughts wandered between a wistful longing for the familiar energy of school and a tentative appreciation for the kindness surrounding her. "Maybe this day isn't so bad," she thought, even as a small part of her mourned the absence of that bright, happy world.

By late afternoon, as the fever began to break and the room grew quieter, Elizabeth found herself curled up on the couch, her eyelids drooping. The earlier chaos of the night had given way to a soft, lingering peace. She listened to the steady breathing of her grandparents and the distant hum of the refrigerator, and for a moment, she allowed herself to believe that perhaps, just for today, she was safe.

"Tomorrow, school will be there," Elizabeth whispered to herself as she clutched her stuffed bunny close. "Maybe tomorrow will be better." Though her voice was low and uncertain, the sentiment was not entirely devoid of hope—it was simply a fragile acceptance of uncertainty.

In that soft, quiet evening, as the shadows lengthened and the light dimmed, Elizabeth realized that even a day spent at home could be a sanctuary—a day of quiet comfort and gentle care. And though she was not entirely optimistic about what the future held, she found solace in the thought that, for now, she was not alone and that this brief respite was enough to carry her through until tomorrow.

A NIGHT OF SAFETY

The night seemed endless, stretching out in layers of darkness and quiet dread. Outside, the wind moaned through barren trees and rustled dead leaves, its mournful song echoing across the empty fields. Inside, the trailer groaned and creaked as though burdened by memories and sorrow. Elizabeth lay in her narrow bed, her eyes wide in the dark as she tried in vain to force herself back to sleep. Every sound—each creak of the floorboards, each whisper of the wind—was amplified in the oppressive silence, reminding her of the isolation that had become her constant companion.

Her small fingers clutched the rough edge of the thin sheet wrapped around her, the fabric feeling like a fragile shield against the encroaching gloom. With every shallow, rapid breath, she sensed the room closing in, as if the walls themselves were eager to press her into invisibility. In a desperate bid to make herself as small as possible, she curled into the tiniest corner of the bed, willing herself to vanish into the darkness.

Then, in a single, heart-stopping moment, the sound became unmistakable. A deliberate rustle—so faint at first, yet growing steadily louder—sent a jolt through her already racing heart. The chilling realization hit her: Julian was awake.

Elizabeth's mind recoiled at the memory of Julian's cold, unsettling gaze from the previous night—a look that had filled her with terror and left an indelible mark on her tender heart. She remembered, even if only in flashes, how his whisper had chilled her, how his presence had always made her feel small and exposed. Now, his being awake transformed the quiet night into something dangerous.

Desperately, she tried to distract herself. She focused on the shifting patterns of shadows dancing across the cracked plaster walls. The silhouettes swirled and merged, their movements momentarily distracting her from the pounding in her chest. "Don't cry," she repeated in a trembling whisper, as if that simple phrase could stave off the encroaching fear. Despite her efforts, tears began to trickle silently down her cheeks, dampening the pillow as they mingled with the raw ache in her heart.

In the midst of this oppressive night, one thought flashed in Elizabeth's mind—a thought both bitter and precious: "School is tomorrow." It was a place where she could simply be Elizabeth, free from the lurking threats that haunted the ranch. But now, even the promise of school felt uncertain—a flicker of escape that might vanish with the dawn.

Elizabeth's senses were keenly attuned to every detail. She felt the cool draft seeping in through the slightly open window, the smooth texture of the worn quilt beneath her trembling hands, and the faint, rhythmic ticking of her heart echoing in the stillness. Every creak of the old floor, every whisper of the wind, deepened her loneliness while simultaneously bolstering a small, desperate resolve: "Tomorrow, I might be free. Tomorrow, I might be safe." But that hope, fragile as it was, came laced with doubt. What if the darkness follows me even into the light?

As the night wore on, Elizabeth tried to cling to these thoughts. The oppressive silence was intermittently broken by the settling of the trailer—a low groan here, a creak there—that somehow both comforted and terrified her. In one quiet moment, she recalled a memory: the way Julian's eyes had flashed with menace during a whispered threat, a memory that made her shiver even now. It was a reminder of why she longed so desperately for the safety of school, for a day when the shadows wouldn't reach her.

Slowly, the relentless tension in her body began to ebb. The persistent sounds of the night, once jarring and loud, blended into a soft, lulling hum that gradually coaxed her toward a fitful sleep. In her dreams, Elizabeth found herself on a swing, soaring high into an endless blue sky. The wind tousled her hair, and the world below shrank away, offering a taste of freedom—a brief, bittersweet escape from the weight of her waking fears. Yet even in that dream, a dark outline lingered at the edges, a subtle reminder that such liberation was as transient as it was illusory.

When the first soft light of dawn crept through the cracks in her window, Elizabeth stirred with a heaviness in her chest. Her eyes, red and swollen from unshed tears, opened to the quiet of a new day. She clutched her beloved stuffed bunny tightly, as if holding onto it might anchor her to the safety she so desperately desired. Though the traces of tears had dried, the emotional residue of the night still clung to her.

In that fragile moment, Elizabeth's mind churned with uncertainty. The promise of school—a place of bright posters, kind voices, and laughter—had once been a beacon of hope. Now, as she lay in the dim pre-dawn light, she was unsure if that sanctuary would be enough to wash away the lingering terror of the night.

Her thoughts wavered between resignation and a cautious, almost reluctant hope. "Maybe today will be safe," she whispered softly, her voice trembling with uncertainty. It was not a promise of complete freedom, nor was it a confident vow; it was simply a tentative wish—a fragile pledge that, in the gentle light of a new day, she might finally find a moment of respite from the darkness that seemed to clutch at her every night.

Elizabeth's heartbeat slowed as she lay there, listening to the faint sounds of the house waking up—the distant creak of wood, the soft rustling of morning air—and the subtle promise of a new beginning. Yet, deep down, she remained unsure. The safety she sought was as elusive as a whisper, and every creak of the floor, every shifting shadow, was a reminder that today might not bring the escape she hoped for. Julian is still asleep, she decided she better get up before him so she can dress in private and begin the day at school.

❧ 38 ❧
A SUMMER OF SHADOWS
AND HOPE

When the school year ended and the sanctuary of the classroom faded into memory, Elizabeth braced herself for a summer that promised both moments of joy and the heavy burden of uncertainty —where even the brightest days were tinged with shadows.

The final bell had rung weeks ago, marking the end of the school year and the slow dissolution of a sanctuary that had once shielded Elizabeth from the harsh realities of life at the ranch. Kindergarten, with its bright posters, cheerful chatter, and the promise of safety, had become a distant memory. Now, as summer stretched out before her like an endless, scorching desert, Elizabeth felt a deep, gnawing dread at the thought of being home all day— with Julian lurking and the oppressive loneliness of the ranch filling every corner.

Yet, amid that overwhelming darkness, there were still small lights to cling to. One of those beacons was her report card. Elizabeth remembered, with a mixture of pride and wistfulness, how her teacher had praised her for her hard work, awarding her five A's. She could still recall the gleam in her teacher's eyes and the promise her grandfather had made at the start of the school year— one dollar for each A earned. That promise had filled her with dreams of shiny coins and crisp bills, dreams that she imagined would one day let her buy her favorite ice cream the next time they went into town.

For a fleeting moment, as she held the report card close to her chest, Elizabeth felt a spark of pride. It was a reminder that, even though school was over, she had once found solace in learning—a place where laughter and friendship made her feel like any other kid. But the end of school meant the loss of that haven, and summer loomed ahead with its own challenges. The absence of school meant facing the ranch every day, where the specter of Julian's presence and the memories of unspoken terrors were ever-present.

Elizabeth had learned to compartmentalize her pain. Over time, she had begun to dull the constant ache by tucking away her memories into the farthest recesses of her mind, treating them as if they were scenes from a movie playing far away. During the long, hot days, she forced herself to focus on the little comforts around her: the warmth of the sun on her face, the gentle blooming of wildflowers near the edge of the woods, and the distant, soothing hum of the creek that wound its way behind the ranch. These small blessings were her lifelines, the tiny threads that kept her tethered to hope even when the days felt overwhelmingly bleak.

Yet, amid these quiet comforts, a single ray of hope had always glimmered: the promise of a visit from her cousins, Lacy and Mia. Elizabeth had eagerly counted down the days until their arrival, imagining the fun they would have together. Mia, who was the same age as Elizabeth, was once her constant playmate; she had spent endless afternoons running barefoot through the fields, laughing as they climbed trees and chased fireflies at dusk. Lacy, a couple of years older than Elizabeth and Mia, had always seemed so mean to the girls, but Elizabeth was happy she was coming too. The more, the better the berry wars.

When the much-anticipated day finally arrived, Elizabeth's heart fluttered with a mixture of excitement and a quiet, unresolved sadness. That morning, as the sun shone brightly over the ranch, Elizabeth stood on the creaking wooden porch, her bare feet padding on the warm planks. The air was thick with the scent of sun-warmed earth and a hint of distant smoke, but today it carried an undercurrent of promise.

Elizabeth clutched her report card tightly—a small treasure that symbolized her achievements—and waited anxiously for the familiar car that would bring her cousins. The distant rumble of the engine stirred a flicker of hope in her heart. For so long, she had grown accustomed to the absence of her mother's comforting voice, the missed calls that had become a painful routine. Yet today, as the ranch basked in summer light, she allowed herself to dream of the joyful moments that the day might bring.

As the car's headlights appeared along the dusty driveway, Elizabeth's eyes widened. With a small squeal of excitement, she dashed toward the gate. The car slowed to a stop, and the door swung open to reveal Mia first—her bright eyes and contagious smile lighting up the scene. "Elizabeth!" Mia cried, throwing her arms around her cousin with an exuberance that made Elizabeth momentarily forget the lingering sadness in her heart.

"Mia!" Elizabeth laughed, returning the hug tightly, though a part of her still wondered why she had to feel this bittersweet mix of joy and loss. Moments later, Lacy emerged, her smirk offering no comfort or reassurance. Together, the three cousins rushed down to the barn to acquire hackamores and head to the upper mile to find some horses, leaving behind the oppressive weight of loneliness that had so often settled over Elizabeth during the long summer days.

The ranch transformed under the warmth of the summer sun. The fields, usually harsh and barren, now glowed with vibrant greens, and wildflowers sprinkled the landscape like bursts of color. Elizabeth and Mia raced through the open fields, their laughter echoing against the distant hills. They kicked off their shoes and ran barefoot over the soft, sun-warmed grass, their giggles mixing with the songs of cicadas in the trees.

"Come on, Elizabeth! I bet you can't catch me!" Mia teased, her voice full of playful challenge.

Elizabeth, her heart light for the first time in months, chased after her, the worries of home momentarily forgotten in the thrill of the race. The girls gathered juniper berries in the bottoms of their shirts and began throwing them at each other. "The one with the largest whelp loses!"

After their frolic, the cousins gathered in the shade of a large juniper tree near the stables. There, a gentle pony waited, its eyes soft and understanding. With a bit of coaxing and a friendly pat from Mia, Elizabeth climbed onto the pony's back. The rhythmic clopping of hooves and the cool breeze against her face made her feel, if only for a fleeting moment, as though she were soaring above the worries that weighed her down. Now they had a ride to the upper mile. Mia got on back with Elizabeth and they headed up.

In the mid-afternoon, as the cousins returned to the ranch house, they set up a makeshift picnic on the sprawling lawn. Lacy unfolded a colorful blanket while Mia and Elizabeth laid out a board game. The laughter that ensued was pure and unburdened. Over checkers and playful teasing—"I'm totally going to beat you this time, Elizabeth!"—the girls shared stories and dreams. Their voices, mingled with the rustling of leaves and the distant sounds of the ranch, created a temporary world of friendship and joy.

"Elizabeth, you look really cool in those new clothes," Mia remarked during a quiet moment, referring to the trendy outfit her mother had sent.

Elizabeth hesitated before responding, her smile fragile. "I don't really like them, but... if you all think they're cool, then maybe I can try to like them."

Her words carried a quiet resignation—a recognition that she might have to adjust to a version of herself she wasn't sure was truly hers. Yet, in the midst of the laughter and gentle teasing, the comment seemed to fit in with the day's lighthearted mood.

As the afternoon progressed, the celebrations continued with more board games and even a brief, spontaneous round of dancing in the open field. As the girls sang popular music off-tune, Elizabeth allowed herself to forget the constant fear that had marred her life at the ranch. The day was filled with small moments of joy—a shared joke here, a warm hug there—that stitched together a tapestry of happiness, however temporary.

But even in these moments, a quiet uncertainty simmered beneath the surface. As the cousins gathered their things for the evening, Elizabeth's thoughts drifted to the inevitable return to the ranch house. The sanctuary of laughter and play would soon be replaced by the harsh reality of home—by the constant reminder of her mother's absence and the haunting presence of Julian.

Later that evening, as the cousins laid out sleeping bags in the living room and whispered secrets in hushed tones, Elizabeth's mind was a swirl of conflicting emotions. The joyous noise of the party contrasted sharply with the quiet dread that lurked in the back of her heart. Despite the warmth of the blankets and the comfort of her cousins, she couldn't shake the sense that the day's happiness was as fragile as a bubble—wonderful but destined to burst.

"I really had fun today," said Mia with a bright smile, but Elizabeth's voice trailed off as she replied softly, "Yeah... it was nice." The simple words carried the weight of uncertainty—she was happy, but she wasn't sure if this joy would last.

As darkness fell over the ranch, the festivities gradually subsided. The cousins retired to their sleeping bags, and the echoes of their laughter faded into the quiet murmur of the house. Elizabeth lay awake for a long while, the flickering light from the fireplace casting shifting patterns on the ceiling. Every so often, she recalled the joyous moments of the day—the laughter in the field, the gentle pat on the pony's back—and felt a pang of longing.

She knew that when morning came, the safety and light of school would be far away, replaced by the relentless, haunting reality of the ranch. Yet, for these few hours, she allowed herself to bask in the warmth of the present. Clutching her stuffed bunny close, Elizabeth whispered into the night, "Maybe tomorrow will be bright too," not as a confident promise but as a tentative wish. It was a fragile hope, easily overshadowed by the uncertainty of what lay ahead.

The night was long and filled with a quiet mixture of joy and sadness—a bittersweet reminder that moments of sanctuary were rare and fleeting. As Elizabeth finally drifted to sleep, the remnants of the day's celebration lingered like a gentle echo. In her dreams, she was not alone; she was surrounded by the soft laughter of her cousins, the bright colors of a hopeful world, and the sense that even in a summer of shadows, there was still room for a glimmer of light.

THE ESCAPE THAT WASN'T

The promise of a new beginning shimmered like a distant mirage on the horizon, but for Elizabeth, every step toward escape only deepened the shadows that clung to her heart.

The news of the trip south had once seemed like a ray of light piercing through Elizabeth's dreary summer—a chance to see her father again, to escape the unyielding confines of the ranch. Now, that promise was tainted by uncertainty. As the plane soared high above, Elizabeth sat silently beside Oliver, stealing glances out the window at the endless sky, her thoughts a tumult of hope, fear, and confusion. When they finally landed, the bustling airport terminal offered a brief distraction. Lucas greeted them with open arms, his booming laughter echoing against the hard walls, while Clarissa stood close by, her smile warm yet tentative. Elizabeth's eyes searched Clarissa's face, trying to read if she was trustworthy, but the uncertainty in her gaze left Elizabeth more troubled than reassured.

Upon arriving at Lucas and Clarissa's apartment—a small, neat space with a faint aroma of fresh paint—Elizabeth and Oliver wandered into the living room. The furniture was modest, and the walls formed a muted backdrop to a life that now felt divided. As they explored, they passed by a bedroom. There, tucked into a quiet corner, was a crib adorned with soft blankets and a mobile of stars and moons gently swaying above it.

"What's that for?" Oliver blurted out, his voice breaking the silence.

In an instant, Lucas's face darkened. Without a word, he snatched a belt from a chair and swung it across his son's back. The sharp snap of leather meeting skin jolted Elizabeth, and she flinched involuntarily. "Shut up," Lucas barked, his voice thick with anger. "Don't you dare upset Clarissa."

Elizabeth's heart clenched as she watched Oliver wince and bite his lip to hold back tears. For a moment, she stood frozen, feeling both anger and helplessness mix within her. She wished desperately to shield Oliver, to protest, but fear chained her to the spot. They learned later that they had a half-brother named Anthony who had passed away at three days old from SIDS.

Later that night, as Elizabeth and Oliver retreated to their shared room, Elizabeth leaned over to Oliver in a hushed tone, her voice shaking with determination. "We don't have to stay here. We can leave," she whispered. Oliver's eyes, still red from the earlier hurt, filled with confusion. "Where would we go?" he asked softly.

"There's got to be somewhere—anywhere but here," Elizabeth replied, her voice quivering as the memory of the belt's snap replayed in her mind, fueling her resolve.

That resolve carried them into the early hours of dawn. Quietly, they packed their few belongings—water bottles, a small blanket, hidden snacks—tucking them into tiny backpacks. Elizabeth's heart hammered as she led Oliver through the darkened hallways of the apartment, careful to avoid any sound that might betray their escape. Outside, the cool pre-dawn air enveloped them as they made their way down the silent street.

After what felt like an eternity, they stumbled upon an abandoned train car nestled in a deserted lot. Rusted metal and broken windows painted a picture of neglect, but to Elizabeth and Oliver, it offered the promise of sanctuary. "This is perfect," Elizabeth whispered, her voice barely audible as she ran her fingers over the worn metal. "We can stay here until we figure something out."

Inside, they spread a tattered blanket over the dusty floor and settled into a fragile cocoon of safety. Elizabeth offered Oliver a granola bar from her bag. "We'll be okay," she assured him, though deep down, uncertainty gnawed at her. For hours, they huddled in that forgotten space, a brief respite from the pain at home. But as the sun began to sink lower, casting long, trembling shadows over the train yard, the reality of their escape began to weigh on them. Hunger gnawed, and the once-safe hideaway now felt claustrophobic.

Back at Lucas's apartment, frantic calls had set off a search. When Lucas couldn't locate them, he immediately contacted Sophia. Within hours, Sophia boarded a flight to Arizona, her worry and sorrow mingling as she raced to rescue her children. As night fell, Sophia drove through the streets of Tempe, her eyes scanning every corner until a kind stranger mentioned seeing two small figures near a train yard. Heart pounding, she followed the lead and soon found Elizabeth and Oliver huddled together in the dim light of the abandoned train car.

"Elizabeth! Oliver!" Sophia's voice cracked with relief as she burst into the train car. Elizabeth's eyes widened in a mixture of guilt and relief.

"Mom?" she whispered.

Sophia pulled both children into a tight embrace. "What were you thinking?" she demanded, more frightened than angry. "You scared me half to death."

Elizabeth's voice trembled as she admitted, "We didn't want to stay there because Clarissa was being mean." The words fell heavily in the quiet space, laden with the complexities of their fractured family life.

Sophia's anger bubbled momentarily, and she turned to Lucas. "You need to get your act together," she shouted, her voice echoing in the small space. Lucas, caught off guard by the confrontation, shifted his gaze from his children to his wife. "I should have never trusted her," he snapped bitterly, directing his anger at Clarissa instead of addressing his own failings.

The confrontation left Sophia feeling as though she had been forced to choose once again between the remnants of her family and her own survival. After a long, tearful discussion, Lucas eventually managed to convince Sophia to give him another chance, promising to change and start anew in Texas—a fresh beginning for their fractured family. Sophia agreed reluctantly, hoping that a new start might mend what had been broken.

Yet, for Elizabeth, the prospect of returning to Texas was

bittersweet. The trip south had offered a fleeting glimpse of hope, but now the uncertainty of her future loomed large. On the plane, Elizabeth watched Lucas sit silently beside Sophia, his eyes shadowed with unresolved conflict. Could things ever truly change?

In that moment, as the reality of her family's situation pressed down on her, Elizabeth felt a surge of both longing and apprehension. The escape they had attempted had not worked as hoped; instead, it had deepened the fissures in their lives. Still, she clung to the thought that every day might bring a new chance—a possibility that even if tomorrow wasn't perfect, it could be different from today.

As the plane's wheels touched the ground in Texas, Elizabeth's heart fluttered with a mix of fear and uncertain hope. The journey had been long, and now, with her family gathered around her once more, she could only wonder if the promise of escape was merely a mirage. The lingering image of the abandoned train car, the taste of temporary freedom, and the harsh reality of her fractured family life merged into one in her mind.

For Elizabeth, the day ahead was a blank slate—a canvas on which she would have to paint her own story, one stroke at a time. As she watched her family shuffle toward an uncertain future, she whispered to herself, "Maybe tomorrow, things will be different." Her voice was small, barely audible above the hum of the airport, yet it carried the weight of a fragile promise—a promise that, perhaps, a new beginning might be possible, even if the escape they had once dreamed of was still just out of reach.

❧ 40 ❧

THE PRICE OF FREEDOM

On a restless Texas night, when silence spoke louder than any words, Elizabeth learned that true freedom sometimes demands a secret, heart-wrenching farewell—one that leaves a family to pick up the shattered pieces in the harsh light of day.

Back in Texas, life had grown heavy with routine and regret. The relentless heat and monotony pressed in on every day, while each evening echoed with the bitter sounds of discontent. Lucas would often grumble as he swirled his whiskey glass in the dim light of their modest apartment. "There's nothing to do with the kids," he would complain, his voice a mix of frustration and resignation that seemed to fill every corner of their home.

In a bid to salvage some spark in their stagnant lives, Sophia had taken a bold step a few weeks earlier: she bought a boat. It wasn't extravagant—a simple, modest vessel—but to Sophia, it represented a promise of adventure, a chance for the family to bond and perhaps reclaim a fragment of hope. One quiet evening over dinner, she had looked into Lucas's eyes and said softly, "Maybe a day out on the water will remind us what it means to be together." For a moment, Lucas's gaze had flickered with a hint of boyish excitement as he ran out to see his new prize. "This might actually be fun," he murmured. In that brief spark, Sophia had dared to hope that perhaps things might change.

But as days turned to weeks, the promise of the boat

transformed. Instead of joining the family for outings, Lucas began using it as his personal escape. Night after night, he would slip away on the water, seeking solace in the anonymity of the open lake, his laughter mingling with the clink of empty bottles. Sophia watched, growing more and more resigned, as the boat that had once symbolized a chance at unity became a painful reminder of Lucas's drifting priorities.

One stifling night, while Sophia sat at the kitchen table reviewing a stack of bills, a subtle sound broke through the quiet—a low murmur and the soft thud of footsteps in the corridor. At first, she thought it was the familiar creak of the apartment settling. But then, as the sound grew more insistent, she sensed that something was amiss. Her heart skipped a beat when she noticed Lucas's favorite jacket was missing from the chair where it was normally rested carelessly draped, she no longer smelled its familiar scent of cologne and whiskey that still clung to the fabric.

Without a word, Sophia crept toward the living room, her footsteps light yet trembling with dread. Peering into the darkened hallway, she caught a glimpse of a figure moving swiftly toward the back door. A chill ran down her spine as she realized that Lucas had once again slipped away—this time, he had taken the boat. There was no farewell, no announcement; he had simply vanished into the night, leaving behind an emptiness that was both physical and emotional.

The next morning, the muted light of dawn found Sophia already awake, a sense of impending dread knotting her stomach. She rushed to the window and peered out, only to confirm her worst fear—the boat was still gone. Her heart sank as she imagined Lucas out on the water with his drinking buddies, his escape now solidified by the silent departure.

Sophia turned away from the window and gathered the children for breakfast. Elizabeth and Oliver sat at the worn dining table, their expressions a mixture of sleepiness and quiet apprehension. Sophia forced a smile as she placed a bowl of cereal before them, but inside, a storm of worry raged.

"Kids," Sophia began gently, "I'm sorry, but Daddy isn't here today."

Elizabeth's eyes, too wise for her age, filled with confusion. "But, Mommy, where is Daddy?" she asked in a small, trembling voice.

Oliver, his lip trembling, whispered, "I want Daddy..."

Sophia pulled them into a tight embrace. "I know, sweethearts," she murmured, her voice soft but resolute. "Right now, we have to take care of ourselves. Let's eat and get dressed."

Though Sophia never mentioned the mounting bills or the burden of the boat payment to the children, the weight of it all pressed down on her. As she set the children off to start their day, Sophia retreated to a quiet corner of the apartment, her mind racing with questions. "How am I going to handle this?" she wondered, staring at the empty space where the boat once sat—a symbol of hope turned financial albatross.

Later that morning, after the children had settled into their routines, Elizabeth and Oliver found a moment together in the living room. The soft light filtering through the window cast gentle shadows, creating a temporary haven in the midst of uncertainty.

"Oliver," Elizabeth began hesitantly, "when do you think Daddy will come back?"

Oliver's eyes fell to the threadbare rug as he replied in a small, wavering voice, "I don't know. I miss him a lot."

Elizabeth's heart clenched as she reached out, taking his hand in hers. "I miss him, too," she said softly. "But Mommy says sometimes grown-ups make choices that hurt, and maybe we have to learn to live without them for a while."

Oliver sniffled. "It hurts so much," he admitted, his voice breaking.

Elizabeth squeezed his hand reassuringly. "I know. But we have to be brave for each other. We'll be okay, Oliver. We'll find a way to be safe, even if things are different now."

A tear slipped down Oliver's cheek as he nodded, and though his voice was barely a whisper, the determination in his eyes shone through.

While the children found solace in their quiet conversation, Sophia remained at the kitchen table, her thoughts heavy as she reviewed the bills spread before her. The boat—a promise of unity and adventure—had become a relentless financial burden, a bitter reminder of Lucas's escape into a world of alcohol and him spending time with his friends. Every number on the page echoed the cost of his choices, and as Sophia sipped her lukewarm tea, she whispered to herself, "I'll find a way. I have to." Her voice was resolute, though undercut by sorrow and the weight of countless sleepless nights.

Later, as the afternoon wore on and the children played quietly in the living room, Sophia found a moment to address the quiet that had settled over her heart. "We'll be okay," she reassured them, her tone firm. "We have each other, and that is what matters. I promise I'll work through this, no matter how hard it gets."

Elizabeth, looking up with red-rimmed eyes, murmured, "I just want Daddy to love us."

Oliver, small and fragile in his understanding, added softly, "I miss Daddy."

Sophia pulled them into another embrace, her promise a quiet vow against the unyielding tide of despair.

That night, as the Texas sky darkened and the distant hum of the city provided a muted backdrop, Sophia sat alone at the kitchen table, wondering where Lucas was. The bills lay scattered before her, a grim ledger. The boat payment, once a symbol of hopeful adventure, now loomed like a heavy chain. She stared at the numbers and sighed deeply. "How am I going to do this if he doesn't come back?" she whispered into the quiet, her voice a mixture of determination and sorrow.

As Elizabeth and Oliver finally drifted into a fitful sleep on the worn couch, Elizabeth's whispered words from earlier echoed in the silent room: "Just make it to tomorrow." The promise was not one of unbridled optimism, but a tentative vow—a fragile hope that another day might bring a little more safety and a small measure of comfort.

In the stillness of that long, difficult night, Sophia understood that the cost of freedom was steep—a burden measured not just in bills and missed promises, but in the emotional scars left behind. And as the first light of dawn began to break through the darkness, she realized Lucas wasn't returning. She resolved, with a heavy but determined heart, to fight for a future where her children could finally find the safety they deserved. She learned later that he had returned to Clarissa with the boat. He never made a single payment. To save money, Elizabeth went back to Arizona.

❧ 41 ❧
A GLIMPSE OF STABILITY

Just as the promise of a better tomorrow began to take root in Texas, Sophia found that even the gentlest glimpse of stability could be shattered by the echoes of a past too stubborn to fade.

Life in Texas had, for a brief while, offered Sophia a taste of what she had always longed for—a chance to rebuild her world on her own terms. Her unwavering work ethic had caught the attention of Brian and Bethany, the warm-hearted owners of the local diner, and through them, she earned an introduction to Skeeter (nicknamed after the sport he loved), their charming yet unpredictable son. Within weeks, Skeeter's easy confidence and generous nature had woven new threads of possibility into her life.

At first, it was as if the weight of endless worries had finally lifted. Skeeter, a man of grandeur with an air of unrestrained optimism, quickly became a central figure in their daily lives. Despite being a chain smoker, Skeeter carried himself with a vitality that belied his habit; he neither indulged in drugs nor succumbed to daily drunkenness. As a trust-fund baby, he had the luxury to devote his time entirely to nurturing this newfound family dynamic. He took delight in spending long afternoons with Oliver and Sophia, ensuring that they enjoyed the simple pleasures life had to offer.

"Sophia, you must join us for dinner at the family cabin this weekend," Skeeter said one breezy afternoon as they sat on the back porch of the apartment. His voice was full of genuine enthusiasm.

"There's nothing quite like a quiet meal under the stars and a round of hunting to remind us what real life feels like."

Sophia smiled, a genuine warmth touching her features. "That does sound lovely, Skeeter," she replied. "It might be just what we need to forget our troubles for a while."

Skeeter's world was one of extravagant simplicity. His family yacht, gleaming under the Texan sun, offered spontaneous trips that turned ordinary days into memorable adventures. One Saturday, he even invited Oliver and Sophia aboard. The gentle rocking of the yacht and the shimmering water provided a rare sense of freedom and luxury that Sophia had never known. "This is what life should feel like," Skeeter declared, his boisterous laugh mingling with the splash of the waves as he helped Oliver board the vessel.

For Sophia, these moments were nothing short of transformative. She had experienced hardship and heartache for so long that the mere act of spending a day out on the water felt like a miracle. Skeeter was, in many ways, the antithesis of everything she had endured with Lucas. Where Lucas had been erratic and distant, Skeeter was exuberant and present, even if his attention sometimes wandered during lively conversations. Once, while they were out at the yacht, Sophia tried to broach the subject of their future together.

"Do you ever think about... marriage?" she asked tentatively as they watched the sunset from the deck.

Skeeter, engrossed in a conversation with a friend about an upcoming charity event, brushed off the question with a laugh. "Oh, come on, Sophia! We're just enjoying life right now. Don't worry about the future," he said, his voice light but his eyes momentarily distant. Though his response left her a bit isolated in that moment, Sophia appreciated his reluctance to force a commitment she wasn't ready to confront.

For several blissful months, life seemed to settle into a new rhythm. Sophia brought Elizabeth back to live with Skeeter and Sophia in a small apartment. Sophia found genuine joy in the little adventures—long afternoons on the yacht, quiet weekends at the cabin, and simple evenings of laughter with her son. It was the first time in years that happiness felt tangible. Even Elizabeth, who had long carried the heavy burden of her mother's absence, began to smile more readily, buoyed by the carefree atmosphere Skeeter helped create.

However, beneath this veneer of stability, old shadows lurked. Despite the joy that had blossomed in their new routine, whispers of the past continued to haunt Sophia. Lucas's memory was never far away, and his absence was felt most acutely in the moments when his presence had once been a source of both pain and twisted comfort. Gradually, these murmurs grew louder until, one fateful evening, they became impossible to ignore.

It started subtly—a familiar ringtone on Sophia's phone that she assumed was a mistake, a whisper of a voice on the other end. But as the days passed, the calls became more insistent, accompanied by hushed arguments in which Lucas claimed, "He won't love those kids like I do. He can't possibly because I am their dad, he isn't." He would continue, "He won't love you like I do. He can't possibly." His words, delivered in moments of drunken clarity, cut deep into the fragile peace Sophia had built with Skeeter.

One night, after a quiet dinner at home, Sophia found herself alone with Skeeter. The tension in the room was palpable. "I can't do this anymore," she said, her voice low and resolute. "I'm tired of these calls, these whispers. I'm tired of feeling like our family is always split apart."

Skeeter frowned, reaching out to take her hand. "Sophia, I know it hurts, but maybe—"

"No, Skeeter," she interrupted, her eyes hard. "I can't keep living like this, caught between what was and what could have been. I have to choose for the kids—for us."

That night, with a heavy heart, Sophia packed the kids' belongings in the quiet darkness. In the middle of the night, while Elizabeth and Oliver slept soundly in the bedroom, Sophia made the painful decision. Without a dramatic farewell or a tearful conversation, she left the apartment with the children and all their Christmas presents, determined to find a new place—a fresh start where the ghosts of the past could no longer dictate their future.

As the car rumbled down the highway toward an uncertain destination, Sophia's mind churned with conflicting emotions. Part of her longed to hold onto the stability that Skeeter had briefly provided. Yet another part of her knew that Lucas's lingering influence had tainted any hope of a truly happy life. When she glanced at the children in the back seat, she whispered, "We'll be okay, sweethearts. We have each other, and that's all that matters."

In the quiet aftermath of another tumultuous day, as the dawn broke over a horizon tinted with both promise and uncertainty, Sophia resolved to forge a new path—one where her children could grow without the heavy price of broken promises and unfulfilled escapes. The cost of freedom had been steep, and she understood that real stability might come only after confronting the painful truths of the past. And so, with a determined heart, she steeled herself for the hard road ahead, hoping that in the struggle, they might someday find true peace.

In the warm Texas afternoon, when a day of carefree laughter and playful games took an unexpected turn, Elizabeth discovered that even innocent mischief could spark confusing secrets—and leave her wondering about the true meaning of family.

It was a bright Saturday morning in Texas when Sophia's voice cut through the calm as she spoke to Elizabeth and Oliver. "I need you and Oliver to spend the day at Aunt Alice and Uncle Richard's house," she instructed briskly yet kindly. "I have work today, so be good, alright?" Sophia's tone, though warm, carried a note of urgency. Elizabeth nodded silently, holding Oliver's hand tightly as they stepped into their car. They had been living with Sophia in their modest apartment for several months now, and although life had its hardships, today promised a change of scene—a break from their routine.

Upon arriving, Aunt Alice and Uncle Richard's house was in a quiet neighborhood. The children were greeted by Lacy, whose confident smile and friendly demeanor immediately put Elizabeth at ease. Moments later, Mia appeared, her cheerful greeting filling the entryway. "It's pool day!" Mia announced, her excitement infectious. The cousins wasted no time; they hurried to change into their swimsuits, their chatter blending with the soft hum of a summer morning.

Under the hot sun, the cool water of the pool offered a welcome relief from the lingering stress of their daily lives. Elizabeth and Mia splashed and played with infectious laughter, while Oliver, with a mischievous grin, showed off his dog paddle. Lacy, ever the responsible older cousin, kept a watchful eye on them as she occasionally dipped her feet into the water while on a call. The atmosphere was light, filled with the easy camaraderie of children enjoying a carefree day.

After their swim, the cousins gathered in the spacious living room of the house, where sleeping bags and backpacks—stuffed with pajamas, snacks, and beloved stuffed animals—were spread out on the floor. The room was transformed into a cozy, impromptu camp, a fortress of soft blankets and pillows that promised hours of shared secrets and laughter.

"Isn't this the best?" Mia exclaimed as the girls arranged the blankets into one giant, plush pile.

Elizabeth smiled faintly, though her thoughts wandered briefly. She remembered the times when home had been a place of worry and solitude, where even small joys were hard to come by. Here, for a few hours, with her cousins gathered around her, Elizabeth felt almost normal—a brief escape from the heaviness of her daily life.

As the afternoon wore on, the children's play turned from swimming to more grounded activities. They played tag in the yard, their laughter echoing under the clear blue sky. Later, after watching a few hours of television, the playful energy shifted when Elizabeth and Mia began searching for their older cousin. "Where did Lacy and Oliver go?" Mia asked, her voice a mix of curiosity and playful teasing.

Elizabeth shrugged, replying, "Maybe they're hiding."

They tiptoed behind the couch, peeking into a dim corner of the room. What they saw made them freeze—there, close together, were Lacy and Oliver. Lacy was leaning forward, planting a quick, awkward kiss on Oliver's lips, with her tongue in his mouth. Mia's immediate reaction was a loud, "Eww!" that burst out in a mix of surprise and mischief, and Elizabeth's jaw dropped in equal parts confusion and amusement.

"What are you doing?" Elizabeth teased, half-mocking yet clearly unsure of what to make of the scene.

Lacy's face flushed a deep red, and she stammered, "It's... it's nothing. You wouldn't understand."

Mia burst into giggles while Elizabeth exchanged a look with her, both of them clearly torn between finding the moment funny and being uncertain about its meaning. The playful teasing soon resumed as the girls dismissed the incident with a shake of their heads and a hurried retreat back to the pallet on the floor, leaving behind a swirl of laughter and a touch of embarrassment.

As the day began to wane, the vibrant energy of the afternoon gave way to quieter moments. The kids all gathered on the living room rug, sharing stories and secrets. The atmosphere was a blend of laughter and gentle murmurs, but an undercurrent of uncertainty still lingered for Elizabeth. Though the playful antics had brought joy, the memory of earlier times remained a quiet shadow in her heart.

Sitting with her cousins, Elizabeth listened as Mia recounted a funny story about a misadventure at the pool, and Lacy talked about an upcoming school project. Amid the chatter, Elizabeth hesitated and then asked in a soft, tentative voice, "Do you think my dad will come back someday?"

Mia frowned for a moment, and Lacy's eyes softened with a mix of regret and resignation. "I don't know, Elizabeth," Lacy replied gently. "Sometimes grown-ups make choices that hurt, and maybe they don't always come back."

Oliver, who had been quietly listening, whispered, "I miss him so much..."

Elizabeth reached over and squeezed Oliver's hand. "I miss him, too," she said, her tone both sorrowful and determined. "But for now, we have each other, and that's what matters."

The conversation, simple yet laden with the weight of their experiences, gave Elizabeth a small measure of comfort, even as she struggled to understand the complexities of grown-up choices.

As the late afternoon light softened into dusk, the cousins began to pack up and prepare to leave. The mood was bittersweet—joy from the day's festivities mingled with the unspoken understanding that these moments of carefree fun were temporary. Soon, Uncle Richard arrived to pick up the children and take them home. With a stern look, Lacy reminded them to keep their voices down and not to mention any of the more private moments they had shared that day.

On the ride home, Elizabeth stared out the window at the

sprawling Texas neighborhood. The vivid images of the day—the laughter, the shared secrets, the warmth of the pool—seemed to recede like a fading dream. Oliver sat silently beside her, his small face reflecting the quiet sadness that had settled over them.

At home, Sophia greeted them with a careful smile, though her eyes betrayed her worry. Later that evening, as they sat together in their modest apartment, Sophia knelt beside Elizabeth and Oliver. "I know today wasn't everything you hoped for," she said softly, "but remember, we have each other, and that's our strength."

Elizabeth's voice was a whisper: "I just want to feel safe."

Oliver murmured, "I miss Daddy..."

Sophia wrapped them in a warm hug, her voice steady but heavy with unspoken pain. "We'll get through this," she promised, though her heart was burdened by the cost of their shattered dreams— especially the boat, which now loomed as a financial chain she had to bear alone.

That night, as darkness fell over the apartment, Sophia sat alone in the quiet kitchen after she put the children to bed, the soft hum of the refrigerator a stark contrast to the turmoil in her mind. The boat payment, a symbol of Lucas's futile escape with Clarissa, stared back at her from the spread of bills on the counter in front of her. With a deep, weary sigh, she whispered, "We'll find a way, I have to..." Her voice was resolute yet tinged with sorrow and exhaustion —a quiet vow to persevere even when the future seemed uncertain.

In the dim light of their bedroom, as Elizabeth and Oliver finally drifted into fitful sleep, Elizabeth's earlier words echoed in the silence: "Just make it to tomorrow." They were not a promise of unyielding hope but a fragile, unresolved plea—a reminder that despite the shadows of the past and the cost of freedom, every new day was a chance to find a glimpse of safety.

As the first light of dawn crept through the window, Sophia gathered her strength. The journey ahead was uncertain, and the scars of her life would not easily fade. Yet, with her children by her side, she resolved to forge a path through the darkness—a path where, perhaps someday, they would all find true stability.

❧ 43 ❧
A NEW DAWN OF THE HEART

Sophia had sworn off love to protect her fragile independence, but when Daniel quietly entered her life like a gentle breeze on a hot Texas day, even her most steadfast vows began to tremble.

Sophia had long prided herself on her self-sufficiency. After years of struggle, she had made a solemn promise—to live a life of celibacy, free from the entanglements that once brought her heartache. The solitude she embraced had become a sanctuary; she was content, even happy, knowing she could depend on herself. Every morning, she woke with a quiet confidence, bolstered by the knowledge that she was in charge of her own destiny.

Then, one seemingly ordinary afternoon, everything began to change. It was at a community event at the local park—a modest affair under a wide Texas sky—where Sophia first encountered Daniel. He wasn't a man of flashy words or grand gestures. Instead, Daniel exuded a steady, calming presence. His dark eyes held a quiet kindness, and his gentle smile spoke of understanding and patience. Over the course of that day, as they worked side by side setting up tables and handing out refreshments, Sophia found herself drawn to his unassuming sincerity.

Later that day, while they sat on a bench beneath an ancient oak, Daniel broke the comfortable silence. "You know, Sophia," he began, his voice warm and thoughtful, "I've watched you work all day, and it's clear you're a very strong person. I admire that."

Sophia, who had grown used to guarding her heart fiercely, looked up, slightly startled. "Thank you, Daniel. I—I've learned to rely on myself after everything."

Daniel nodded slowly. "Sometimes, relying solely on ourselves can be lonely. I don't mean to intrude, but if you ever need a friend —or maybe more—I'm here. No pressure, no expectations."

For a long moment, Sophia searched his eyes, feeling a stirring she hadn't allowed herself in years. In that quiet exchange, she felt something shift—a delicate crack in the wall she had built around her heart.

Over the following weeks, Daniel became a constant presence in Sophia's life. They met for coffee, took leisurely walks along tree-lined streets, and spent evenings talking about their pasts, dreams, and disappointments. His words were always gentle, never pushing her beyond what she was ready to share. Slowly, Sophia found herself laughing again, her heart warming to the possibility that she might not have to stand alone forever.

One cool, star-studded night, as they sat on the back porch of Sophia's apartment, Daniel grew quiet. The only sound was the soft murmur of crickets and the distant rustle of the wind. Daniel looked at Sophia with an intensity that belied his calm demeanor. "Sophia, I know you've sworn off relationships—sworn to a life of independence—but I can't help the way I feel. I care for you deeply, more than I ever thought possible. I want to build a future with you, if you'll let me."

Sophia's breath caught in her throat. The night, which had been filled with the usual comfortable quiet, now seemed charged with possibility and apprehension. "Daniel, I... I've been alone for so long," she murmured. Her eyes searched his face for any sign of reproach, but all she saw was earnest hope. "Sometimes, I wonder if it's safer to be on my own."

Daniel reached out, gently taking her hand. "I understand your fears, and I'm not here to change you. But love doesn't have to steal your independence; it can be a partnership where we share our burdens instead of carrying them alone."

Sophia's mind flashed with memories of heartbreak and solitude, but the sincerity in Daniel's eyes was hard to ignore. With the urgency of someone who had long been starving for connection, she whispered, "Yes. Yes, I'll try."

In that tender moment, Sophia's resolve to live a life alone began to crumble. The decision was not made with grand declarations or promises of perfection. It was a quiet, desperate acceptance—the kind that comes from a heart that has been waiting too long for the nourishment of genuine care.

In the weeks that followed, Sophia and Daniel cultivated a gentle, steady relationship that was as unassuming as it was real. Daniel, with gentleness and kindness, remained reliable and consistently supportive. He brought a sense of stability to Sophia's life; his presence was a reminder that she didn't have to face the world's hardships alone. Their days together were simple but comforting—quiet mornings over coffee, shared walks, and long conversations in which Daniel listened more than he spoke.

Sophia began to notice subtle changes in herself. She found that, for the first time in years, she could laugh without a trace of bitterness and dream of a future not dominated by fear and financial burdens. Yet, even as this new life blossomed, the memories of past hardships—of broken promises and isolation—lingered like shadows at the edge of her vision.

One evening, after a particularly peaceful day, Daniel and Sophia sat together on the back porch. The Texas sky was clear, the stars bright against the midnight canvas. Daniel gently asked, "Do you think you're ready to let someone in completely, Sophia?"

Sophia looked down at her hands, then back at him. "I'm scared," she admitted quietly. "I've built my life around being independent, and now I'm not sure if I can ever trust myself to share that space."

Daniel took her hand, his tone soft yet resolute. "We can take it one day at a time. I'm not asking for everything all at once. I just want to be here for you through every step."

Her eyes glistened with unshed tears, and with a trembling smile, she replied, "I need that more than I ever thought I would."

They sat in companionable silence, the soft murmur of their shared breaths filling the night. In that quiet space, Sophia began to believe that perhaps the future could hold something gentle and enduring—even if it wasn't the life she had once sworn to lead.

Despite the budding stability in her personal life, Sophia's mind still wrestled with the weight of past burdens. The financial strain of going it alone remained a silent worry. However, Sophia kept these concerns hidden from her children and Daniel, determined to protect the relationships that were important to her.

Over time, the steady rhythm of Daniel's care and the small moments of genuine happiness in her new life began to chip away at the loneliness that had once defined her. She discovered that while her past was filled with heartache and solitude, the future might hold unexpected joys if she were willing to embrace uncertainty.

One quiet morning, as Daniel and Sophia prepared breakfast together, she paused and said, "I never imagined that I'd feel this way again. I used to think I'd sworn off love for good, but now... I'm not so sure."

Daniel smiled softly. "Maybe it's not about giving up who you are; it's about sharing that strength with someone who truly cares."

Sophia's eyes met his, and for a moment, the scars of her past seemed to fade into the background. "I'm willing to try," she said, her voice steady yet filled with cautious hope. "For you, for us."

In that moment, Sophia resolved to face the future with all its uncertainties. The road ahead would not be easy—old ghosts and new challenges would continue to test her resolve—but she now had a partner by her side, someone who believed in sharing the burdens rather than letting them define her.

As dawn broke on a new day, Sophia stood by the window, watching the soft light of the Texas morning creep over the horizon. Her thoughts wandered to the promise she had made to herself long ago—to be strong, independent, and free. Yet now, with Daniel in her life, she understood that true freedom did not mean living in isolation; it meant having the courage to share one's life, even when it was frightening.

The promise of a shared future was tentative, marred by the scars of past betrayals and the lingering cost of old choices. But as she listened to the gentle murmur of the apartment complex coming to life and the distant laughter of children on the street, Sophia allowed herself a small, hopeful smile. She whispered softly to the breaking day, "Maybe tomorrow, everything will be just a little bit brighter."

In that quiet moment, Sophia resolved to forge ahead—one step at a time—trusting that with Daniel by her side and the support of those who loved her, she could build a future where the ghosts of her past would no longer hold her captive.

❧ 44 ❧
A HOUSE DIVIDED

When the fragile promise of stability shattered under the weight of favoritism and unspoken resentments, Elizabeth discovered that even a house filled with family can feel as divided as broken glass.

Sophia's hope for a stable future had once seemed within reach when she married Daniel. His calm demeanor, steady job, and unassuming kindness had, at first, brought a glimmer of light to Elizabeth's troubled world. Daniel was nothing like her father, Lucas—he didn't drink, didn't smoke, and he appeared determined to provide the warmth and structure their family so desperately needed. In the early days, Elizabeth cherished the way Daniel praised her artwork and eagerly helped her with school projects. His gentle encouragement, calling her "the light of the house," filled her with a sense of belonging that had long been missing.

Yet as time passed, subtle fissures began to emerge. It started with the small things. Daniel's patience, though ample with Elizabeth, seemed to wither when it came to Oliver. In quiet moments, when no one was looking, Daniel's own guilt over his limited relationship with his son simmered beneath the surface and soon morphed into resentment. The warmth he bestowed on Elizabeth was accompanied by a growing coldness toward Oliver.

One evening at dinner, the tension became painfully clear. Oliver accidentally knocked over his glass of water. Daniel's tone, sharp and unyielding, cut through the gentle murmur of family conversation.

"You need to be more careful, Oliver. How hard is it to sit still for one meal?" Daniel snapped, his eyes narrowing as he fixed his gaze on the trembling child.

Sophia's fork paused mid-air as she interjected softly, "Daniel, it was an accident."

But Daniel's response was immediate and dismissive. "That's the problem—everything with him is an accident."

Elizabeth's eyes darted between her mother and her younger brother. Oliver's face flushed with embarrassment, and Elizabeth felt a pang of guilt. She remembered how differently Daniel treated her—how his praise made her feel valued—while Oliver received only criticism. The disparity stung; it was as though Daniel reserved kindness solely for Elizabeth, leaving Oliver to bear the brunt of his unresolved feelings about his own son.

Over the next few weeks, Daniel's favoritism became harder to ignore. He showered Elizabeth with art supplies and accolades for her academic achievements, spending time nurturing her hobbies. Meanwhile, when Oliver sought help or a comforting word, Daniel brushed him aside or scolded him. One Saturday morning in the yard, while Elizabeth sat drawing on the porch, Oliver approached Daniel with a basketball in hand.

"Can we play for a little while?" Oliver asked, his tone hopeful yet tentative.

Daniel, his attention fixed on tending to the garden, barely looked up. "Not now, Oliver. I'm busy," he said curtly. Oliver sighed and walked away, tossing the ball half-heartedly as he disappeared around the corner. Elizabeth's heart sank as she watched him go. She wanted to call out to him, to remind him that every child deserved kindness, but the sting of Daniel's dismissal left her speechless.

The tensions escalated further during a family game night—a hopeful attempt by Sophia to bring everyone together. The living room was abuzz with laughter and the clatter of game pieces. Elizabeth, Oliver, and their cousins gathered around the board, and for a brief period, the air was filled with the promise of unity. However, the atmosphere darkened when Oliver, in his innocent confusion, misread the rules of the game.

"That's not how you play," Daniel said sharply, his voice cutting through the merriment.

"I didn't know," Oliver mumbled, shrinking into his seat.

"Maybe if you paid more attention, you wouldn't mess things up," Daniel snapped, his words echoing in the stunned silence that followed.

Sophia's eyes flashed with anger as she interjected, "Daniel, stop. He's just a kid. You don't have to be so harsh."

Daniel's response was defensive. "Maybe if Oliver had some discipline, he wouldn't be so difficult," he retorted, his tone heavy with unspoken pain about his own son.

Sophia's face flushed. "You're not being fair. You treat Elizabeth like she's perfect and act as if Oliver can't do anything right," she countered, her voice trembling with both anger and sadness.

The argument grew louder, and soon the room filled with clashing voices. Elizabeth, caught in the crossfire, reached over to squeeze Oliver's hand under the table—a silent plea for unity in the midst of a divided household.

In the days that followed, the fights became more frequent. Sophia and Daniel argued nearly every night about Oliver's behavior, and Elizabeth found herself caught in the middle. One evening, as the children lay in Oliver's bedroom, Oliver's small voice finally broke the silence.

"Why does Daniel hate me?" he asked, his tone filled with quiet confusion and hurt.

Elizabeth hesitated, unsure of how to answer. "I don't think he hates you," she said softly. "He's just... sad about his own son."

Oliver turned to her, his expression skeptical. "That doesn't mean he has to be mean to me," he murmured.

Elizabeth's heart clenched. "I wish I knew how to make it better," she admitted, feeling helpless as she watched her brother struggle under the weight of unwarranted criticism.

Later that night, after another heated argument with Daniel, Sophia came in and sat on the edge of Lucas's bed. Her eyes were tired, and her voice was barely a whisper as she said to Oliver, "I'm sorry, baby. I thought Daniel would be good for us."

Oliver, his eyes filled with sorrow, leaned against her, letting the silence speak volumes. "I miss Daddy," he murmured softly, the words lingering in the heavy air.

Sophia wrapped an arm around him. "I'm trying to fix this," she whispered, a promise more to herself than to anyone else.

Over time, the division within the house grew more pronounced. Sophia found herself withdrawing, her eyes avoiding Daniel's accusatory glances and her voice growing quieter whenever he was near. Elizabeth felt the shift keenly. The warm, safe home she once knew had fractured into a place of tension and conflict. Even as she clung to the small moments of happiness—a whispered joke with Oliver or a quiet smile during a shared secret—she longed for the simplicity of the past, even if it meant missing the familiar chaos of the ranch and, sometimes, even the presence of Julian.

One night, as the day wound down, the family gathered for dinner—a meal that had once been a symbol of unity but now felt laden with unspoken resentments. Daniel's criticisms echoed at every turn, and Sophia's attempts to soothe the children only deepened the rift. In the midst of this, Elizabeth could only watch, her young mind grappling with the complexities of favoritism and the harsh reality of adult emotions.

Late that night, as the echoes of another argument subsided into silence, Elizabeth lay awake in her room. The soft light from a lamp cast long shadows on the wall, and the quiet was punctuated only by the distant sound of a television in another room. In that fragile solitude, Elizabeth's thoughts drifted unbidden to her family—her mother's overcompensation to Oliver, Daniel's harsh words, and the loving warmth that now felt so elusive.

"I just want things to be different," Elizabeth whispered to herself, her voice trembling with the weight of her confusion and longing. Yet even in that whisper was a spark of determination—a small, unresolved hope that one day, somehow, the pieces of their fractured home might be mended.

In the quiet aftermath of that long, troubled day, Sophia sat alone in the living room, her eyes scanning all the things they owned. The house, once a haven, now felt divided—a place where love and resentment, hope and despair waged a silent war. As she looked over the scattered remnants of dinner on the dining table and the empty space that once brimmed with laughter, she resolved to fight for a future in which her children could truly feel safe.

Though the cost of freedom had left deep scars, and the pain of broken promises lingered like a stubborn shadow, Sophia knew she must forge ahead. With each new day, she would work to heal the divisions, even if the path was fraught with uncertainty and the ghosts of the past refused to fade.

Elizabeth, nestled against Oliver as they slept on his bed, softly repeated her familiar, fragile mantra: "Just make it to tomorrow." It was not a promise of unyielding hope but a tentative vow—a reminder that even in a house divided, the possibility of unity and peace was worth striving for, no matter how uncertain the future might be.

❧ 45 ❧

SHATTERED GLASS

In the eerie stillness that followed the storm, when broken glass scattered like cruel confetti across cold tile, Elizabeth learned that even the safest home can fracture—and the harsh words between adults can shatter more than just windows.

The house was quiet—the kind of stillness that falls after a storm, heavy and oppressive. Elizabeth lay in bed, eyes fixed on the ceiling, as the low hum of the air conditioner filled the silence. At first, she tried to ignore the muffled voices drifting from the other side of the house. Over the past few weeks, the constant, stilted arguments between Sophia and Daniel had become a backdrop to her days. But tonight, the voices began to rise with an unusual intensity. Elizabeth's stomach churned as she strained to listen.

"...we need to fix this, Daniel," came Sophia's voice, sharper than usual.

Daniel's reply was low and clipped: "It's just money, Sophia. And you know Oliver isn't the problem." His tone made Elizabeth's heart race faster with unease.

Unable to ignore the escalating conflict, Elizabeth sat up in bed. "Mommy?" she whispered into the darkness, but her call was swallowed by the rising voices. The argument seemed to be about money, about Oliver, about fairness—topics that were all too familiar, yet tonight carried a bitter edge.

Then, suddenly, a loud crash reverberated through the house, shattering the remaining calm. For a moment, everything was silent —a stunned pause that lasted long enough for Elizabeth's heart to nearly stop. In a burst of alarm, she threw off her covers and scrambled out of bed. Her bare feet hit the cold carpet with a jolt, and she rushed toward the source of the noise.

Peeking out of her door, Elizabeth's eyes widened at the sight before her: shards of glass glittered on the kitchen floor like cruel, tiny stars. The window to the atrium in the kitchen was shattered, and in the middle of the chaos, Sophia lay on the hard tile, her hands braced against the floor as if to catch herself from falling again.

Daniel stood a few feet away, his face a furious shade of red and his chest heaving. "You're overreacting," he snapped, his tone defensive as he tried to dismiss the commotion. "It was an accident."

Sophia slowly pushed herself up and met his gaze, her eyes blazing with fury. "You pushed me, Daniel," she said in a low, trembling voice that carried the weight of accumulated pain. "You crossed a line."

Daniel ran a hand through his hair, his anger flaring then sputtering into frustration. "You're making this into something it's not," he said. "I didn't mean—"

"Enough," Sophia cut him off sharply. "I won't do this. Not again. Not ever."

A heavy silence fell over the room. Elizabeth, overwhelmed by the intensity of the moment, ducked back into her own room, her heart pounding with fear and uncertainty. She knew better than to intervene, even as every fiber of her being wanted to do something.

Hours passed in a tense, suffocating hush. Then, Sophia appeared in Elizabeth's doorway, her face set with determined resolve. Her voice, though soft, carried an undeniable finality. "Get dressed," she said quietly, gently rousing Elizabeth. "Pack a bag. We're leaving."

Elizabeth blinked in disbelief, her voice catching as she asked, "What about Daniel?"

Sophia's eyes were hard, her tone unyielding. "We're done here. Just do as I say."

Without another word, Elizabeth hurried to retrieve her school backpack and began stuffing it with clothes, her sketchbook, and a few cherished trinkets that recalled happier memories. From the adjacent room, she heard Sophia calling out in Oliver's room, giving him the same urgent instructions. Oliver protested in a sleepy, muffled tone, but his defiance faded as soon as he caught the determined look on their mother's face.

Within fifteen minutes, the house was in a state of quiet disarray. Sophia led Elizabeth and Oliver through the dim corridors, careful to avoid disturbing Daniel, who had retreated to the master bedroom—whether in anger or indifference, Elizabeth could not tell. Stepping out into the cool Texas night, the trio slipped quietly through the front door, leaving behind a home that had once promised safety but now felt irreparably broken.

The car ride that followed was shrouded in a heavy silence. Sophia gripped the steering wheel tightly, her knuckles turning white in the faint glow of streetlights. Elizabeth sat in the backseat with Oliver leaning against her shoulder, his small form half-asleep, his favorite toy clutched close. As the car sped along empty, moonlit streets, Elizabeth's mind buzzed with unspoken questions. Where are we going? What will happen next? Will Daniel chase after us? Though she longed to voice her fears, the uncertainty of the moment left her silent.

After what seemed like an eternity, Sophia finally broke the silence. "We're going to figure this out," she murmured, her voice barely rising above a whisper as if to keep the fragile hope intact. "I don't know how yet, but we'll find a way."

Elizabeth listened, her heart heavy yet clinging to that distant promise of a new start. "Maybe this is the last time we have to run away in the middle of the night," she thought, though the words remained unspoken.

Glancing at her mother's reflection in the rearview mirror, Elizabeth saw determination etched on Sophia's face—a look that, for the first time in a long time, made her believe that her mother was no longer overwhelmed by chaos but was ready to protect them at all costs. Suddenly, in a burst of youthful urgency, Elizabeth spoke up. "Let's go to Tracy's house!" she exclaimed, her voice trembling with a mixture of excitement and desperate relief.

Sophia's expression softened immediately, relief mingling with her steely resolve. "That's a great idea," she said warmly. "Tracy's mom is my best friend, and Tracy is your best friend. We'll be safe there."

46

MORE TRANSITIONS

When home became too heavy to bear, a modest refuge at Tracy's house offered a brief escape—a promise of safety in a world that had learned to shatter, only to be pieced back together with the laughter of childhood.

After leaving Daniel in the dead of night, Sophia, Elizabeth, and Oliver arrived at the home of Elizabeth's best friend, Tracy. The modest one-story house, with its worn welcome mat and a backyard cluttered with well-loved toys, felt to Elizabeth like a small slice of heaven—a place where, even if only for a day, she could forget the bitterness of her own home.

Tracy's parents greeted them warmly. "Welcome, come on in," said Tracy's mom with a gentle smile as she led Sophia and the children to a small guest room furnished with a fold-out couch and an old dresser. "It's a bit cramped, but we'll make it work," she added reassuringly. Elizabeth noticed how Tracy's dad silently hefted their bags with a sturdy, quiet assurance that made her feel unexpectedly safe.

Once inside, Elizabeth and Tracy slipped quickly into their usual rhythm. They spent hours giggling over cartoons in the living room and trading secrets in the cozy corner of Tracy's room, where the walls were decorated with faded pop posters and bright stickers. Their conversation flowed easily, punctuated by bursts of laughter as they played with Tracy's collection of dolls. For a few precious hours, Elizabeth could forget the chaos that had forced her family to leave home.

Meanwhile, Oliver, now eight and full of restless energy, was not content to blend into the background. One bright afternoon, as the girls were busy whispering secrets in Tracy's room, Oliver burst in with an exuberant grin.

"Come on, let's go outside!" he declared, bouncing on his heels.

Elizabeth frowned. "We're busy, Oliver. Go play by yourself," she chided lightly, though her tone held a trace of resignation.

Oliver rolled his eyes dramatically. "You're so boring. Come on— Tracy's dad set up the sprinkler in the backyard!" he announced, his voice rising with excitement.

Tracy's face lit up instantly. "The sprinkler's the best! Let's go, now!" she chimed, grabbing Oliver's hand and tugging him toward the door.

Elizabeth sighed but eventually relented, trailing behind them as they stepped into the backyard. The yard was a chaotic mix of muddy patches and overgrown grass, but at its center, the sprinkler burst forth like a beacon of childhood magic, sending shimmering droplets into the sunlit air and scattering tiny rainbows.

"Wow, look at those rainbows!" Oliver shouted, already dashing through the spray with uncontainable glee. Tracy laughed, shrieking as the cool water hit her face, and Elizabeth hesitated at the edge for a moment. But when Oliver grabbed her hand and pulled her into the fun, she couldn't help but laugh as well.

They spent the entire afternoon soaked and happy, slipping and sliding in the muddy grass. Their laughter echoed around the yard, a joyful rebellion against the hardships they had left behind. Later, as the children returned inside, dripping and beaming, Tracy's mom handed them fresh towels and chuckled, "You kids sure know how to have fun."

Elizabeth wrapped a towel around herself and glanced at Oliver, who was grinning from ear to ear. "You make it all better, Oliver," she murmured softly, a pang of gratitude warming her heart.

As the day wore on, the atmosphere at Tracy's house grew more relaxed, yet a hint of underlying tension remained. Later that afternoon, while the children played in the living room, Elizabeth and Oliver found a quiet corner together with Tracy. The soft light streaming through the window cast gentle shadows, and for a moment, the day felt almost normal.

"Oliver," Elizabeth began hesitantly, "do you think Daniel will ever come back?"

Oliver looked down at the patterned rug and then up at Elizabeth, his small face etched with worry. "I don't know... I hope not," he whispered.

Elizabeth squeezed his hand. "Me too," she replied quietly.

Oliver sniffled, his voice barely audible. "It still hurts, though..."

"I know, Oliver," Elizabeth said, wrapping her arm around him. "But we have to be brave. We'll be okay as long as we look out for each other."

Their soft conversation lingered in the quiet room, a fragile thread of resilience weaving them closer together.

As evening approached, the joyous moments at Tracy's began to blend with a growing awareness of the instability back home. While the children prepared for dinner, Sophia received a terse phone call from Daniel, whose voice carried an undercurrent of anger and regret. Later, as Sophia spoke in hushed, strained tones with Tracy's parents in the living room, her eyes betrayed a mix of relief and lingering worry.

"You know," Sophia confided quietly, "I don't know how much longer I can keep doing this... all these conflicts, all these reminders that home isn't safe."

Tracy's mom nodded in sympathy. "You did what you had to do," she assured her. "For now, you're safe here. And sometimes, safety is just a temporary state."

Sophia's face grew somber. "I only wish the children didn't have to suffer the consequences," she murmured, her voice thick with unspoken pain.

As the day came to a close, a heavy decision weighed on Sophia's mind. With a steady, tired resolve, she informed the children that they would soon be moving to a new apartment. "After school tomorrow, we're going straight home and staying inside," she declared firmly. "Elizabeth, you're in charge of Oliver. If he gets into trouble, so do you."

Elizabeth nodded, feeling the weight of responsibility settle upon her shoulders. Even though the promise of safety at Tracy's had offered a brief escape, the reality of their situation at home still loomed large.

Later, as the children played in their new temporary routine—sometimes sneaking out to the back alley for a few stolen moments of freedom—Elizabeth and Oliver had a quiet conversation.

"Oliver," Elizabeth said one evening as they sat together on a worn-out couch, "I wish things could be different."

Oliver's eyes filled with unshed tears. "I miss Dad, and I miss the way things used to be," he whispered.

Elizabeth took his hand gently. "I know. But we have to be strong, Oliver. Mom always says that even when everything feels broken, we must hold on to hope and try to make tomorrow better."

Oliver sniffled, nodding silently. Their shared silence said more than words could; it was a promise to stick together despite the uncertainty.

That night, as Tracy's house settled into a peaceful quiet and the echoes of the day's laughter faded, Elizabeth lay in her temporary room. The soft glow of a bedside lamp illuminated her thoughtful face, and she found herself replaying the day's events—the joyful splashes in the sprinkler, the teasing, the gentle reassurance among friends, and the underlying tensions that still haunted her thoughts.

"I just want things to be different," she whispered into the darkness, her voice trembling with a blend of sorrow and fragile resolve. Then, with a determined exhale, she repeated her familiar vow, "Just make it to tomorrow." Each repetition was a tender promise—a small, steadfast hope that despite shattered moments and unspoken truths, there was a chance for healing, for rebuilding, for a new beginning.

Across the hall, in the quiet solitude of the kitchen, Sophia sat with a stack of bills spread out before her—a stark reminder of the challenges that lay ahead. Though the numbers were a constant burden, Sophia's mind was fixed on the promise of a future where her children could finally be safe. With a deep, steady breath, she murmured, "I'll find a way. I have to, for both of them." Her words, though resolute, were tinged with the sorrow of all that had been lost.

As the first light of dawn crept over the horizon, Sophia gathered Elizabeth and Oliver on the couch and held them close.

"Good morning, my loves," she said softly, her voice steady despite the pain in her eyes. "Today is a new day, and we'll take it one step at a time."

Elizabeth, still processing the events of the day, looked up at her with cautious hope. "Mom, do you really think things can change?" she asked in a small, trembling voice.

Sophia pulled Elizabeth into a tight embrace. "I promise, we'll do everything we can to make it better," she whispered, her tone firm yet tender. "It might not be perfect, but we'll rebuild together, piece by piece."

In that quiet, tentative morning, as Tracy's house offered a temporary haven from the chaos of their past, Elizabeth's soft refrain—"Just make it to tomorrow"—echoed in her heart as a fragile vow. Despite the uncertainty and the scars of yesterday, there remained a small, stubborn spark of hope for a future where the pieces of their shattered world might one day be mended.

47

A LESSON UNLEARNED

In a day that began with the simple joys of homework and shared laughter, the unexpected crash of conflict would shatter Elizabeth's fragile sense of normalcy and force her to confront the painful lessons of responsibility and love.

The day had started off so normally that, for a brief while, Elizabeth and Oliver had almost forgotten about the chaos that often lurked in the corners of their lives. In the quiet of their modest apartment, Elizabeth had helped Oliver finish his homework before they settled at the kitchen table to draw pictures together. They squabbled over crayons and exchanged teasing remarks, their laughter mingling with the soft hum of the air conditioner. For those precious moments, they were simply siblings enjoying a peaceful morning.

Then, as the afternoon unfolded, the familiar phone rang—a call from Mom that signaled the end of their carefree time. Elizabeth answered in a polite, practiced tone. "Hello?"

Her mother's voice came through, strained yet insistent: "Elizabeth, you're in charge today. I need you and Oliver to be home when I return. Don't go outside."

Elizabeth's heart sank slightly at the reminder, though she responded dutifully, "Yes, ma'am." The weight of responsibility settled on her small shoulders, a burden she had grown accustomed to over time.

After the call ended, Elizabeth glanced around the apartment and, to her mounting alarm, noticed that Oliver was nowhere to be seen. "Where did he go?" she muttered under her breath. She quickly looked around their small apartment, and it didn't take long to figure out that Oliver wasn't inside. Without hesitation, she grabbed her shoes and bolted out the door, determined to locate her brother.

The playground was only a short walk away, but as Elizabeth approached, her heart pounded faster at the sight before her. Oliver was climbing the jungle gym, swinging from the bars as if completely unaware of the urgency in Elizabeth's voice.

"Oliver, we have to go!" Elizabeth called, jogging toward him.

He continued to swing, his eyes fixed on his play, as though he had not heard her. Frustration surged in Elizabeth's chest. "Oliver!" she repeated, louder this time, her voice cracking with exasperation. She hurried up to him, grabbed his arm firmly, and tugged him toward the apartment. "Come on, we need to go home now!"

But Oliver, determined to assert his independence, twisted free. His small face scrunched in defiance. Before Elizabeth could even process his actions, Oliver balled up his fist and, in a flash of anger or misunderstanding, punched her square in the nose.

Pain exploded across Elizabeth's face. She stumbled backward, clutching her nose as tears sprang to her eyes. "Oliver!" she cried out, a mix of shock and betrayal lacing her tone.

Oliver did not pause—he darted away, leaving Elizabeth standing alone in the middle of the playground, her nose throbbing and her heart sinking. The painful echo of his defiance haunted her as she slowly made her way back to the apartment.

Upon returning, Elizabeth found the door locked. "Oliver, let me in!" she shouted, pounding on the door with mounting desperation.

From the other side came a muffled, mocking reply. "Nope! You shouldn't have grabbed me like that. Now you stay out there!"

Desperation crept into Elizabeth's voice as she pleaded, "Please, Oliver, Mom's going to be home soon. We'll both get in trouble if you do this!"

But Oliver's tone remained cold and dismissive. "Nope. You will. Not me."

With those words, Elizabeth slid to the ground, leaning her back against the door as tears streamed down her face. She felt utterly helpless—trapped in a situation that spiraled out of her control. All she could do was wait, silently hoping that Mom would understand her side of the story.

When Sophia finally arrived, her presence filled the entryway with a mixture of stern authority and sorrowful disappointment. "What are you doing outside?" Sophia demanded, her tone sharp as she hurried over to Elizabeth.

"I—I was getting Oliver," Elizabeth stuttered, her voice trembling with fear and confusion.

Sophia's gaze hardened as she listened, and without further discussion, she turned to Oliver's side. "You're in charge, and you were outside. Go to my room and wait for me," she instructed firmly.

Elizabeth's heart sank. She wanted to protest, to argue that Oliver had locked her out, but she knew that arguing would be futile. Instead, she silently trudged back to her room, the weight of responsibility pressing down on her even further.

Later that evening, as the household fell into a heavy, oppressive silence, Sophia entered Elizabeth's room. Her expression was set, and her tone was cold as she pulled open the closet and retrieved a worn leather belt. "Since you don't listen when I speak, we're going to try something different today," she said. "Every time I have to spank you for letting Oliver get away, I'll double the number of swats. Maybe that will finally teach you to be responsible."

Elizabeth's stomach churned with fear. "Mom, please," she whispered, her voice barely audible. "I was just trying to get him to come inside."

Sophia's voice was firm, her resolve unyielding. "You were outside, and you let him go out. It's your job to keep him safe."

"Please, Mom," Elizabeth begged, tears streaming down her cheeks. "I promise I'll do better."

Without further response, Sophia pointed to the bed. "Turn around," she commanded.

Elizabeth obeyed, trembling as she leaned over the edge of the bed, bracing herself. The first lash struck sharply, and by the third, she bit her lip to stifle a cry. The punishment escalated, and before she knew it, the count exceeded fifteen swats. Pain overwhelmed her, and she collapsed to the floor, unable to stand as Sophia's anger continued unabated. The belt hit wherever it could land.

After what felt like an eternity, Sophia finally ceased, stepping back with heavy breathing. "Get up," she ordered, her tone final. "And don't ever go out again."

Elizabeth struggled to her feet, her body quivering with pain and humiliation. As Sophia stowed the belt away, Elizabeth's thoughts darkened with a wish that Oliver might share her punishment—but instead, she later heard his distant laughter echoing from the dining room, where he and Sophia sat together for dinner, their voices light and carefree.

Alone in her room, Elizabeth lay on her bed, her stomach aching and tears continuing to fall silently. "Maybe one day," she thought bitterly, "she'll see the truth." But even as that thought passed through her mind, a deeper uncertainty settled in—one that left her wondering if she would ever be heard.

The next day, the morning began with a mix of routine and lingering tension. Elizabeth and Oliver woke up and prepared for school in the small apartment, their movements subdued by the events of the previous night. In the quiet of the morning, Sophia's voice cut like a knife. "After school, you come straight home and stay inside," Sophia said firmly as she ensured everything was in order. "Elizabeth, you're in charge of Oliver. If he gets into trouble, so do you."

Elizabeth nodded, her voice barely audible. "Okay, Mom."

At school, as Elizabeth tried to concentrate on her classes, her thoughts drifted back to the events at home. During a quiet moment, she confronted Oliver in the hallway, "You better stay in today?"

Oliver looked down, his voice small. "I will. I don't want you to get into trouble again."

Elizabeth sighed, squeezing his hand. "You better, or I will give you what she gives me," she said firmly.

Oliver sniffled, his eyes glistening. "Does it still hurt?" he asked.

"No," Elizabeth replied, her voice resolute. "I will be fine. We just have to stick together."

Their words, though simple, resonated deeply—a small pact between siblings to face a broken world together.

That night, as the house settled into its uneasy quiet, Elizabeth lay in her room and stared at the ceiling. Every detail of the previous night—the escalating voices, the crash of shattered glass, and the sound of the belt—replayed in her mind with painful clarity. In the dim glow of her bedside lamp, she whispered to herself, "I just want things to be different."

After a long, heavy silence, she repeated softly, "Just make it to tomorrow." Each repetition was a fragile promise—a small, determined vow that, despite the pain and the injustice, she would endure, hoping that one day her voice might be heard and the broken pieces of her world might be mended.

Across the hall, Sophia sat in the quiet solitude of the kitchen, staring at the remnants of the night's chaos—an unspoken testament to the cost of trying to keep the family together. Though she never spoke of the punishment to Elizabeth, the heavy burden of responsibility and regret weighed on her. With a deep, weary sigh, she murmured, "I'll find a way. I have to, for both of them."

As the first light of dawn crept through the window, Sophia gathered Elizabeth and Oliver close and said softly, "Good morning, my loves. Today is a new day, and we'll take it one step at a time."

Elizabeth, her eyes still red from tears, looked up at her with a mix of sorrow and hesitant hope. "Mom, do you think things can really change?" she asked, her voice trembling.

Mom pulled Elizabeth into a tight embrace. "I promise we'll do everything we can to make it better," she whispered, her tone a quiet vow against the uncertainty that lay ahead. "It might not be perfect, but we'll rebuild together—piece by piece."

❧ 48 ❧

THE BREAKING POINT

In a single, agonizing moment, when every lash of the belt spoke of broken trust and unending blame, Elizabeth realized that the one place called "home" had become the crucible of her deepest betrayal.

Elizabeth jolted awake to a sudden, searing pain slicing across her back. Disoriented and half-asleep, she could barely register what was happening before the belt struck again—a cruel, swift blow that ripped a gasp from her lips. Through the haze of confusion, she heard her mother's voice, raw and unyielding.

"You were supposed to be watching him!" Sophia's words rang out, her tone trembling with anger as she raised the belt for another strike.

Elizabeth scrambled backward, her heart pounding as she tried to protect herself from the relentless assault. "Mom, please!" she begged through sobs, her voice breaking. "I told him to stop—I told him!"

Sophia's response was a sharp swing of the belt that landed across Elizabeth's arms. "You're in charge," she snapped, her words low and harsh. "You're supposed to make sure he behaves!"

The pain surged through Elizabeth's body, tears streaming down her face as her cries turned from shock to despair. Despite the onslaught, she knew better than to fight back; arguing or resisting would only worsen the punishment.

Finally, Sophia dropped the belt, leaving Elizabeth trembling on the bed, her face pressed into the rumpled sheets. The momentary reprieve was shattered by Sophia's command, her voice cold and resolute.

"Get up and bend over the bed."

Elizabeth's stomach twisted. She wanted to refuse, to stand up for herself, but the weight of fear pinned her in place. Slowly, she rose on shaking knees and bent over the bed, clutching the blanket in white-knuckled hands. Behind her, Sophia's voice took on a grim finality.

"This time, it's double the lashes—eighty. Count them."

Elizabeth's mind spun. She remembered the last time, the agony left behind by the belt. The thought of enduring twice as much made her entire body quake. Her voice was a hoarse whisper as she pleaded, "Mom, please... I tried to stop him. I didn't do anything wrong."

Sophia's only response was a curt dismissal as she placed the belt across Elizabeth's back, punctuating each new lash with biting anger. "You let him destroy those books," she said through gritted teeth. "You're responsible."

Elizabeth began counting, her voice quivering. "One. Two. Three..."

By the third blow, tears were streaming down her cheeks; by the tenth, her knees buckled entirely, and she collapsed onto the floor. Yet Sophia did not relent. The strikes landed on Elizabeth's back, shoulders, arms, and even her head when she tried to shield herself. The pain overwhelmed her senses until the act of counting dissolved into raw sobs.

At last, Sophia's arm stilled. Elizabeth lay crumpled on the floor, her body quivering in a mixture of pain, disbelief, and grief. Sophia stood over her, the belt dangling loosely in her hand.

"Don't leave your room," Sophia commanded, her tone devoid of sympathy. She turned on her heel, slamming the door behind her.

Elizabeth crawled onto the bed, her entire body aching with every movement. Stinging welts crisscrossed her skin, but it was the ache in her heart that throbbed the hardest. She closed her eyes against the unyielding brightness of the overhead lamp, tears slipping silently down her cheeks.

"She always says I'm in charge," she thought bitterly, recalling Sophia's accusations. "But I can't control him—he never listens..."

She pressed her face into the pillow, her sobs muffled by the fabric. In the other room, she heard soft laughter and the clinking of cutlery. The realization that her mother and brother were enjoying a dessert while she lay bruised and alone felt like a stab through the chest. She swallowed the lump in her throat, unable to shake the burning sense of betrayal.

The following day dawned with a pall of tension lingering in the air. Elizabeth moved gingerly, her muscles protesting with every step, but she forced herself to dress for school. The bruises made even the lightest brush of fabric a sharp reminder of the night before.

In the living room, Sophia offered clipped instructions. "You'll come straight home today—no playing outside. Understood?"

Elizabeth nodded, her voice subdued. "Yes, ma'am," she said, her eyes focused on the floor. She caught sight of her brother watching from the corner of the room with a faint smirk. A fresh wave of anger and resentment roiled inside her, tightening her jaw.

When they boarded the bus, Elizabeth kept her distance, sliding into a seat far from her sibling. She stared out the window, arms folded protectively over her aching torso. Every breath reminded her of the lashes, and every thought was laced with resentment toward the one she blamed.

She could still hear the mocking voice, the sound of those books being ruined, and the defiance that had cost her so much pain. Oliver had not kept his promise to watch her back; instead, he seemed to be enjoying getting her into trouble lately.

That afternoon, they arrived back at the apartment in tense silence. As they stepped inside, Elizabeth summoned her courage. She grabbed Oliver by the arm, her voice trembling with anger. "Don't even think about going outside," she warned, her eyes flashing. "Because if you do, I'll... I'll make you sorry."

A flicker of fear crossed Oliver's face, replaced swiftly by sullen acceptance. He shrugged off her grip and mumbled something under his breath, retreating to another room without argument. Elizabeth stood there, a small surge of triumph mixing uneasily with her guilt.

For a moment, she wondered if this was what her mother felt

when she punished her—some twisted sense of control that came at the cost of someone else's pain. The realization chilled her. She dropped her gaze, releasing a shaky breath as the adrenaline coursing through her veins subsided.

That night, Elizabeth lay awake, the dim glow of the hallway light casting faint shadows on her bedroom walls. Every twitch of her bruised muscles reignited the memory of the belt's unforgiving bite. She could hear the distant murmurs of her mother's conversation on the phone, and she thought about how all this had started with a child who wouldn't listen—yet somehow, the punishment had fallen squarely on her.

"It's always me," she whispered to the stillness. "I'm always to blame." A few silent tears trailed down her cheeks, and she wondered if there would ever come a day when her voice would carry weight, when her pleas would be heard without ridicule or dismissal.

She closed her eyes, recalling past nights of similar anguish, the echo of harsh words, and her mother's firm refrain: "You're in charge." It felt like a twisted joke—she could never truly control Oliver, and in failing that impossible task, she suffered the consequences. Her stomach churned with equal parts anger and sorrow.

"Maybe one day," she thought desperately, "she'll see how unfair this is." But even as the thought crossed her mind, doubt gnawed at her. What if her mother never saw it? What if this was her life from now on?

The next morning, Elizabeth gingerly got dressed for school, each movement sending fresh pangs of pain along her bruised arms and back. Her mother glanced at her from the kitchen, a fleeting expression of something—guilt or worry—crossing her face before it hardened once more. Elizabeth swallowed the lump in her throat, determined not to betray her lingering hurt.

"Remember," Sophia said, her tone firm, "straight home after school. And make sure your brother does the same."

"Yes, ma'am," Elizabeth replied softly, her gaze focused on the worn linoleum floor.

As she walked to the bus stop, Oliver trailed behind her, the distance between them feeling impossibly wide despite the short walk. The hush between them was louder than any argument, a testament to the night's aftermath. Elizabeth cradled her bruises and her simmering resentment, unsure which hurt would fade first.

Sinking into a seat near the bus's rear, Elizabeth let her head rest against the window. The vehicle rumbled forward, carrying her toward yet another day of routine tasks and unspoken tension. In her mind, she repeated her familiar, fragile mantra—"Just make it to tomorrow"—each word a desperate vow to endure the pain, the injustice, and the fractured sense of what should be home. Yet she couldn't help but wonder if tomorrow would truly bring anything different.

"Someday," she thought, "someone will see the truth." But as the bus groaned to a stop at school, Elizabeth's hope faltered. For now, survival was all she could manage—a lesson unlearned, a future uncertain, and a heart weighed down by too many secrets.

She missed Julian.

49

GROWING RESENTMENT

In the hush of a new apartment and a stifling summer stretching ahead, Elizabeth discovered that the weight of unfair rules and a mother's unwavering favoritism could spark a resentment more enduring than any bruise.

The school year ended with a muted farewell. Without fanfare or ceremony, Elizabeth and Oliver quietly packed up their desks, handed in their textbooks, and said soft goodbyes to teachers and classmates they would likely never see again. Elizabeth felt a small pang of sadness at leaving school behind, but the emotion quickly gave way to a heavier sense of dread. Summer loomed like an endless road, an uncharted horizon with no real destination.

In the first week after they moved into the new apartment, Sophia called a family meeting. It was early evening—long shadows fell across the walls, and the air in the cramped living room felt sticky and heavy with unspoken tension. Elizabeth perched on the edge of the couch, arms crossed over her chest, eyes fixed on the beige carpet.

"Listen up," Sophia began with a stern tone. She stood by the window, arms folded. "The rules are the same as before. You don't go outside unless there's an emergency. Do I make myself clear?"

Oliver nodded, feigning solemn obedience, his wide eyes betraying only the faintest flicker of rebellion. Elizabeth, for her part, barely registered Sophia's words, lost in her own brooding thoughts. "It's always the same rules," she reminded herself bitterly. "And the same punishments, too."

"Elizabeth," Sophia snapped, breaking her out of her reverie, "are you listening?"

"Yes, ma'am," Elizabeth muttered, her voice lacking conviction.

Sophia's gaze lingered on her, daring her to speak up, to challenge the edict. When Elizabeth offered no further response, Sophia continued, "No excuses. No exceptions. If I catch either of you outside, there will be consequences."

The word "consequences" made Elizabeth's stomach twist. She remembered all too well how "consequences" felt—a stinging belt, tears, and the unshakable sense of injustice. Her back twinged at the thought, recalling the lingering aches of a recent punishment.

After the meeting, Elizabeth retreated to her new room—a small, bare space with a window that overlooked the courtyard outside. She threw herself onto the bed, sighing at the faint lines of sunlight that seeped through the blinds. From somewhere outside, she caught snippets of laughter and the distant thud of a ball hitting the pavement. The sound felt like a cruel taunt.

"They're free," Elizabeth thought bitterly, hugging a pillow to her chest. "Why can't I be?"

As the days of that first week dragged on, the monotony weighed heavily on Elizabeth. She tried, and often failed, to keep Oliver out of trouble. He was eight—restless, impulsive, and constantly testing boundaries.

One humid afternoon, Elizabeth found him hovering by the front door, fiddling with the lock. Immediately, a spike of panic and frustration hit her. She strode over, her voice low and urgent, "What are you doing, Oliver?"

He glanced at her, shrugging. "I'm bored," he whined. "I want to see what's out there."

Her eyes widened. "Mom said no," she reminded him, reaching out to stop him from turning the doorknob. "Don't you remember what she said? We'll both be in trouble if you go outside?"

Oliver smirked, that mischievous glint in his eyes sending a chill through Elizabeth. "She won't know if you don't tell her."

She tightened her grip on his arm, her tone a harsh whisper. "I swear, if you go out there—"

"Fine," he cut her off, jerking his arm free. "I won't go." He stomped off to the living room, threw himself onto the couch, and switched on the TV with a huff.

Elizabeth watched him, anxiety churning in her gut. She didn't trust his sudden compliance. He'd lied and manipulated his way out of trouble before. "And I'm always the one who pays for it," she thought, a bitter taste creeping into her mouth.

Two weeks into the new arrangement, the dull routine of "stay inside and keep Oliver contained" proved harder every day. The apartment was small, the summer was stifling, and Sophia's rules felt increasingly suffocating to Elizabeth, who longed for fresh air and the sight of the outside world. She missed the Ranch.

Every time Oliver concocted a new scheme—attempting to sneak out the door or rummaging through Sophia's belongings—Elizabeth's resentment deepened. She watched her brother bounce around the apartment like a caged animal, yet he always seemed to shift the blame onto her. And Sophia, worn down by stress or simply unwilling to listen, took his side more often than not.

One evening, after yet another near miss with Oliver attempting to slip outside, Elizabeth cornered him in the hallway. "Oliver," she said, her voice trembling with both anger and desperation, "you have to stop. I can't—" She paused, her eyes burning, remembering how the belt had found her the last time he defied the rules. "I just can't do this anymore. Do you understand?"

Oliver looked at her, his expression briefly uncertain. "I'm sorry, okay?" he muttered, glancing away. "I'm just so bored."

Elizabeth swallowed. For a moment, her anger waned. "We both are," she said quietly, exhaustion lining her words. "But it's not worth the beating, is it?"

He said nothing more, shrugging before walking off to watch cartoons. Elizabeth stood there, her heart heavy. She knew he'd likely try again tomorrow, the cycle repeating.

As the days stretched on, every defiant act from Oliver planted a fresh seed of resentment in Elizabeth's heart. She hated that she was always to blame for his impulsiveness. She hated the way Sophia coddled him, excusing his misdeeds while expecting Elizabeth to bear the responsibility. And she hated how powerless she felt, enduring punishments for transgressions that were never truly her fault.

Late one night, Elizabeth lay awake in the darkness of her room, staring at the thin cracks in the ceiling. Outside the window, she could hear distant laughter from neighbors enjoying the summer night. "They're free," she thought, the same bitter lament echoing in her mind. "Why can't I be?"

In that raw moment, a new realization took shape—one that was as painful as any beating. Perhaps the problem wasn't just her. Perhaps her mother's affections were truly skewed, an unspoken favoritism that let Oliver roam free from punishment while Elizabeth bore every lash. A knot of hurt and anger coiled tightly in her chest.

"Maybe she doesn't love me the same way she loves him," Elizabeth admitted to herself, the thought piercing her heart like a jagged knife. For a fleeting second, she felt tears burn her eyes, but she blinked them away. "Crying doesn't help."

Within another week, Sophia noticed a shift in Elizabeth's demeanor. The normally obedient, albeit resentful, child had grown silent, her eyes carrying an edge of defiance. One sweltering evening, as the relentless sun dipped below the horizon, Sophia confronted Elizabeth in the living room.

"What's with that look on your face?" she demanded, hands on her hips. "Do you have something to say?"

Elizabeth shook her head, her jaw set. "No, ma'am," she replied in a subdued tone.

Oliver sat on the couch, flipping channels and pretending not to notice. Sophia's frustration was evident in her narrowed eyes. She stepped closer to Elizabeth, her voice loaded with tension. "I'm tired of the attitude. If you can't handle this responsibility, I'll make sure you learn how to follow the rules."

Elizabeth felt the familiar spike of fear. "I am following them," she protested softly, but her voice lacked the conviction to stand firm. She recalled Oliver's smirk from earlier, the way he always seemed to slip away from blame, and her resentment flared anew.

"Then keep your brother inside," Sophia snapped, her tone final. "And watch your attitude."

Elizabeth glared at the floor, refusing to let her mother see her eyes brimming with tears. "It's not my fault, it's not my fault," she repeated internally, each iteration fueling her silent rebellion.

That night, Elizabeth curled up on her bed, tension thrumming beneath her skin. The stifling heat of summer pressed against the thin apartment walls, and she could still hear the faint buzz of neighbors enjoying the evening air in the courtyard. Every fiber of her being longed to step outside, to taste even a moment of the freedom she yearned for.

Instead, she lay in bed, fists clenched around the worn edges of a blanket, her mind looping through every injustice: Sophia's strict edicts, her own bruises from punishments past, the smirk on Oliver's face whenever he got away with mischief. He never suffers, she thought, bitterness coiling in her chest. "It's always me."

Overcome by the suffocating sense of futility, Elizabeth exhaled a shaky breath. "It's not fair," she whispered into the dark, her voice trembling with suppressed rage. "Maybe... maybe she doesn't even care about me." The idea twisted her heart painfully, but she couldn't deny the weight it carried.

As sleep edged closer, her last conscious thought echoed the mantra that had carried her through so many painful nights: "Just make it to tomorrow." But in the stagnant heat of that new apartment, it felt more like an uncertain wish than a hopeful promise. Even so, she clung to it because hope—no matter how small—was all that kept her afloat in a life where resentment grew as relentlessly as the scorching summer sun.

She missed Julian.

50

A SURPRISE TRIP

When a new face arrived in Sophia's life—a man whose generosity sparkled as brightly as the diamonds he gifted—Elizabeth discovered that momentary luxuries could cast shadows of doubt and that some trips promised more than just a change of scenery.

Sophia recognized that a more sustainable income was essential to adequately support her family. Securing a position as a secretary appeared to be the perfect next step—yet she had no idea this new role would soon upend her entire life. The children's world also took an unexpected turn when Sophia met Caleb. His arrival was swift and somewhat mysterious. He worked at the same company as Sophia, yet he handled money with effortless ease, as though an endless supply flowed just beneath the surface of his charming demeanor. Elizabeth noticed how her mother's eyes lit up around him—a mixture of fascination with his dark, actor-like looks and the allure of his unrestrained spending habits.

From the moment he stepped into their small apartment, Caleb made his intentions clear: he was here to transform their modest life into something more glamorous, if only for a fleeting season. Sophia, eager for a break from the routine of harsh discipline and financial strain, seemed hypnotized by the promise of luxury. Her new companion reminded Elizabeth of an actor straight out of a mob movie—handsome, confident, and exuding a subtle danger beneath his charm.

"Pack your bags," Sophia announced one afternoon, a week into Caleb's frequent visits. Her tone was abrupt, leaving no room for questions. "We're going on a trip. Caleb has arranged everything."

"A trip?" Elizabeth repeated, blinking in confusion. She searched her memory for any previous mention but came up blank. "Where?"

"I told you about this," Sophia retorted sharply, though Elizabeth was certain she had heard nothing of the sort.

Despite her reservations, Elizabeth trudged to her bedroom. Stuffing a few changes of clothes into a duffel, she also grabbed her battered Walkman and favorite Duran Duran cassette—if she was going somewhere unknown, at least her music would keep her company. She glanced at Oliver, who was tossing random items into a small backpack, apparently just as clueless but much less bothered.

The drive felt long and uneventful. Elizabeth sat in the backseat, headphones on, "Hungry Like the Wolf" looping as she gazed out the window at the passing scenery. Next to her, Oliver flipped through a magazine, occasionally glancing up to ask if they were almost there. Sophia and Caleb exchanged quiet words in the front seat—snippets of conversation about directions, local seafood, and half-hinted promises of a grand time.

After several hours, the landscape began to shift to coastal hues. Elizabeth's eyes widened as they pulled into a sandy driveway that ended at a house overlooking the beach. "No way," she whispered, pressing her face to the glass. The ocean stretched out in shimmering blues, a stark contrast to the cramped apartment life she had known.

Caleb parked the car, flashed a grin in the rearview mirror, and said, "Welcome to Pensacola, kiddo."

Elizabeth's jaw dropped. She felt an instant thrill as she stepped out, the salty breeze brushing her cheeks. Oliver hopped after her, whooping at the sight of the crashing waves. Even Sophia, who usually wore a stern mask, allowed a small smile to tug at her lips.

The house was beautiful—white walls and large windows, perched right on the sandy shore. Caleb ushered them inside, unveiling spacious rooms and an expansive kitchen filled with gleaming appliances. "Pick whichever bedroom you want," he told Elizabeth and Oliver, gesturing to the second floor. "There's plenty of space."

Elizabeth wasted no time. She raced upstairs, eventually claiming a room with two balconies: one overlooking the front entry and another with an oceanfront view. The sweeping view of the beach made her feel like she was in a postcard. She let out an involuntary gasp. "This is incredible."

That evening, Caleb took them to a bustling local market. The air smelled of fish and brine, intermingled with the sharp tang of lemons and spices. Elizabeth's eyes darted to every stall, intrigued by the array of seafood—some of which she'd never seen before. Caleb encouraged her to pick out whatever she liked. He turned to Sophia with a charismatic grin. "Let's treat Elizabeth tonight," he said. "She looks like she could use a good meal."

They returned to the house with bags of shrimp, lobster, oysters, and fish whose names Elizabeth couldn't remember. Caleb transformed the ingredients into a feast—steamed, grilled, chilled. The kitchen counters groaned under the weight of platters kept at the perfect temperature on a specialized bar. As Elizabeth savored her first bite of succulent shrimp, she felt a gentle surge of happiness. Maybe, just maybe, this trip really was a gift.

Outside, the waves lulled them into a peaceful rhythm, and for once, Elizabeth fell asleep easily. Her last conscious thought was how the ocean's steady roar replaced the hush of arguments and rules back home.

Early the next morning, Elizabeth leaped out of bed, eager to run to the water. She tugged on shorts and a T-shirt, bounded down the stairs, and rushed outside. But within minutes, her excitement dissolved into disappointment. The shoreline was dotted with bright blue jellyfish everywhere, their translucent bodies glistening ominously under the sun.

Caleb, spotting her crestfallen look, came up behind her. "They wash in sometimes," he explained gently, "and their sting can still hurt, even if they're dead. Stay clear for now, okay?"

Elizabeth nodded, biting back her tears. She had imagined splashing in the waves, building sandcastles, and maybe even discovering shells. Instead, a parade of jellyfish barred her from the water. Oliver tried to poke one with a stick, earning a swift reprimand from Caleb.

"That's enough, bud. Let's not tempt fate."

"Aw, man," Oliver grumbled, kicking sand. Elizabeth stifled a giggle at his sulking—sometimes, she felt a strange camaraderie with her mischievous sibling, but mostly, she braced herself for the trouble he attracted.

To salvage the day, Caleb led them to another house down the beach, where his adult children were staying. Elizabeth initially felt nervous—Caleb's children were older, strangers—but they greeted her warmly, ushering them onto a deck that overlooked the ocean. Laughter, dancing, and more seafood followed. Despite the jellyfish's unwelcome presence, Elizabeth found herself smiling at the day's unexpected joys.

On the third morning, Elizabeth woke to an amazing sight: the jellyfish had disappeared overnight. She peered out the balcony window, thrilled by the idea of finally dipping her toes in the water. Grabbing a T-shirt and shorts, she dashed downstairs, only to be intercepted by Sophia's stern voice.

"Where do you think you're going?" her mother demanded, arms crossed.

"The water," Elizabeth replied, unable to hide her excitement.

"Not without a bathing suit," Sophia snapped.

Elizabeth's heart sank. "I don't have one. I didn't know we were coming to the beach, so—"

"That's your problem," Sophia interrupted. "You can't go in the water without a swimsuit, so I guess you're staying inside."

Elizabeth felt a hot flush of anger and disappointment, tears pricking her eyes. "I only want to dip my feet," she tried to plead, but Sophia shook her head in grim finality.

"Go back upstairs. Now."

Frustrated, Elizabeth stormed up to her room. Tears blurred her vision as she sank onto the bed, burying her face in her hands. "It's so unfair. I didn't even know about this trip. The freedom and fun the beach promised felt suddenly distant—a cruel tease."

A soft knock at the sliding glass door of her balcony startled her. She looked up to find Caleb standing on the balcony, a sympathetic smile on his face. "May I come in?" he asked gently.

Sniffling, Elizabeth gave a small shrug. "I just... want to be alone."

Caleb hesitated, then ventured, "If you let me in, how about I take you to the surf shop in town? We'll pick any bathing suit you like. Then you can enjoy the water."

Elizabeth stared, torn. A swirl of hope and skepticism tightened in her chest. "Is he serious?" Yet the promise of freedom was too tempting to refuse. She unlocked the balcony door, stepping aside to let him in.

"Thank you," Caleb said quietly, placing a light hand on Elizabeth's shoulder. "I know you're upset, but trust me—this trip can be fun for you, too."

Elizabeth followed him downstairs, where Sophia stood in the hallway, arms still crossed. Her glare softened the moment Caleb approached, distracting her with a gentle peck on the cheek before steering Elizabeth through the front door.

The drive to the surf shop was short. Elizabeth's heart pounded with anticipation as she entered a space brimming with racks of bright, stylish swimsuits. The smell of sunscreen and the sight of boogie boards and beach trinkets flooded her senses. So many choices!

Caleb nudged her forward. "Pick any suit you want. If you like more than one, we'll get them both."

Elizabeth's eyes widened. "I—I don't think Mom would let me have a two-piece," she admitted quietly, eyeing a bright blue bikini that caught her interest.

Caleb winked. "I won't say a word if you don't," he said, his grin mischievous yet reassuring. "Now, go on. Have fun."

Elizabeth tried on several, hesitating between two favorites. At one point, she felt the old fear creep in—Sophia's rules, Sophia's anger. But Caleb dismissed her worries with a casual wave, taking both suits from her. "We'll just get them both," he declared, as though money were no object.

Her heart soared with a rush of unfamiliar joy. For once, her wishes mattered. For once, she wasn't an afterthought or a burden. Clutching the shopping bag, she thanked the cashier, practically skipping out of the shop.

Returning to the beach house, Elizabeth felt like the day's oppressive cloud had lifted. She held her bag protectively, determined to head straight to the water. But the moment she walked inside, she sensed tension thrumming in the air. Sophia stood in the kitchen, her gaze cold and suspicious at the sight of Elizabeth carrying newly bought swimsuits.

"What is that?" Sophia barked, pointing at the bag.

"Swimsuits," Elizabeth answered softly, bracing herself for the explosion.

Caleb, as if anticipating the conflict, stepped in smoothly with a calm smile. "Hold on," he said, turning to Sophia. He slipped a small velvet box from his pocket, revealing a glimmering diamond tennis bracelet that made Sophia's sharp words die on her lips.

"You're getting worked up over nothing," Caleb murmured, fastening the bracelet around Sophia's wrist. "I saw this and thought of you."

Sophia's frown vanished, replaced by wonder as the diamonds caught the overhead light, scattering tiny rainbows. "It's beautiful," she murmured, her voice unsteady as she admired the refraction in the polished gems.

Elizabeth watched the transformation in silence, her earlier excitement fading. "So this is how it works," she realized. Caleb had dazzled her with swimsuits, and now he was mesmerizing Sophia with extravagant jewelry. A fleeting sense of empowerment turned hollow as she recognized how easily they were all being played.

"Go try on your suits," Sophia said, her eyes never leaving the sparkling bracelet. She waved Elizabeth off dismissively, any anger she might have held now eclipsed by the brilliance on her wrist.

Elizabeth retreated upstairs with her new suits. Yet, the initial rush of joy she'd felt at the surf shop had dulled. She tried on the bright blue bikini, staring at herself in the mirror with a mixture of pride and unease. "It's beautiful," she acknowledged, but she also felt a pang of guilt—knowing Sophia would never have allowed this without Caleb's interference.

Stepping onto the balcony, Elizabeth breathed in the salty air. Below, she glimpsed Caleb and Sophia sitting on the patio, Sophia's wrist glittering in the sun as she showed off the bracelet. Caleb lounged in a chair, exuding that same effortless cool, as though he orchestrated every moment to perfection.

So who's really in control here? Elizabeth wondered, clutching the railing. She couldn't help but sense that each gift—her swimsuits, her mother's bracelet—was a currency Caleb used to maintain power in this uncertain dynamic.

Moments later, clutching a towel, Elizabeth descended the stairs toward the beach. She paused by the front door, the memory of

Sophia's earlier scolding dancing on the edge of her mind. Caleb's easy manipulation had granted her a brief pass, but at what cost?

Glancing once more through the sliding glass doors, Elizabeth caught sight of Sophia smiling, the diamonds on her wrist shimmering in the midday sunlight. Her mother's contented laughter drifted up, mingling with the gentle hush of the sea. Despite the sudden turn of events, Elizabeth felt a hollow ache in her chest.

"I should be happy," she told herself. "I'm free to enjoy the beach now." But deep down, she recognized that Caleb's lavish gestures were a bandage over a wound, not a genuine cure for the family's fractures.

Stepping outside, Elizabeth inhaled the salt-tinged breeze, letting it fill her lungs with a fleeting sense of possibility. "For now," she decided, "I'll enjoy the water." Because the tides could shift at any moment, she sensed that nothing in this new arrangement was truly secure. She walked across the warm sand toward the crashing waves, the bright new bikini providing a rare taste of freedom—and a subtle reminder that every gift carries a price in a world where loyalty and control can change as swiftly as the incoming tide.

51

AN UNANNOUNCED VISIT

When Alice arrived unannounced, trailing curiosity and veiled envy in her wake, Elizabeth sensed that her family's newfound splendor was a fragile disguise—one that Alice's mischief could unravel with a single, pointed remark.

It had been only a few weeks since the Florida trip, and the memories of sunlit beaches and lavish meals were still fresh in Elizabeth's mind. Sophia and Caleb had returned to their routine in the modest apartment, though the subtle changes lingered. Sophia wore her new bracelet with quiet pride, and Caleb's charismatic presence cast a lingering glow of prosperity over their day-to-day life.

Elizabeth, meanwhile, drifted through the halls of her new summer break, torn between excitement for the respite from school and unease at the unspoken tensions that simmered beneath the surface. She was in her room, halfheartedly rearranging her books when the shrill ring of the doorbell jolted the household. Moments later, Sophia's voice carried through the apartment.

"Alice," Sophia greeted, forcing a smile that strained against her cheeks.

At the sound of her aunt's name, Elizabeth's heart leapt. "Aunt Alice? And maybe Mia..." She dashed into the living room, her eyes lighting up at the sight of her cousin. The two girls squealed in unison, rushing into each other's arms.

"You're here!" Elizabeth gasped, hugging Mia tight. "I can't believe it!"

"Me neither," Mia replied, matching Elizabeth's grin. The girls exchanged a flurry of inside jokes and quick updates, picking up exactly where they had left off.

Sophia, meanwhile, turned to her sister. "So," she said, her tone clipped, "what brings you here, Alice? You didn't even call."

Alice's eyes sparkled mischievously. "Oh, you know, family visits —and I couldn't resist checking out this fancy new lifestyle Elizabeth has been writing about," she teased, her gaze sweeping the modest living space.

Elizabeth felt her cheeks warm. "I only wrote about the Florida trip in my letter to Mia," she thought guiltily. She hadn't intended to stir any drama, but she recalled detailing the beach house, the feasts, and the diamond bracelet Sophia had flaunted.

Caleb, who had been lounging on the couch, stood up. "And you must be Sophia's sister," he said, flashing his trademark smile. "I'm Caleb. It's a pleasure to meet you."

Alice paused, studying Caleb with an almost predatory interest. "The pleasure's all mine," she replied, her voice low and flirtatious, lingering in her handshake a beat too long.

Elizabeth caught the flicker of annoyance in Sophia's eyes. "Alice, how long are you staying?" she asked, her voice tight.

Alice shrugged casually, but her gaze remained fixed on Caleb. "Not too long. Just wanted to see my darling niece and nephew and... get a glimpse of what you've been up to." She let the last words hang in the air.

Sophia's jaw clenched. "We're doing just fine," she said. "Caleb's been very kind."

Alice arched an eyebrow. "I can see that." She nodded toward the diamond tennis bracelet gracing Sophia's wrist, a small smirk curving her lips. "You must be in excellent hands."

Caleb stepped forward smoothly, intercepting the rising tension. "Alice, how about dinner tonight? I'll whip up something special. We can celebrate your arrival."

At that, Alice's face brightened with calculated delight. "Now isn't he the charmer, Sophia? You sure know how to pick them."

Sophia mustered a tight smile,. murmuring, "Yes, well, he's wonderful." Her eyes flicked to Caleb, silently telling him to guide

Alice to the kitchen—anything to avoid further barbs in the living room.

As Alice followed him, Sophia bent down to Elizabeth, her voice hushed. "Keep your eyes open, Mouth," she said in a cryptic tone. Elizabeth blinked in confusion, uncertain whether the warning was about Alice's meddling or something else entirely. Regardless, she nodded obediently, her heart thudding with the sense that trouble was brewing.

While the adults moved into the kitchen, Elizabeth and Mia slipped away to Elizabeth's room. Collapsing onto the bed, they stared at each other with excitement and relief.

"I can't believe you're really here," Elizabeth breathed, pulling Mia into another hug.

"Me neither." Mia's smile wavered, her voice lowering. "Mom's been talking nonstop about meeting Caleb ever since she read your letter. She seemed... kinda jealous, I guess."

Elizabeth frowned. "Jealous? But why?"

Mia gave a small, knowing shrug. "You know how Mom is. The moment she sees someone with something shiny or new, she wants it too. She kept going on about the beach house and all this fancy stuff, like a diamond bracelet." Mia's gaze flicked to Elizabeth's bare wrist. "She's got her sights set on something, that's for sure."

Guilt churned in Elizabeth's stomach. She recalled how, in her letter to Mia, she had gushed about Caleb's generosity: the seafood feasts, beach sunsets, and Sophia's dazzling jewelry. "I didn't mean to stir anything up," she said, her shoulders sagging. "I was just excited about the Florida trip."

Mia patted her cousin's arm lightly. "Don't worry. Mom's not staying long. She just wants to see how 'the other half' lives, I guess."

Yet Elizabeth couldn't shake a creeping dread. She had known Sophia and Alice long enough to suspect this wouldn't end quietly or cleanly.

That evening, Caleb outdid himself preparing dinner. The aroma of herbs and sizzling vegetables filled the apartment, mingling with the distant hum of air conditioning. Elizabeth set the table while Mia organized plates and silverware. Oliver hovered nearby, sneaking bites when he thought no one was watching.

When Sophia and Alice emerged from a terse conversation in

the hallway—faces tight with forced civility—they joined the rest at the table. Caleb unveiled an impressive spread: grilled fish, stir-fried vegetables, and a shrimp dish coated in some aromatic sauce. Alice cooed in delight, showering Caleb with compliments that grew more effusive (and increasingly flirtatious) as the night went on.

"Caleb, you really know how to treat a lady," Alice purred, leaning forward. "Sophia's so fortunate to have found someone so... skilled."

Sophia's eyes narrowed, her smile taut. "Yes, I am," she said, placing a possessive hand on Caleb's shoulder. "And Caleb's fortunate too—not everyone can appreciate a man's talent."

Alice's smirk deepened, her gaze flicking between Sophia and Caleb. "I bet," she said, her tone tinged with hidden meaning. A tension-laden silence settled over the table.

Sensing the growing friction, Caleb kept the conversation light, asking Mia about her upcoming plans, teasing Oliver about the sneaked bites, and encouraging Elizabeth to talk about her summer. But Elizabeth noted how her mother's hand clenched around her fork, knuckles white with suppressed annoyance. Mia nudged Elizabeth beneath the table, casting a look that said, "Told you so."

Elizabeth forced a small smile, her appetite fading despite the delicious meal. She could feel the weight of the conflict pressing in around her, a silent storm on the verge of erupting. The once-cozy dinner now felt like a performance for Alice's benefit—and perhaps Caleb's as well.

After dinner, the tension continued to simmer. Caleb quickly offered to clear the table, and Alice hovered around him, feigning interest in the dishes. Sophia stood by, her jaw set, watching every move with hawk-like attention. Elizabeth and Mia slunk back to the bedroom, closing the door to shut out the sound of fake laughter echoing through the apartment.

"Does she always behave like that with other people's men?" Elizabeth asked quietly, hugging her knees as she sat on the floor.

Mia sighed. "Honestly, she can't help herself. It's like she sees a challenge and can't resist. The more glamorous or successful someone is, the more she needs to see if she can... you know."

A knot formed in Elizabeth's stomach. "I hope Caleb's smart enough not to fall for it."

Mia hesitated, choosing her words. "He seems to like the attention. Guys like him usually do."

Elizabeth swallowed hard, recalling how easily Caleb had won over Sophia with gifts and gentle flattery. A new worry surfaced—what if Caleb's loyalty was as fleeting as the Florida sunshine?

As night wore on, the adults eventually retreated to the living room. Elizabeth peeked out to see Alice perched on the couch, tossing playful remarks at Caleb while Sophia glared from the recliner. The entire apartment felt charged with unspoken strife. The glare of fluorescent lighting on Sophia's diamond bracelet reminded Elizabeth of the beach trip—a temporary wonder that might be overshadowed by deeper familial conflicts.

Slipping back into her room, Elizabeth found Mia picking at a loose thread on the bedsheet. "I'm sorry," Elizabeth whispered, sinking onto the mattress. "I didn't mean for your mom to feel jealous. I was just excited when I wrote to you about everything."

Mia offered a faint, sympathetic smile. "Don't worry. Mom's jealousy isn't your fault. Trust me, she's always been that way."

Elizabeth nodded, hugging a pillow to her chest. Down the hallway, she heard a raised voice—Sophia's, sharp and clipped—followed by Alice's careless laugh. "They're going to blow up soon," Elizabeth thought, her heart heavy. "And I'm stuck in the middle again."

"Let's just stay in here," Mia whispered, reading her cousin's mind.

Elizabeth agreed, turning off the overhead light to cast the room in soft shadows. The two girls settled in, whispering about music, old memories, and their own hopes for the future—anything to drown out the muted argument that threatened to boil over in the other room.

As the apartment sank into an uneasy hush, Elizabeth lay awake, her mind racing. Caleb's charm, Sophia's anger, Alice's calculated flirtation—it felt as though each piece was pushing the family closer to a precipice. "I wish things could be simple," she thought desperately, recalling the fleeting calm of Pensacola's beach. But here in the cramped apartment, simple felt like a distant dream.

Eventually, Alice announced she'd be leaving the next day, and a semblance of calm settled over the apartment. But Elizabeth sensed that beneath the forced smiles and empty reassurances, the family's fractures only deepened. Caleb's show of hospitality had staved off open conflict, but resentments now lingered in the stagnant air.

As Alice retreated to the couch for the night, Mia squeezed Elizabeth's hand in a silent goodbye, knowing the morning departure would be quick and uneventful. Elizabeth nodded, swallowing the dread that had been clawing at her all evening.

Lying in bed, Elizabeth forced her eyes shut, the dim glow of a streetlamp seeping through the curtains. She repeated her usual mantra—"Just make it to tomorrow"—aware that tomorrow might bring yet another confrontation. Yet even in her fear, a sliver of hope remained: perhaps Alice's departure would restore some measure of peace. Perhaps the tensions swirling around Caleb's lavish gifts, Sophia's hardened pride, and Alice's meddling would settle back into the uneasy normal that had preceded Alice's visit.

But that's all it ever is, Elizabeth thought bitterly. An uneasy normal. She drifted off to uneasy dreams, the last echo of her consciousness replaying Alice's smirk, Sophia's clenched jaw, and Caleb's smooth grin—reminders that in this family, spontaneity was never a promise of joy but a prelude to fresh discord.

❈ 52 ❈

A DESPERATE ESCAPE

When Alice announced her departure as suddenly as she had arrived, Elizabeth realized that the fragile pretense of peace in their home was about to shatter—and in a moment of desperation, she would risk everything for a chance at freedom.

Alice emerged from the kitchen, her movements swift and resolute. A half-folded shirt dangled from her grip, and a hairbrush poked out of her back pocket. She hadn't planned to stay long, but something about her urgency now felt final. Every step she took seemed to punctuate her growing impatience.

"Mia!" Alice called, her tone clipped. "Gather your things. We're leaving."

From her perch on the living room couch, Mia glanced up, startled. She caught Elizabeth's wide-eyed stare and shrugged helplessly. Meanwhile, Elizabeth's heart dropped like a stone. She had dreaded this possibility ever since Alice arrived—a looming departure that might take Mia, her closest confidante, away for good.

Elizabeth edged into her bedroom, where Alice was already cramming odds and ends into a worn duffel bag. The tension in the air crackled.

"You're leaving?" Elizabeth whispered, her voice trembling with dismay.

Alice didn't stop folding. "Yes. We're going. Now." Her words allowed no room for negotiation. "Mia, hurry up!" she barked, raising her voice.

Elizabeth's thoughts spun. "I can't lose Mia this quickly. Not again."

Moments later, Elizabeth found Mia hunched over a small suitcase in her bedroom, zipping it shut with a resigned sigh. The sense of departure weighed on both of them, each unspoken second throbbing with the knowledge that this reunion was ending too soon.

"I don't want you to go," Elizabeth murmured, her voice thick. She hesitated, then swallowed hard, a risky plan forming. "Take me with you. Please."

Mia's eyes widened. "You really mean that? You want me to ask my mom if you can come with us?" She shot an anxious glance toward the hallway.

Elizabeth nodded fervently. "I can't stay here. Everything's wrong—my mother, the punishments... I just... I need to get out."

Mia paused, torn. "All right," she said at last, exhaling slowly. "Let's try—together."

They approached Alice near the apartment's front door. Alice was tugging a blanket free from a rumpled couch cushion, her expression tense.

"Mom," Mia began cautiously, "can Elizabeth come with us for a little while?"

Alice froze, blinking in surprise. She turned slowly, meeting Elizabeth's beseeching gaze. "Absolutely not," she said after a beat, her voice stern. "I can't just take someone else's kid. That's—" She waved a hand dismissively. "Look, I know it's not easy here, but your place is with your mother."

Elizabeth's throat went dry. "But—Aunt Alice... she's... I can't—"

Alice cut her off, regret flickering in her eyes. "I'm sorry, Elizabeth. This is final."

Crushed, Elizabeth stumbled back to her bedroom, tears pricking her eyes. She could hear Alice and Sophia's voices escalating in the living room. They always fight, Elizabeth thought, and I always pay the price.

A flash of determination took hold of her. If Alice wouldn't take her voluntarily, maybe she could force her hand. She rummaged through her closet, yanking out a small backpack. Rapidly, she stuffed in a couple of shirts, some rolled-up jeans, and a toothbrush. Her heart pounded as she zipped the backpack closed, pulses of adrenaline thrumming in her veins.

Bolting from her room, Elizabeth marched past Sophia and Alice, who were hissing heated words at each other—something about meddling, about control. She caught Mia's wide-eyed look but said nothing, determined to keep her plan hidden. Throwing open the front door, she made a show of slamming it behind her.

They'll think I'm throwing a tantrum, Elizabeth reasoned, darting around the side of the building to where Alice's little red car was parked. She opened the back door quietly, her breath hitching. The space was cramped with luggage and random items. She shoved a blanket aside, wedged herself between two bags, and crouched low. Every second that passed felt like an eternity.

Inside, her pulse thundered in her ears. What if she doesn't drive away? What if Sophia stops her? But she pushed the fears down, hoping no one would check the back seat.

Meanwhile, in the apartment, the argument between Sophia and Alice built to a crescendo. Mia hovered near the doorway, looking torn as her mother and aunt hurled accusations.

"You've always meddled in my life," Sophia spat, her fists clenched.

Alice shot back, "Someone has to protect these kids from your twisted rules and punishments."

Finally, Alice snatched her keys from the coffee table, glaring at Sophia one last time. "We're leaving now, and if you've got a problem with that, too bad." She stormed out, with Mia trailing behind, a small suitcase in hand.

They piled into the car—Alice in the driver's seat, Mia up front, the trunk already stuffed with hastily packed bags. Neither noticed the slight shift in weight as Alice tried to adjust her seat.

"Are you okay, Mom?" Mia asked hesitantly.

Alice started the engine, her jaw set. "I'll be fine once we're away from here." She spared Mia a small, reassuring smile, then pulled out onto the road.

For several tense minutes, the only sound was the hum of the engine and the faint hiss of the air conditioner. Elizabeth, hidden beneath the blanket in the back seat, held her breath, adrenaline surging with each bump in the road. She dared to hope that Alice might drive far enough that returning her would be too much trouble.

They were halfway down the street when Alice grumbled, "Why can't I move this seat back?" She twisted around, frowning at the lack of space. Her hand fumbled against a mass of soft fabric—and then landed on something warm: hair.

"What the—!" Alice yelped, slamming the brakes. The car lurched to a stop. Mia jerked around, her eyes flying wide as Alice shoved the blanket aside.

"Elizabeth?!" Mia gasped, her voice part shock, part disbelief.

Elizabeth surfaced from the crumpled pile, heart thudding, her eyes meeting Alice's furious glare. "I told you," Elizabeth said, struggling to keep her voice steady, "I can't stay there."

Alice's face burned with anger. "Are you out of your mind?" she shouted, turning off the ignition. "You can't just sneak into someone's car, Elizabeth! Your mother will call the cops if she thinks I've kidnapped you."

Elizabeth, still trembling, fixed Alice with a pleading look. "Then let her. I'd rather deal with that than go back."

Mia's gaze flicked anxiously between them. "Mom, maybe... maybe we can keep her for a bit? Just until it's safe—"

"No," Alice snapped, her tone wavering between outrage and guilt. "This isn't a matter of a few days. It's illegal, and I can't just waltz off with my sister's kid."

Elizabeth's shoulders fell, tears glimmering in her eyes. "Please. You know what it's like in that house."

Alice closed her eyes, pressing her lips together. For a moment, it seemed she might relent. Then her face hardened. "I'm sorry, Elizabeth. I just can't."

Quietly, Alice turned the car around. Nobody spoke. Mia watched Elizabeth with a look of sympathy, her own disappointment etched across her face. Elizabeth felt numb—her bold escape plan disintegrating before her eyes.

They pulled up once more to the apartment, the sun dipping low in the sky and casting long, defeated shadows across the parking lot. Steeling herself, Elizabeth climbed out of the car, meeting Sophia's thunderous expression with as much composure as she could muster.

Sophia stood on the stoop, arms crossed, anger radiating off her.

Alice glowered in return, tensions still simmering from their earlier fight. Elizabeth lingered by the car door, unsure whether to approach her mother or flee again.

Alice sighed, finally breaking the silence. "I'll talk to her, Elizabeth," she said softly, trying to temper her frustration. "I'll do what I can... I promise."

Elizabeth nodded, tears threatening to spill. She backed away as Alice and Mia drove off, the red car disappearing around the corner. The emptiness in her chest felt immeasurable—a broken longing for a rescue that never materialized.

Sophia's voice cut the silence like a blade. "What number are we on now, Elizabeth? One hundred sixty?" she asked, almost triumphantly. Her eyes held a gleam that sent a shiver through Elizabeth's already trembling frame—suggesting yet another punishment in the unending cycle.

Elizabeth lowered her gaze, her heart pounding. The audacity of her attempted escape would cost her dearly; she could already feel the weight of impending consequences pressing on her.

"Inside. Now," Sophia commanded, stepping aside for Elizabeth to enter. As Elizabeth walked past, she felt Sophia's gaze boring into her back, a silent promise that the price for her disobedience would be steep.

Once inside, Elizabeth drifted to her room, each step heavier than the last. She dropped her small backpack by the bed and sank onto the mattress in exhaustion. The stillness of the apartment pressed in around her, broken only by Sophia's sharp footsteps down the hall.

In the dim light filtering through the curtains, Elizabeth hugged a pillow to her chest, recalling Alice's parting words: "I'll do what I can... I promise." It felt hollow, a faint echo in a world that rarely gave her any reprieve. "Words never change anything here," she thought bitterly.

She let her eyes drift to the window, where the last rays of daylight were fading. The apartment walls that once felt merely oppressive now felt suffocating, as if they were closing in, eager to see her fail. Despite her dashed hopes, a flicker of defiance stirred within her. "Maybe next time," she told herself. "Maybe next time, I won't get caught. Maybe next time, I'll find a real way out."

Yet even as she clung to that faint spark, the heaviness in her chest remained. No matter how many times she vowed to escape, she was still trapped in this place—under Sophia's rules, under the specter of new punishments. With a shaky breath, Elizabeth closed her eyes, bracing herself for whatever her mother had in store. Even a desperate escape, it seemed, was still not enough to break the chains that bound her. Sophia called Elizabeth to her bedroom...

A SECRET HIDEAWAY

Elizabeth and Oliver had promised each other to stay out of trouble. After all, they were tired of enduring constant spankings, and they hoped to show Sophia that they could be responsible. But being on their best behavior proved more difficult than expected—especially when the urge for independence tugged at them relentlessly.

Their first venture into adulthood was a morning coffee stand, cleverly set up just outside Elizabeth's bedroom window. Each dawn, they would open the window and place a wooden plank across the sill as a makeshift counter. The plan was simple: sell hot coffee (brewed with their mother's coffee pot) to neighbors rushing to work. Elizabeth handled the money, while Oliver poured the steaming beverage into paper cups they had scavenged from various sources. For a few days, it worked surprisingly well. A handful of bleary-eyed workers stopped by, amused by the children's entrepreneurial spirit. Elizabeth and Oliver pocketed their small earnings with pride. But their ambitions weren't limited to coffee. They had recently gotten into trouble for selling off some old toys to afford shaving razors and cream—hoping that shaving would make them feel more mature. Sophia had been furious, scolding them for throwing away their childhood for a "crazy scheme."

Spankings came thick and fast after that. Sophia was already stressed from life in the cramped apartment, and her patience with the kids was wearing thin. Every little misstep seemed to warrant a swift punishment. Fed up and desperate for a break, Elizabeth and Oliver devised a plan to escape the barrage of discipline. They discovered that the apartment next door was vacant—its door locked, but one of the windows slid open with minimal effort. A new world of possibility lay beyond that dusty threshold. They crept inside one afternoon, hearts hammering. The place was small and unfurnished, the air stale from disuse. But to the children, it felt like an oasis. "This can be our secret hideout," Elizabeth whispered, peering into the tiny living room. Oliver nodded, eyes shining with excitement. "No more spankings—just us, doing whatever we want."

Over the next week, Elizabeth and Oliver spent their free hours sneaking into the vacant apartment. Armed with a broom, a rag, and a bucket of water, they cleaned every corner, sweeping away cobwebs and wiping down the musty floors. To them, it felt like turning a rundown space into a cozy sanctuary. "We can play house," Elizabeth suggested one afternoon, positioning a few boxes as makeshift chairs around an imaginary dining table. "I'll be the mom, and you can be the dad."

Oliver rolled his eyes. "Why do I always have to be the dad?"

"Because you're a boy," Elizabeth teased, sticking out her tongue. They giggled and bantered, losing track of time as they rearranged cardboard boxes to form a couch and a rudimentary bed. The emptiness of the apartment was a canvas for their imagination —a place where they could be grown-ups, hosting dinner parties and sipping invisible tea, far from the constraints of real life.

As the days went by, the siblings began to dream bigger. What if they could invite their friends over? They could expand on the coffee shop idea or hold secret late-night gatherings, no adults allowed. The lure of freedom was intoxicating, but caution quickly tempered their excitement. They knew if Sophia discovered their "secret hideout," the consequences would be severe. Still, Elizabeth and Oliver toyed with the idea, whispering about it as they plotted decorations made of old magazines and scraps of fabric. "Just imagine," Elizabeth said, her eyes gleaming, "Mia and Lacy could come over, and we'd have a real party." Oliver grinned at the thought. "Yeah—but we'd have to keep it super quiet." Their fantasies grew more elaborate each day, though they never quite found the courage to extend invitations. Deep down, Elizabeth suspected it was better to enjoy her private little refuge alone. The fewer people who knew, the safer it was from discovery.

Each morning, they'd slip out of the apartment, careful to leave no trace of their presence. The apartment remained vacant and untouched by the outside world, an ever-ready sanctuary from Sophia's frustration. Even their minor coffee shop profits went into small items to spruce up the place—like cheap curtains to hide their comings and goings from any nosy neighbors. For a brief time, Elizabeth and Oliver found solace in that tiny apartment. When the world outside felt too heavy—when the spankings loomed or the grown-ups' disappointments overshadowed them—they disappeared into their secret hideout. There, behind closed doors and locked windows, they were just two kids, safe from the prying eyes of adults, building their own version of life where the only rules were the ones they created themselves.

Elizabeth and Oliver had been careful—at least they thought they had. They snuck into the vacant apartment at odd hours, leaving no mess and making sure to slip out before anyone grew suspicious. But the day finally came when the property manager caught them. Maybe it was the faint sound of their giggles through the walls or the slightly ajar window that hadn't been quite re-locked. Either way, a single knock on Sophia's door was all it took to unravel their secret.

Elizabeth and Oliver were in their room when they heard muffled voices at the front door. The moment Sophia called for them, they knew something was wrong. Her tone was colder than usual—no trace of warmth or caution, just a terse demand: "Get out here."

The siblings shuffled into the living room to find Sophia talking with the apartment manager. His face was stern, arms crossed. "They've been using a vacant unit without permission," he told Sophia, his voice clipped. "We can't allow that."

Sophia's knuckles turned white around the doorknob. "I understand," she said, forcing politeness. "It won't happen again."

The manager's eyes flicked to Elizabeth and Oliver, a mixture of disapproval and exasperation in his gaze. "If it does, you'll be evicted," he warned. "No exceptions."

With that, he stepped back out of the apartment, and Sophia closed the door behind him. The silence in the living room felt suffocating. Elizabeth and Oliver locked eyes for a heartbeat, both bracing for the inevitable. Sophia turned, her mouth set in a grim line.

"You had to push it," she said quietly, her voice shaking with barely contained anger. "You just couldn't stay out of trouble."

Elizabeth opened her mouth to explain, but no words came. How could she possibly justify sneaking around when the risk was so high? Oliver's eyes darted to the floor, his cheeks burning.

"You both know what this means," Sophia said, gesturing for them to follow her into the cramped master bedroom. Her voice was taut, edged with fury and disbelief. "We've talked about consequences, haven't we?"

She made them stand side by side, recalling the "normal double spankings" from their last major offense. Elizabeth's heart pounded in her chest as she realized Sophia was about to repeat the same punishment she had promised before: one for defying the rules and another for risking their home.

Neither Elizabeth nor Oliver argued. There was no point. The shame of their discovery and the apartment manager's threat to evict them hung over them like a storm cloud. Sophia delivered the spankings, her anger fueling each strike. Both siblings gritted their teeth, tears pricking at the corners of their eyes, but they refused to cry out. It was worse than usual, maybe because Sophia's fear of losing their home had heightened her frustration.

When it was over, Sophia stood there, breath shaky, eyes hollow. "You could have cost us everything," she said, her voice hoarse. "Do you understand that?"

Elizabeth and Oliver nodded, bowing their heads. Neither spoke. What could they say?

"Go to your rooms," Sophia finished, dismissing them with a wave of her hand.

They retreated in silence, the sting of both their bodies and their pride heavy in each step. The small room, once a refuge of sorts, now felt as suffocating as the outside world. Elizabeth sat on the floor, knees drawn to her chest, while Oliver curled up on his bed, his face pressed into the pillow.

After a long stretch of silence, Oliver finally got up and walked to where the two bedroom doors met and whispered, "Sorry, Elizabeth."

Elizabeth forced a small nod, tears threatening to spill over. "Me too," she murmured.

In the living room, Sophia could be heard pacing, talking to herself about rent, rules, and the fragile stability they all relied on. Elizabeth and Oliver exchanged a look, both grasping the same bittersweet truth: their brief escape in that vacant apartment had almost cost them their home. And now, they were stuck, bound tighter by the consequences of growing up in a place that left them with so few ways to be free.

🦋 54 🦋

MAKING WAVES

When a simple plan to break their boredom turned the bathtub into an impromptu disaster, Elizabeth and Oliver discovered too late that their small act of defiance could unleash a wave of consequences—one that would wash away their fragile sense of home.

The morning started with the usual routine: a rushed breakfast, a stern lecture from Sophia to stay indoors and "be good," and a dutiful nod from Elizabeth and Oliver as they left for school. They had promised each other to avoid trouble, weary of the spankings that had become all too frequent. Yet, by mid-afternoon, once they returned to the empty apartment, the siblings felt an old itch for adventure begin to surface. The small living space felt stifling, and Sophia's constant warnings echoed like a storm cloud in their minds.

Elizabeth sank onto the couch, flipping through the same channels on television, her thoughts drifting. She tried to focus on the cartoon in front of her but found her gaze wandering to the window. "I wish we could just do something fun, something that's ours..." Oliver, too, restlessly paced, running his hands through his hair.

"I'm bored," he groaned, collapsing beside Elizabeth and yawning dramatically. "I want to swim!"

"We can't," Elizabeth reminded him, rolling her eyes. "Mom said not to go anywhere, remember?"

Oliver sighed, but a mischievous spark glimmered in his eyes. "Then let's do something here—like a pool in the bathtub."

Elizabeth snorted, half amused, half skeptical. "Uh, no. That's definitely not allowed."

"Come on," he insisted, his face brightening. "It's just water. We can drain it afterward. Mom will never know."

After a moment's hesitation, Elizabeth relented with a reluctant shrug. "Fine, but let's keep it small. I'm not getting spanked again, okay?"

"Deal," Oliver grinned, leaping to his feet.

In the narrow bathroom, the siblings set about creating their clandestine "pool." Oliver turned on the faucet full blast, and water poured into the tub. Elizabeth grabbed an old bath towel, carefully tucking it under the closed door to contain any accidental spills.

At first, they stuck to the tub itself, giggling as water rose, splashing over the edges. The warm steam fogged up the mirror, and the bathroom took on a playful air. Elizabeth perched on the edge, letting her feet dangle into the water. Oliver sat in the tub, grinning as he scooped water into plastic cups and poured it over his arms.

"This feels so silly," Elizabeth said, though a small smile tugged at her lips. "We're practically swimming—without leaving the house!"

Oliver's eyes twinkled with glee. "Exactly," he said, splashing her lightly. "A perfect plan."

Their laughter rose, echoing off the tiled walls. Emboldened by their success, they dared to expand their mischief: If they placed extra towels along the base of the door, maybe they could flood the floor, turning the entire bathroom into a shallow pool.

"Are you sure?" Elizabeth asked, chewing her lip. "Mom would freak if she knew."

Oliver shrugged, excitement outweighing caution. "We'll just mop it up before she gets home. She'll never notice."

They laid a second towel, pressing it firmly under the door's edge, then turned the faucet on full force. The water quickly overflowed from the tub, creeping across the tiles. Elizabeth and Oliver danced around in the growing puddle, giggling as they kicked up gentle splashes.

"We have our own private water park!" Oliver exclaimed, holding up his arms triumphantly. Elizabeth's heart soared briefly with the thrill of rebellion, the water lapping at her ankles in a half-inch wave.

But the fun turned to panic when Elizabeth realized the water had begun slipping past their makeshift barrier. A thin rivulet snaked out into the hallway. Alarmed, she lunged for the faucet handle, shutting off the water.

"It's still going under the door!" she yelped, yanking towels from the rack to push against the leak. Their playful smiles vanished as they realized how much water had already spread.

They scrambled for a mop and bucket, but each frantic attempt only seemed to slosh more water around. The hallway carpet began to soak, and fear coiled in Elizabeth's stomach. A series of furious knocks jolted them, and when Elizabeth cracked the door open, she was met by the scowling face of the building manager.

"Are you—are you flooding the apartment?" the manager barked, water seeping past his polished shoes. Behind him, neighbors peered from their doorways, their expressions a mixture of worry and annoyance.

Oliver appeared at Elizabeth's side, dripping and speechless. "We were just—uh—" he stammered.

"I don't want excuses," the manager cut him off, glaring. "Get this cleaned up. And you," he pointed at Elizabeth, "are in serious trouble. This water is leaking into all the neighboring apartments, and I won't have it!"

Elizabeth's cheeks burned. She wished the floor would swallow her up. "Why did we do this?" she thought, panic knotting in her chest. By now, the manager was already on his phone, calling Sophia or possibly the police. The siblings locked eyes, both realizing they couldn't hide this mess.

Shortly afterward, Sophia arrived to find the hallway soaked, the manager waiting by the door, arms folded in fury. The moment she saw the water-damaged carpet and the angry neighbors, a grim understanding settled over her features.

"What happened?" Sophia demanded, her voice trembling with rage. She turned on Elizabeth and Oliver, her eyes flashing. "Explain yourselves!"

"We—uh—wanted to—" Elizabeth began, her voice quavering.

She cast a quick glance at Oliver, who looked ready to cry. "We only meant to have some fun. We were bored."

"That's no excuse for this," the manager interjected, his glare not softening in the slightest. "The landlord has had enough. Your children keep causing trouble, and this was the last straw. You're evicted, effective immediately."

Sophia's breath caught. "Evicted?" She looked at the manager, a flicker of panic in her eyes. "Wait—there has to be something we can do. I can pay for the damage, or—"

He shook his head, his expression unyielding. "No third chances. You have to leave."

Emotion tightened Sophia's features, and she glared at her children with a mixture of fury and heartbreak. Neighbors retreated into their apartments, satisfied or unwilling to witness the family meltdown. Sophia turned away from the manager, her voice trembling as she spat out, "Start packing. Now."

Even as Sophia began gathering boxes, the siblings knew a severe punishment loomed. "We messed up again," Elizabeth thought, dread filling her stomach like a lead weight. They trudged to their bedroom to collect clothes and trinkets, hearts pounding at what might come next.

Sure enough, Sophia soon appeared at the doorway, belt in hand, eyes aflame with anger fueled by terror at losing their home. "This is for your carelessness," she hissed, tears brimming in her eyes. "You cost us our apartment!"

Neither child resisted. Each knew that protests would only enrage Sophia further. Elizabeth braced herself as the belt struck, her back burning under the furious blows, tears slipping down her cheeks. Oliver endured his share, gulping back sobs.

She missed Julian.

When Sophia finished, she collapsed onto the edge of the bed, shoulders heaving. The siblings watched her uncertainly. For a moment, it looked like she might hug them—but then she steeled herself, her face closing off.

"We have to be out in two weeks," she said quietly, bitterness dripping from every word. "Because of you two."

With red-rimmed eyes, Sophia resumed hurriedly stuffing clothes and kitchen utensils into boxes. Elizabeth and Oliver trailed after her, forced to help pack while nursing fresh bruises. Outside, the sun dipped below the horizon, casting long shadows across the chaos.

"This was just supposed to be fun," Oliver murmured hoarsely to Elizabeth, his arms full of towels still damp from their failed indoor pool. "I never thought..." His voice cracked.

Elizabeth swallowed hard, tears threatening anew. "Neither did I. We just wanted to—" She paused, recalling the morning they woke up bored, longing for a taste of freedom. "We just wanted to break out of the monotony..."

By the time they taped up the last box, darkness had settled, and the apartment echoed with emptiness. Sophia gave the siblings one last glare before retreating into her bedroom and slamming the door. Elizabeth heard muffled sobs from within, a reminder that Sophia, too, suffered the consequences of their impulsive act.

Standing in the half-empty living room, Elizabeth surveyed the mess. Stacks of boxes, the soggy bathroom rugs tossed haphazardly in a corner, and the faint smell of chlorine from the tap water that had flooded their world. Everything felt bleak and precarious.

Oliver hovered by her side, hugging his arms. "I'm sorry," he mumbled, his eyes averted. "I messed up."

Elizabeth bowed her head, recalling how she had willingly participated in the plan. "We both did," she admitted, her voice barely above a whisper.

Through the open window drifted the muffled hum of traffic, a reminder that life outside continued uncaringly. For Elizabeth and Oliver, the guilt and the harshness of their mother's response cut deep. They had wanted only a few moments of childish excitement, but that desire had drowned the family's already fragile stability.

"We'll find somewhere else," Elizabeth said softly, more to comfort herself than Oliver. Yet, as the words left her lips, she felt the sting of reality: no matter where they went next, Sophia's anger and the threat of punishment would follow. And beneath it all lingered the unspoken truth: each bid for freedom carried a cost— sometimes as high as losing their home.

EXPOSED IN THE GYM

When the bruises Elizabeth tried so hard to hide threatened to be seen in gym class, even her armor of long sleeves and forced smiles could not protect her from the truth—and from those who might finally question it.

Elizabeth woke with a jolt, her body instantly reminding her of the beating she'd endured the night before. Each bruise on her arms and back pulsed with a dull ache, and when she dragged herself to the mirror, she froze. Deep purples and blues marred her skin, forming a jagged map of pain. She squeezed her eyes shut for a moment, forcing herself not to cry. "No time for tears," she thought grimly.

She rummaged through the closet, choosing her usual disguise: a loose long-sleeved shirt and loose pants—clothes that wouldn't cling and reveal the damage beneath. Then came the careful dance of covering the bruises on her face. Elizabeth dabbed on cheap concealer, hand-me-down powders, anything to fade the mottled coloration. Minutes passed in anxious silence until she stepped back, satisfied that she had masked the worst of it.

A hollow quiet filled the house. Elizabeth braced herself as she moved into the kitchen. Sophia was there, sipping tea, her expression void of warmth. The newspaper rustled in Sophia's hands, and she barely spared Elizabeth a glance.

"Behave today," Sophia said coolly, finally meeting Elizabeth's eye with a stern glare. "No more nonsense."

"Yes, ma'am," Elizabeth whispered, her heart pounding at the memory of last night's punishment. She slipped away to grab a piece of toast, shuffling back to her room without daring to say another word.

School felt like a reprieve, yet Elizabeth's movements were slow, each bruise screaming a reminder. She made her way through first period in a haze, carefully sidestepping bumps in the hallway and plastering a polite smile whenever a teacher asked if she was okay.

By lunchtime, one of her classmates, Regina, noticed Elizabeth cradling her right arm. They found a moment by their lockers, Regina's inquisitive look scanning Elizabeth's overlong sleeves.

"Hey, Elizabeth, you all right?" Regina asked softly. "You're moving like you're hurt."

Elizabeth forced a tiny grin. "I'm fine. Just... twisted my arm at home."

Regina's eyes lingered on the edge of a faint bruise poking out from under Elizabeth's shirt cuff. "Are you sure?"

Elizabeth's stomach clenched. She dropped her gaze to the floor. "Yeah, I promise I'm okay."

With a reluctant nod, Regina backed off. "Okay, if you say so. Just... let me know if you need anything."

Elizabeth offered a quiet "thanks" before scurrying to her next class, silently praying no one else would look too closely.

As the day wore on, an ache of dread coiled tighter in Elizabeth's chest. Gym class was the last period—an hour she'd been dreading since sunrise. Changing into shorts and a T-shirt would expose everything. "Maybe Ms. Novak will let me sit out," she told herself, though she doubted it. Ms. Novak was strict but not unkind. Yet the threat of defiance lingered. If Elizabeth refused to dress out, the teacher could report her to the office, and Sophia's wrath would be inevitable.

When the bell rang, she trudged to the locker room, her heart pounding. She nodded a vague greeting to a few classmates, offering excuses that she wasn't feeling well in hopes they might accept her standoffishness. The smell of rubber mats and disinfectant filled the air, amplifying her anxiety.

Elizabeth found a quiet corner near the showers, hoping to

change in secrecy. She quickly pulled the gym shirt over her long sleeves, ignoring the odd stares from two girls who paused mid-conversation to watch. Just a few minutes, Elizabeth thought, and I'll be out in the gym; no one will see...

But Ms. Novak's voice echoed across the rows of lockers: "Elizabeth! Stop hiding in the corner. Change properly like everyone else."

Elizabeth froze, her cheeks flushing hot. "I'm not feeling well, Ms. Novak. Can I please just sit out today?"

"No excuses," Ms. Novak replied briskly, approaching with her arms folded. "You know the rules. Out with the long sleeves. Let's go."

"I'm cold," Elizabeth muttered, her voice trembling. "It's just—"

"Elizabeth." The teacher's tone remained firm, but Elizabeth detected an undercurrent of concern. "Take it off. Now."

A hush spread through the locker room, curious eyes turning on Elizabeth. Her stomach churned, and her hands quivered as she peeled off the baggy top, revealing the mottled bruises that lined her arms and shoulders. For a moment, all sound seemed to vanish.

The sight of those bruises pulled a shocked gasp from a few onlooking classmates. Elizabeth could only stare at the ground, humiliated tears burning at the corners of her eyes. Ms. Novak inhaled sharply.

"Elizabeth..." she began, gentling her tone. "How did—who—" She cleared her throat, seemingly choosing her words. "Did someone hurt you?"

Elizabeth's mind raced. She could almost feel Sophia's fury if she confessed. "I can't. She'll kill me if I tell." She swallowed, summoning a quivering lie. "I—I fell down the stairs," she whispered, her voice shaking.

Ms. Novak didn't look convinced. She directed the other girls to continue dressing and head out to the gym, leaving her and Elizabeth alone in a corner of the locker room. Once the others were gone, Ms. Novak lowered her voice, her eyes flicking toward the bruises again.

"You fell down the stairs multiple times?" she asked gently, crossing her arms. "I'm worried about you, Elizabeth."

Elizabeth simply nodded, unable to meet her teacher's gaze. "I'm okay," she insisted, though her tone betrayed her.

Ms. Novak sighed, torn between pressing further and respecting Elizabeth's clear fear. "All right. Get dressed for class, at least. We'll talk about this later if you want."

Elizabeth breathed a small, shaky sigh of relief, grateful that Ms. Novak wasn't dragging her to the nurse or principal—yet. Still, the teacher's warm concern and watchful eyes hinted that the secret might not remain buried much longer.

Reluctantly, Elizabeth changed, pulling on her gym shorts and T-shirt. The fabric clung uncomfortably to her bruised back, each movement sending a jolt of pain. Stepping into the gym, she felt the stares of classmates who had glimpsed her injuries. She avoided their eyes, focusing on Ms. Novak's instructions to stretch and jog warm-ups. Every jolt of her sneakers on the polished floor reminded her of the deeper bruises hidden under cloth and makeup.

A couple of classmates whispered, but no one openly confronted her again. Elizabeth forced herself to jog, biting her lip whenever a ripple of pain seared her muscles. Her mind drifted to Sophia, the spankings, and the fear of what would happen if Ms. Novak or another adult pried too deeply.

Near the end of class, Ms. Novak pulled Elizabeth aside discreetly. "If you need to sit out, say so," she murmured. "I can tell you're hurting."

Elizabeth mustered a thin smile. "I'll manage," she whispered, grateful that the teacher offered a sliver of compassion. Yet her chest tightened at the thought of explaining the real cause behind her pain.

When the final bell rang, Elizabeth hastily changed back into her long sleeves, wincing as the fabric brushed her bruises. The locker room buzzed with post-gym chatter, but Elizabeth kept her head down, swallowing the knot in her throat. "Don't let them see you cry."

She left school in a haze, ignoring Regina's concerned wave goodbye. The hot swirl of humiliation and fear loomed large. What if Ms. Novak reported her suspicions? Elizabeth's mind spun worst-case scenarios: Child Protective Services, Sophia's explosive rage. She walked home slowly, as if each step delayed the moment she would face Sophia's sharp gaze again.

Arriving at the apartment, she found it empty—Sophia was still working. In the silence, Elizabeth collapsed onto the couch, hugging a pillow tight. The day's events washed over her: the near discovery, Ms. Novak's concerned eyes, the hush that fell over the locker room when her bruises were laid bare.

"Maybe someone will help me," she thought, a spark of hope flickering. But just as quickly, she remembered Sophia's looming wrath if word got out. If they find out... I can't risk it. What if it gets worse?

She pressed a hand over her sore ribs, closing her eyes. Yet it had never been this obvious before. The bruises on her arms, the faint welts peeking above her collar—it all threatened to undermine her carefully maintained façade. Sooner or later, someone might push for answers, Ms. Novak or a concerned friend, leaving Elizabeth trapped between the terror of Sophia's punishment and the faint promise of escape.

As evening approached, Elizabeth sat alone in the dimming light, her sleeve pulled up just enough to stare at one of the largest bruises. Each dark splotch was a silent testament to the cycle she couldn't break. "You have to stay quiet," she reminded herself, chewing on her lip. But what if I don't? What if...? The thought dissolved under a wave of dread. She lowered her sleeve again, shutting away the bruises as though hiding them might erase the truth.

In the hush of the apartment, the world felt suspended— Sophia's next outburst not yet triggered, Ms. Novak's gentle interrogation paused. For a fleeting moment, Elizabeth allowed herself to imagine a future without hiding, without bruises. She envisioned a day when she could walk into gym class in a tank top without fear. But that vision evaporated as quickly as it surfaced, leaving her with the stinging memory of Ms. Novak's question: "Did someone hurt you?"

The answer was one she wasn't ready to give. So she waited in the stillness, sore and trembling, determined to endure just a little longer—though she knew, deep down, that each day made it harder to keep her secrets concealed. If the bruises grew more obvious, if the questions grew louder, if her will to hide it all cracked just a bit more... how long before the lies gave way, exposing the truth that lived in every painful mark on her body?

❧ 56 ❧

FALSE HOPE

When Ms. Novak let Elizabeth leave without another word, Elizabeth couldn't help but hope—but the closer she got to the school doors, the more she wondered whether grown-ups kept secrets or if she was walking into a trap waiting to snap shut.

Elizabeth woke with a gnawing sense of dread, her body still aching from the previous night's punishment. As she eased her way off the bed, each bruise and welt reminded her of Sophia's anger, sharp and unforgiving. Yet Ms. Novak let her leave without another word—an unspoken promise Elizabeth both clung to and distrusted all at once.

She dressed carefully, as always—long sleeves to hide the dark bruises on her arms, loose pants to conceal the marks on her legs. The mirror reflected a small, wary girl, eyes shadowed with worry. She whispered to herself, "Don't let them see." Satisfied that her clothes would keep her secrets safe, she slipped out of her bedroom.

The kitchen was silent except for Sophia's quiet rustling at the table. Sophia glanced up once, flicked her gaze over Elizabeth, then returned to reading. "You'd better keep in line today," she said coolly, with no trace of warmth in her voice.

"Yes, ma'am," Elizabeth replied, forcing her tone to remain steady. Toast in hand, she ducked away, relieved that Sophia didn't press further. If only I could stay invisible all day, she thought, heading out the door toward the school bus.

The bus ride felt longer than usual. Elizabeth sat alone, the roar of chatter around her turning into a dull hum as she replayed yesterday's events in her mind: Ms. Novak discovering her bruises, the hush that fell in the locker room, her feeble lie about falling down the stairs, and then the teacher's quiet assurance in letting her leave with no other conversation.

A gnawing voice whispered, "What if she doesn't do anything? What if she does, and Mom finds out?" The conflicting fears twisted Elizabeth's stomach, leaving her trembling by the time the bus jolted to a stop at the school entrance.

Stepping onto the sidewalk, she steeled herself for another day. If Ms. Novak followed up, what would that look like? Would she call Sophia? The dreaded letters—CPS—floated through Elizabeth's mind, though she barely knew what they meant. All she knew was Sophia's reaction would be explosive if she learned Elizabeth had "told."

Elizabeth approached her first-period classroom with heavy legs, each step feeling like wading through deep water. As she reached the door, laughter and chatter from inside felt overwhelming, a noise barrier she couldn't face. She lingered in the hallway, eyes fixed on the polished floor, inhaling shaky breaths. "Don't cry. Don't cry. Don't let them see."

Forcing herself to push forward, she slipped through the doorway, head down, ignoring a few inquisitive looks. At her desk, she laid out her notebook, though her hands shook as she tried to steady her pencil. The teacher's lecture droned on, but Elizabeth caught none of it—her mind looping around Ms. Novak and the looming dread of Sophia's wrath.

Regina, sitting beside her, leaned over at one point. "You okay, Elizabeth?" she whispered. "You look really pale."

Elizabeth managed a faint nod, not daring to speak. If she opened her mouth, she wasn't sure she could hold back tears. Regina's concerned stare lingered, but the bell's sharp ring cut the moment short.

In the hallway between classes, Elizabeth ducked her head to avoid eye contact, hugging her books to her chest as if they might shield her from whispers. She spotted Ms. Novak at a distance, speaking with another teacher, and the sight made Elizabeth's heart leap into her throat. She didn't even look at me, Elizabeth thought, half relieved and half disappointed.

Would Ms. Novak pull her aside for a private chat? Or had she already forgotten? Each scenario felt terrifying—being ignored or being singled out. As if sensing her turmoil, Regina came up beside her, wearing a soft frown.

"Elizabeth, are you sure nothing's wrong?" Regina pressed gently. "You seem... I don't know, scared."

Elizabeth swallowed hard. "I'm okay," she managed, her tone flat. "Just tired."

Regina hesitated, wanting to probe more, but the surge of students heading to the next class separated them. Elizabeth gripped her books, weaving through the crowd, anxiety coiling tighter with every step.

Shortly before lunchtime, Elizabeth lingered by her locker, considering skipping lunch to avoid the cafeteria's chaos. Suddenly, a familiar figure approached—Ms. Novak again. Elizabeth's heart lurched at the teacher's determined expression.

"Hey, Elizabeth," Ms. Novak said softly, placing a hand on Elizabeth's shoulder. "I wanted to check on you. There's someone who'd like to meet you—over in the guidance office. Come on, it'll just take a bit."

Elizabeth's eyes widened, panic battling with a faint glimmer of relief. "Am I... in trouble?" she asked, her voice quavering.

Ms. Novak shook her head, offering a small, reassuring smile. "No, not at all. I promise, it's just a friendly meeting." Then, lowering her voice, she added, "Everything will be all right, Elizabeth."

Though her mind screamed with doubts, Elizabeth found herself nodding, letting Ms. Novak guide her down a quieter hallway. "Is it the counselor?" she wondered. "Will they call Mom?"

At the guidance office, a kind-faced woman with warm eyes greeted them. "Elizabeth, hi! I'm Mrs. Abernathy," she said brightly. "How are you doing today?"

Elizabeth shrank back. "I... I'm not in trouble?" she repeated nervously, stepping into a small, cozy office. Two other women—Ms. Cathy and Ms. Linda—were setting out juice boxes and a plate of cookies on a round table. The room's walls boasted motivational posters about asking for help and being brave. Elizabeth's heart pounded.

Mrs. Abernathy shook her head. "No trouble at all, sweetheart. Ms. Novak mentioned you could use a break, and we thought a girl's lunch might cheer you up."

Elizabeth eyed the cookies, her mouth watering despite her worry. She nodded faintly, edging toward a chair while Ms. Novak lingered at the doorway, offering a nod of encouragement before stepping back toward the door. The two other women smiled, gesturing for Elizabeth to sit.

"Elizabeth," Ms. Cathy said softly, handing her a juice box, "it's nice to meet you. We just wanted to chat, see how you're doing. Maybe share cookies—sound good?"

Elizabeth peered at the women, unsure. "O-okay," she replied in a near whisper, taking the juice box. The sweet scent of cookies and the gentle warmth of their smiles felt comforting, but her chest remained tight with caution.

For several minutes, they talked about small, harmless topics— her favorite subjects, if she liked to draw, and whether she had any pets. Elizabeth answered in subdued tones, still fearing any slip that might bring Sophia's rage. Ms. Linda occasionally asked a slightly deeper question—"Are you getting enough rest?"—but quickly backed off when she noticed Elizabeth stiffen.

Finally, Ms. Cathy cleared her throat, her gaze flicking to Ms. Abernathy. "Elizabeth, we also wanted to ask about something Ms. Novak mentioned. She saw some bruises on you yesterday. We just want to make sure you're safe."

Elizabeth froze, the cookie halfway to her mouth. Her stomach lurched. She set the cookie down, heart pounding. "I'm... fine," she lied, her voice shaking. "I... fell down some stairs."

Mrs. Abernathy exchanged a careful glance with Ms. Cathy, then leaned in. "Elizabeth, we just want to help. Sometimes, if you're hurting, it can be really scary to talk about it. But we promise you're not in trouble, and we'd like to keep you safe."

A momentary silence followed before Ms. Cathy spoke, her tone gentle. "Would it be okay if we took a look at your bruises, just to see if you need any help? We need to be sure you're all right."

Elizabeth felt her breath catch in her throat. Her eyes flicked between the two women, recalling Ms. Novak's promise. Could they actually protect me? She hugged her arms protectively. "I—um... I don't want Mom to find out," she managed, tears pricking her eyes.

Ms. Abernathy nodded sympathetically, her voice soft. "We understand, Elizabeth. But we need to document what's going on so we can really help you." She paused, then gently asked, "Do you mind showing us the bruises? I know it's scary, but this is important."

Elizabeth swallowed. She thought about Sophia, about what might happen if she discovered Elizabeth was showing people the marks. But these grown-ups seemed sincere, and Ms. Novak had insisted they wouldn't let her get into trouble. Slowly, Elizabeth nodded, trembling as she tugged up her sleeves to reveal the bruises on her arms.

A sharp intake of breath filled the small office, Ms. Linda's eyes reflecting shock and sorrow. Elizabeth kept her gaze down, her cheeks flushing with shame. Ms. Abernathy, determined yet gentle, reached for a small digital camera on the table.

"Elizabeth, honey," Ms. Abernathy said, her tone calm but resolute, "I need to take photos. I promise we'll handle them carefully. We just need to document everything, okay?"

Elizabeth's stomach twisted at the thought, but she gave a timid nod. She stood, removing her long-sleeved shirt slowly, revealing more bruises across her shoulders. Ms. Abernathy inhaled shakily at the sight but kept her voice steady.

"Thank you for trusting us," Ms. Abernathy said. She snapped a series of pictures, the camera's soft click echoing in the silence. Ms. Cathy placed a gentle hand on Elizabeth's back, murmuring, "You're doing great, Elizabeth. We know this is hard."

Elizabeth flinched, forcing herself not to recoil from Ms. Cathy's touch. Once the pictures were taken, she quickly pulled her shirt back on, tears burning in her eyes. Ms. Abernathy set the camera aside, her face a blend of compassion and resolve.

"We'll keep these photos safe," Ms. Abernathy whispered, giving Elizabeth's hand a small squeeze. "Thank you for letting us see."

Eager to end the scrutiny, Elizabeth sank back into the chair, her head bowed. Ms. Linda spoke up, her voice gentle yet serious. "Elizabeth, can you tell us anything about how these bruises got there?"

Elizabeth's heart hammered. She pictured Sophia's glare, the belt in her hand. Her mind screamed, "No, no, no," but a small part of her yearned to share the truth. She glanced at Ms. Abernathy, Ms. Cathy, and Ms. Linda—adults who seemed to genuinely care.

Finally, in a shaking whisper, she offered the same flimsy excuse: "I fell down some stairs." Even as she said it, she felt the tears escaping, betraying her façade. "I... I just fell. That's all."

Ms. Cathy and Ms. Linda exchanged a sorrowful look. Ms. Cathy tried once more, "Elizabeth, if someone at home—"

But Elizabeth shook her head vigorously, cutting her off. "I—I can't talk about it," she stammered, the tears coming faster. "Please. I'm not... I'm not allowed."

The women's comforting words came gently, assuring her she wasn't at fault and that they would help. But each time Elizabeth glanced at Ms. Abernathy's camera, she remembered Sophia's likely reaction if she learned of these photos. The knot of fear in her chest grew, overshadowing Ms. Novak's reassurance.

Eventually, Ms. Cathy sighed, noticing how pale Elizabeth had become. "Let's take a break for now, okay, Elizabeth? We can talk again soon."

Mrs. Abernathy handed her a tissue, her voice kind. "You've been very brave. We know this is scary."

Elizabeth nodded numbly, wiping her tears. Ms. Novak reentered the room briefly, the same comforting yet cautious look on her face. "Elizabeth, you'll head back to class soon. But remember, we're here. Things might feel confusing, but you're not alone."

In a whirl of muted goodbyes and half-promises, Elizabeth was guided back into the hallway. No immediate rescue, no grand solution—just the echo of Ms. Abernathy's camera clicks lingering in her memory. Ms. Novak gave her a gentle pat on the shoulder before urging her to return to class.

"Am I... going home normal?" Elizabeth finally asked, her voice trembling.

Ms. Novak paused, her face tight with sympathy. "For now, yes. But we'll do our best to help. Trust me."

Elizabeth swallowed her disappointment. She walked back through the corridors, each step weighted by the knowledge that her secrets were out—or at least partially out—but no immediate change seemed forthcoming. Was that all? Another adult promise that might vanish by tomorrow?

The final bell rang, and Elizabeth trudged outside. It was onto the bus home, just like any other day. She boarded quietly, ignoring the curious stares from other students.

Staring out the window, she tried to quell the anxiety roaring in her chest. "They took pictures," her thoughts hissed. "If Mom finds out, it'll be so much worse. But if they do nothing, I'm still stuck." The bus jolted forward, carrying her into a sinking twilight of uncertainty.

Stop by stop, kids disembarked, leaving Elizabeth alone in her window seat. The hum of the engine grew more oppressive as she neared her apartment complex. By the time the bus halted at her stop, the sky had darkened, reflecting the dread churning in her mind.

She stepped off, backpack slung over her shoulder, and trudged toward the apartment building. The door felt heavier than usual, as though crossing its threshold sealed her fate. Inside, the lights were on—she could hear faint movement in the kitchen. "Mom's home," Elizabeth realized with a jolt of fear.

Easing open the door, she slipped inside. The smell of cooking oil and detergent hung in the air, an all-too-familiar mix. She paused in the living room, every bruise throbbing in tandem with her racing heartbeat.

Sophia emerged from the hallway, eyebrows arched. There was no immediate explosion of anger, just a scrutinizing look that made Elizabeth's skin crawl. "Does she know?" The question rattled around Elizabeth's head. She forced her face into neutrality, willing herself not to tremble.

"You're late," Sophia said simply, her voice devoid of warmth. "What took you so long?"

Elizabeth swallowed. "Bus... route messed up," she mumbled, half-lie, half-truth.

A tense pause followed, the silence thick. Sophia studied her for a moment longer, then turned away with an air of disinterest. "Don't make a habit of it," she muttered, disappearing back into the kitchen. Elizabeth exhaled shakily, relief and dread warring in her chest. For now, she didn't know.

Standing alone in the hushed living room, Elizabeth's thoughts wandered to Ms. Abernathy's camera, the soft click recording her bruises. She pictured the gentle assurance in Ms. Cathy's eyes, Ms. Novak's promises echoing in her head, and the cookies left uneaten on the table. It felt surreal—like a fragile bubble of concern that popped the moment she stepped back into real life.

She wasn't sure what tomorrow would bring. Maybe Ms. Abernathy and Ms. Cathy would follow through; maybe they wouldn't. "False hope," her mind whispered. Another adult pledge that might dissolve under Sophia's looming shadow.

Closing her eyes, Elizabeth inhaled a shaky breath. She had dared to let them see, to let them document what had been done to her. And yet here she stood, still tethered to the place that hurt her most. One day, perhaps, those pictures would make a difference. But tonight, she was still alone, still bruised, and still terrified that the next belt strike could come at any moment.

57

MRS. MARINO

When Sophia calmly severed Elizabeth from the family, the girl realized that cruelty can sometimes wear a calm, collected face—and that even the quietest decree can splinter a child's world beyond repair.

Sophia emerged from the kitchen with a measured air, as though she'd simply finished cooking dinner and had ordinary orders to give. But the words she spoke struck like a lightning bolt.

"You are no longer a member of this family," she said coolly, setting her apron aside. She glanced over the living room, where Elizabeth stood uncertainly. "You will not speak to your brother at all. Not a word. You will only address me, and you will call me Mrs. Marino. I am no longer your mother, and Oliver is no longer your brother. You will go to school, come home, silently do your homework in your room, and eat in your room. Keep your room immaculate. Keep your bathroom clean by yourself. The maid will not clean up after you. She is for family only. Is that understood?"

Elizabeth's heart pounded so loudly it seemed to echo in her ears. She couldn't believe Sophia's calm, almost bored tone, as though renouncing her child's place in the family was a small administrative note. She swallowed hard, forcing her voice to remain steady. "Yes, ma'am," she whispered, her voice tight with confusion.

Sophia's expression didn't waver. "Now, go to your room and do your homework. I'll bring your dinner when it's time."

Elizabeth managed a subdued nod and turned to leave, but Sophia's voice followed her.

"And don't let me see you wandering around the house," she added, her tone cold.

Elizabeth stepped quickly down the hallway, feeling the heat of tears threatening to fall. "Don't cry—she'll only use it against me," she reminded herself, clenching her fists as she slipped into her bedroom.

Once inside, Elizabeth closed the door quietly behind her. The room, once a comforting space with her books, stuffed animals, and neatly arranged trinkets, felt stifling. She let out a shaky breath, leaning against the door for a moment before crossing to her bed. The bedspread was spotless, the shelves carefully lined—just the way Sophia demanded. Yet it no longer felt like hers.

She sank onto the edge of the mattress, shoulders slumped as a wave of numbness settled over her. "What did I do to deserve this?" The question circled her thoughts relentlessly. Her gaze landed on her small desk beneath the window, where a stack of homework waited, but she found no energy to tackle it.

A soft laugh from the kitchen drifted down the hallway, the sound twisting like a knife in her chest. She recognized Oliver's distinctive giggle—once a source of joy, now barred from her life. Memories of them joking around or sneaking cookies behind Sophia's back flitted through her mind, intensifying her sense of loss.

Elizabeth whispered to herself, "He's not my brother anymore... I don't have a brother. I don't have a family."

Her voice trembled with bitterness, tears prickling at the corners of her eyes.

Sophia's decree felt like a cruel punishment. Elizabeth replayed the moment in her head: Sophia standing there, casually delivering a life-altering sentence.

"Why does she hate me so much? What did I do wrong?" Elizabeth wondered.

She recalled the fleeting hopes she had placed in the women at school—Ms. Novak, Ms. Abernathy, Ms. Cathy—adults who had promised help. Yet here she was, locked away in her own home, forbidden to speak to her brother. If those grown-ups had intervened at all, it hadn't stopped Sophia from cutting her off.

A surge of anger and disappointment welled up. She clenched her fists, feeling the tears threaten again. "They said they'd help, but everything's worse," she lamented silently.

Elizabeth forced herself to stand and shuffle to her desk. She flipped open a math book, hoping to lose herself in numbers and forget her misery. But her eyes blurred over the pages, the neat columns of problems dissolving into a meaningless jumble. Each time she tried to focus, an echo of Sophia's decree rang in her head.

Just then, a burst of muffled laughter from the kitchen carried down the hall. Oliver's voice again. Elizabeth's chest tightened. She missed him, missed how they used to share jokes or watch each other's backs. But now, Sophia had forbidden any conversation.

Elizabeth thought, "I don't care. It doesn't matter. I don't need them," she lied to herself, blinking back tears. But the steady drip of sorrow in her chest told her otherwise.

Her eyes stung, and her breathing grew unsteady. She pressed her palms flat on the desk, trying to ground herself. "Crying won't make her love me," she reminded herself harshly.

The hours dragged, and the sky outside shifted to an orange glow. Eventually, a soft knock startled Elizabeth from her homework's half-hearted progress. She rose, crossing to the door. Opening it a crack, she found the maid standing there, tray in hand —a plate of food and a drink. The woman wore a subdued expression.

Without a word, the maid handed Elizabeth the tray. For a second, their eyes met. Elizabeth thought she saw a flicker of sympathy. She opened her mouth, contemplating a whispered "thank you," but the maid merely bowed her head and retreated down the hall, footsteps quiet on the carpet.

Closing the door, Elizabeth eyed the dinner with little appetite. She set it on her desk and sat down, picking at the food and finding it tasteless. "I'm a ghost," she thought, swallowing around a knot in her throat. Unseen, unheard... unimportant.

Finishing her meal, she placed the tray by the door and returned to her chair, burying herself in the last bits of homework. The equations and vocabulary words blurred, but she forced her mind to remain there, anywhere but on the emptiness inside.

Darkness enveloped the room, the overhead light casting harsh shadows on the walls. Elizabeth eventually changed into her pajamas, each movement mechanical. The ache in her chest grew heavier as the night deepened—she was still banished, still severed from the family by Sophia's cruel decree.

Sliding under the covers, she stared at the ceiling. Memories flickered of earlier in the day when Ms. Abernathy gently took photos of her bruises, Ms. Novak's assurances, and Ms. Cathy's kind voice. Yet those promises felt remote, overshadowed by Sophia's final words: "You are no longer a member of this family."

Elizabeth thought to herself, "Maybe they've all forgotten me. Maybe they never meant it in the first place."

She pictured Oliver's laughter from earlier, so warm, so carefree. The laughter felt like a mockery of her isolation. She thought about the vow she had made to protect him, how she used to stand up to Sophia for his sake. Now, Sophia had effectively stripped that role away.

A tear slid down Elizabeth's cheek. She pressed a hand over her mouth to stifle a sob, not wanting Sophia to hear her crying through the thin walls.

Elizabeth whispered softly, "I miss you, Oliver. I miss us, and I miss Julian."

As sleep weighed on her eyelids, Elizabeth's last thought clung to a faint, desperate prayer for something—someone—beyond these walls. She pictured a person who might see her, truly see her, and remind her that she mattered.

In the corridor, Sophia's voice murmured once, but Elizabeth couldn't discern the words. She tensed, waiting to be called or reprimanded, but the house remained still. The silence was as sharp as any belt strike, carving out an emptiness in Elizabeth's heart.

"Tomorrow... maybe tomorrow something will change," she thought. "It has to."

Yet even as the thought flickered, she felt how unlikely it was, the ache of Sophia's decree echoing in her mind. Nothing could fill the hollow space she now occupied—not a daughter, not a sister, just another presence in a house that no longer felt like home.

With that grim acceptance, she drifted into a restless sleep, tears drying on her cheeks. The last spark of hope glimmered faintly in her mind, the notion that somewhere in a bigger world, compassion might wait for her. But here and now, in the stillness of a once-familiar bedroom, all she felt was the heavy shadow of her mother's verdict: exiled from the only family she'd ever known and left with nothing but the silent question of "why."

58

THE WEIGHT OF SILENCE

A week had crawled by since Elizabeth last saw Ms. Abernathy and Ms. Cathy. Each day, she dreaded Sophia discovering the truth—those photographs capturing her bruises—and her worst fear was about to be realized.

A week passed in a haze of tension, every moment a balancing act between Elizabeth's wish for help and her terror that Sophia might find out she'd allowed Ms. Abernathy to take pictures of her injuries. When she came home from school on the seventh day, her stomach churned at the sight of Sophia waiting in the living room, arms folded and posture rigid.

Sophia's gaze bored into her. "Go to your room," she said curtly, her voice simmering with an undercurrent that Elizabeth couldn't quite place.

"Yes, ma'am," Elizabeth whispered, her pulse accelerating. She slipped quietly down the hall, her heart pounding.

She sat on her bed, a swirl of dread knotting her insides. Minutes ticked by. Suddenly, a knock from the entryway drifted down the corridor. Elizabeth heard voices—muffled, urgent. "That's them; they're here... Ms. Cathy and Ms. Abernathy?" Her pulse jumped. Sophia had discovered the pictures, hadn't she? That was why Elizabeth was banished.

Shortly after, Sophia came to her door, shoving it open with a clipped motion. "Come," she ordered.

Following in Sophia's shadow, Elizabeth rounded the corner into the living room. Her breath caught: Ms. Cathy and Ms. Abernathy stood there, expressions drawn, concern etched into their features. Elizabeth's heart lurched with a complicated blend of relief and fear.

Cathy and Ms. Abernathy exchanged a glance, both of them noticing Elizabeth's tense posture. She hovered uncertainly, arms locked in front of her. Sophia stayed a few steps behind, her face set like stone. The entire room felt charged with unspoken conflict.

"Elizabeth," Cathy said softly, kneeling a bit so they were level, "we're here to talk again. You can tell us if anything's wrong. We just want to help."

Elizabeth's tongue felt glued to the roof of her mouth. She could feel Sophia's glare on her back, a silent warning that any mention of the photos or the bruises would not end well. Instead of speaking, she nodded stiffly, her gaze fixed on the floor.

Ms. Abernathy stepped forward, her voice kind but firm. "We heard from someone—" She paused, glancing at Sophia, who glowered in response. "We just need to confirm you're safe, Elizabeth. If there's anything you need to tell us, now is the time."

Sophia's eyes flashed. "She's told you plenty already," she snapped, crossing her arms even tighter. "My daughter doesn't need a private conversation. Whatever you have to say, you can say it here."

A tight knot of fear twisted in Elizabeth's stomach. She glanced at Ms. Cathy, who gave her a small, encouraging nod. "Mrs. Marino, sometimes children feel more comfortable speaking alone. Please, let us—"

"I know what you're trying to do," Sophia interrupted icily. "You think you'll get her alone and she'll 'confess' to something. But I've already found out about your little photography session." Her glare fixed on Elizabeth. "She went bragging about her bruises, didn't she?"

Elizabeth's blood ran cold. "She knows," rang through her mind. Sophia thought she had boasted about them? Her heart pounded a ragged beat. "I—I didn't brag," she stammered, her voice barely audible. "I didn't—"

Sophia shot Elizabeth a furious look. "Quiet. Don't you dare make excuses."

Ms. Cathy's brows knitted. "Bragging? Mrs. Marino, Elizabeth didn't come to us like that. We approached her because we were worried. Any photographs we took were strictly to ensure her well-being was documented. Elizabeth had no part in bragging or showing off."

Ms. Abernathy tried to keep her voice gentle. "We just wanted proof of her injuries in case she needed help. Elizabeth—would you like to talk about that?"

Elizabeth risked a glance at Sophia, whose stare could have sliced through steel. She could almost feel the violence simmering beneath her mother's calm exterior. "No," Elizabeth murmured, tears threatening. "I... I'm fine now."

Cathy took a slow breath, stepping between Sophia and Elizabeth. "We really should speak with her alone for a few minutes." Then, turning to Elizabeth, she asked gently, "Is that okay with you, Elizabeth?"

Fear coiled in Elizabeth's chest. She could sense Sophia's fury emanating behind her. Despite that, a glimmer of hope flared. Maybe if she just had a moment without her mother looming, she could correct Sophia's twisted accusation. "Yes," she whispered shakily, her gaze flicking to Sophia's clenched fists. "I'd like that."

Sophia's jaw set in a rigid line, but after a tense moment, she huffed, stepping aside. "Fine," she spat. "But don't you dare lie about me again." Her eyes bored into Elizabeth, as if daring her to speak the truth.

Elizabeth led Ms. Cathy and Ms. Abernathy into the small kitchen, her heart thudding. The overhead light cast stark shadows, illuminating the swirl of dust motes in the air. She perched on a chair, hands twisted in her lap. Ms. Cathy and Ms. Abernathy pulled up chairs nearby, trying to keep their voices low.

"Elizabeth," Ms. Cathy began, leaning forward with a soft earnestness, "I want you to know: no one thinks you were bragging. We know you're scared. The pictures were just to protect you."

Ms. Abernathy nodded. "The bruises we documented weren't something to flaunt. We only took them to show the authorities, if needed, that you're being hurt." She paused, gently adding, "Are you still being hurt, Elizabeth?"

Elizabeth's eyes welled with tears. She pressed her lips together, recalling Sophia's threat from just minutes ago. "If she thinks I said anything, I'll pay for it..." The fresh bruise on her leg twinged, shaped like a handprint. She swallowed hard.

"I—I'm okay," she managed, her voice unsteady. "I didn't tell you on purpose, I swear. I wasn't bragging. I'm sorry you took pictures."

Ms. Cathy's expression softened further. "Oh, Elizabeth, we're not upset with you. We just want to keep you safe from harm."

A flicker of frustration crept into Ms. Cathy's voice. "You can be honest if you're still in danger. Has your mother done anything new since the last time?"

Elizabeth's breath caught. She thought about the bruise from two nights ago. But Sophia's threat resonated loudly: "If I lose Oliver because of you, I'll make sure you regret it for the rest of your life." She trembled, choosing her words carefully. "She's... not happy. But... no, I'm fine."

Ms. Abernathy gently touched Elizabeth's hand. "We know she found out about the photos. We're sorry if that made things difficult. This isn't your fault, Elizabeth."

Elizabeth nodded, tears burning her eyes. She hated how powerless she felt, hated Sophia's assumption that she'd boasted about bruises. As if I'd be proud of them. But she couldn't bring herself to fully contradict Sophia while still under her roof.

A sudden clearing of a throat made them all jump. Sophia stood in the kitchen doorway, arms folded. "Enough," she said, her voice dangerously low. "Time's up. Elizabeth has studying to do."

Ms. Cathy's jaw tightened slightly. "We hadn't finished—"

"It's finished," Sophia snapped, flicking a glare at Elizabeth. "She has nothing more to say." She gestured impatiently for them to exit. "You can leave now."

Ms. Abernathy rose, shooting Elizabeth a resigned, sorrowful look. "We'll check in again soon, Elizabeth," she promised softly. "Please remember you can tell us anything. We won't let you get in trouble for telling the truth."

Elizabeth forced a small nod, her heart racing as Ms. Cathy and Ms. Abernathy slid past Sophia, heading for the front door. Sophia didn't move until they were gone, the door shutting with a dull thud.

The silence that settled was thick, charged with unspoken fury. Sophia advanced a few steps, eyes narrowed. "So you let them take pictures, did you?" she hissed.

Elizabeth's mouth went dry. "I... I didn't tell them anything," she managed. "I didn't brag about my bruises. They took pictures without me showing off. They said—"

"Shut it," Sophia snapped, her tone icy. "I know you wanted them to see. You wanted them to pity you. Making me out to be a monster, yes? So you get your precious attention?"

Elizabeth felt tears prick her eyes, but she refused to let them fall. "I didn't... I just—"

"Liar." Sophia's voice dropped, dripping with contempt. "If I lose Oliver over your little stunt, I'll make sure you regret it every day of your life." She stepped closer, forcing Elizabeth to step back until her heels bumped against the kitchen table. "Do you understand?"

Terror twisted Elizabeth's insides, but she managed a stiff nod. She knew better than to speak now; any word might detonate Sophia's simmering rage.

"Go to your room," Sophia commanded, stepping aside. "And keep that mouth shut next time they come snooping."

Elizabeth skirted around Sophia, her legs quaking. She nearly stumbled as she escaped down the hall, her breath coming in ragged gasps. Re-entering her bedroom, she shut the door, leaning against it for support. Her heart hammered, and tears stung her cheeks.

She thought about Ms. Cathy and Ms. Abernathy's kind faces, their quiet determination to help, and the photographs meant to protect her. Instead, they had led Sophia to believe Elizabeth was boasting about her bruises. Could it have made things better if I spoke up? Or would she just punish me more?

With a trembling sigh, she sat on the edge of her bed. The exhaustion of constant vigilance weighed on her like a stone. She pressed a hand against the fresh bruise on her leg, shaped like Sophia's handprint, recalling how it still ached with each step.

Elizabeth thought to herself, "I told them I'm fine, but everything's worse now. She knows about the pictures." A shiver ran through her. "It wasn't bragging—why would I be proud of these marks?"

She lifted her gaze to the ceiling, tears threatening again. "I didn't do anything wrong," a small, defiant voice inside whispered. But fear and shame mingled, reminding her that Sophia's wrath was never far. "Why does she blame me for everything?"

Yet a faint glimmer of resolve flickered amid the dread. Ms. Cathy and Ms. Abernathy hadn't abandoned her; they had come back. They insisted on seeing her despite Sophia's hostility. Perhaps they'd keep trying, keep pushing, until one day Elizabeth might break free from this oppressive hush.

For now, though, she was still trapped in a house where any mention of the truth was twisted into betrayal. Elizabeth swallowed, burying her face in her hands and letting the tears fall silently. "Maybe one day," she told herself. "Maybe one day these pictures will help me find a way out—and she'll see I never bragged at all."

59

FIVE FINGER DISCOUNT

A new city, a nicer car, and Sophia's promotion at the title company promised a smoother life for Elizabeth and Oliver—until one reckless decision turned Reno's bright allure into another fleeting illusion.

After the flood fiasco that cost them their previous apartment and brought in a brief CPS inquiry, Sophia orchestrated yet another move—this time with far greater optimism. Armed with a promotion at a title company that would boost her income, she traded in their battered old mini-truck for a modest but respectable sedan. The vehicle's smooth ride felt like an omen of better days.

"This place will be different," Sophia said, her eyes flicking to Elizabeth and Oliver in the rearview mirror. "I've got a better position now—more pay, fewer worries. We'll be fine."

Elizabeth offered a small nod, glancing out the window as they rolled into Reno at dusk. Neon lights illuminated the skyline, and the siblings couldn't help but feel a spark of hope. Soon, they pulled into the parking lot of a nice apartment complex—no modest apartment this time, but a middle-class building with clean and well-maintained landscaping.

Sophia popped open the trunk of her new car, smoothing her blouse as she stepped out. "Unpack quickly," she said. "I start my new job tomorrow, and I need you two to stay out of trouble."

Elizabeth and Oliver exchanged cautious glances. If Sophia was truly stable this time—new job, better car, better home—maybe the family could finally find peace.

Within a week, the siblings found a way to earn their own money: running paper routes at dawn. Each morning, they biked through hushed residential streets, tossing rolled newspapers onto doorsteps before the city fully stirred. Elizabeth relished the independence, the crisp air, and the sense of accomplishment as she collected her earnings.

"I can't believe I'm actually saving money," Elizabeth said one morning, counting out her tips in the faint glow of a streetlamp.

Oliver grinned, zipping his jacket. "I know—feels good not to beg Mom for every dollar. I just hope she stays off our backs."

Back at the new apartment complex, Sophia often left early for her job. The slight lift in her mood reflected her better income and position, and for a short while, it seemed the family might finally gain some traction in life.

Oliver, though, quickly burned through his paper route pay on trifles: a new girlfriend he tried to impress and random gadgets he never used. When the paper company asked for fees—rubber bands, protective sleeves—Oliver was broke, leaving Elizabeth to bail him out.

"Pay me back," she warned, pressing a few crumpled dollars into the paper office's hand.

Oliver shrugged sheepishly. "I will, I promise."

Despite the annoyance, Elizabeth still found her route exhilarating—her small claim of freedom in a world where Sophia's rules often loomed large.

As the novelty of pre-dawn deliveries wore off, Elizabeth's craving for something more grew. She roped Oliver into post-route wanderings through parking garages and nearby complexes, all in search of little "treasures" left in unlocked cars.

"It's just a quick peek," Elizabeth insisted one day, testing a car's handle. "I'll bet people leave money lying around."

Oliver hesitated, scanning for pedestrians walking by. "Are you sure? If Mom finds out..."

Elizabeth smiled wryly, a spark of daring lighting her eyes. "She won't—unless we get sloppy."

At first, they took only loose change or an abandoned CD here and there, telling themselves it was harmless. But the rush of discovering small valuables emboldened them. Soon, the siblings escalated to breaking into locked cars, snagging sunglasses, spare bills, and anything that looked worthwhile.

"We'll stop soon," Oliver kept saying, rummaging through a glove box one brisk morning.

Elizabeth felt adrenaline surging like a drug. "Not yet," she murmured, her heart hammering in her chest. "We're making easy cash. Why quit?"

All illusions of invincibility dissolved one chilly autumn morning. The siblings were rifling through a sedan in a dimly lit parking lot when a stern voice froze them in place.

"Freeze!"

They spun to see a security guard, flashlight pinned on them, already calling the police. Elizabeth's stomach plummeted. Oliver dropped a stolen pair of sunglasses, his face turning ashen.

"Mom's gonna kill us," he breathed, panic edging his voice.

Within minutes, red and blue lights flickered across the lot. The police discovered the small trove of stolen items in Elizabeth's bag —coins, CDs, and random trinkets. A landlord from the complex, furious at finding out that thieves lived on his property, insisted on immediate eviction.

Sophia arrived, color draining from her face. She glared at Elizabeth and Oliver, then hissed at the landlord, "They're just kids. I'll pay for whatever they took."

The landlord refused to budge, brandishing an eviction notice. "Your children have been rifling through people's cars for weeks. You have one week to be gone."

The police took Elizabeth and Oliver in for questioning. Fearful of Sophia's wrath, they admitted nothing about her discipline except that it was strict. Hoping to dodge deeper scrutiny, Sophia unleashed a desperate gambit:

"Take them away if you think I'm a bad mother," she said, her voice dripping with sarcasm. "Adopt them out. I'm done with their nonsense." She was serious; she wanted nothing more to do with Elizabeth and Oliver's poor behavior.

But the police, already occupied with the siblings' theft charges, hesitated to involve CPS further. Eventually, Sophia relented, agreeing to take them home rather than risk more investigation into her parenting. The family was effectively forced to leave the apartment—again.

Oliver rubbed his arms, shivering despite the warm day. "I can't believe we screwed up so badly that we're losing this place."

Elizabeth bit her lip, tears stinging her eyes. "Guess we weren't as slick as we thought."

The siblings returned to the apartment, which Sophia had once viewed as a symbol of her rising prospects at the title company. Now, they packed boxes under the glow of flickering street lamps. Suitcases and hastily stuffed garbage bags formed a sad echo of their last hurried departure.

Sophia's voice, low and furious, cut through the silence: "We're heading back to Texas. I'm going back to my old job."

Elizabeth glanced at Oliver. She recalled how proud Sophia had been of her new position, the higher pay, and the chance to finally escape their pattern of chaos. And here they were, once again, undone by impulsive decisions.

Oliver slouched against a suitcase, cap pulled low over his eyes. "Sorry," he mumbled.

Sophia's lips tightened. "Sorry doesn't change anything. We haven't even been here six months yet, and you two have already got us kicked out again. Load up; I am done."

The car trunk filled with boxes, each item a reminder of a chance wasted. Elizabeth swallowed her guilt. She remembered the thrill of rummaging through cars at dawn—the false sense of power overshadowed now by shame. Sophia, shaking with rage and disappointment, slid behind the wheel.

As they pulled away from the complex's lot, the neon sign flickered overhead, and Reno's skyline receded behind them. Elizabeth sat in the back seat, hugging her backpack, tears threatening to spill. Another eviction, another broken promise of stability. She cast a final glance at the city lights.

Oliver nudged her, his voice barely above a whisper. "I know we messed up," he said. "I'm sorry, Elizabeth."

She nodded, her voice too tight to answer. "How many times can we start over before we realize we're just repeating the same mistakes?" she wondered.

Sophia gripped the steering wheel, knuckles white. "Texas," she muttered. "We're finished here."

But Elizabeth recalled half-hearing mention of Arizona in a previous plan—no one truly knew where Sophia might steer them next. The only certainty was that they had left another "fresh start" behind in the dust, the neon lights of Reno fading in the rearview mirror.

The car rumbled onto the highway, the hum of tires the only sound as they drove into the night. Elizabeth stared out at the dark horizon, the weight of her choices pressing heavily on her chest. She yearned for a place they could finally call home without packing up in disgrace—but the glow of Reno's neon was already a memory, and the next unknown awaited on the open road.

❧ 60 ❧

A FRAGILE DEPARTURE

Returning to Texas with a promising promotion, Sophia's new apartment hinted at stability—but when lingering resentments flared, Elizabeth found herself shipped to Arizona with barely a goodbye.

The Reno disaster—complete with theft and evictions—led Sophia straight back to Texas. This time, her old title company position had turned into a better-paying role, and she was quick to tout her promotion as the key to a smoother life. After a few days of shuffling between hotel rooms, she managed to secure a decent two-bedroom apartment in a respectable complex.

"This is good enough," Sophia declared, stepping through the apartment's threshold with an air of impatience rather than relief. "I don't want either of you messing this up."

Elizabeth set her small bag down, exchanging a wary glance with Oliver. They both understood Sophia's thinly veiled warning. Though the new place boasted clean carpets and freshly painted walls, the tension in Sophia's voice remained palpable, hinting that her resentments still simmered beneath the surface.

Barely settled, Elizabeth found herself walking on eggshells. While Sophia vanished daily for her new position at the title company, Elizabeth and Oliver were left to navigate school and the apartment grounds on their own. Oliver spent his after-school hours drifting between television and half-hearted attempts to help around the house.

One evening, Elizabeth finished her homework at the new dining table. Sophia arrived home in a crisp office suit, setting her purse down with a tired sigh.

"Is dinner ready?" she asked, her eyes scanning the kitchen counters.

Elizabeth blinked. "Um, I... was waiting for you to—"

"Don't make excuses," Sophia snapped, her frustration peeking through. "We have a routine now. That means you do your part without me telling you."

Elizabeth bit her lip, nodding. Even with a better paycheck, Sophia seemed as short-tempered as ever.

A few days later, Elizabeth returned from school to find Sophia standing by the living room window, arms crossed, lips pressed tight. The sight made Elizabeth's stomach knot. She quietly closed the door, setting her backpack on the floor.

"Pack your things," Sophia said, her tone strangely calm. "You're leaving."

Elizabeth's heart lurched. "What did I do?"

"You heard me." Sophia's glare cut through any argument. "I've had enough of you here. You'll stay with your grandparents in Arizona." She gave Oliver, peering from the hallway, a quick glance. "Just you. Now go. Pack."

Shock welled up in Elizabeth, tears stinging her eyes. "She's throwing me out," she thought, wondering yet again what invisible line she had crossed. "But... I just—"

"Don't talk back," Sophia snapped. "Hurry."

Elizabeth trudged into the second bedroom, her mind reeling. She'd barely unpacked her belongings. Now, she stuffed clothes and schoolbooks into her worn duffel bag, her heart pounding with a mix of confusion and happiness. The new apartment was supposed to be a fresh start, but it felt like every move just pushed her closer to the edge of Sophia's anger.

As she zipped her bag, she glanced at a small keepsake—a stuffed dog she'd had since childhood. Her hand hovered over it. She recalled Sophia's past warnings: "Don't take anything I paid for." With a sinking heart, she left it behind, not daring to defy her mother's decree.

Stepping back into the living room, she spotted Oliver lurking by the couch, watching television. Neither sibling said a word. They both knew Sophia wouldn't tolerate arguments.

Sophia stood by the front door, keys in hand, impatience etched into her features. "Come on," she said curtly, stepping outside with Elizabeth trailing behind. The late afternoon sun cast long shadows over the apartment's manicured lawns, and a faint breeze rustled the shrubs.

"Mom—" Elizabeth tried, her voice shaking with the desire for one last plea, but Sophia shut down any appeal.

"No," Sophia said flatly. "This is settled. Get in the car."

Elizabeth slid into the passenger seat of Sophia's sedan. The ride was tense and silent. She stared out the window, tears prickling. "She never wanted me here at all," a bitter thought crept in.

After a short, uneasy drive, they arrived at a gas station parking lot on the outskirts of town. Elizabeth was surprised to see her grandparents' car parked nearby, waiting. Her grandmother waved hesitantly from the driver's seat.

"Get out," Sophia snapped. "They'll take you from here."

Clutching her duffel, Elizabeth stepped out of Sophia's sedan. Her grandmother opened her arms, concern flooding her expression. "Oh, Elizabeth—come here."

Elizabeth let her grandmother fold her into a brief hug. Meanwhile, Sophia leaned against her own car, arms crossed, her face devoid of warmth. After a tense pause, she threw Elizabeth's duffel bag to the ground.

"There," Sophia said. "Done."

Elizabeth lifted the bag, tears threatening again, but her grandmother ushered her gently into the back seat of their older pickup. Her grandfather offered a stiff nod.

"Alright," her grandmother said quietly to Sophia. "We'll make sure she's cared for."

Sophia only shrugged, turning away as if everything were a casual transaction. With a cold finality, she got into her sedan and drove off without a backward glance.

Elizabeth buckled up, scarcely able to process the abrupt change. Her grandmother offered a soft, worried smile. "It'll be okay, sweetheart. We'll take care of you. We're your family."

Elizabeth swallowed hard, her eyes fixed on the passing scenery as they left Texas behind. She thought of the half-unpacked apartment, how the entire "fresh start" disintegrated in an instant. She wondered if Oliver was watching from the window or if he was relieved to see her go. The conflicting emotions churned in her chest.

Her grandfather cleared his throat. "You'll be in with the girls this time. You are getting too old to share a room with a boy."

Elizabeth mustered a nod, tears finally escaping. She tried to blink them away, but her grandmother caught a glimpse. She reached over to pat Elizabeth's hand reassuringly.

"That's it," her grandmother said. "Just rest. It's a long drive."

It was nightfall the next day by the time they reached her grandparents' modest home in Arizona. Porch lights glowed warmly, a stark contrast to Sophia's icy departure. As she climbed out of the car, Elizabeth felt a strange mix of relief and loss. She knew her grandparents meant well, but she couldn't shake the hollow ache left by Sophia's abrupt rejection.

"Go put your stuff away," her grandmother said, "the girls have set aside room for you."

Elizabeth dropped her duffel beside the bed, noticing a small window facing the forest. The silence of the house felt foreign after the constant tension in Texas. She managed a small "thank you," though her throat tightened with unshed tears.

Hours later, after her grandparents turned in, Elizabeth lay awake under a borrowed blanket, staring at the bottom of the top bunk where Evelyn and Isabelle lay. The day's events replayed over and over—Sophia's flat decree, the short drive, the quick hand-off as though Elizabeth were cargo. Her grandmother's gentle reassurance provided little solace.

"Did she ever want me around at all?" Elizabeth whispered into the darkness, tears finally escaping. "Why can't we ever just be... a real family?"

She thought of Oliver, left behind with Sophia's unpredictability. At least he wasn't usually the target. Clutching her pillow, Elizabeth closed her eyes and wondered if her grandparents' house could ever feel like home. The notion of safety was overshadowed by a numb sense of having been cast aside.

Elizabeth thought to herself, "Maybe it's better this way—maybe I can heal here. But does she even care that I'm gone?" Then she remembered Julian. Could he get to her when she was in with Isabelle and Evelyn?

The darkness offered no answers, only the lingering memory of Sophia's final, icy words and the memory of the last time Elizabeth stayed at the Ranch. As sleep gently pulled her under, Elizabeth held onto the faint wish that, in this new place, she might learn what a quiet life without constant upheaval really felt like—despite the deep hurt etched in her heart.

61

A BEST DAY EVER

When Elizabeth woke up that morning, she had no idea her laughter in the chicken coop would soon give way to a frantic race against time—proving that, on the ranch, even the best days can change in an instant.

Elizabeth stepped outside into a morning bathed in warm sunlight, her heart light for the first time in ages. She inhaled deeply, savoring the ranch air—an earthy mix of hay, dew, and distant wildflowers. She practically skipped down the worn path toward the chicken coops, where her aunts, Isabelle and Evelyn, were already chatting away.

"Morning, sunshine!" Isabelle called, waving a small broom.

"Morning!" Elizabeth answered, her voice bright. She felt a buoyancy in her chest that had been missing for a long time. No gloom, no heaviness, just... happiness, she mused.

As she neared the coops, Elizabeth soaked in the ranch's sounds: hens clucking in their enclosures, a tractor humming from afar, and Isabelle and Evelyn's occasional laughter. The day felt ripe with possibilities, and for once, Elizabeth's mind wasn't consumed by worry.

"Okay, Elizabeth, you can start by raking out that coop," Evelyn said, handing her a rake. "Be thorough—we don't want old straw piling up."

Elizabeth nodded. "I'm on it," she said, flashing a grin. She entered the coop, carefully raking straw into neat piles.

Isabelle brushed some straw aside and, with a playful twirl, used her rake like a dance partner. "Guess who's in a good mood today?" she teased, swinging the makeshift partner around.

Evelyn giggled. "What are you singing now, Isabelle?"

Isabelle burst into a peppy tune Elizabeth didn't recognize, her voice echoing in the dusty coop. Elizabeth paused her raking, enthralled by her aunt's carefree twirling.

"I'll teach you the words if you join in," Isabelle teased, extending an imaginary microphone made of straw.

Elizabeth giggled, feeling bold. "I'll try... maybe just hum first?"

As Evelyn joined the melody, Elizabeth mimicked the tune, half-laughing at her own tentative voice. The repetitive chorus flowed easily, and soon Elizabeth was humming along, rake in hand, swaying to the beat. Each sweep felt lighter, the chore transforming into a silly dance fueled by shared laughter.

By the time they finished with the chickens, Elizabeth's cheeks were glowing pink from exertion and joy. She couldn't remember the last time she had done something so mundane yet felt so free.

"Time for rabbits," Isabelle announced, leading the way to the hutches. The pens were lined under a shady overhang, and the rabbits perked up at the trio's approach.

Evelyn knelt by one hutch, carefully lifting a tiny bunny into her arms. She beckoned Elizabeth closer. "Here, hold it gently," she said, transferring the squirming fluff into Elizabeth's hands.

Elizabeth's heart melted as she stroked the rabbit's soft fur. "He's so warm," she whispered, smiling. "But... I wish we could keep him as a pet."

Evelyn sighed softly, her eyes serious. "Don't get too attached. These rabbits aren't exactly pets; they are dinner."

Elizabeth nodded, glancing at Isabelle, who was refilling a water dispenser. She sensed an undercurrent of reality—life on the ranch meant some animals were for livelihood, not companionship. Still, holding the bunny felt magical, if only briefly.

As they cleaned the rabbit hutches, removing old bedding and spreading fresh straw, the girls' chatter floated in the warm air. Elizabeth found herself humming the song from earlier, buoyed by a rare feeling of belonging.

"Well, you're in a good mood," Isabelle joked, noticing Elizabeth's tune.

Elizabeth placed a rabbit gently into a temporary pen. "I really like this... you know, working together, with no one yelling. It just... feels good."

Evelyn flashed a smile. "That's the ranch for you—when it's calm, it's the best place on Earth."

They finished the chores quickly, a testament to how smoothly they worked as a team. The grass outside felt soft beneath them as they flopped down to watch the rabbits hop around in their makeshift enclosure.

"You did great," Isabelle said, nudging Elizabeth's arm. "You've got the perfect touch with those bunnies."

Elizabeth beamed, glancing around at the peaceful ranch landscape. In that moment, it truly felt like the "best day ever," the morning's trifling tasks turned into a joyful dance of shared laughter and gentle responsibility.

Before Elizabeth could fully settle into her contentment, Evelyn noticed a colt approaching, covered in blood.

A bolt of tension flickered through the air. Elizabeth sat up, her heart pounding. "What's wrong?"

Look, turning to the others with alarm. "One of the young horses got tangled in barbed wire. He's cut up."

Isabelle sprang up. "Let's go," she said, her voice urgent. "Elizabeth, come on."

In a matter of seconds, their cheery banter was replaced by a surge of adrenaline. Elizabeth raced after her aunts across the field to the colt they called "Rab," the dusty path sweltering under the sun. Laughter from earlier vanished, replaced by a knot of fear in Elizabeth's gut.

They found the Rab near a fence, skin nicked and torn around his flank and chest. The barbed wire dangled precariously, biting into his flesh. Elizabeth's stomach didn't churn at the sight of blood; instead, she became focused. Rab was panicked, eyes wide and nostrils flaring. Elizabeth found the peace in herself to calm him in spite of his injuries.

Isabelle knelt by the horse's head, speaking low and soothingly. "Easy, boy, easy. We've got you," she murmured, running a calming hand along his neck.

Evelyn hastily ran to the house, her voice trembling as she spoke. "Dad—get the truck. Rab's in bad shape. Hurry."

Elizabeth, startled but determined, grabbed a rag from Evelyn's kit. "What can I do?"

Isabelle glanced up, her expression taut. "Help keep him still. Don't let him move around too much."

Heart hammering, Elizabeth approached Rab's side, placing a gentle palm on his neck. Her breath caught at the sight of blood staining his coat. She stroked softly, trying to exude calm. "It's okay," she murmured. "We're here."

Within minutes, Henry and Margaret arrived in the truck, concern etched on their faces. Margaret rushed over with wire cutters while Henry turned the truck around.

"Let's free him from that fence," Margaret commanded, her voice steady. She motioned to Elizabeth. "Stay by his head; keep him as calm as you can."

Isabelle crouched next to Margaret, carefully unwinding the barbed wire from Rab's flesh. Each movement made Rab spasm, and Elizabeth's heart thundered with empathy. She whispered soothing nonsense as the horse quivered under her touch.

Finally, the wire came loose. The colt teetered, flanks heaving. "We have to load him," Henry said, opening the truck's tailgate. "He's got to go to the vet."

Evelyn, Isabelle, and Elizabeth rallied, guiding Rab into the truck bed. Rab balked, his eyes rolling, but they managed to coax and then lift him in, forcing him to lie down. Margaret grimaced at the blood still seeping from his cut.

"We'll keep pressure on the wound," Evelyn said, pressing a clean cloth to Rab's chest.

Without wasting a moment, Henry hopped behind the wheel, taking care not to jolt the injured colt. Elizabeth and her aunts climbed into the back with Rab, their arms steadying him as the truck rumbled toward the vet's clinic.

Each bump in the road sent pain rippling through the colt, who whimpered in distress. Elizabeth felt the earlier elation fade into grim resolve, her hands shaking from the adrenaline. She locked eyes with Isabelle, who nodded encouragement.

"You're doing great, Elizabeth," Isabelle said quietly over the hum of the truck. "Hang in there."

The trip seemed endless, yet every mile felt like an eternity. Rab's ragged breathing was all Elizabeth could focus on, her earlier laughter replaced by a fierce determination to help. She inhaled, recalling how quickly one perfect day had twisted into near tragedy.

At last, they pulled into the veterinarian's lot. The staff rushed out, sedating Rab before lifting him onto a rolling table and vanishing into the clinic. Elizabeth, Isabelle, and Evelyn collapsed against the truck bed, relief and fear churning in equal measure. None of them noticed the amount of blood that had soaked into their clothing. None of them cared.

While Margaret and Henry handled paperwork inside, Elizabeth and the girls waited by the truck. Isabelle paced, her voice tight with residual worry. "That wire really tore him up."

Evelyn wiped sweat from her brow. "He's tough, though. He'll pull through."

Elizabeth leaned against the tailgate, her heart still pounding from the chaos. "I've never seen a horse so hurt," she said softly. "I'm glad we got there fast enough."

After what felt like hours, Margaret emerged, her expression calmer. "Rab's sedated and stitched up," she reported. "We have to keep the wound clean for the next few weeks, but the vet says he'll recover."

Elizabeth let out a shaky breath. "Thank goodness," she whispered. She remembered the gentle bond she had felt just that morning with the ranch animals and how easily life could become an emergency.

The ride back was mercifully smoother, Rab still sedated but stable. Once they arrived, they settled him into a stall, administering pain medication as he slowly came to. Evelyn turned to Elizabeth.

"You did really well today," she said, placing a gentle hand on Elizabeth's shoulder. "If you're up for it, I'll show you how to handle the bandages and give him injections for his recovery."

Elizabeth nodded, tears of relief stinging her eyes. "Yes, please. I want to help."

Isabelle offered a tired smile. "We'll all make sure he heals up right."

For the next few days, Elizabeth diligently cared for Rab alongside Evelyn, learning to clean and dress the wound and gently administering injections when needed. Though the morning's carefree chores felt distant, Elizabeth recognized that the day had brought out a new determination in her. The "best day ever" soared from singing in the coops to saving a life.

By the time Rab healed, no scar remained to mark the ordeal. Elizabeth, however, found a lasting reminder in her own heart: life on the ranch could spin from joy to emergency in a heartbeat, but she wasn't powerless. She had a role, a purpose, and a sense of unity with the people around her—an experience every bit as precious as the morning's laughter.

That evening, as dusk settled over the ranch, Elizabeth stood by Rab's stall. She reached through the bars, stroking his now-smooth flank. A soft, content snort escaped the colt. Elizabeth smiled, recalling how the day began in song and ended in resilience.

"This really was the best day," she murmured under her breath, her mind drifting back to the laughter, the frantic rescue, and the renewed confidence she felt in the ranch's embrace—where each moment, no matter how tumultuous, formed part of a growing sense of belonging she never thought she'd find.

62

THE CIRCLE OF LIFE

When Elizabeth set foot on the ranch, she believed she knew how life worked—but in her first week, the raw reality of daily chores, life and death, and her family's unwavering pragmatism would challenge everything she thought she understood.

From the moment Elizabeth arrived at the ranch, she sensed how different it was from anywhere she'd lived before—no bustling city noise, no cramped apartment walls. Instead, she awoke each morning to a wide sky, a chorus of roosters, and the earthy scents of hay and soil. Within days, she discovered that living on a ranch meant embracing a raw honesty about food, animals, and survival that both fascinated and unsettled her.

She had always thought of chickens as curious, clucking creatures that pecked at the ground and made for lively barnyard scenes. But one morning, she found herself staring, wide-eyed, as her grandmother calmly butchered a hen. The air was thick with the sharp smell of fresh feathers and raw meat. She couldn't look away from the process, her heart pounding.

Her grandmother glanced over at her. "It's all right to be startled, dear. Are you okay?"

Elizabeth nodded mutely, her eyes still on the bird. "I—I guess I didn't realize how... how real this is," she managed to say, her voice trembling.

Her grandmother gave a soft, understanding smile. "This is how we eat, sweetheart. This hen lived a good life, and now it's giving us a meal. We use everything we can—no waste."

Elizabeth swallowed hard, recalling how she'd just fed the chickens the day before. They weren't just pets, she thought; they were future meals all along. It rattled her, but she couldn't help but feel a new respect for the effort behind every dinner plate.

Later that day, as they prepared the chicken for supper, Elizabeth stood beside her aunt Isabelle in the kitchen, helping to rinse the cuts of meat. She noticed that not a single piece was thrown away; every part found a use.

Isabelle, sensing Elizabeth's continued unease, gave her a quick nudge. "You holding up okay?"

Elizabeth nodded slowly. "Yeah... I just never imagined eating something I saw alive just yesterday."

Isabelle handed her a small dish towel. "We get it, kiddo. It's not easy at first. But when we do it ourselves, we know the animals are treated right. They're not just some mystery from a supermarket shelf."

Hearing that gave Elizabeth a small dose of comfort. She realized how disconnected she had been from the reality of where food came from, and though she felt squeamish, she also recognized an odd gratitude for the chicken's life.

A few days later, Elizabeth was raking up the chicken coops when she heard her grandfather calling out, his voice echoing across the yard.

"Hey, Elizabeth, come on over here. Your uncle just brought in a deer."

Confusion swirled in her gut. Another butchering? She glanced around, noticing Isabelle and Evelyn heading that way too, chatting as if this were an everyday event. Determined to push past her discomfort, Elizabeth followed after leaning the rake against the side of the chicken coop.

At the far side of the barn, her uncle had tied a deer up under a large oak tree. Elizabeth's grandfather stood beside him, sharpening a knife with calm efficiency. The air carried a brisk tang of metal and fresh earth, laced with the musky scent of the deer.

Evelyn beckoned Elizabeth over, her gaze gentle. "Come see. It's not so different from the chicken—but bigger, and it will provide a lot more food."

Elizabeth took a cautious step forward. "So we—um, we do everything here too? Like the chicken?"

Her grandfather nodded, gesturing to the deer's hind leg. "We process it ourselves. That means steaks, ribs, roasts—nothing wasted. This is how we respect the animal's life."

Uncle Julian, smirking, handed Elizabeth a piece of venison jerky. "Try this—made it last week from my last hunt. It's good, see?"

She hesitated, then took a small bite. The smoky, slightly gamey flavor popped on her tongue. It was strange, but not unpleasant. "Huh... it's kind of tasty," she admitted, her cheeks warming at Julian's approving grin.

With brisk efficiency, her grandfather and uncle started butchering the deer. They explained each part: which cuts become steak, which do better in stew, and how the bones could be boiled for stock. Elizabeth observed quietly, an odd blend of fascination and squeamishness building inside her. She noticed how, even though the men worked steadily, there was a solemn quality in how they spoke about the deer's final moments.

Her uncle paused to show her a particularly tender cut, pointing with his knife. "This might look gruesome, but if I do this right, the deer feels minimal pain. It's better than any random butcher shop; trust me."

Elizabeth tried to nod, though she still felt her stomach knot at the sight of raw venison. "So... you always hunt like this? For the family?"

"Pretty much," Julian answered. "We raise some animals here, but the deer come from the wild. It's part of how we live now."

That evening, Elizabeth washed up for dinner, her mind spinning with the day's events. The table was laden with fresh venison steaks, mashed potatoes from the garden, and even a small bowl of chicken soup from the previous day's leftover stock. Before anyone took a bite, her grandfather raised a simple toast:

"To the animals that keep us going," he said quietly. "We honor them, and we don't waste their gift."

Elizabeth's gaze drifted to her plate, the deer steak still sizzling slightly. She swallowed, recalling the moment she'd laid eyes on that deer hanging in the tree, how it had once walked free. Yet here it was—her meal.

She lifted her fork, heart thumping, and tasted the venison. It was rich and savory, a flavor she'd never truly experienced before. As the family chatted, praising the tenderness of the meat, Elizabeth found herself surprisingly appreciative, not repulsed. The hush in her mind allowed a strange sense of gratitude to settle in.

After dinner, her grandmother joined her on the porch swing, the evening air still and warm, cicadas humming in the distance. They rocked gently, gazing out at the last streaks of sunset.

Her grandmother tucked a loose strand of Elizabeth's hair behind her ear. "I noticed you handled the butchering pretty well—better than most kids might. How are you feeling?"

Elizabeth's shoulders lifted in a small shrug. "It's still scary. And... sad, I guess. But I get it now. Animals aren't just—" she paused, struggling for words. "They're not just random. They're part of what keeps us alive."

"That's right," her grandmother said softly. "We raise them, respect them, and when it's time, we do our best to make it quick and use every part. That's the circle of life here."

Elizabeth stared at the dim horizon, recalling the chickens pecking in the yard and the deer's glassy eyes. "I never knew how much work went into food. I used to just see it in the grocery store."

A gentle breeze ruffled their hair. Her grandmother patted her knee. "We all learn something new when we face life this directly."

By the end of the week, Elizabeth had grown more accustomed to the rhythms of ranch life. While the sight of blood still made her stomach tighten, she no longer felt the urge to bolt from the room. Instead, she focused on the sense of purpose—collecting eggs, watering livestock, and even participating in the butchering process.

One afternoon, Isabelle teased her as they cleared feathers from a butchered bird. "Bet you never thought you'd do this in your wildest dreams, huh?"

Elizabeth shook her head, a small smile tugging at her lips. "No way. But... it's kind of cool in a weird, honest way. I get it now."

Evelyn chimed in, "You're braver than most city folk. Some can't handle the blood."

Elizabeth flushed, remembering how squeamish she had felt at first. But she realized that witnessing these harsh realities was changing her view not just of animals but of herself. She felt oddly stronger, as though each confronting moment chipped away at her old fears.

On the last night of her first week, the family gathered for dinner around a simple stew made from leftover chicken and fresh vegetables. Grandpa clinked a fork against his glass. "To a good harvest, good stock, and good folks around this table," he said gruffly.

Elizabeth chewed slowly, absorbing the warmth of the meal. She remembered the shock of watching her grandmother butcher that first hen and the chill that ran through her upon seeing the deer on the table, but also how each day's chores had taught her something profound—about sustainability, respect for animals, and her place in this interwoven life cycle.

After dinner, Elizabeth went outside and lingered by the coop, listening to the gentle clucking as the hens settled for the night. She inhaled the scent of hay, letting the quiet envelop her. In her mind, she whispered a small thanks—to the hens, the deer, the ranch, and perhaps even to the uncertain journey that had led her here.

She smiled to herself, recalling how days ago she could hardly stand the sight of butchering, yet now she felt at peace with it—an appreciation for the difficult, necessary tasks that fed her family. Tomorrow, more lessons would come. But for tonight, she embraced the deep contentment that came from facing the circle of life head-on and discovering her own resilience in the process.

63

A SHADOW IN THE NIGHT

Elizabeth believed the quiet ranch evenings might finally offer her some peace—but one dark night, a familiar shadow reminded her that true safety was far more elusive than she had ever imagined.

It was late. The ranch house was mostly dark, lit only by the muted glow of a single lamp in the living room and the flicker from a low-volume TV program. Curled up on the couch, Elizabeth tried to lose herself in the sketchbook her grandparents had gifted her. They had insisted she needed a creative outlet, and she cherished every page.

Her grandparents and aunts had retreated to their bedrooms hours ago, their distant snores or shifting footsteps the only background hum in the house. Elizabeth's eyelids grew heavy, yet she resisted sleep, savoring the gentle hush and the sense of relative calm.

She moved her pencil in slow arcs, attempting to capture the shape of a nearby lamp. A part of her mind drifted back to earlier that day—collecting eggs with Isabelle, laughing at Evelyn's joke about the rooster. "This is better than anything I had before," she reminded herself, exhaling softly. "I can breathe."

Just as she found a small pocket of relief, a hinge squeaked from down the hallway.

A chill ran down Elizabeth's spine. She glanced toward the hall leading to Julian's room, her heart skittering. The ranch, once so lively by day, felt ominous now in the late hours. She forced her gaze back to her sketchbook, hoping Julian would just walk past without noticing her.

But his silhouette, tall and imposing, emerged from the dark corridor. He paused, stretching as though he'd just woken. Elizabeth's breath caught in her throat. Don't look up. Don't speak. She swallowed, focusing on the faint hum of the television, wishing she could vanish into the couch.

"Still awake?" came Julian's casual drawl.

Elizabeth's pencil stilled on the page. "I'm just drawing," she mumbled, keeping her eyes low.

Julian shuffled closer, the soft pat of his bare feet loud in the quiet. "Don't you trust me?" he asked, his voice holding a too-familiar edge.

Her chest constricted. Trust him? No. Yet fear made her comply with his small talk. "I'm not tired yet," she offered, her voice trembling at the edges.

He leaned an arm on the back of the couch. "You should be, though. We've all got chores tomorrow." The tone was casual, but Elizabeth felt the tension crackling under his words—an unspoken threat that left her skin crawling.

She forced a thin smile, hands gripping her sketchbook. "I will soon." She tried to focus on the half-drawn lamp, ignoring the gaze she sensed on her.

As Julian lingered, Elizabeth's mind flickered with memories of other nights—nights when a harmless conversation turned into a terrifying ordeal. She remembered how, even in a house full of people, no one had heard, or at least no one had intervened. The sense of entrapment gnawed at her.

"You've always liked drawing," Julian commented lightly, his eyes on the pages in her lap. "I guess that's why you're so quiet—you've got your own little world, huh?"

Elizabeth bit the inside of her cheek. "It's all I have that's mine." She gave a tiny nod but didn't speak. A faint rustling from the hallway teased her with the possibility that someone else might be stirring. Please let it be Evelyn or Grandma, she silently begged. But no rescue came.

Julian stepped forward, slipping the sketchbook from her grasp and dropping it onto the floor. She stiffened. "No…"

He moved in, pressing too close, forcing Elizabeth back against the couch cushions. Her breath came in shallow gasps. She whispered a protest—"I—I'll go to bed, okay? Julian, please..."—but he didn't stop.

Time blurred into a haze of dread. She braced herself, her mind whirling with how to escape, but fear locked her limbs. The faint rattle of the TV provided no salvation; the house's silence betrayed her once more.

When it was over, Julian stood up, breathing heavily, and with a smirk that made her stomach lurch, he padded back down the hallway. The soft click of his door shutting echoed like a final condemnation.

Elizabeth lay unmoving for several long moments, tears gathering at the corners of her eyes but refusing to fall. The living room lamp cast a dull yellow glow over the rumpled blanket, her discarded sketchbook lying on the floor like a testament to her shattered bubble of calm.

She slowly reached over, picking up the book and placing it on the coffee table. "It's still better than living with my mother," she told herself, half-lie, half-hope, a hollow attempt at self-reassurance. At least Julian doesn't... doesn't hurt me physically. But the tremor in her limbs told her that pain came in many forms.

Pulling the blanket around her shoulders, she nestled into the couch cushions, too afraid to walk the dark hallway to her bed. The air felt stifling, the tension of the moment refusing to dissipate. She stared at the static shadows on the ceiling, her mind spinning.

She tried to doze off. Every noise—the groan of the fridge, the creak of a settling floorboard—sent a jolt of panic through her body. "Is he coming back?" The question kept her eyes flickering open. Eventually, weariness caught up with her. She drifted into an uneasy sleep, tears drying on her cheeks.

Before darkness claimed her, she forced herself to compare: yes, better than with Mom. Yet that statement felt hollow. The lingering memory of Julian's smirk haunted her final moments of consciousness, and all she could do was survive another night.

She curled into a tighter ball, hoping morning chores would bring enough distraction to keep her from falling apart. "I can't let this break me," she resolved, a quiet vow in the silence. Because if the ranch couldn't be her refuge, then what hope was left?

64

A NEW SUNDAY TRADITION

Elizabeth hoped Sundays at the ranch might offer a break from the usual grind. But one morning, a forced haircut and a sermon on "God's plan" made her question whether this new tradition was truly better—or just another way to control her.

Sunday dawned gently, with soft sunlight spilling into the girls' room. She rose early for chores; her grandparents had assured her that Sundays were different—work today is limited to feeding and watering. Excitement fluttered in her chest at the idea of a slower morning, bacon sizzling in the kitchen, and a new routine she didn't fully understand yet.

Her nose twitched at the aroma of cooking bacon as she pulled on the outfit she'd laid out. Yet, before she could dash to the kitchen, her grandmother intercepted her in the hallway.

"Hold on, sweetie," she said in a mildly stern tone. "Let's fix that hair of yours first."

Elizabeth blinked. "Sure... I can brush it."

Her grandmother shook her head, guiding Elizabeth toward the living room. There, a chair sat in the center, with a small table nearby holding a comb, brush, and—Elizabeth's heart lurched— scissors. She shifted nervously. "What's all this?"

Margaret patted the chair. "We're giving you a trim. Your hair is too long and gets tangled. Trust me, you'll thank me later."

A jolt of worry raced through Elizabeth. "I like it long. I can comb it on my own," she insisted, her voice faltering. She recalled how, back with her mother, no one had cared if she let it grow or not. This sudden concern of Margaret's felt unsettling.

"It's for the best," her grandmother replied, her voice firm but seemingly kind. She guided Elizabeth onto the seat, securing the length of hair at Elizabeth's nape in one swift motion.

"Wait," Elizabeth managed, a tremor in her tone, "you're really cutting it short?"

"Don't fret," Margaret said, not unkindly. "We just need something simpler for ranch life."

Before Elizabeth could protest again, she heard the scissors clamp down on her thin hair. A sharp snip, and the tension of her ponytail vanished. She gasped as the severed hair fell in a dark heap to the floor. Her hands flew up to the raw, uneven ends now skimming her neck.

Her grandmother smiled, oblivious to Elizabeth's shock. "All done. So much easier to handle, see?"

Elizabeth stared at the scattered locks, tears burning in her eyes. She fought them back, unwilling to show how upset she was. "Yes, ma'am," she whispered, swallowing the lump in her throat. This was the ranch's Sunday morning, apparently—obeying without question.

Still reeling, Elizabeth slipped into the bathroom to splash water on her face, avoiding the mirror that would confirm her new, rough-edged hairstyle. She forced deep breaths, hoping to quash the sense of violation roiling in her gut.

When she arrived in the kitchen, the table was laden with eggs, bacon, and biscuits. Grandpa sat sipping coffee, and Aunt Evelyn hummed as she stacked plates. The scent should have been mouthwatering, but Elizabeth felt hollow. She slid into a chair, her eyes downcast.

Her grandmother looked over. "There you are. It'll be time to leave for church soon, so eat up."

Elizabeth nodded. She poked at the eggs, struggling to summon any appetite. She felt a gentle nudge from Evelyn on her shoulder. "You look nice, Elizabeth," Evelyn offered softly, noticing the short hair. "It really shows your face."

Elizabeth forced a thin smile. "Thanks," she managed, though it felt like swallowing shards of glass. She took a few bites of bacon, the taste failing to comfort her.

After breakfast, Margaret ushered everyone into the old truck for the drive to church. Elizabeth clutched a thin set of scriptures her grandmother had given her, anxiety building in her chest. "What if I do something wrong?" she asked quietly, peering at the worn leather cover.

"Just behave," her grandmother replied simply. "Sit quietly, listen, and smile if folks greet you. You'll be fine."

Henry, at the wheel, navigated the roads with practiced ease. Elizabeth gazed out the window at the passing fields, mulling over her jarring haircut and the newness of attending church with her grandparents. A part of her felt excitement at trying something different, but the tightness in her chest refused to ease.

When they pulled up at the small white church, Elizabeth was startled by how crowded it was—dozens of cars lined up, families chatting on the lawn. The moment the family stepped out, people waved, calling her grandparents by name.

"Henry, Margaret! So good to see you both," someone called.

"And who is this young lady?" asked another, turning a friendly smile at Elizabeth.

She swallowed, forcing a polite nod. "I'm... Elizabeth."

Her grandmother gave her an approving look, and they headed inside.

Inside the church, the wooden pews gleamed under shafts of colored light from stained-glass windows. Elizabeth followed the family to seats near the front, her nerves prickling. She hugged her scriptures, remembering her grandmother's instructions.

As the service began, the minister stepped to the pulpit. Elizabeth's eyes widened when she recognized him—Uncle James, the one she'd barely met. She hadn't known he was the minister there.

He opened with a warm greeting, then delved into a sermon. "Today, we reflect on the great truth of God's plan," he proclaimed, his voice rich and deep, scanning the congregation with conviction. "Every moment of our lives is known to Him; every trial is part of His wise design. And why? Because in every sorrow, God has lessons to teach us. He loves us enough to let us learn."

Elizabeth gripped the edge of the pew. "God allowed sorrow?" The words lodged in her mind, stirring up memories of pain: her mother's cruel discipline, Julian's violation, even the forced haircut that morning. Her heart hammered. So this is part of His plan?

Uncle James's sermon grew more impassioned, referencing hardships as divine lessons and how God's love was behind it all. Each phrase felt like a dagger to Elizabeth's chest, her confusion blossoming into a quiet anger. "If He's so loving, why let me suffer?" she thought, tears prickling at her eyes.

After the sermon, the family stationed themselves at the church door, greeting the departing congregation. Elizabeth stood awkwardly beside her grandparents, forced to smile at strangers praising Uncle James's message. Her grandmother nudged her gently whenever she spaced out.

"You must be Elizabeth," a kindly older woman said, shaking her hand. "Lovely service, wasn't it?"

Elizabeth mustered a nod, her throat tight. "Yes, ma'am," she whispered, though inside she churned with the question: Could that sermon really justify all I've been through?

Eventually, the crowd thinned, and the family slid into the truck for the promised after-church ice cream. Elizabeth sat quietly, letting the sweetness of vanilla ice cream melt on her tongue. She tried to let the treat numb her confusion, but her thoughts kept drifting back to Uncle James's sermon and the cut hair that lay in a trash can at home.

Once back at the ranch, the sun hanging low in the sky, Elizabeth returned to her room. She placed her scriptures on the shelf as instructed, feeling an odd dissonance between the polished leather and her raw emotions. "If this is God's love, I don't want it," she thought grimly.

She brushed a hand over her newly shorn hair, the ragged ends reminding her how little say she had in her own life. Her grandmother's words—"You'll thank me later"—echoed, making her realize how little her feelings seemed to matter.

"Witches turn away from God's plan," Uncle James had warned during his sermon. "They reject His light and choose darkness. But Elizabeth couldn't see how darkness could be worse than a life where she was forced to accept every indignity as 'God's plan.' She'd survived her mother's house, Julian's shadow, and now a place where even a haircut wasn't her choice."

She stared at the small cross hanging by the door in the girls' bedroom, a gift to Margaret from her own mother. Slowly, she removed it and placed it into a drawer, her hands shaking. "I'm done." A sense of finality settled over her. If rejecting this plan labeled her a witch, then so be it—she would find her own path, a glimmer of control in a life that felt ruled by others.

Elizabeth peered out her window at the sprawling ranch, the fields dimming in twilight. She remembered how, earlier, she had sought to believe the ranch would be better than all she'd known. But illusions were cracking fast. She turned away, her shoulders tense. Then, with resolve, she thought it was better than living with her mother. At least the ice cream was sweet, she thought with bitter humor.

The day's events—her hair snipped away without permission, the sermon insisting her pain was preordained—stirred a growing rebellion in her chest. She inhaled, steadying herself. "I'll find my own truth," she silently vowed. No matter what names they gave her —"witch" or "sinner"—she'd rather claim the power to shape her fate than accept a destiny that condoned her suffering.

In the gathering dusk, Elizabeth stood straighter, a quiet anger fueling her determination. Tomorrow, she'd wake again to ranch chores, forced smiles, and everyone else's rules. But tonight, she let herself hold onto this small flame of dissent, a spark of will that might, one day, set her free.

65

UNINVITED SHADOWS

Elizabeth hoped Sunday nights on the ranch might finally mean rest —but when her grandparents drove Isabelle and Evelyn to a girls' event at the church, she realized she was left behind with Julian and Uncle James, and no one could keep the lurking menace at bay.

The Sunday sun dipped low, casting warm light through the ranch house windows as everyone gathered around the table for an early meal. Isabelle and Evelyn chatted about their upcoming girls' event at the church—some special evening activity they had been looking forward to all week. Their excitement filled the room, but Elizabeth found herself too tense to share it.

Henry methodically cut into his roast chicken, occasionally glancing at the clock. "We'll leave soon, so we're not late driving the girls," he said. "It's a bit of a drive to town."

Margaret nodded as she scooped mashed potatoes onto everyone's plates. "Elizabeth, honey, you've hardly touched your food."

Elizabeth shifted in her seat. "I'm just not very hungry," she said softly.

Across the table sat Julian, slowly sharpening a knife with slow, deliberate strokes. The metallic scrape echoed in her ears, each rasp sending a shiver up her spine. She could feel his eyes on her from time to time, though she avoided meeting them.

"Elizabeth," her grandmother prompted again, more firmly this time, "please try to eat. You need your strength for tomorrow's chores."

Swallowing her apprehension, Elizabeth took a few bites. "It's not the chores I'm worried about." Despite the aroma of roast chicken and freshly baked bread, anxiety settled heavily in her stomach, leaving no room for food.

When the meal ended, Margaret pushed back her chair. "We should clean up quickly so we can head out. Isabelle and Evelyn, gather your things. Henry, can you help me load the truck?"

Isabelle hopped to her feet, grabbing her purse. "Yes, ma'am. We don't wanna be late." She smiled at Elizabeth. "We'll bring you something fun from the church, maybe some goodies, okay?"

Elizabeth forced a nod, mustering a weak grin. "Sure, thanks."

Evelyn turned to her. "We'll only be gone a couple of hours. You'll be all right here with Uncle James and Julian, yeah?" The casual question lanced Elizabeth's heart.

She managed another nod, though her mind raced. Alone with Uncle Julian and Uncle James... who won't do anything if Julian decides to bother me. She pictured Uncle James absorbed in his own world, unlikely to interfere.

Margaret began stacking plates in Elizabeth's hands, snapping her out of her thoughts. "Here, sweet girl. Help me rinse these."

Elizabeth complied, moving to the sink. The soft swirl of water and soap comforted her momentarily as she scrubbed, but she remained acutely aware of Julian's presence behind her. He lingered at the table, still honing the knife blade.

A faint conversation drifted over from the living room, where Henry and Uncle James were discussing tomorrow's fence repairs. Isabelle and Evelyn bustled around, collecting jackets and church items. Yet, amid the normal family bustle, Elizabeth's dread only grew.

"All set," Henry called, stepping into the kitchen. He glanced at Elizabeth with a small, reassuring smile. "We won't be too long. You mind the house with Uncle James, okay?"

Elizabeth's grip on the dish towel tightened. "Yes, sir," she answered, her voice subdued.

Margaret offered a quick hug. "Be good, Elizabeth. If you need anything, Uncle James is in the study. He might be reading, but knock if you want him."

Elizabeth said nothing, her throat too tight for words. She felt a rush of guilt for not being able to express her fear, but what could she say? "Don't leave me with Julian." She had tried that once and had been dismissed as overreacting.

Isabelle and Evelyn each gave Elizabeth a passing wave and "See you soon!" before hurrying out the door. Uncle James walked behind them, apparently headed outside to check on something before returning to the study. The screen door banged shut, and within moments, she heard the truck engine start.

When the vehicle finally rattled away, silence flooded the house. Elizabeth kept her back to Julian, pretending to re-rinse a clean dish. Surely, Uncle James might keep Julian in line if he were awake, she told herself. But a part of her doubted it.

She heard Julian's footsteps on the floor, that measured, lazy gait. Her pulse thrummed. "Stay calm," she commanded herself, setting the dish on a rack to dry.

"Elizabeth," Julian drawled, leaning against the kitchen doorway. "You're awful quiet tonight."

She gripped the edge of the counter. "I'm just cleaning," she managed, her voice tight. "I'll go to bed soon."

Julian gave a low chuckle, the sound making her skin crawl. "With Mom and Dad, plus the girls, off at church... it leaves us with a free evening." He paused, letting the implication hang. "Uncle James is in the study, you know—he won't bother us. Don't you want to talk?"

Her heart hammered. "I'm... I'm tired," she whispered, trying to push past him.

Julian shifted, blocking her path with a casual step. "Not too tired for a little chat. Don't be rude."

Hating how her voice trembled, Elizabeth risked a glance at the hallway leading to the office. A faint yellow glow seeped from under the door, but she suspected Uncle James was too engrossed in reading or sermon prep to notice anything else.

"I—um," she began, "I just remembered some chores left in the barn. Maybe I should—"

"Liar," Julian said flatly, crossing his arms. "Isabelle did the barn chores hours ago. No chores for you."

Tears pricked her eyes. "I... I don't want to watch TV or anything," she murmured, forcing a polite tone. "I just want to rest."

He leaned in, his voice dropping to a menacing hush. "You used to be friendlier, Elizabeth. Don't you trust me?"

Her stomach lurched, remembering how trust had been betrayed so many times. She clutched the dish towel to hide her shaking hands. "I'm just tired," she repeated.

Julian smirked. "Fine, be that way." He stepped back, motioning to the living room with a jerk of his chin. "But you're not going to bed yet."

Mind-numbed, Elizabeth followed him to the living room. The lamp cast dim shadows across the worn couch. She perched stiffly on the cushion's edge, bracing for the worst. The television flickered with some random late show, but she couldn't focus on anything except the tension pulsing between them.

Julian sank down beside her, uncomfortably close. The slight squeak of the couch springs set her teeth on edge. He stared at the TV for a moment, then glanced at her. "You know, it's rude to ignore me," he said.

She swallowed. "I'm not... ignoring you."

He reached out, brushed a strand of her hair aside—an act that made her flinch. "Sure feels like it," he murmured.

A wave of helpless anger swelled in her chest. She wanted to recoil, to scream, "Stop touching me!" but she knew that defiance would only provoke him. Instead, she inhaled shakily, tears burning her eyes.

Minutes passed, or maybe hours—time lost meaning as Julian occasionally tried to draw her into conversation. She responded in monosyllables, trying not to provoke him. Uncle James's door remained shut. The faint sound of pages turning in the study was her only awareness that he even existed, and he seemed oblivious to the tension in the living room.

Finally, Julian let out a bored sigh. "I'm getting a drink," he said, sliding off the couch and padding to the kitchen. "Don't go anywhere."

The moment he disappeared, Elizabeth exhaled a trembling breath, her fingers digging into the couch cushion. She felt tears trickling down her cheeks. "No one's coming to save me," she thought, resentful of how easily her grandparents and aunts had left, unaware or unconcerned.

She stood, moving toward the hallway, hoping to slip away. But halfway there, she heard Julian rummaging in a cabinet—he'd be back any second. Uncle James's door was still closed. She stifled a sob, returning to the couch as footsteps approached.

Julian re-entered, glass in hand, noticing her attempt to stand. "You going somewhere?" he asked, his voice cold.

She forced a small smile. "Just stretching my legs."

He nodded, collapsing onto the couch again. Tension thickened like a weight in the air. She sat with a rigid posture, praying the family's errand wouldn't last much longer.

Julian didn't waste any more time. He penetrated Elizabeth, then dressed and plopped onto the couch to watch television.

Elizabeth's tears began to fall without her permission. She pressed her sleeve to her face, tasting the salt on her lips. She yearned for the rumble of a vehicle returning, for her grandmother's voice, for anyone to break this awful hush. The clock read just past nine.

She lingered a moment longer, too drained even to stand. "Better than living with her mother?" Elizabeth wondered bitterly in the dark. "Maybe," but the dread felt the same. She inhaled a shaky breath, letting the tears roll silently. Another night survived, another threat endured. One day, she promised herself, she'd break free of every uninvited shadow haunting her life.

66

UNINVITED GUESTS

Elizabeth believed the ranch's quiet evenings might shield her from further turmoil—until James's so-called friends arrived, and she learned no place was safe from uninvited shadows.

Sunday night draped the ranch in deepening darkness. Only the faint glow of the television pierced the hush inside the living room. Elizabeth sat stiffly on the worn couch, her heart pounding despite the seemingly mundane backdrop. She noticed Uncle James in his study down the hall and Julian idly flipping channels—those two presences offered anything but peace.

Earlier in the day, Henry and Margaret had taken Isabelle and Evelyn to a girls' event at the church, leaving Elizabeth behind. They expected to return later, trusting Elizabeth would be "under good care" with her uncles, Julian and James. But the knot of unease in her stomach insisted otherwise.

She heard a sudden knock at the front door. At first, she froze, thinking maybe her grandparents were finally back. A faint surge of hope fluttered in her chest. But then Uncle James's footsteps emerged from the study, crossing the house to greet unexpected company. Voices floated in, male and unfamiliar, jovial in a way that instantly put Elizabeth on edge.

"Come on in," James's voice boomed, followed by the creak of the door. Elizabeth risked a glance from the couch. She caught sight of two men entering—friends of James's, judging by their easy banter with him. They removed dusty hats and shook out the chill of the night air, chatting casually as they drifted into the living room.

Her heart thudded. "Why is James inviting them here so late?"

One of the men offered a lazy grin, scanning the modest furniture and settling into a chair. "Aren't you got the whole house to yourself tonight, James? Lucky man."

James shrugged. "Yep. Family's out." He flicked a gaze toward Elizabeth. "We've got some discipline to attend to tonight, anyway."

Elizabeth's skin prickled at the phrase, dread coiling in her chest. She saw Julian linger in the background, arms crossed. He looked annoyed, but at whom or what, Elizabeth couldn't tell.

A brief conversation ensued: the men joked about ranch tasks and chuckled about the daily grind. But their attention kept drifting to Elizabeth, an unsettling heaviness in each passing glance.

Elizabeth tried to shrink into the corner of the couch, hoping to vanish into the faded cushions. "Maybe they'll leave soon." But the clinking of metal from the kitchen shattered that fragile hope.

James reappeared, hefting a large metal basin—one she recognized from dog-bathing chores. He set it on the floor at the room's center, water inside sloshing with each step. The hush that followed felt suffocating.

Her throat turned dry. "He's done this once before," she realized with a sick jolt.

One friend cocked an eyebrow, a smirk tugging at his lips. "What's this about, James?"

James knelt by the basin, filling it further from a pitcher of steaming water he'd retrieved. "Teaching this girl some manners," he said coolly. His eyes locked onto Elizabeth. "Because they think they can do whatever they want. Not on my watch."

The men exchanged knowing looks, leaning forward in their seats. Julian hovered by the doorway, his expression unreadable. In an abrupt motion, he left for the bathroom, returning moments later with wet hair and annoyance etched across his face.

James's head snapped up at Julian's arrival. "Get on to bed," he ordered, waving a dismissive hand. "We don't need you here."

Julian paused, glancing at Elizabeth, tension flickering across his features. "Fine," he muttered, brushing past them. His door shut with a dull thud, leaving Elizabeth alone with James and the two strangers.

Elizabeth's heart roared in her ears. "If Julian is being dismissed, this must be worse," she realized. She shifted on the couch, her hands twisting in her lap.

James looked at her with grim finality. "You—get up. Come here."

She rose slowly, limbs trembling, eyes darting from James to the men. One friend gave a low chuckle; the other settled back as if awaiting a show. Elizabeth swallowed, attempting to find her voice, but no words emerged.

"Undress," James said, his voice so devoid of emotion it chilled her more than if he'd been shouting. "You'll bathe right here."

Elizabeth's breath caught. "P-please... can't I go to the bathroom to—?"

"Did I ask for your suggestions?" James's tone cut her off, a razor edge to his authority. "Now. And be quick about it."

Humiliation flushed through her body, but her mind screamed helpless warnings. "Arguing will only make it worse." She fumbled with the hem of her shirt, tears stinging her eyes. She heard the men's hushed remarks and caught glimpses of leering gazes.

Stepping into the basin felt surreal, the warm water a stark contrast to the cold pit in her stomach. She tried to crouch low, arms hugging her knees. "I have to disappear... but James wouldn't allow that."

"Stand up," he barked, grabbing a rough cloth. "I can't clean you if you're hiding."

Choking back a sob, Elizabeth rose, her arms shaking as she fought the urge to cover herself. James began scrubbing, each pass of the cloth biting into her skin. The men watched, murmuring idle comments that made bile rise in her throat.

Her cheeks burned, tears silently rolling down her face. She glimpsed one friend nodding in amusement, the other crossing his arms as if impressed by James's "discipline."

Occasionally, James growled, "Hold still," or "Stop flinching," as if her flinches were inconveniences rather than natural reactions to dehumanizing treatment. When he focused his thorough scrubbing between her legs, she began to cry out in pain. "Oh, shut up," he commanded.

Minutes dragged like hours, each second an assault on her dignity. She kept her gaze averted, unwilling to meet any of their eyes. A swirl of shame, fear, and bitter anger surged within her, but she felt too powerless to manifest it.

Finally, James tossed the cloth aside, satisfied with his grotesque display of control. "That's enough," he said, sounding bored. He pointed to her clothes in a heap. "Get dressed and go to bed. I'll see you next Sunday."

Stifling a shudder, Elizabeth stepped out of the basin, water trickling off her legs and leaving small puddles on the floor. She snatched her clothes, cheeks flaming, and dressed with trembling hands, careful to avoid looking at the smirking men.

Without another glance, she fled down the hall, each footstep a frantic desire to escape. Behind her, she heard faint laughter—like the men discussing a successful evening's entertainment. The sound twisted her insides.

When she reached the girls' room, she locked the door, though she knew it was a fragile barrier at best. Pressing her forehead to the wood, she exhaled shaky breaths, tears threatening anew. "He can pick locks anyway... but it's all I have." She quietly flipped off the light, letting the darkness envelop her.

She crawled onto the narrow bed, hugging her knees, her skin still stinging from the harsh scrubbing. Her mind raced through questions: "Would her grandparents sense her distress tomorrow? Could she hide the red marks on her arms and legs? What if they dismissed her fear as an exaggeration—yet again?"

No answers came. She blinked into the blackness, recalling how she once viewed the ranch as a refuge from her mother's tyranny. The suffocating quiet of the night reminded her that monstrous behaviors weren't confined to any single household. Everywhere she turned, a new shadow rose.

She lay there motionless, listening for the men's voices in the living room. A wave of relief washed over her at hearing no footsteps approaching. But the questions pounded, leaving her cold with dread. When does it stop? Does it ever stop?

"Better than living with my mother?" She wondered bitterly if her life was cursed to be a series of predators, each more brazen than the last. One day, she resolved in a silent vow, "I'll break free from every uninvited guest, every horrifying threat." "Yes," she whispered to herself, "better than with my mother."

Until then, she waited—another night endured, another haunting memory added to the pile. She squeezed her eyes shut, forcing herself to remain quiet, tears trickling onto the pillow. Dawn felt too far away, and the only armor Elizabeth had left was her silent promise to survive whatever darkness followed her tomorrow.

Then the moment she dreaded arrived: the doorknob was being turned.

67

THE CART RIDE

For Elizabeth, a battered old golf cart was more than a dusty relic— it was a fleeting chance to reclaim the carefree spirit of childhood, if only for one thrilling, wind-tossed moment.

After countless weeks of backbreaking chores on the ranch, the arrival of Aunt Linda and her children, Emma and William, brought a surge of excitement that permeated the entire house. Linda's energetic laughter echoed through the living room as she greeted her parents, Henry and Margaret, and chatted cheerfully with her sisters.

Elizabeth hovered at the edge of the conversation, a hint of a smile tugging at her lips. She felt a wave of relief seeing Emma and William again—two faces that reminded her life could be a lot worse. Their father was an alcoholic and drug addict who sometimes beat the children beyond recognition. They eventually moved to the ranch to keep prying eyes from calling the police. However, this visit was a fun vacation for everyone.

"Elizabeth!" Linda called, waving her over. "It's so good to see you. Your cousins have been dying to show you something outside."

Emma and William burst into the living room, backpacks flopping at their sides, eyes shining with anticipation. "Elizabeth, come on!" William blurted, tugging at her hand. "We've got to go— there's not much daylight left!"

Any formalities were forgotten as Elizabeth dashed out the back door, with Emma and William close behind. The sky was painted with orange and pink streaks, and a warm summer breeze rustled the grass underfoot. A faint squeak of the ranch gate accompanied their footsteps as they sprinted toward the bottom of the hill.

"I've missed you guys so much," Elizabeth said between breaths, her heart pounding with an unusual mix of joy and adrenaline. "It feels like forever since we played together."

William grinned. "Us too; we couldn't wait!"

Emma, adjusting her ponytail, shot William a teasing look. "He basically counted down every mile," she joked, giving Elizabeth a playful elbow. "He said we had to hurry up and get to the cart."

Near the bottom of the gently sloping hill sat the old golf cart, its paint chipped and faded by years of sun. The once-padded seats were long gone, leaving only a hard metal shell. No engine, no frills—just an empty frame perched on four squeaky wheels. Yet, to Elizabeth and her cousins, it was a treasure waiting to be revived for one more daring ride.

"There it is!" William announced as though he had made some grand discovery. His dramatic flair made Emma roll her eyes affectionately.

Elizabeth pressed a hand to the worn frame, the dull metal cool beneath her palm. She gave a small laugh. "It still looks as beat-up as ever. Didn't Grandpa say we might break our necks on this one day?"

Emma shrugged, her eyes dancing with mischief. "He said that last summer. And we're still alive, right?"

William grinned. "Let's push it uphill before it's fully dark and give it a good try."

They each grabbed a side of the cart—Elizabeth and Emma on one flank, William on the other—shoes digging into the dirt as they heaved. The squeak of the wheels and the crunch of gravel filled the air, accompanied by their labored breaths.

"Come on... we've got this," Elizabeth panted, summoning determination. A soft breeze ruffled her hair, carrying the scent of evening blossoms. The hill felt steeper than she remembered, each footstep heavier than the last.

"Hardest thing I've ever done," William wheezed dramatically, pausing to pretend-swoon. Emma snorted. "Stop being a baby. You say that every time."

Their banter lightened Elizabeth's load in ways more than physical. She smiled, pushing with renewed vigor. Finally, after much grunting and encouragement, they reached the crest of the hill, breathless and triumphant.

William dropped onto the cart's makeshift seat—a plank of wood they'd wedged in. Emma perched at the rear, while Elizabeth clung to one side, her heart pounding with excitement. She glanced at the rolling slope below them, her pulse already racing in anticipation.

"Are you ready?" Elizabeth asked, the corners of her mouth lifted in a genuine grin she seldom wore these days.

"Ready!" Emma cheered, bracing herself. "Push off, William!"

William gave a grunt of effort, and the cart tipped forward. Gravity seized them, sending the cart hurtling downhill. Wind whipped across their faces, the warm summer air roaring in their ears. The wheels squeaked and rattled against the uneven ground. Elizabeth let out a scream of both terror and delight, her arms tensing to keep from flying off.

For an instant, she forgot everything: the ranch chores, the fear, the tension that had knotted her chest day after day. They were kids —gloriously reckless, unstoppable. Laughter spilled from them like water from a broken dam.

Then, as often happened, the cart thumped against a large oak at the bottom of the hill. Its balance teetered dangerously. Elizabeth felt her stomach drop. "Oh no—" she managed before the cart lurched onto its side.

They tumbled free in a chaotic tangle, shrieks turning into breathless laughs. Elizabeth landed on her shoulder, the impact jarring but not devastating. A heartbeat later, Emma and William sprawled next to her, the cart lying on its side, one wheel spinning fruitlessly.

For a moment, they lay there, gulping for air. Then the first giggle escaped from Emma. Elizabeth followed, a giddy chuckle rising in her throat, and soon the three of them were laughing so hard they could barely breathe.

"That was... awesome!" William declared, his face smeared with dirt and his eyes shining with triumph.

"My elbow's scraped, but I'm fine," Emma announced, wincing

as she examined a small cut. She shot the others a grin. "No pain, no gain, right?"

Elizabeth sat up, patting dust from her knees. Despite the stinging bruise forming on her hip, a wild grin claimed her face. "Let's do it again," she said, her voice buoyed by adrenaline.

They whooped in agreement, pulling themselves upright. The cart might be a battered shell, but in this moment, it felt like a gateway to unbridled freedom. The burdens they carried—be it the ranch's constant chores or Elizabeth's heavier secrets—faded against the simple thrill of racing down a hill with cousins who shared her wonder.

With youthful defiance of exhaustion, they spent the next hour repeating the cycle—pushing, climbing in, and barreling down—until the sun slipped past the horizon, leaving streaks of purple and gold in the sky. Each crash ushered in fresh laughter; each scrape a new badge of daring.

Emma's hair flopped in her eyes, William's shirt gained another tear, and Elizabeth's cheeks hurt from smiling. As the final ride ended in another dusty tumble, they collapsed in a heap, sweaty and filthy but glowing with victory.

"We must be the bravest kids in the world," Emma declared, echoing her earlier sentiment, her voice quivering with laughter.

William flopped onto his back, gasping. "Definitely braver than any grown-up around here," he teased.

Elizabeth grinned at them both, her chest swelling with a sense of kinship she rarely felt these days. "And a little crazier too," she added, brushing grass from her jeans.

Nightfall crept in, a gentle breeze cooling their flushed faces. The three trudged back to the main trailer, clothes stained with mud and their arms peppered with minor bruises. Elizabeth inhaled the evening air, feeling more alive than she had in weeks.

"Think Mom will scold us for being this dirty?" William teased, wiping a smudge from his chin.

Emma rolled her eyes. "She can't complain. It's the ranch, after all."

Elizabeth chuckled, though her thoughts flickered to how her grandmother might comment on her torn clothes or scuffed elbows. Even so, the sense of freedom lingered in her chest. She couldn't shake the exhilaration; for that short while, she had tasted unbridled joy.

As they reached the porch, the golden glow from inside beckoned them with the promise of a normal evening—Linda chatting with Henry and Margaret, the clatter of plates, perhaps some friendly banter. Elizabeth quietly hoped the easy camaraderie would last.

Emma draped an arm around Elizabeth's shoulders. "We have to do that again tomorrow, right?"

Elizabeth gave her a warm smile. "Absolutely."

Inside, Linda's welcoming laughter spilled into the hallway. Elizabeth caught a glimpse of her grandmother glancing at their grubby state but breaking into an indulgent smile. It was worth the risk of mild scolding to see that affectionate amusement.

As Emma and William bustled into the house, regaling Linda with the tale of their cart escapades, Elizabeth lingered for a moment on the threshold. She replayed the hill's thrill in her mind —wind in her face, shrieks of laughter, and the astonishing feeling of being a normal kid, albeit briefly.

Despite the heavier shadows that haunted her daily, tonight, for a precious evening, she found solace in a simple cart ride. Each tumble and bruise somehow reaffirmed her resilience. If only every moment on the ranch could be so liberating.

A soft ache in her knee reminded her it couldn't always be. Still, as Elizabeth stepped inside, cheeks still flushed from smiling, she clung to the hope that these intervals of childlike joy might fortify her for the darker days—reminding her that not every shadow in her life was unrelenting, that sometimes, "laughter at sunset could be enough to carry her through."

68

GRANDPA'S TREASURE AND
JULIAN'S TARGET

Elizabeth expected an ordinary afternoon scouring "Pop's Treasures" with her cousins, but she never anticipated that Julian's twisted game would turn a dusty scrapyard into a battleground of fear and outrage.

Late afternoon light bathed the ranch in soft gold as Elizabeth led her cousins, Emma and William, up the gentle slope behind the house. They were fresh from riding the makeshift cart, knees still scraped from tumbles and hearts still thumping with excitement. But the trio craved new adventure—a chance to explore beyond the daily drudgery.

"Elizabeth," Emma asked, shading her eyes from the sun, "where exactly are we going again?"

She smiled faintly, gesturing at the silhouette of rusted vehicles and farm equipment sprawled across the hill's crest. "Up there," she said. "My mother calls it 'Pop's Treasures.' It's basically a giant junkyard, but we've always found cool stuff lying around."

William bounced on the balls of his feet. "Yes! Race you to the top!" He shot forward, prompting Emma and Elizabeth to laugh and sprint after him. The air smelled of sun-baked grass and dust, each footstep stirring the warm earth beneath their sneakers.

At the hill's peak stood a clutter of broken tractors, dented car doors, and full vehicles missing engines or other crucial parts. There was even an old, rusted engine still hanging in a tree. Here,

Grandpa's decades of collecting odd parts and junk converged into a bizarre labyrinth. The kids slowed, panting, as they surveyed the scrapped relics.

"This place is so cool," William breathed, as though spotting hidden treasure. "I bet there are a million things we can turn into a fort or something."

Elizabeth, mindful of her earlier cut on jagged metal, cautioned him. "Just watch out for sharp edges. Grandpa hates it when we move anything, anyway."

Emma stepped over a half-buried tire, her gaze roaming curiously. "He told me once that each piece here has its own story, like a broken puzzle of ranch history. It could be neat to see if we can figure any out—"

Her sentence died off as she spotted Julian perched atop the roof of an old, rusted VW Microbus. He was silhouetted against the deepening sky, a BB gun resting across his lap. Elizabeth's heart lurched. "Why is he here?"

"What's he doing?" William whispered, his voice hushed as though Julian might overhear from across the junkyard.

Elizabeth swallowed, uneasy. "He's always messing around out here. I—I don't know." Her gaze flickered to Julian's tight hold on the gun. A memory surfaced—Julian's casual cruelty from earlier days—and her chest tightened with fear.

Emma inched closer to Elizabeth. "Should we say something?"

Before Elizabeth could respond, Julian lifted the BB gun, squinting through the scope. Alarm flooded her. "Julian!" she called, her voice shaking. "Stop—what are you aiming at?"

He didn't answer. The gun's muzzle pivoted, triggering a wave of dread in Elizabeth's gut. Suddenly, a sharp pop split the air. The kids flinched, their hearts pounding. A startled bleat from behind them made them spin around, eyes wide.

A goat stumbled, reeling from a BB lodged painfully in its flank. William's jaw dropped. "He shot the goat?"

Elizabeth's anger surged, eclipsing her fear. "What is wrong with you?" she shouted up at Julian, fists clenching at her sides. "Why would you do that?"

Julian hopped off the car roof with a thud, boots kicking up dust. He leveled a cold stare at Elizabeth, the BB gun still in his grip. "It's just a stupid goat," he muttered dismissively. Then, ignoring their shock, he sprinted after the bleating animal, gun raised once more.

"No!" Elizabeth screamed, racing after him. Emma and William followed, eyes brimming with dread. They watched in horror as Julian steadied the gun on the fleeing goat and pulled the trigger once more.

This shot hit the goat square in the testicles. The creature collapsed with a yelp of agony, trembling on the ground. Emma gasped, covering her mouth in disbelief, while William let out a furious cry, "Leave it alone, Julian!"

Elizabeth's chest burned with outrage. "Stop that, you big jerk!" she shouted. Adrenaline shoved aside her usual caution—she had to stop him.

Julian spun on his heel, his scowl deepening. "You don't tell me what to do," he snarled. Lifting the BB gun menacingly, he aimed in Elizabeth's direction.

Emma and William fell silent, their faces pale, each step arrested by fear. Elizabeth's breath caught, but her anger burned brightly. "Put the gun down," she demanded, her tone wavering but resolute. "You're just hurting animals for no reason. That goat never did anything to you."

A twisted grin tugged at Julian's lips, though his eyes remained cold. "You think you can lecture me? Maybe I should shoot you next." He paused, letting the implication hang.

Elizabeth's heart hammered. She refused to look away, even as terror coiled inside her. "I can't let him think I'm backing down."

"Go on," she challenged quietly, though tears threatened to fill her eyes. "Show everyone what a coward you are—shooting goats, pointing guns at kids. I am pretty sure Grandma and Grandpa will have an opinion as well."

Julian's smirk faltered. He slowly lowered the BB gun, but not before firing another shot into the dirt near the goat's head, sending it stumbling away. The poor creature scrambled off, bleating pitifully and disappearing behind a twisted hunk of tractor metal.

Julian whipped around, frustration pouring off him in waves. "You think you're so brave, Elizabeth?" he hissed. "You and these punks want to boss me around? No." Anger radiated from him as he gestured with the BB gun. "I'll teach you all a lesson."

Nearby, an old truck bed cover rested on cinder blocks—

makeshift storage, another piece of Grandpa's random collection. Julian flicked his gaze there, a cruel glint sparking. "Under there," he snapped. "All of you."

William stepped forward, fists clenched. "We're not going anywhere—"

"Shut up," Julian growled, pointing the gun at William. "Move." The cousins exchanged alarmed looks, fear overshadowing any defiance. Elizabeth's limbs felt numb, but she nodded at them to comply, her heart racing. Don't make this worse.

The kids crawled under the low truck bed cover, stooping awkwardly amid shadows and debris. Elizabeth's mind spun. "He can't seriously—

He barked another command. "Clothes off. Now."

Emma choked on a sob. "Please—no—"

Julian brandished the BB gun, his face twisted in anger. "I said now. Unless you want me to show you what a real bullet can do."

Elizabeth's fingers shook as she tugged at her shirt hem. She shot a helpless glance at Emma and William, who likewise wrestled with their clothing. In the fading light, tears glistened on their cheeks.

As they shivered, half-dressed, an abrupt voice echoed from behind a rusted car. "What in the world is going on here?"

Elizabeth's head snapped up. Uncle James emerged, his face thunderous. Tension bled into her relief. "He's no saint," she recalled from past experiences, "but maybe he'll stop Julian's madness."

Julian whirled, frustration flashing across his features. "Mind your business, James."

But James advanced, eyes blazing at the sight of the shaken kids and Julian's raised BB gun. "The hell I will," he snapped. "Put that down, now."

Two of James's longtime buddies, who had been scouting for old tractor parts, followed him. The men took in the scene—Elizabeth and her cousins trembling, half-clothed, and Julian bristling with anger.

"Enough!" James's voice cracked like a whip. "Julian, you step away. Now."

Julian's scowl deepened, but he relented, lowering the BB gun.

"They were messing with me," he muttered petulantly, shooting Elizabeth a venomous glare.

With surprising swiftness, James seized the BB gun from Julian's hand, tossing it aside. His glare encompassed all the kids. "What the hell is this? I can't leave you alone for two minutes without chaos."

Elizabeth wanted to protest, to explain Julian's cruelty to the goat, how he'd threatened them. But the words stuck in her throat, uncertain whether James would care or blame them anyway.

William, fists balled at his sides, spoke up. "He—he shot the goat. Twice. And he threatened us with the gun."

Emma nodded through tears. "We... we didn't do anything."

Julian sneered. "Lies."

James shook his head, gesturing for the kids to quickly gather their clothes. "I'm punishing the lot of you. It doesn't matter how it started; I told you not to get into trouble around here."

Elizabeth's heart sank. "We're all in trouble? Even though Julian's the monster here?" She bit back tears, hurriedly redressing, shame burning her face.

At least James forced Julian to retreat. "Get to the house," he barked at Julian. "And you kids, too. This is done."

Slowly, the kids emerged from under the truck bed cover, reclaiming a shred of dignity in their rumpled clothes. Julian stomped off, muttering curses. Elizabeth shuddered, her thoughts lingering on the injured goat and the horror of Julian's threats. No real justice for that poor animal, she realized.

James turned to the men. "Take a look around, see if there's anything we missed for the tractor repair." His tone was gruff, as though brushing the matter aside with no real attempt to differentiate between victims and aggressors.

He then shooed the kids toward the path leading back to the ranch house. Elizabeth, Emma, and William trudged along, hearts heavy, each step feeling like a betrayal of their innocence. William's face was red with indignation, and Emma's tear-streaked cheeks reflected confusion.

Elizabeth's head spun. How did a simple quest for Grandpa's old treasures transform into another horrifying close call? She turned back to see Julian's silhouette vanishing into the twilight. She swallowed a mix of relief and anger.

As they neared the house, the last rays of daylight cast long shadows across the yard. Emma wiped her eyes, trying to regain her composure. "I can't believe he shot that goat," she whispered hoarsely. "What if it's hurt really badly?"

Elizabeth's chest tightened. "We should check on it tomorrow," she said softly, though she dreaded the possibility that no one would care except for them.

William rubbed his elbow, still trembling with adrenaline. "I hate him," he muttered. "He's a monster."

Elizabeth placed a tentative hand on his shoulder. "I know," she murmured. "We'll... figure something out. Just... don't provoke him alone, okay?"

They reached the porch, Uncle James trailing behind. He opened the door with a glower, motioning them inside. "Wash up. I'll deal with you brats in the morning."

Elizabeth sighed, stepping over the threshold. The ranch house's warm lamplight felt hollow after such a violation. No comfort awaited them, just another harsh reminder that safety remained elusive. She ushered Emma and William toward the bathroom, wanting at least to calm them, if not herself.

As they crossed the threshold, Elizabeth silently vowed to keep watch over her cousins. She recalled the goat's anguished bleat, the truck bed cover overhead, and Julian's twisted smirk. Another vicious memory was added to her life's stack of wounds.

But we survived. The thought flickered, a stubborn ember of resilience. For tonight, that would have to be enough.

69

A FLAMING START

Elizabeth hoped this bigger, nicer apartment might finally quell the chaos that had been her constant companion. But despite her reluctance, her brother Oliver's reckless ideas ignited a blaze, turning their fresh start into yet another scorched memory.

Elizabeth trudged into her mother's latest apartment with a duffel bag slung over her shoulder. She paused in the entryway, struck by how different it looked from their usual cramped, peeling-wall places. The floors were bright linoleum, the rooms open and well-lit, and even the furniture seemed newer. It felt more like a real home than any she'd known in a long time.

Her mother, flipping through envelopes at the sleek dining table, barely glanced up. "Elizabeth, put your stuff in my room; we will be sharing. And behave—I'm not getting evicted again."

"Yes, ma'am," Elizabeth murmured. A familiar knot of anxiety twisted in her chest. Even if the surroundings were pleasant, old patterns could shatter anything.

Oliver, sprawled on a white recliner, smirked at her. "Hey, sis. Not bad, right? At least we've got space."

She managed a small shrug. "I guess." The sunny windows and clean paint couldn't erase the memory of past disasters. Still, a flicker of hope surfaced in her mind: maybe this time they could avoid repeating the cycle.

For several days, calm lingered. Then, one afternoon, Elizabeth was in her bedroom—a wide, airy space that actually smelled of fresh paint—when Oliver barged in. His eyes danced with the mischievous energy that always spelled trouble.

"Did you notice that unit next door?" he asked, lowering his voice conspiratorially. "Vacant. Window's partly open. We should check it out."

Elizabeth tensed. "Oliver... I just got here. If Mom finds out we're snooping—"

He rolled his eyes. "We'll get spanked anyway if nothing happens, so we might as well have fun, right?" A grin tugged at the corner of his mouth. "Come on, we'll be quick."

A pang of unease clutched her. She wanted to refuse, but Oliver's logic stung. "We do get punished for things big or small." Steeling herself, she sighed. "All right, but let's keep it short. Let's try not to get caught."

He winked, leading her to the hallway. "Short and sweet. Trust me."

They slipped outside and across the corridor. The adjacent door was locked, sure enough; its window was slightly ajar. With a little effort, Oliver eased it open, gesturing for Elizabeth to come in.

She hesitated, glancing around. "Okay, hurry," she whispered, her heart thumping. They clambered inside, feet landing on the spotless floor. It smelled faintly of cleaning solution and stale air.

Oliver scanned the bare living room. "There might be leftover stuff," he said, rummaging through a half-open closet. Elizabeth's guilt rumbled in her gut. "We shouldn't be doing this." But she kept silent, drifting to the kitchen area and checking the cupboards. They were mostly empty.

Before long, they concluded there was nothing of value. Elizabeth felt relief trickle in. "Let's get out," she said, her voice quieter now. "I don't want to push our luck."

Oliver shrugged and agreed, climbing back out the window. Elizabeth followed, exhaling as they reentered their own apartment. "At least we didn't get caught—this time."

But Oliver's restlessness only grew. Late one evening, Elizabeth woke to a bitter, acrid smell creeping in through her open bedroom window. Fear sparked in her chest. Racing to the living room, she found Oliver standing at the window, his gaze locked on the apartment next door—now lit by the glow of flickering flames.

"You started a fire next door?" she gasped, her heart pounding.

Oliver's eyes shone with adrenaline and guilt. In his hand, she glimpsed a can of hairspray and a lighter. "I was messing around," he admitted, his voice unsteady. "I tried to, like, write my name in fire. I didn't think it would catch the walls."

"Are you crazy?" Elizabeth cried, her voice trembling. "You'll burn this building down!"

Sirens wailed outside, the bright reds and blues dancing through their windows. Oliver grabbed her wrist. "We need to hide," he hissed. "The police will come asking questions."

Her stomach knotted. "We can't face them." But a surge of fear overtook any rational thought. "Alright," she managed, letting him pull her toward his bedroom.

They darted into Oliver's room, slamming the door behind them. The faint stench of hairspray still clung to his clothes. "Get under here," he said, pointing beneath the bed. "We wait until they're gone."

Elizabeth's heart hammered as she dropped to her knees, crawling under the wooden frame. Dim light filtered through the bed slats. She could hear shouting in the hall, the distant crackle of radios, and muffled orders from firefighters or neighbors. Adrenaline pumped through her veins, stirring an odd blend of terror and the reckless thrill of having participated.

Oliver pressed a hand over his mouth, breathing quickly. "See? Told you it'd be fun," he whispered, a twisted grin betraying his nerves.

Elizabeth shot him a glare. "Fun? We could get arrested," she hissed back, her voice shaking. Yet beneath her anger, she felt a jolt of rebellious exhilaration. *He's not entirely wrong. I'll get spanked no matter what—*

They lay there, time stretching painfully. The sirens eventually dimmed, and frantic voices receded. After several agonizing hours, it all quieted. Oliver smirked. "They're gone."

Elizabeth exhaled shakily, guilt tangled with the lingering rush of near disaster. "But will they really not figure it out?"

The following day, the building manager banged on their door, accompanied by a furious mother who waved a fine notice in Sophia's face. "The police know it was kids messing around next door—yours!" the manager seethed, scowling. "You're paying to fix the damage." Sophia closed the door. The manager slapped a final ultimatum: cover the damages or face eviction. Tension suffocated the apartment.

In the bedroom, Sophia glowered, belt in hand. "You think I'm made of money? First, I get complaints about you two prowling, now a fire? You can both get ready for the whipping of your lives."

Oliver looked away, sullen. Elizabeth swallowed, shame coiling deep. She understood they had gone too far—but for a flicker of time, it had felt freeing to rebel. Now all that remained was the sting of consequences.

Their mother's fury erupted in belt lashings, both siblings yelping at each turn. Elizabeth winced under each blow, thinking, "We deserve some of this, but do we deserve all of it?"

Paying for repairs crippled their mother's finances. Within days, the building manager delivered the eviction notice. Elizabeth discovered it pinned to the door after an errand. Her breath caught, reading the word "Evicted" in bold. That's it. Another place lost.

The final evening in the once-hopeful apartment oozed resentment. Their mother snarled at them while boxing up possessions. "Couldn't even last a month without a fiasco. Do you know how good we had it here?"

Elizabeth stared at the wide windows that had once made the space feel bright. Now, the walls reminded her of black scorch marks and a near disaster.

Oliver rolled his eyes as he tossed his clothes into a box. "We'll find someplace else," he muttered. "Mom can't blame you for everything."

Elizabeth almost snapped back but felt drained. Maybe they both shared blame—he'd gone along with her, after all. Shoulders slumped, she packed her own things. A pang of regret mixed with a rebellious aftertaste from their near arrest. We definitely had "fun," but at what cost?

Nightfall draped the complex in shadow as they hauled boxes to their mother's car. Elizabeth paused at the entrance, remembering how she had first stepped inside, naïve enough to hope. The overhead light flickered, mocking any notion of a fresh start.

Her mother stormed out, scowling at the pile of belongings. "Get in," she spat. "We're gone. I'm done wasting money on fines."

Climbing into the car, Elizabeth sank against the window. She watched the apartment's bright lights disappear behind them. Another place, ruined. Another chance, gone. She glanced at Oliver, who gazed at passing streetlights, wearing a mix of irritation and apathy.

A swirl of conflicting emotions raged in her: regret, guilt for the damage, and an odd longing for the rebellious thrill that had momentarily made her feel alive. But mostly, she felt weary. "A new spanking, a new home," she thought sourly, tears stinging her eyes.

Even in the hush of the back seat, she formed a silent vow: one day, she would break free from this relentless pattern, no longer a prisoner of her own family's recklessness. For now, the taillights receded down the road, leading them to yet another uncertain tomorrow, leaving only the scorched memory of what might have been a stable home.

70

A FRAGILE NEW HOME

Elizabeth welcomed the idea of staying in the same school district, convinced that the proximity would make the move easier. Yet even a new address couldn't shield her from the wrenching betrayal that would soon unfold.

Evicted from their previous place—for what felt like the tenth time—Elizabeth's mother, Sophia, managed to secure a modest, single-story house still within the same school zone. Elizabeth couldn't hide her relief; at least she wouldn't have to say goodbye to teachers and friends yet again.

Though older in style—complete with a wide porch and original wooden shutters—the house was in good condition. The paint showed gentle wear, and the porch steps squeaked, but the inside boasted spacious rooms and sturdy floors. Sophia, who had recently landed a better-paying position at her company, seemed untroubled by finances for once. She looked almost pleased as she supervised the movers.

"Elizabeth, take these boxes to your room," Sophia directed, her tone brisk but not irritated. "We should have everything set up before dark."

Elizabeth nodded, maneuvering around the couch and coffee table. She allowed herself a tiny spark of optimism. "Maybe we can stay here longer." She glanced at Oliver—her brother—who was shoving electronic cables into a box.

"This place isn't bad," he said, flashing her a quick grin.

Elizabeth shrugged, a half-smile forming. "I like it. And same school, so I'm not complaining."

Within a week, they settled into a familiar, if uneasy, rhythm. The house felt comfortably lived-in: old floorboards creaked in the evenings, and a light breeze carried the scent of cut grass through the wide windows. Despite the chill of moving again, Elizabeth clung to the relief of consistent classes and friendships.

After school, she split her time between homework in her bedroom and helping Sophia with chores. Sophia's new job kept her out late many nights, but at least the bills were no longer a looming threat. Occasionally, Elizabeth glimpsed a weary relief in her mother's eyes, as though a stable paycheck smoothed a part of life's rough edges.

Still, tension hovered beneath the surface. Sophia had made it clear: "No more trouble, or we're out again." Neither Elizabeth nor Oliver cared to test her patience.

In the midst of this fragile calm, Elizabeth found an unexpected bright spot: a boy named Mike. They crossed paths at school— introduced casually by a mutual friend during lunch break. With an easy smile and a gentle demeanor, Mike captured Elizabeth's attention instantly.

They clicked in small ways at first: chatting about shared teachers, trading quick jokes about the cafeteria's questionable food. Then came a day when he walked her home, offering to carry her books. His tall frame, calm stride, and the way his eyes lit up when he smiled all gave Elizabeth a disorienting sense of comfort she rarely felt.

A few afternoons later, he left a note on her locker—just a short, sweet message about how her eyes lit up in geometry class. Elizabeth blushed so fiercely that she pressed the paper to her chest, grinning despite herself. "He's so sweet," she thought, half-disbelieving that someone could be so openly kind.

Over the following weeks, their bond deepened. Sometimes, Mike snuck her a flower—stolen from a neighbor's garden, he'd admit with a cheeky grin—and teased that even a swiped rose was better than none at all. Elizabeth savored these small gestures, each an antidote to the lingering turmoil of home. She found herself daydreaming about his gentle laughter and the way he spoke softly whenever she talked about her life.

One chilly afternoon, he offered to carry her backpack again. "It's heavy," he said, hunching his shoulders in mock exhaustion. "What are you hiding in here—bricks?"

She giggled, feeling a warmth spread in her chest. "Textbooks, obviously. You're just weak."

He laughed, leaning a bit closer than usual. "Blame the school system, not me. They say education is key, but my arms are paying the price."

For a fleeting moment, Elizabeth allowed herself to hope that this new environment—a stable house, a sweet boy—could foster something almost normal for her.

One Thursday after school, Elizabeth invited Mike over while Sophia was still at work, wanting to share a quiet hour watching a show or listening to music in her bedroom. The house was calm, with older walls muffling the outside world.

Her cheeks burned with excitement and nerves. "He's so caring," she reassured herself as they sat on her bed, discussing weekend plans. But when their playful banter moved to gentle kisses, something in Mike's demeanor shifted.

Suddenly, his kisses became rougher, insistent. He nudged her back onto the mattress, pressing his body against hers. Elizabeth tensed—this is too much, too fast, she thought. "Wait, Mike—" she murmured, half-laughing, half-uncertain. But he didn't pause, his hands roaming with a fierce urgency.

Her heart pounded in alarm. "Mike," she tried again, her voice cracking, but he ignored her quiet protests, pinning her wrists. A wave of confusion and fear crashed over her. He fumbled with her clothing, determined to take "what all men take," never asking if she agreed.

Elizabeth fought a gasp, her mind reeling at the betrayal. "This can't be happening; he was so sweet—but the reality of his weight on her, his unrelenting push, shattered any illusions. Her pleas softened into a numb shock, tears slipping unheeded. He finished with a triumphant sort of calm, then patted her hair as though everything were normal."

"We're closer now," he said quietly, almost smug. Then he

adjusted his shirt and left her lying there, her body trembling with the raw sting of violation.

In the days that followed, Mike maintained his outwardly charming facade at school—carrying Elizabeth's books, leaving sweet notes—but behind closed doors, whenever he came over, the forced acts continued. "We're just having fun," he'd insist, pressing kisses that turned into stifled pleas and pinned limbs.

Elizabeth found herself frozen, torn between the warmth of his public gestures and the horror of his private demands. Each time she considered breaking free or screaming for help, the fear of blame or scorn silenced her. She recalled all the times Sophia or others hadn't believed her about lesser issues. "No one will believe me now," she thought bleakly, shame creeping in every time she endured Mike's visits.

At school, people noticed how Mike and Elizabeth seemed inseparable, assuming a cute romance. Elizabeth attempted smiles, trapped in a swirl of conflicting emotions. She still felt something for the gentle boy he presented outside the bedroom, though she dreaded the moment he would corner her again.

Elizabeth's mother, preoccupied with her new job and the house's minor repairs, paid little attention to her daughter's reverted demeanor. Oliver was too busy flirting with trouble to sense Elizabeth's distress. And so, the walls of their home offered no protection from the daily dread building in Elizabeth's heart.

One afternoon, after another forced encounter, Elizabeth sat on the edge of her bed, eyes hollow. "Is this what love is supposed to be?" she wondered, hugging her knees. Even the memory of Mike's stolen roses felt tainted now.

She toyed with telling a teacher or counselor, but the swirl of fear—of not being believed, of being blamed—won out. She locked the secret away, letting her silent tears soak into her pillow.

71

CALIFORNIA FRESH

As the car rumbled away from Texas, Elizabeth's heart soared at the prospect of sunny skies and new beginnings in California—her chance to leave the past behind and embrace a future filled with promise.

Sophia's recent promotion and transfer had finally granted the family a fresh start in California, and as the sleek sedan glided smoothly along the highway, Elizabeth felt something she hadn't experienced in years: excitement. The spacious car, with its gleaming interior and modern comforts, was a stark contrast to what Elizabeth was used to, and her eyes sparkled as the vast Texas plains gave way to rolling hills and distant city lights.

"Mom, look at those trees!" Elizabeth exclaimed, pressing her face to the window. "It's as if the whole world is changing right before our eyes."

Sophia smiled in the rearview mirror. "That's right, honey. We're leaving behind old troubles and stepping into something new. You'll have a fresh start in California—a new school, new friends, and even a new home."

Oliver, sitting beside her, grunted, "New place, new rules, huh?"

Elizabeth giggled, her heart light. "Maybe new rules mean fewer fights and more fun. I can't wait to see what's out there!"

Sophia's voice was warm and reassuring as she continued, "I

want you both to enjoy every moment, and I promise this move will be the best thing that's ever happened to us."

Elizabeth's pulse quickened with anticipation as they rolled down the highway. She couldn't help but imagine the vibrant life that awaited her—sunny beaches and endless opportunities for adventure. Every mile they covered seemed to wash away a bit of the past.

After nearly two days on the road, the sedan pulled into a charming apartment complex nestled in a quiet California town. The building boasted a tasteful blend of old-world character and modern upgrades—well-manicured hedges, polished entryways, and large windows that spilled golden light into the corridors. Elizabeth's eyes widened in delight as she stepped out of the car.

"Wow, Mom, this place is amazing!" she said, her voice filled with wonder as she took in the neat façade and inviting atmosphere.

Sophia nodded, her expression proud. "I worked hard for this, Elizabeth. I wanted us to have a fresh start, a safe space where we can build a better future."

Elizabeth's heart soared. "I can't believe we're really here," she whispered, a smile spreading across her face. "Maybe I'll even make some new friends."

Inside, the apartment was spacious and bright. Due to the higher cost of this complex, Sophia could only afford a two-bedroom. She decided that Oliver would have one bedroom and Elizabeth would sleep on the couch. "Make sure you keep the living room clean at all times."

Elizabeth sighed. "Yes, ma'am," she said with obvious disappointment.

Later that evening, as the family sat down to a hearty dinner prepared by Sophia, the conversation was lighter than it had been in a long while. Over plates of fresh salad and warm bread, Sophia asked, "Oliver, what do you think about your new room? Any ideas on how you'd like to decorate it?"

Oliver beamed, his excitement palpable. "I'd love to hang up some of my posters—some of cars and my favorite bands!"

Elizabeth, half-listening, mumbled, "Sounds cool, Oliver."

Sophia smiled softly. "We'll make it happen. This is our new start, and I want you both to feel at home here."

The next morning, Elizabeth woke early with a sense of purpose.

Stepping out the front door, she took a deep breath of the crisp California air—a far cry from the arid heat of Texas. The distant murmur of the ocean mixed with the gentle rustle of leaves, and for a moment, Elizabeth allowed herself to believe that perhaps this new beginning could be different from the past. She was mesmerized by the smell of salt in the air.

At breakfast, Oliver and Elizabeth chatted animatedly about their new school, their friends, and the exciting possibilities ahead. "Do you think they'll have a cool art club at my school?" Elizabeth asked, her eyes sparkling with hope.

Oliver shrugged nonchalantly. "Maybe. You always had the best ideas, anyway."

Their mother joined the conversation. "I know change is hard, but I promise you, California is a place for new opportunities. You both deserve a fresh start." Her tone was gentle, yet filled with determination—a stark contrast to the past.

Elizabeth's smile widened. "I'm really looking forward to it, Mom. I'm going to try my best to make this work."

Yet, amidst the excitement, Elizabeth couldn't shake a tinge of sadness at the thought of leaving her old friends behind in Texas. Later that day, while on a brief phone call with her best friend back in Arizona, Amy, Elizabeth's voice trembled with a mix of joy and sorrow.

"Amy, I'm really excited about this move," she confessed, her eyes bright as she imagined her new life. "But I will miss you so much."

Amy's voice was soft and understanding. "I know, Elizabeth. But sometimes a fresh start is exactly what you need. Promise you'll write, okay?"

"I promise," Elizabeth replied, feeling the weight of the promise settle on her. "I'll keep you updated on everything."

As the sun set over the new apartment, Elizabeth sat on her makeshift bed in the soft glow of the setting light, a gentle smile playing on her lips. Outside, the warm California night whispered of hope and change.

Sophia came to check on her, her face softening as she looked at Elizabeth. "How are you feeling about everything?" she asked, genuine concern lacing her voice.

Elizabeth's eyes sparkled with cautious optimism. "I'm excited,

Mom. I know it won't be perfect right away, but I feel like this time might really be different."

Sophia's smile deepened. "I believe it too, Elizabeth. We're starting fresh, and I promise I'll do everything I can to make this work."

For the first time in a long while, Elizabeth allowed herself to believe in the possibility of stability—a chance to build new friendships, discover fresh opportunities at her new school, and perhaps even heal from the pain of her past. As she settled under her cozy quilt that night, she closed her eyes with the thought that, in California, the future might finally be hers to shape.

72

UNFAMILIAR AFFECTION

Sometimes, the softest whisper can change everything—if you're brave enough to listen.

Elizabeth's heart pounded with a strange new hope as she stepped into her first day at her new California school. The promise of a fresh start had arrived like a gentle breeze after years of stormy skies. Everything felt different—lighter, somehow. In the corridors, the cheerful strains of Beach Boys songs crackled over the intercom. The rule was simple: one song's worth of time to get to your next class. As she walked the brightly lit halls, Elizabeth found herself humming along, each note a small reminder that this place might be different from the past.

Her teachers, warm and encouraging, took the time to explain assignments and answer questions, and for the first time in what felt like forever, Elizabeth sensed that she wasn't merely surviving; she was beginning to thrive.

After classes ended, a new experience awaited her on the school bus. The bus was overcrowded, and most students took the city bus home instead. Nervous and unsure, Elizabeth climbed aboard, her stomach fluttering with uncertainty. But as soon as she stepped onto the bus, her eyes fell upon him.

Jeremy.

He was a high schooler with dark hair that fell just above his eyes; his quiet, brooding presence was unmistakable amid the chaos of the bus. His dark, mysterious gaze drew Elizabeth in like gravity, and she found herself unable to shake the thought of him for days afterward.

A week later, Elizabeth noticed him again—in the same seat at the back. Something stirred inside her, a mix of bravery and curiosity. Gathering her courage, she left the front seats and slid into the space next to him. In that small, silent proximity, her heart raced, and her cheeks warmed with excitement. No words were exchanged for many days, each journey reinforcing the quiet, unspoken connection until, finally, one day, Jeremy broke the silence.

"Hey," he said as she settled into her seat. His voice was calm, carrying a gentle amusement that sent a nervous flip through her stomach.

Caught off guard, Elizabeth's cheeks flushed as she managed a timid "Hi."

"You're new, right?" he asked, his tone casual and inviting.

Elizabeth nodded. "Yeah."

"I've seen you around," he continued with a small, encouraging smile. "You're always so quiet."

For a long moment, her heart pounded so fiercely she was sure he could hear it. Then Jeremy leaned back, his gaze steady and warm as he introduced himself. "I'm Jeremy. What's your name?"

"Elizabeth," she replied, her voice trembling with a mix of awe and uncertainty.

"Nice to meet you, Elizabeth," he said, and in that simple phrase, something in her stirred.

The bus ride that day seemed to stretch on endlessly, but Elizabeth didn't mind. For the first time, she felt seen—truly seen by someone who didn't simply brush her aside. When the bus finally slowed at his stop, Jeremy turned to her with a relaxed grin. "Wanna come over?" he asked, as naturally as if inviting a friend for a walk.

Elizabeth hesitated for only a fraction of a second before nodding. "Sure," she whispered, her voice barely above the hum of the engine.

As she followed him off the bus, her pulse fluttered wildly. The neighborhood was a world away from the cramped apartments and shadowed memories of her past—a place of sprawling homes with manicured lawns and towering trees. Jeremy led her up the driveway of one of the largest houses—a sprawling two-story home that seemed plucked from a movie set. Inside, the ceilings soared, and every surface shone with meticulous care, a stark contrast to everything Elizabeth had known.

"Come on," Jeremy said, motioning her toward the kitchen. The space was enormous—modern, with shiny countertops and a central island that gleamed in the soft light. As he opened the fridge and began pulling out ingredients for sandwiches, he asked casually, "Are you hungry?"

"A little," Elizabeth admitted.

He handed her a plate, piling his sandwich high with layers of turkey, cheese, lettuce—and something unusual: a generous heap of green sprouts.

"What's that?" Elizabeth asked, her curiosity piqued as she pointed to the sprouts.

"Sprouts," Jeremy replied with a shrug. "They're good. You should try some."

Hesitant but intrigued, Elizabeth added a small handful to her own plate. When she took a bite, the fresh, slightly nutty flavor surprised her. "Not bad," she murmured, and Jeremy's smile widened in quiet satisfaction.

They spent the afternoon at the kitchen island, sharing sandwiches and stories. Elizabeth talked about her love for art and her favorite songs, carefully skimming over the darker parts of her past. Jeremy spoke of his school, his friends, and even his dreams of becoming a musician. In that simple, unguarded conversation, Elizabeth felt herself slowly opening up. For once, she wasn't weighed down by the burdens of her past; here, in Jeremy's comfortable, kind presence, she felt like just a regular girl—laughter replacing old fears, hope mingling with each shared secret.

Yet even as the hours melted away in their newfound connection, a shadow of doubt lingered in the recesses of Elizabeth's mind—a tiny, persistent voice that reminded her of the pain and betrayal she had known before. She couldn't fully trust the moment, even as Jeremy's gentle kiss on her cheek—a spontaneous, tender gesture as the duo waited at the bus stop—made her heart flutter in a way that was both exhilarating and terrifying.

For days, this quiet courtship continued. Elizabeth would board the bus, sit next to Jeremy, and let her heart race in the silent intimacy of that shared journey. But with each passing day, her hope for connection battled with the echo of past hurts.

"Wanna come over?" echoed in Elizabeth's dreams.

As the sun dipped low one evening, Elizabeth finally stepped through the front door of her own home, and that fragile bubble burst. Her mother, Sophia, stood there—arms crossed, face etched with worry and anger.

"I was worried you got hurt. Where have you been?" Sophia demanded sharply.

Elizabeth opened her mouth to explain, but before she could utter a word, Sophia's face darkened with confusion and then something colder—something that made Elizabeth's blood run cold.

"I know that smell," Sophia hissed, her nostrils flaring as she took in Elizabeth's disheveled appearance. "What have you done?"

Before Elizabeth could answer, Sophia's hand struck her hard across the face. The blow sent Elizabeth staggering to the floor, shock and pain intertwining with the bitter taste of betrayal.

"Go to your room, you whore!" Sophia thundered. "And you will never see him again."

The words stabbed through Elizabeth like a blade. Tears welled in her eyes as she scrambled to her feet, clutching her burning cheek. There was no point in protesting; Sophia's decision was always final.

Elizabeth fled to her room, slamming the door behind her as her heart shattered under the weight of that cruel decree. She could still feel the echo of Jeremy's soft kiss on her lips—a moment of tenderness now buried beneath the sting of her mother's abuse and rejection. Alone in the darkness, she resolved to hide Jeremy's number deep within her secret stash, a small, defiant rebellion against the harshness of home.

As she sat on the edge of her bed, tears mingling with a fierce, quiet determination, Elizabeth whispered into the silence, "Just make it to tomorrow."

It was a fragile vow—a desperate promise that, despite the familiar, unyielding cruelty waiting for her at home, she would try to survive another day with hope flickering in the darkness.

73

A STRANGER AT THE DOOR

The knock came unexpectedly—sharp and insistent—shattering the fragile calm Elizabeth had grown accustomed to. In that split second, everything changed.

One warm afternoon, Elizabeth sat at her small desk, textbooks spread before her on an otherwise ordinary day. The familiar murmur of the neighborhood was interrupted by the distant sound of an approaching car. Expecting nothing more than routine, she glanced out the window—only to see Sophia entering the apartment, accompanied by a man she didn't recognize.

He was short and rugged, his hands rough as if carved by years of hard labor. His clothes bore stains of grease and dust, yet his smile—friendly, though tinged with hesitation—hinted at hidden depths.

"This is Logan," Sophia announced briskly as she set her purse on the counter. "He ran into my car at the gas station today. He's going to fix it for me."

Logan offered a polite nod and a quick, "Nice to meet you," in a low, gravelly voice that seemed to echo off the bare walls. Elizabeth managed a quiet, "Hello," unsure whether this was just another transient acquaintance in Sophia's long list of unexpected visitors—or something more.

Then, with an unusual lightness in her tone, Sophia added, "And we're going to church with him on Sunday."

Elizabeth's brow furrowed. "Church?" Not because she disliked the idea of attending, but because the thought of her mother suddenly embracing religion felt as alien as Logan's unexpected arrival. Sophia had never been particularly spiritual, and this abrupt enthusiasm seemed out of place.

Elizabeth said nothing further. She had learned early that silence was often the safest response. "Okay," she replied simply, followed by a polite, "Nice to meet you, Logan," before retreating to her room. Once inside, she closed the door behind her and let out a soft sigh, trying to refocus on her homework while her mind lingered on the strange man in the living room. Was he merely a passing fixer-upper, or would he become a fixture in their lives?

Sunday morning arrived with an air of uncertainty. Elizabeth, Oliver, and Sophia piled into the car, and as Sophia drove with an oddly calm demeanor, Elizabeth's curiosity deepened. When they reached the destination, the ride along a long dirt road led them through tall, whispering trees to a sprawling campground unlike any church Elizabeth had seen before. Scattered cabins, lazy tendrils of smoke from chimneys, and clusters of people moving quietly under the rustle of leaves set a surreal stage.

At the end of the drive stood a modest welcome center with a faded sign reading, "May God Light the Way." Beyond it, a large white tent billowed gently in the breeze. The makeshift sanctuary, incongruous against the natural serenity, sent a small shiver down Elizabeth's spine.

Outside the welcome center, Logan waited—hands tucked casually in his pockets and a warm smile that now seemed less tentative. "Morning," he greeted. "Glad you could make it."

Sophia beamed, and Elizabeth, along with Oliver, offered polite hellos as they stepped out of the car. Elizabeth couldn't help but notice the curious stares from the adults around them—mostly men in worn but neat clothes and a few quietly observing women. Elizabeth and Oliver were the only children in sight.

"This way," Logan said, gesturing toward the tent.

Inside, rows of folding chairs faced a simple wooden platform. The air smelled faintly of damp earth and candles. Elizabeth noticed that the men filled most seats, while the women sat quietly at the edges. Although the atmosphere was hushed and reverent, there was an undercurrent of tension that prickled at her senses.

They took seats near the middle, and Logan introduced them to a few members of the congregation. "This is Sophia, and these are her kids, Elizabeth and Oliver," he said with pride, as if presenting cherished family to old friends. The men greeted Sophia with nods that lingered a moment too long, making Elizabeth shrink instinctively closer to her mother.

The service began. A tall, broad-shouldered man stepped onto the platform, his booming voice welcoming everyone as "brothers and sisters" gathered under God's watchful eye. He preached of obedience, purity, and the roles that God had designed for men and women—painting a picture of a community set apart from the corruption of the outside world. Elizabeth glanced at Oliver, who slumped in boredom, then at Sophia, whose serene expression made it hard to tell if she truly believed the sermon or was caught up in the novelty.

As the preacher spoke of submission and sacrifice, each word stirred memories of pain and betrayal from Elizabeth's past. The idea that every hardship was part of "God's plan" made her stomach twist with uncertainty.

Then, amid the solemnity, a gentle strumming broke through the preacher's sermon—a soft, melodic sound that drew Elizabeth's eyes to the corner of the stage. There, a man sat on a stool, plucking the strings of a well-worn guitar. His fingers moved with ease, producing a warm and inviting sound that filled the tent and stirred something deep inside Elizabeth. He was perhaps in his mid-thirties, with kind eyes partially hidden behind a neatly trimmed beard. Their eyes met briefly, and he offered a small, welcoming smile that made Elizabeth's heart flutter.

Unable to contain her curiosity, she leaned toward her mother and whispered, "Mom, can I go talk to him?"

Sophia's gaze dropped to Elizabeth with a firm but gentle expression. "Not now, Elizabeth. We're here for service," she replied, leaving no room for debate.

Reluctantly, Elizabeth kept quiet, stealing glances at the guitarist as his music wove through the hymns. Throughout the service, although the congregation's singing filled the tent with unity, Elizabeth's thoughts kept returning to him. Who was he? How long had he been playing? Did he teach music? The questions swirled in her mind until the service ended.

As people began to mingle and greet each other, Elizabeth stayed close to Sophia, who was deep in conversation with Logan. Desperate to catch one last glimpse of the guitarist, Elizabeth stole a glance toward the stage. There, he was packing up his instrument and, for a fleeting moment, his eyes met hers once more. He nodded in a quiet farewell, sending a thrill through her.

Later, as the day stretched on and the sun dipped low over the campground, the atmosphere grew livelier. Laughter and the rustling of leaves mixed with soft chatter as people began to leave the tent. Elizabeth felt both out of place and inexplicably focused on the thought of lingering music in the background.

Suddenly, the gentle strumming of the guitar returned. Elizabeth's eyes darted to the edge of the gathering, and there he was again—perched casually on a half-wall, his sandy blonde hair tousled and his fingers dancing over the strings. His eyes lifted and locked with hers; he smiled warmly, and for a moment, Elizabeth's unease melted into shy wonder.

Before she could process the encounter, her mother's voice cut through, crisp and laden with warning. "Don't wander off," Sophia snapped as Elizabeth neared her. "All these men are criminals, and this is a rehab camp. They're dangerous."

The words stung, and Elizabeth's stomach twisted at the thought. Yet, drawing a deep breath, she stepped closer to Sophia, allowing her mother's presence to shield her from further unwanted attention. In that moment, as Sophia surveyed the scene with a mix of irritation and resolve, Elizabeth silently vowed to obey the rules —even as the memory of the guitarist's gentle strum lingered like a forbidden secret.

As they made their way back to the car, Elizabeth felt a fleeting sense of relief. The camp receded into the background along with the unsettling presence of Wade—the memory of his kind yet unnerving smile etched in her mind. Yet the day's events would remain with her, a reminder of the fragile line between new hope and old fears.

Was this encounter merely a fleeting spark of kindness or the beginning of something that might one day change everything? Elizabeth wondered, her heart both heavy and hopeful as she stepped into the car, determined to brace herself for whatever mysteries tomorrow might bring.

74

SHATTERED TRUST

Elizabeth couldn't pinpoint exactly when the tension had snapped—only that it was late one California afternoon, when the sun dipped low and the walls of the apartment began to vibrate with raised voices. She and Oliver had been in the living room, quietly reading, when suddenly the sound of shouting erupted from somewhere deep within the house. Accusations and angry retorts, layered with palpable desperation, seeped through the thin walls. Then, as abruptly as it had started, the noise ceased, leaving behind a silence that chilled her to the bone.

Moments later, the front door burst open. Sophia staggered out, tears streaming down her face, one hand clutching her back as though trying to hold herself together. Logan followed, his expression a hard, unreadable mask of anger before he turned and walked away without another word.

Sophia's voice, trembling and raw, broke the silence. "Take me to the hospital," she cried, and Elizabeth's heart clenched at the sound. Oliver's eyes widened in horror as he immediately nodded, his small hands reaching out. "I'll help you get in the seat," he offered, his voice barely above a whisper.

Before Oliver could fully support their mother, Elizabeth bolted back into the apartment and returned with the car keys clutched tightly in her hand. Without hesitation, she slipped behind the driver's seat. Sophia, clearly in pain, sagged onto the seat beside

Oliver as Elizabeth's fingers fumbled with the ignition. Every jolt and bump on the road made Sophia cry out, and with each shudder, Elizabeth felt panic surge through her.

On the drive to the nearest hospital, Elizabeth tried desperately to focus on the road. "Just hold on, Mom," she murmured between rapid breaths, her knuckles white on the steering wheel. She forced herself not to glance at the rearview mirror too often, though the image of Sophia's pained, pale face burned in her mind.

At the emergency room, hospital staff whisked Sophia away on a gurney. Elizabeth barely managed to fill out the intake forms—her hands shaking so badly she could barely write. Oliver sat with his head in his hands, tears silently streaming down his cheeks. "She'll be okay," Elizabeth whispered, though deep down, she wasn't sure she believed it.

Several hours later, a doctor emerged. "Sophia has suffered a fractured vertebra in her lower back," he explained gently, outlining the need for rest, care, and possibly surgery if complications should arise. Elizabeth's stomach churned at the thought of her mother's pain, and she glanced at Oliver, who simply stared blankly into the distance.

But what stunned Elizabeth most wasn't the diagnosis—it was what came next. Despite the severity of the injury, Sophia, in a voice that was strangely even, insisted on returning home with Logan rather than pressing charges. Later that day, she left the hospital in a back brace, every step a painful reminder of the fight that had erupted at home. Elizabeth and Oliver trailed behind her, their faces etched with disbelief.

Outside the hospital entrance, Logan appeared to pick up Sophia. His eyes were sullen and devoid of remorse as he offered no apology—only a heavy silence that made Elizabeth's skin crawl.

In the days that followed, Sophia rarely mentioned the incident. She spent hours resting on the couch while Logan hovered around her, his concern feeling superficial and rehearsed. Then, one evening, as they sat together in a tense silence over a sparse dinner, Sophia finally spoke words that sent Elizabeth's blood boiling.

"I forgive him," Sophia declared softly, almost too casually, as if absolving the act of violence could be reduced to a simple statement.

Elizabeth's fury erupted. "He broke your back!" she shouted, her voice cracking with a mixture of disbelief and rage. "How can you say that's okay?"

Sophia's eyes flickered—there was a mix of regret and resignation in them. "He didn't mean for it to happen," she murmured, her tone dismissive as though the accident were just that—an accident.

Elizabeth's voice shook as she demanded, "Mom, you have to see —Logan's presence is toxic! You're letting him hurt you again, and it's tearing us apart." But Sophia only offered a flat look, dismissing her outburst. Oliver, usually so lively, withdrew into a sullen silence whenever Logan's name was mentioned.

Mealtimes turned bitter. Elizabeth refused to speak to Logan, and Oliver ate in silence. Sophia, desperate to maintain an appearance of normalcy, filled the silence with mundane chatter about bills and errands, even as her children seethed internally.

That night, in the sanctuary of her dimly lit room, Elizabeth clutched her pillow and wept quietly. "I just want you to see the truth, Mom," she sobbed. "I want you to understand that you deserve better than this!" But Sophia's forgiveness formed an invisible wall—unyielding and unbreakable—that neither Elizabeth nor Oliver could penetrate.

As the dark hours deepened, Elizabeth lay awake, haunted by a single, persistent thought: Could this violation of trust ever be mended, or was their family destined to crumble beneath the weight of silence?

75

A RUN FOR THEIR MONEY

The moment the last golden ray of California vanished behind the horizon, a shocking announcement over dinner shattered the fragile calm—a promise of change that no one could have predicted.

At dinner that evening, the table buzzed with subdued conversation when Sophia suddenly announced, "I'm marrying Logan—and we're moving to New Mexico to lease a dog kennel!" Her voice rang out with unexpected cheer, and for once, Elizabeth felt a genuine flicker of excitement deep inside her.

"A dog kennel?" Elizabeth repeated, her eyes widening with disbelief as she exchanged a look with Oliver. Despite his usual grumbling at the idea of change, Oliver's pale face softened slightly as he mumbled, "That sounds... cool, I guess."

Sophia continued, "Yes, we'll be running it ourselves. There will be dogs of all sizes—so many dogs! It's going to be hard work, but it's an opportunity for all of us. Oliver, you'll be staying at the tabernacle church while we get things set up. Elizabeth, I need your help to get the kennel up and running."

Elizabeth's heart lifted at the thought of being surrounded by animals. Hard work wasn't new to her, but the idea of spending her days knee-deep in puppies and wagging tails felt almost like a dream. She barely noticed when Oliver groaned in protest about leaving his friends behind. All she could think about was the vision of her laughing among playful pups.

Later that night, as Elizabeth lay on her bed staring at the ceiling, she imagined the future vividly. The prospect of leaving behind the painful memories of California made her chest feel lighter. In her dreams, golden retrievers and border collies bounded through open fields, and the thought of escaping old wounds brought a hopeful smile to her lips. For the first time in years, her future felt like it held something wonderful—a chance to start anew.

The weeks leading up to the move were a whirlwind. Boxes were packed with haste, tearful goodbyes were exchanged with the few friends she had made at school, and the family's belongings were loaded into a moving truck that seemed to seal the past behind them. Although Elizabeth felt a sting of sadness at leaving her familiar life, the promise of a new beginning in a place full of dogs softened the blow.

One evening at dinner, as the family gathered around the table, Logan—Sophia's soon-to-be husband—spoke with animated passion. "I've been brainstorming ways to build a real reputation for our kennel," he explained, leaning forward as if sharing a secret. "We'll offer top-notch care, create a training area, and even set up a small adoption center. This isn't just a business; it's a fresh start for all of us."

Sophia's eyes shone as she reached for Logan's hand. "I truly believe we're on the right track," she added with a proud smile. Elizabeth watched them, noticing the almost reverent way her mother looked at Logan. It was a side of Sophia she rarely saw—a genuine hope that maybe, just maybe, things would be different.

The day of the move finally arrived. As the family piled into the car, Elizabeth stole one last glance at their California apartment. There was no longing or regret—only a determined focus on the road ahead. "Goodbye, California," she thought silently, facing forward as the miles melted away. The long drive was tiring, but with every passing mile, Elizabeth's excitement grew. She chattered to Oliver, "Imagine the kennel—wide-open spaces, puppies running everywhere, maybe even a few that we get to name!" Oliver grunted his agreement, though his expression remained unreadable.

After dropping Oliver off, the remaining family traveled for nearly two days before the sedan pulled into a parking lot in New Mexico. The air was dry and warm, and the vast desert landscape stretched out before them like a promise. Tucked on the outskirts of a small town was the kennel—a modest, unassuming building surrounded by open land and a scattering of scrappy trees. To Elizabeth, it looked like a slice of heaven.

Sophia and Logan unlocked the front door, and they all walked into a quiet, dirty, smelly building. The kennel was not in good condition; it was filthy and needed a thorough cleaning before opening. This didn't dismay Elizabeth. "This is amazing!" she exclaimed, barely able to contain her delight.

Later, as the family toured the property, Logan and Sophia discussed their plans in animated conversation. "We'll need to renovate the main building, set up a proper training course, and don't forget the grooming station," Logan declared. Sophia nodded, adding, "And Elizabeth, I want you to help organize the supplies. You have a great eye for detail."

Elizabeth's eyes sparkled at the thought of puppies and playful dogs. "That sounds incredible," she whispered, her voice filled with cautious hope. For a brief moment, the painful memories of the past seemed to fade, replaced by the promise of a new, joyful beginning.

That night, as the sun dipped below the horizon and painted the desert in hues of gold and crimson, the family gathered for dinner in their new home. Over plates of fresh salad and warm, homemade bread, Sophia and Logan shared their vision for the kennel with lively dialogue, their voices full of promise. Elizabeth listened, her mind drifting between the warmth of the moment and the lingering echo of old pains.

After dinner, Logan pulled Sophia aside. "I'm really excited about our future here," he said quietly, his hand lingering on hers. "I promise we'll make this kennel a place where every dog feels loved and every one of us feels like we belong."

Sophia's smile was gentle. "We're starting over, and I believe this is our chance to finally leave the past behind."

As the family settled in for the night, Elizabeth sat by the window, gazing out at the expansive desert sky. In that quiet, transformative moment, she felt a fragile joy stirring—a hope that even in the midst of change and uncertainty, new beginnings could mend broken dreams.

76

TRADING COMFORT FOR COMPANIONSHIP

The promise of a fresh start had never felt so tangible—until reality revealed its harsh face. Elizabeth's heart pounded as she stepped into the kennel, expecting a sanctuary of barking joy, only to be met with a wave of mildew and dust that clung to every rusty gate and grimy concrete floor.

The family had gathered early that morning, determined to transform the dilapidated space into a home for animals. Sophia and Logan wasted no time in assigning tasks. "Elizabeth," Sophia instructed briskly as she handed out cleaning supplies, "you're on debris duty in the pens. Get those cobwebs off the walls and scrub every inch of that floor."

Elizabeth's stomach churned as she surveyed the grimy kennel runs. "This isn't what I imagined..." she thought to herself, masking her disappointment with a determined nod. She glanced at her mother, hoping her excitement for the work would carry her through, though the disrepair was noticeable from every rusted gate to the dusty floors.

For the next two weeks, from sunrise to sunset, the family labored tirelessly. Elizabeth scrubbed, swept, and wiped until her arms ached, each stroke a mix of frustration and hope.

"Look!" Logan called one morning as he repaired a sagging gate. "That's one less rust spot to worry about."

Sophia, busy organizing the indoor grooming area, added with a smile, "Every little improvement counts."

Between grueling tasks, Elizabeth found small moments of pride. One early morning, as she worked alone in the quiet of the kennel, she paused and whispered to herself, "This is my space now." The sounds of barking dogs and the purrs of cats filled her with an inexplicable warmth.

Opening day arrived sooner than expected. Cars pulled into the driveway one after another, each bearing a nervous dog or a curious cat. Elizabeth's heart swelled as she watched the chaos unfold—a chaotic symphony of barks, meows, and excited panting. "This is it," she said to herself, smiling at the breakthrough. "The dream is happening."

Later that day, as the family gathered around for dinner after a long day's work, Logan clapped his hands. "Great job, everyone! Today, the kennels truly came alive."

Elizabeth smiled at his praise, but it felt hollow. "This is it; this is our path now," she thought, her hands sore from the labor. Elizabeth had been assigned to feed the animals and clean their pens. It wasn't glamorous, but it was far easier than the backbreaking chores she'd endured on the ranch. Here, she didn't have to pluck feathers or deal with the slaughter of livestock. Her work now was filled with the wagging of tails, the soft purring of cats, and the occasional sloppy kiss from a friendly dog.

Elizabeth's favorite moments came in the early mornings when she was able to clean the runs before anyone else arrived. The quiet of the morning was hers alone. She loved to pretend that it was her kennel and that nobody else was around, cleaning with the pride of ownership and responsibility that filled the space as the animals settled into their new lives.

The one downside to this new life, however, was her own uncomfortable living situation. Elizabeth's "room" was little more than a curtained-off corner in the back of the house. She slept on the floor, her clothes folded neatly in a plastic bin next to her makeshift bed. At first, the absence of a proper bed stung more than she cared to admit. She missed the small comforts she had left behind in California. But seeing the animals settling into their cozy pens with clean bedding in the evenings slowly helped her accept the trade-off. "At least I'm giving them a home," she thought as she crept into her blanket pallet each night.

One afternoon, as Elizabeth took a break from her chores, Logan joined her in the kennel. "You've got a real gift with these animals, Elizabeth," he said, gently ruffling her hair. "I'm telling you, one day people will know the name of this kennel, and it'll be because of you."

Elizabeth's heart swelled with pride at the compliment. "Thank you," she murmured, her voice filled with a quiet appreciation that hadn't been there in years.

Logan's tone softened further. "And I want you to know—your work here matters. This place is full of happy barks and purrs, and you, Elizabeth, will always be a part of that story."

His words were like a balm to her tired soul, making the intense work feel slightly more meaningful. Yet, as the weeks passed, an unexpected tension began to creep into their routine. One evening, while the family gathered at the table for takeout in the newly organized indoor grooming area, Logan's tone shifted. "Elizabeth," he said, leaning in as if sharing a secret, "you could learn so much more here with me. Why spend your time in school when you're already a natural at this?"

Sophia, sitting nearby, furrowed her brow. "Logan, she's just a kid. She needs her education." Logan's eyes flashed with irritation. "Her education is right here—learning to care for and train animals. What's she going to learn in a classroom that really matters?" He waved dismissively, his tone growing sharper.

Elizabeth listened from the corner, her stomach twisting. She knew she loved the kennel work, but school had always been an escape for her. It was a place where, for a brief time, she wasn't defined by her circumstances and struggled to hold onto the life she knew. The idea of letting that go, of abandoning school for more kennel work, felt terrifying.

In the days that followed, Sophia, perhaps sensing the change in Elizabeth's mood, pulled her aside. "We'll get you a GED," she reasoned matter-of-factly. "No more school. Logan says you're learning so much here. You won't have to waste your time with that."

"What? But I—" Elizabeth began, her voice weak. She still wanted school. She wanted to be normal.

Sophia waved her hand dismissively. "It's better for you. Logan's right. You'll enjoy being here, in your element. We've all made sacrifices, and this is your chance to make something of yourself. Don't you want to become something?"

Elizabeth's chest tightened, but she had no choice. The decision was final. With no room for protest, she reluctantly agreed. Soon, she was sitting for her GED exam, and although she passed with ease, there was no celebration, no moment of pride—just an overwhelming sense of loss.

Elizabeth's world became smaller. The kennel consumed her days, and her nights were filled with exhaustion, punctuated only by Logan's praise. "You're doing fantastic," Logan would say, running his fingers through her hair as he watched her clean. "You're a natural."

Elizabeth kept working, hoping the praise would stop, hoping things could go back to the way they were before school disappeared. It wasn't long before she found herself retreating further inward, giving up things she once enjoyed. Her sketchbook lay abandoned, her conversations with her mother grew less frequent, and the world she had built seemed to shrink, confined entirely to the kennel and Logan's relentless gaze.

When Elizabeth tried to talk to her mother, wanting answers, Sophia was too preoccupied. "You're doing fine, Elizabeth," she would say. "You're lucky to be here. Not everyone gets an opportunity to work with animals."

But Elizabeth wasn't sure she loved it anymore. The once breezy joy she had felt with every dog was fading into a tiring routine, and worse—Elizabeth began to fear Logan was becoming her new "Julian."

But buried beneath Elizabeth's exhaustion and the weight of expectations, a secret rebellion started to stir—a quiet hope that one day she would reclaim her life and her dreams, no matter the price.

77

NEWFOUND FREEDOM

The keys to Old Yeller gleamed in Elizabeth's hand like a promise of escape—a promise that, on that dusty summer afternoon, might finally set her free.

When Elizabeth turned sixteen, a subtle shift took place in the New Mexico household. With Oliver now a steady part of the family and Logan stepping in to offer guidance, everything seemed poised on the brink of transformation. That afternoon, under the relentless New Mexico sun beating down on the kennel, Logan handed Elizabeth the keys to his small yellow mini-truck—a vehicle he affectionately called "Old Yeller."

"It's all yours, kid," Logan said with a gentle but determined smile, his deep voice low and gravelly. "You shouldn't have to rely on your mom forever."

Elizabeth's pulse quickened as she climbed into the driver's seat. The cracked leather pressed warmly against her legs, and for a moment, every worry of the past faded into the promise of independence. "I can do this," she whispered to herself, though her hands trembled slightly as she gripped the steering wheel.

Over the next few weeks, Logan took it upon himself to teach Elizabeth how to drive. On empty, dusty roads outside of town, he explained every detail with patient clarity.

"Always check your mirrors, Elizabeth," Logan instructed one sunny morning, his tone both firm and encouraging as he pointed to the side-view mirror. "And ease gently into traffic—you don't want to startle anyone."

Elizabeth listened intently. "Okay," she replied, her voice quavering with equal parts excitement and fear. With each lesson, she grew a little more confident.

When she successfully shifted gears on a quiet stretch of road, Logan clapped her on the shoulder. "Good job," he said. "You're really getting the hang of it."

True to his word, Logan eventually let her keep the mini-truck as a token of trust. For Elizabeth, "Old Yeller" wasn't merely a vehicle; it was her ticket to freedom, a symbol of her new life away from the constant constraints of kennel chores. She drove it everywhere—running errands, picking up supplies, and even taking long, solitary drives to clear her mind.

But that taste of freedom was shattered one fateful evening. As twilight deepened and the air grew cool, Elizabeth was startled awake by the sound of the mini-truck's engine rumbling outside. Rushing to the window, her heart pounded as she saw, to her horror, that the truck was moving—and not in the usual gentle manner. She dashed back to the house, fear and frustration knotting her insides.

"Oliver!" she called urgently, her voice echoing through the hall. Moments later, Oliver appeared at the doorway, his face ashen and his eyes downcast. His friend, trailing behind him, looked equally guilty.

"What did you do?" Elizabeth gasped as she stepped outside into the fading light. Before her stood the once-bright mini truck, its front end crushed and headlights shattered.

Oliver avoided her gaze. "We took it for a joyride," he mumbled, his voice barely above a whisper. "We... tried to follow someone we thought was cool."

Elizabeth's anger flared as she crossed to inspect the wreck. "You know how important this truck was to me!" she cried, her voice cracking with a mix of betrayal and sorrow. "It was my lifeline —my chance to be independent!"

Oliver's friend shuffled uncomfortably. "We're sorry, Elizabeth. We didn't mean for it to go so far," he added softly.

Soon after, Logan and Sophia emerged from the kennel. Logan's jaw set hard as he surveyed the damage. "You nearly killed yourselves with that reckless stunt," he said in a voice that was calm yet laced with underlying fury. "This isn't just about a truck—it's about trust."

Sophia's eyes flashed with disappointment as she glared at Oliver. "Get inside, now," she commanded. Without waiting for an explanation, she ushered everyone back into the house. In the living room's heavy silence, Logan pulled Elizabeth aside and placed a steady hand on her shoulder—his touch was meant to be warm and reassuring.

"Elizabeth, I'm sorry you have to bear the consequences of their foolishness," Logan murmured quietly. "I know you're hurting. But we'll figure this out—together."

Elizabeth's eyes brimmed with unshed tears as she struggled to find the right words. "I just... I trusted this freedom," she whispered, her voice trembling with disappointment. "I thought things would be different."

Logan sighed, his expression softening. "Sometimes, freedom comes at a price, Elizabeth. It's up to us to learn from these mistakes and become stronger. I believe in you."

Later that night, as Elizabeth lay in her room listening to the steady hum of the house settling, she replayed the evening's events in her mind. Every dent in "Old Yeller," every harsh word, and every moment of reckless joy coiled together in a bittersweet tapestry of newfound freedom and shattered trust.

"Tomorrow," she vowed silently, "I'll be more careful. I won't let Oliver hinder me again." Yet, as sleep pulled her under, Elizabeth couldn't help but wonder if true independence was ever truly within her grasp—or if each step toward freedom would always be marred by the weight of others' mistakes.

In that quiet, fragile space between wakefulness and dreams, Elizabeth clung to a small ember of hope: that despite the chaos and heartbreak, one day she would drive further than the wreckage of "Old Yeller" and learn to trust in her own strength once more.

78

SOLUTIONS

In the dead of a starless night, when the only guide was a faint line on a deserted road and every bump of the car felt like a heartbeat, Elizabeth realized that survival sometimes depended on trust in the most precarious of routines.

In the wake of Oliver's impulsive joyride and the crash that nearly totaled the yellow mini-truck, life at the kennel had taken on a new, fragile rhythm. The truck's battered front end was held together by nothing more than makeshift repairs—wire and sheer hope—but it still limped along. Its headlights were dead, and the starting mechanism was unreliable at best. Gone were the days when Elizabeth could hop behind the wheel at any hour; now, daylight was their only ally.

Push-starting the truck had become a dreaded yet essential part of their routine. Elizabeth and Oliver would park it facing downhill whenever possible. Then, with quiet determination and a shared sense of responsibility, one of them would jump in to pop the clutch and, once the vehicle gained enough momentum, push-start the engine. The process was clumsy and time-consuming, a constant reminder of the consequences of Oliver's reckless behavior.

"Ugh, if only you hadn't done that, Oliver," Elizabeth grumbled as she wiped sweat from her brow, her voice heavy with resignation.

"I know, Mon—" Oliver would start, only to fall silent under the weight of guilt.

One particularly tense evening, they stayed out later than planned. The sun had dipped below the horizon faster than they expected, and suddenly, they found themselves at the edge of town in utter darkness. With no headlights to guide them—or even a flashlight to break the black veil—they both felt a surge of panic.

"Elizabeth, I can't see a thing!" Oliver said, his voice barely above a whisper as he squinted at the road.

"We have to keep moving," Elizabeth replied firmly, gripping the steering wheel until her knuckles turned white. "Just help me watch the road."

They opened both doors and inched forward slowly, their senses strained by the darkness. The absence of streetlights transformed every twist and turn into a perilous guessing game. Occasionally, a distant set of headlights would provide a fleeting glow, but mostly, they relied on the thin white lines painted on the road.

"Steer left!" Oliver suddenly hissed as the truck began to drift.

"I am!" Elizabeth shot back, her heart thundering in her chest as she adjusted the wheel with trembling hands.

After what felt like an eternity, they finally pulled into the kennel's dirt driveway. The pale glow of the kennel lights revealed the truck's dented hood and the jagged, broken fender—a stark testament to the night's ordeal. Elizabeth killed the engine, her hands still shaking. Oliver exhaled slowly, running a hand through his hair.

"Don't tell Logan," Oliver murmured, his voice low and regretful.

Elizabeth shook her head firmly. "Never. You know he'd kill us if he found out."

They slid out of the truck and gently closed the doors behind them. The familiar chorus of barking dogs greeted them from behind the chain-link fences—a sound that, for a moment, offered comfort amidst the chaos. It reminded Elizabeth that, despite the damage and the fear, the kennel was still their home, imperfect and makeshift as it was.

Later that night, as Elizabeth lay in her small room on her pallet, she replayed the drive in her mind. The oppressive darkness, the frantic steering, the barely visible white lines on the road—all of it had sent a jolt of adrenaline through her body. Yet, even as she recalled the surge of relief upon safely arriving at the kennel, a lingering knot of fear remained in her stomach.

Her thoughts drifted, and she resolved silently, "I have to be more careful. One misstep in this dark world could leave us stranded with nothing but our wits to rely on."

As she closed her eyes, Elizabeth whispered to herself, "Just make it to tomorrow," a fragile vow echoing in the stillness of her room—a promise to herself that, even in this precarious new normal, she would endure.

79

STARS OVER THE LAKE

Under a sky ablaze with fading orange and pink hues, Elizabeth clung to the back of a pickup truck as it rattled along the country road. The music from the speakers—loud and defiant—drowned out all thoughts of responsibility. Today promised a break from the drudgery of daily life. The truck's driver, a boy from her school with a mischievous grin, had promised a party by the lake, and the thrill of a nighttime adventure was irresistible.

When the truck finally rolled to a stop by the lake, the sun had just dipped below the horizon, leaving behind streaks of vibrant color that danced on the water's surface. A bonfire blazed nearby, its flames leaping into the gathering dusk, while laughter and playful chatter filled the air. Elizabeth's heart soared as she and her friends disembarked, feeling, for the first time in ages, an unburdened sense of freedom.

The driver—whom everyone called Jake—led the group with an easy confidence. "This is gonna be epic," he promised as he spread a bundle of blankets neatly in the bed of the truck, far from the bonfire's glare. Elizabeth joined him, her skin tingling with excitement and a hint of nervous anticipation. As she settled into the makeshift seating, the chill of the truck's metal seeped through her jeans, a small but steady reminder that she was alive and free.

Later, as the bonfire's light flickered against the darkening sky,

Jake whispered to Elizabeth, "What's your favorite band?" His tone was playful, inviting her to share a piece of herself.

Elizabeth hesitated, then replied softly, "I—I like Depeche Mode. Their music makes me feel like everything's okay." Her voice wavered slightly as she spoke, the confession hanging between them.

Jake's eyes lit up. "Me too. You know, sometimes a good song can change your whole night." He leaned in, and for a long, charged moment, their faces were inches apart. Then, with an urgency that startled her, he kissed her.

For a split second, Elizabeth's world narrowed to that rough, intense kiss—an encounter that awakened both desire and dread. Her heart pounded in defiance of her mind's protest, and even as her body yielded, her thoughts screamed in silent alarm. "This isn't what I wanted," she thought, even as the kiss deepened. But the moment passed, and when Jake finally pulled away, he flashed a half-smile as if nothing were amiss.

"See you around," he said casually, leaving Elizabeth with a tumult of conflicting emotions. Relief mingled with lingering fear, and as the crowd began to disperse, Elizabeth felt a bittersweet sense of relief that he was finally gone.

After the bonfire faded into memories, Elizabeth's best friend, Christy, caught up with her.

"Elizabeth, what now?" Christy asked eagerly as they huddled outside, the cool night air wrapping around them.

Elizabeth's eyes sparkled with a blend of excitement and uncertainty. "Elman said he's having people over at his place. We could go for a bit—just to chill."

Christy grinned. "Sounds like a plan. Let's head out."

They hopped into another friend's car and soon found themselves at Elman's house—a stark contrast to the lively energy of the lake party. The interior was dimly lit, the air heavy with smoke and a laid-back, almost lethargic atmosphere. Elman, always respectful and kind, greeted them with a warm smile.

"Hey, girls. Welcome. I know it's a bit wild in here, but I promise you, it's a safe space," he said as he led them into a cozy corner of the living room.

Christy and Elizabeth exchanged a look; Elizabeth's earlier excitement was now tinged with cautious curiosity.

In a low, friendly tone, Christy remarked, "It's nice to have a change of pace, huh?"

Elizabeth nodded silently, her mind still buzzing with the night's events. Later, as the evening wore on and the music mellowed, Elman offered, "You know, if you want to try something new, I could show you a way to take the edge off without it being too harsh."

Before Elizabeth could ask what he meant, Elman took a gentle hit from a joint, then leaned in and, with careful precision, blew the smoke into her mouth as she inhaled. The moment was almost tender—a brief, unexpected intimacy that both startled and soothed her.

But the euphoria was short-lived. Elizabeth soon found herself high, yet the buzz was tainted by a lingering headache. Laughter and conversation faded into a sleepy haze as the night deepened.

As the party dwindled, a knock at the door brought Dale into their orbit. Dale, with an easy charm, greeted Elman with a handshake and exchanged a few words about weekend plans. His eyes then found Elizabeth, and in that brief glance, a spark of interest ignited.

"Hey," Dale said, approaching her with a friendly tone. "I'm Dale. I haven't seen you around. What's your name?"

"Elizabeth," she replied softly, her voice steady despite the flutter in her stomach.

They settled into a worn armchair in a quieter corner of the room. Dale spoke about his school, his truck, and casually inquired, "So, how do you know Elman?"

Elizabeth smiled faintly. "We're best friends. He's always been good to me and Christy—why don't you stay awhile and hang out?"

Dale nodded, his eyes kind. "I can't tonight, but can I call you sometime? I'd like to get to know you better."

Elizabeth's heart skipped a beat. "Yeah, that'd be nice," she whispered, exchanging numbers with him as the ambient chatter of the party blurred into the background.

Later, as Elizabeth and Christy moved to the kitchen for water, Elman greeted them.

"Are you all right?" he asked, his eyes briefly looking around at all the guests who still lingered.

Christy grinned. "Better than a lot of folks, I guess."

Elizabeth forced a relaxed smile, though inside she wondered what these new connections meant for her future. As the night wore on, Elizabeth eventually announced she was leaving because some of the partygoers were getting too wild.

"I'm heading out," she said, scratching her head. Then, with a sudden light in her eye, she decided to call Dale and see if he was still awake and if he was up for visitors.

"It's cool if you come over," he replied. Then he gave her his address, and Elizabeth hitched another ride for the night.

At Dale's place—a modest condo with soft, early morning light spilling through the windows—Elizabeth carefully made her way upstairs, trying not to disturb anyone. A mishap with the door woke Dale's brother, Jason, who instantly popped his head out briefly and then went back to bed. But not before muttering, "Don't let Dad catch you."

Finally, when Elizabeth and Dale were alone, the tension that had haunted her seemed to melt away. Dale's kiss was gentle and sincere, and for once, Elizabeth felt a genuine warmth without an undercurrent of fear. Their conversation flowed naturally, and when they exchanged a passionate kiss that left her heart fluttering, Elizabeth allowed herself to bask in the feeling—no longer shadowed by dread or the need to escape.

For hours, Elizabeth and Dale lived in a bubble of youthful camaraderie, the promise of new beginnings etched into every whispered laugh and shared secret. As they cuddled together in a queen-size bed that night, Elizabeth felt, for the first time in a long while, that the future might hold a gentle promise of hope—a fragile yet beautiful new chapter waiting just around the corner.

80

THE BREAKING POINT

Elizabeth felt lighter than she had in a long time. Meeting Dale felt like a turning point—something to finally quell the chaotic restlessness in her life. In just a few weeks, his warm eyes and easy laugh had become the core of her daydreams, and she allowed herself to believe she had found the person she wanted to spend her life with. Even his father welcomed her with open arms, treating her like the daughter he'd always wanted. It was easy to imagine a future in which she was part of Dale's family, free from the shadows of her past.

But Elizabeth carried a secret burden—a flaw she couldn't quite name—that would soon unravel everything she had built with Dale.

One weekend, Elizabeth slept over at Dale's house. Dale had invited her to hang out, watch movies, and just enjoy each other's company. The evening was perfect. They cooked a simple dinner, laughed at inside jokes, and huddled under a soft blanket in his bed, watching classic films until they both dozed off.

But late into the night, Elizabeth found herself unable to sleep. The stillness of the house pressed in on her, and her thoughts refused to settle. She slipped out of bed quietly, trying not to wake Dale, and wandered into the living room.

There, she found Jason—Dale's brother—sitting by himself, his posture slouched and his expression clouded by some private sadness. He looked up, startled, when she entered.

"Are you okay?" Elizabeth asked gently, keeping her voice low to avoid disturbing the rest of the house.

Jason exhaled shakily, running a hand through his disheveled hair. "Not really. My girlfriend—ex-girlfriend—broke up with me today."

Elizabeth's heart went out to him. She couldn't stand to see someone hurting. Without thinking, she sat beside him, laying a reassuring hand on his shoulder. "I'm sorry," she said softly. "That's rough."

He turned to face her, his eyes glistening with grief. They talked for a while—about heartbreak, regrets, and the fragility of love. The more Jason confided in her, the more Elizabeth felt compelled to comfort him. She offered a hug, intending nothing more than simple support. But in that moment of vulnerability, Jason took it further.

He leaned in, pressing his lips to hers. Elizabeth stiffened, surprise and alarm colliding in her mind. She had no interest in Jason, but an old, ingrained pattern of not refusing overtook her. When he pushed for more, she couldn't bring herself to say no. Confusion churned in her stomach, but she didn't resist as lines blurred in the quiet living room.

The early morning light brought a heavy sense of dread. Elizabeth returned to Dale's room before dawn, slipping beneath the covers with her heart pounding. Guilt washed over her in waves. She wanted to pretend the night's incident hadn't happened, to compartmentalize it as she had so many times before in her life. She told herself she wouldn't mention it to Dale—there was nothing to be gained from hurting him.

But Jason had other plans.

Later that day, Dale confronted her, eyes flashing with hurt and betrayal. "Jason told me everything," he said, his voice shaking with anger. "He said you slept with him."

Elizabeth's mind reeled. She tried to explain, stumbling over words that sounded weak even to her own ears. She wanted to tell Dale that she didn't know how to refuse, that she was scared and trapped in old patterns. But she couldn't find the words to make him understand. She saw the raw pain in Dale's eyes and knew no explanation would suffice.

"How could you do this?" Dale demanded. "I trusted you—I thought you... you were different."

Tears blurred Elizabeth's vision. She reached for him, but he stepped back, recoiling as though her touch were poison. "Dale, please, it wasn't... I never wanted this," she pleaded.

"Then why?" he whispered, his voice cracking.

Elizabeth had no answer that would soothe him. Dale shook his head, snatching his keys off the table and storming out. In that moment, Elizabeth's world collapsed. The one stable piece of her life she had begun to believe in—her future with Dale—was gone in the blink of an eye.

At night, she cried into her pillow, replaying that moment in the living room over and over. She wondered how it all went wrong so quickly, how she could have been so foolish. A small part of her realized that the flaw wasn't that she had a weakness for attention or affection—it was that she'd never learned how to say no, to stand up for her own boundaries. She didn't have the right to say no; she was a girl, and that's what guys do to girls.

She thought about Dale's eyes, the kindness that once dwelled there, replaced by heartbreak and anger. She whispered apologies into the empty darkness of her room—apologies she would never get to say to his face.

As the days went by, the sting of losing Dale remained. Elizabeth learned to survive the pain, to carry on with her daily tasks at the kennel or at school. But she never forgot the lesson: one moment of confusion and inability to refuse could shatter everything she'd worked so hard to build. And things were about to change even more.

81

PUPPY LOVE

Elizabeth's shoulders slumped as she crouched in the kennel's makeshift birthing pen. It was late in the day, and her limbs ached from hours of cleaning pens, delivering food, and handling countless grooming tasks that Logan had insisted were hers to complete. Tonight, however, she faced a new, delicate challenge—helping a pregnant shepherd whelp her litter. The bitch, Zoe, trembled, her anxious eyes flitting toward Elizabeth as though pleading for reassurance.

"Easy there, girl," Elizabeth murmured, gently stroking the dog's smooth fur. "You're doing just fine." Her soft, soothing words were meant to calm both the animal and herself. Each time Elizabeth leaned forward to check on the progress, a sharp stab of pain shot through her aching back, and she winced. I have to see this through, she thought, swallowing her exhaustion. The momma needs my comfort while she delivers.

At last, a tiny puppy wriggled free—a slick, whimpering bundle of life that made Elizabeth's heart pound with relief and renewed adrenaline. "Oh, look at you, little one," she cooed as she carefully dried the pup with a soft cloth. "Welcome to the world." As she cradled the tiny creature, she marveled at its fragility and the miracle of life unfolding right before her eyes.

Logan ambled over, toolbox in hand, and gave her a brief nod.

"Good job, Elizabeth," he said in a quiet tone that carried a mixture of approval and indifference.

"Thanks," she replied, her voice soft despite the physical strain. His few words were enough to fuel a small flicker of pride within her. It was moments like these—each tiny life emerging despite her own weariness—that made the endless, backbreaking work seem worthwhile.

As more puppies began to arrive—each needing gentle handling to be guided toward their mother—Elizabeth's voice grew softer, murmuring repeated reassurances: "There, there... you're safe now." When a particularly fragile pup started to shiver, she leaned in closer. "You're doing so well. I'm right here with you," she whispered. The Zoe's deep brown eyes locked with Elizabeth's, and in that silent exchange, a warm connection sparked between them, momentarily easing the physical pain in Elizabeth's limbs.

Yet even as these small victories brightened her spirit, the physical toll of the day was relentless. Her arms burned from constant scrubbing, her thighs ached from hours of crouching on cold concrete, and every movement blurred her vision for a moment. During a brief pause, she sank against the wall, muttering to herself, "I can't let this fatigue win. I must keep going." Her determination was fierce—there was no room for surrender when so many tiny lives depended on her vigilance.

"Elizabeth, take a break if you need it," Logan called from across the pen as he walked by, his tone softening just a bit.

"I'm fine," she replied, forcing a smile despite the exhaustion that threatened to overwhelm her. "Just a little tired, that's all." Logan gave a quick nod, his eyes lingering on her for just a second before he returned to repairing a loose gate. That brief look of concern warmed her, though a part of her longed for someone else to step in and say, "Elizabeth, I'll finish this for you," so she wouldn't have to carry the burden alone.

Time wore on, and as twilight deepened, the kennel fell under the soft glow of a solitary floodlight. Elizabeth's focus never wavered; she continued her work until the final puppy emerged near midnight. Its tiny whimpers grew fainter until Elizabeth's careful massage awakened it, and she guided it to nestle safely against its mother. With a deep, exhausted sigh, she watched as Zoe finally lay back, nuzzling her newborns contentedly.

Dragging herself out of the whelping pen, Elizabeth wiped her brow with the back of her hand and glanced at the overhead clock —almost one in the morning. Her body, worn and weary from the day's relentless labor, threatened to collapse. The buzzing kennel light and the gentle sound of puppy whimpers filled the night air, mingling with her own ragged breathing.

Stepping outside for a breath of cool air, Elizabeth paused near the kennel. "Just a few more minutes," she whispered to herself. "I have to get home to rest—and maybe meet some friends later." The thought of a midnight rendezvous, a brief escape into the normalcy of teenage life, sparked a rebellious thrill within her, even as fatigue weighed her down.

Inside the house, Oliver snoozed peacefully on the living room couch—one sock missing, as usual. Elizabeth's gaze lingered on him with a pang of envy, longing for the simple comfort of sleep that eluded her. Yet, she had plans beyond exhaustion. Even though her body screamed for rest, she had made a promise to herself: when the alarm went off in a few hours, she'd muster the strength to sneak out and reclaim a piece of her youth.

Walking back toward the house, her legs wobbled, and she paused at the door, listening as the low whimpers from the kennel mingled with the hum of the refrigerator. With a deep, steadying breath, Elizabeth vowed silently, "I won't let exhaustion win tonight. I'll get a few hours of sleep, and tomorrow, I'll meet my friends for that midnight escape." The promise, though fragile, was a spark of defiance that she desperately needed to keep pushing on.

Back in her small room, Elizabeth carefully changed out of her soiled kennel clothes, every movement met with protest from her aching muscles. Her trembling hands set the alarm clock with painstaking care. As she nestled onto her hard pallet under a thin blanket, she allowed herself to close her eyes for just a short rest. Before sleep overtook her, she whispered a silent promise, "I'll be ready in the morning to tackle another day."

In those precious moments between wakefulness and dreams, as she drifted into an uneasy sleep, Elizabeth's thoughts swirled with images of the newborn puppies, Zoe's gentle nuzzle, and the memories of the joy she felt as she welcomed each puppy into the world.

She hadn't been asleep long when she felt it. The pressure on her hip was like someone was rubbing a dow rod against her body. As she began to wake further, she noticed that her shirt was off and Logan was rubbing her back gently. She soon realized that it was he who was rubbing against her hip, trying to satisfy himself. She lay there paralyzed for a few moments while she tried to grasp what he was doing. She knew he was overly comfortable with her sometimes, but he had never made any aggressive moves toward her in the past—just passive brushing of the hair and patting her on the shoulder. All innocent. But then it finally occurred to her that if she didn't say something now, he would become her new Julian, and she wouldn't be safe here either.

Elizabeth was frozen with fear until the moment changed. He was now trying to pull Elizabeth's panties down when she abruptly sat up, covered herself, and turned to face him. For the first time in her life, she mustered the courage to stand, or sit up, and face the man whom she didn't want inside her.

"What are you doing?" she asked abruptly. "If you don't get out of my room, I am going to tell my mother."

Logan did not stop, and Elizabeth fought against him for the first time. However, she wasn't strong enough, and Logan ultimately took what all men take.

For the first time after these events, Elizabeth felt weak and scared. She realized that fighting back didn't do anything to benefit her. As a matter of fact, it caused the act to hurt. When Logan finally left her room, she rolled over on her hard pallet and tried to find some sleep that was clearly elusive that night.

❧ 82 ❧

A TWO-WEEK TAKEOVER

As the final check was stowed and the phone fell silent, Elizabeth's pulse hammered with a mix of triumph and terror—each tick of the clock a reminder that the two-week takeover was not just a daring bid for independence but also a race against the inevitable moment when their secret might finally unravel.

The morning after Sophia's abrupt departure, the silence in the house felt deafening. Elizabeth and Oliver discovered a hastily scrawled note pinned to the kitchen table. In Sophia's rushed handwriting, it read: "Logan and I are off to California on dog business. We'll be back in two weeks. Hold down the fort." There were no warm goodbyes, no extra explanations—just that one note that now weighed heavily in Elizabeth's hand.

Elizabeth looked up at Oliver, who had just finished reading the note over her shoulder. "They just... left?" he asked, his voice small and uncertain.

Elizabeth sighed, her heart a jumble of emotions. "Yes, they left. Two weeks, they said," she murmured. A part of her was shocked at the sudden abandonment, while another part—a rebellious spark—saw it as an opportunity.

They both stood in the quiet living room, the note sagging in Elizabeth's grasp. The air felt charged with unspoken responsibility. Elizabeth's eyes narrowed as she scanned the room. "We have to run the kennel," she declared firmly, more to herself than to Oliver. "We can't let everything collapse just because Mom and Logan are gone."

Oliver gave a tentative nod. "Yeah, but what are we supposed to do? We're just kids."

Elizabeth exhaled slowly and walked over to the desk where a stack of bills lay scattered alongside check stubs and receipts. "We're in charge now," she said, her voice a mix of determination and worry. "I wonder—what if we use the checks that customers give us to cover the kennel's expenses, deposit them, and use checks to pay the bills? And then... keep all the cash for ourselves?"

Oliver's eyes widened in surprise, then lit up with a mischievous grin. "That's genius, Elizabeth!" he exclaimed, his voice bubbling with excitement. "Imagine all the things we could do—buy snacks, maybe even that new video game I've been eyeing."

Elizabeth quickly rummaged for an old shoebox and labeled it "Kennel Account." "Okay," she said, carefully placing each check inside. "These go to pay for feed, utilities, and other necessary expenses. And all the cash? We can use it for extra treats and fun, as long as nothing raises suspicion."

The siblings spent the next few days establishing their routine. Every morning, they would get up and be in the kennel before the staff, greeting employees with practiced smiles and rehearsed lines. "Good morning, we're taking care of things today," Elizabeth would say, her tone professional despite her youth. Oliver was in charge of feeding and cleaning, while Elizabeth managed the schedule, answered the phone, and oversaw appointments.

At one point, a particularly curious employee asked, "Where are your parents today? I haven't seen them in a while?"

Elizabeth exchanged a quick look with Oliver before replying confidently, "They ran a supply errand. They'll be back soon." The employee nodded, satisfied with the answer.

As the weeks passed, the kennel operations ran almost seamlessly under Elizabeth and Oliver's management. Every check deposited into the shoebox was carefully recorded in Elizabeth's neat ledger, and every cash payment was discreetly stashed away. Yet, with every passing day, a sense of anticipation—and a growing knot of anxiety—settled in Elizabeth's stomach. What if her parents returned early? What if someone noticed a discrepancy in the books?

Late one afternoon, while Elizabeth was reconciling the day's receipts with her ledger, Oliver ambled into the office. "Hey, Liz, you look worried," he said softly, dropping his backpack with a thud. "What's up?"

Elizabeth sighed, rubbing her temples. "I don't know, Oliver. Every time I double-check these numbers, I worry that something might go wrong. What if Mom and Logan come back and find out we've kept some cash aside?"

Oliver shuffled his feet, his tone trying for reassurance. "You're doing great, Liz. Look, we're careful, right? And besides, we need this money to survive? We can't buy groceries with a check."

Elizabeth managed a small smile. "Yeah, you're right." She forced herself to focus on the ledger again, but her mind drifted to the possibility of facing her parents' anger.

Each day unfolded with a mix of mundane routine and small victories. The kennel sparkled under their meticulous cleaning, and the employees rarely questioned the sudden efficiency. In the afternoons, the phone rang with reservations and appointment requests, and the siblings handled them with a professionalism that belied their age.

One quiet afternoon, as Elizabeth was tidying the lobby, an employee named Carla stopped by the desk. "You two have really done a fantastic job," Carla remarked, her tone warm and genuine. "The place has never looked better."

Elizabeth's chest swelled with a mix of pride and apprehension. "Thank you, Carla," she replied, forcing a cheerful smile. "We're just trying to keep everything running smoothly."

Carla leaned in conspiratorially. "I'm sure your parents would be proud, too. When will they come back?"

The remark sent a jolt through Elizabeth. She forced herself to nod, but inside she wondered if that pride would ever be real. "Real soon," her voice cracked.

As the two-week mark drew near, Elizabeth found herself oscillating between relief and dread. On one hand, the smooth operation of the kennel filled her with a sense of accomplishment. On the other, every tick of the clock reminded her that soon her mother and Logan would return, and the fragile façade of their independence could shatter in an instant.

One evening, as the sun dipped below the horizon, casting long shadows over the kennel's yard, Elizabeth and Oliver closed the day's books. The campus was quiet, and the only sound was the soft murmur of a cooling breeze and the distant barking of dogs. Elizabeth sat at the front desk, gazing at the neat piles of receipts and the steadily growing stash of cash.

"Do you ever wonder what we'd do if they came back and found out about our little secret?" Oliver asked, his voice low, almost contemplative.

Elizabeth looked up, her eyes narrowing. "Every day," she admitted. "But I think we're doing what we have to do. We're keeping the kennel running, and that's what matters most right now."

Oliver nodded, a look of determined resignation on his face. "We're in charge now. We're making our own rules."

Elizabeth's mind swirled with conflicting emotions. The freedom was exhilarating, but it was also a heavy responsibility. In the back of her mind, she couldn't shake the fear of being caught or the guilt of diverting money meant for the kennel. As she tucked the last receipt into her ledger, she whispered, "I'll make sure nothing goes wrong."

The final morning before her parents were due to return arrived with an uneasy calm. Elizabeth and Oliver arrived at the kennel early, double-checking that every pen was spotless and every transaction was accounted for. Elizabeth deposited the last batch of checks and carefully balanced the ledger, while Oliver tidied up the grooming area. They exchanged a look—a silent mix of triumph and trepidation.

Later that afternoon, as Elizabeth sat in the quiet office, the phone rang unexpectedly. Her heart leaped into her throat as she picked it up. "Hello?"

A gruff voice on the other end said, "Is this the kennel? I have a question about an appointment." Elizabeth's mind raced—could this be a sign that someone might start asking too many questions? She answered the call calmly, her voice steady despite the pounding of her heart.

After hanging up, she exhaled shakily. Oliver peeked into the room. "Everything okay?" he asked.

"Yeah," Elizabeth replied, though her eyes betrayed her worry. "Just... we need to be extra careful now."

As the day turned into evening, Elizabeth could feel the tension building. Every so often, she glanced at the tethered phone, half-expecting it to ring with a call from Sophia checking in. But the line remained silent, leaving her with an unsettling mix of relief and anxiety.

That night, after the kennel had closed for the day, Elizabeth sat by the front desk under the soft glow of a single lamp. The night was quiet, the kind of silence that promised either peace or impending chaos. She reread her ledger one last time, making sure every check was in place and every expense noted. Oliver joined her, and they spoke in hushed tones about the past two weeks.

"Elizabeth," Oliver said, his voice barely above a whisper, "do you think Mom and Logan will be proud when they come back?"

Elizabeth shook her head slowly, her eyes fixed on the ledger. "I don't know, Oliver. I just hope they don't find out about the extra cash." Her tone was heavy with worry.

Oliver's expression hardened slightly. "We did what we had to do. We kept the kennel running. That's what matters."

Elizabeth sighed, though she couldn't help but feel a twinge of guilt. "I just—sometimes I wonder if all this freedom is worth the risk. What if one day we mess up, and then... then everything falls apart?"

Oliver placed a comforting hand on her shoulder. "Hey, we're in this together, right? We'll figure it out, just like we always do."

Elizabeth managed a small smile, grateful for Oliver's reassurance, even as the silent threat of their parents' return loomed over her. With a final glance at the quiet phone and the neatly balanced ledger, she whispered, "Tomorrow, we'll face whatever comes. We'll do it together."

The night deepened, and the only sounds in the empty kennel office were the gentle hum of the refrigerator and the steady tick of the wall clock. Elizabeth turned off the light and closed her eyes, the echo of her whispered promise mingling with the anxious beats of her heart. In that fragile, silent moment, the two-week takeover felt like a small victory—a secret rebellion against a life dictated by uncertainty. Yet deep down, she knew the greatest challenge was yet to come, and every moment of freedom came at a price.

As the clock neared midnight, Elizabeth couldn't shake the ominous feeling that the quiet might shatter at any moment—a prelude to a return that would either cement their newfound independence or destroy it forever.

❧ 83 ❧

ONE NIGHT TOO FAR

Elizabeth never imagined that a party meant to celebrate their newfound freedom would descend into a nightmare. Two weeks had stretched into three, and with Sophia and Logan still absent on their California trip, the kennel had become both a sanctuary and a stage for dangerous rebellion. That night, the once-cheerful gathering had spiraled out of control.

The living room buzzed with music and laughter as classmates and neighborhood adults mingled freely. Elizabeth and Oliver had been caught up in the excitement—until the alcohol flowed too freely. At first, the shots and laughter had filled the air like a promise of escape from their daily drudgery. But as the hours wore on, the festive mood darkened. Oliver flitted from group to group, his carefree grin a mask for growing recklessness, while Elizabeth, trying to remain sober, clutched her cup tightly.

"Hey, Elizabeth, come over here!" Oliver shouted at one point, laughing with a group of older kids near the makeshift bar. She forced a smile and moved past Oliver, determined to make it to the bathroom before anyone else. Suddenly, an unfamiliar man—tall, with cold eyes and an air of entitlement—cornered her in the hallway.

"Another drink?" he offered, holding out a glass. His voice was low and suggestive. Elizabeth hesitated, and his hand reached out to gently brush against her arm.

"Leave me alone," she murmured, trying to pull away.

But the man persisted, his tone shifting from inviting to commanding. "I'm just trying to help you loosen up," he said, drawing her toward a quieter room. His grip tightened, and the once-distant sound of the party faded into a menacing hush. Elizabeth's heart pounded furiously. The soft murmur of laughter from the living room contrasted sharply with the cold, oppressive silence of the hallway.

"I don't want this," Elizabeth whispered, her voice trembling. Yet as he pressed her against the wall, the memories of past abuses and the constant pressure to submit left her feeling frozen— paralyzed by a familiar, haunting fear. The man pushed his body against Elizabeth's, lifting her off the floor, sliding himself under her skirt and pushing himself into her clumsily.

At that precise moment, Dale burst into the room. His eyes widened as he took in the scene: the man had Elizabeth pinned against the wall, and she looked utterly terrified. "What the hell is going on here?" Dale demanded, his voice shaking with both anger and hurt.

Elizabeth's eyes met Dale's, silently pleading for help. But Dale's shock quickly warped into a storm of emotions. "I can't believe you'd let this happen," he spat, misunderstanding the situation entirely. His tone was laced with betrayal. Before Elizabeth could say another word, the intruder, startled by Dale's sudden presence, pulled out, adjusted his pants, and bolted into the night.

Dale stepped forward, concern etched on his face. "Elizabeth, are you okay?" he asked urgently. Tears welled in her eyes as she tried to explain, her voice choked. "It wasn't what you think... I... I froze... I just—"

"No," Dale interrupted bitterly, his face hardening. "I can't handle this, Elizabeth." With that, he turned and stormed off, disappearing into the darkness and leaving her heart shattered and raw.

Elizabeth's stomach twisted as guilt, shame, and despair crashed over her. She wandered back into the bustling living room, where the remnants of the party lay scattered: half-empty cups, spilled alcohol, and abandoned laughter echoing in the empty space. The room felt like a wreckage of lost promises—a stark contrast to the vibrant chaos of earlier.

In the kitchen, a bottle of rum sat unopened on the counter, its label now a bitter reminder of the night's horror. Her hands trembled as she unscrewed the cap and took a long, desperate drink. "Maybe this will make it all disappear," she whispered to herself, her voice barely audible. Each swallow burned, dulling the immediate pain but deepening the sorrow.

Oliver was nowhere to be found—likely lost in his own dark thoughts or passed out in a corner. Elizabeth slumped onto the couch, the taste of rum bitter in her mouth. She recalled Dale's disappointed expression and the crushing weight of his departure. The betrayal she felt from his misunderstanding cut deeper than any physical blow could. "I just wanted someone to save me," she thought, tears streaming silently down her cheeks. "I want him to see that I am not weak."

As the night began to quiet, Elizabeth finished her rum bottle; her mind churned with memories of past abuse, the times she had been forced into silence. She recalled the suffocating atmosphere of her home, the relentless demands, and the fear that had ruled her life. Now, as the room spun slowly around her and the party's echoes faded into a heavy, oppressive quiet, she was left alone with her despair.

A distant clock ticked, each second marking the time she felt more lost. "Why can't I just be free?" she whispered, her voice trembling with hopelessness. The question hung in the air, unanswered, as the room remained dim and lifeless.

Elizabeth clutched the bottle tightly, determined not to let this night define her, yet feeling utterly defeated. The weight of loneliness, the constant betrayals, and the stark reminder of her inability to protect herself coiled inside her like a viper. She resolved silently that she would never allow herself to be so helpless again— that someday, she would find the strength to stand up, to speak out, and to reclaim her voice from the shadows of silence.

For now, however, the darkness pressed in, and Elizabeth sank deeper into a numb stupor, her mind echoing with the shattered remnants of trust. Another night had passed—one night too far— and with it, a bitter lesson on the cost of vulnerability in a world where help often came too late and betrayal lurked behind every corner.

In the cold stillness of the early hours, Elizabeth's thoughts finally began to clear, a flicker of resolve piercing through the haze of despair. "I won't let this be my forever," she vowed softly to herself. "Tomorrow, I will find a way to be heard." But as the darkness outside persisted, she knew the road ahead was long, and the scars of tonight would take time to heal. She chugged the remaining rum as fast as she could in hopes of quieting the noise in her head.

84

THREE DAYS OF DARKNESS

Elizabeth had never imagined that a single moment of despair could spiral into three days of near oblivion. After Dale had stormed out, leaving her in a torrent of tears, she'd snatched a bottle of rum off the kitchen counter and drank with abandon—hoping, desperately, to drown the sting of betrayal and her own crushing sense of failure. Soon enough, the alcohol swept her into total blackout. She remembered nothing of stumbling through the house or collapsing on the living room floor—nor that Oliver had found her and fought to drag her onto her pallet in her room.

For Oliver, those three days were a relentless, agonizing nightmare. At just thirteen, he had been thrust into the impossible role of caretaker for his unconscious sister. Every time he passed by her room, he peered through the crack in the door, looking for any flicker—a flutter of her eyelids, a shallow shift in her breathing— that would signal she was coming back. Hours stretched into an eternity as he tried to rouse her with urgent whispers.

"Elizabeth, come on... please, open your eyes," he pleaded softly one time, shaking her shoulders gently. His voice trembled as he repeated her name, his desperation mounting with every passing minute. But she lay as still as a rag doll, unresponsive.

Panic clawed at Oliver's heart. He had heard stories—whispers of people dying from alcohol poisoning—but the very idea of calling an ambulance sent icy dread racing through his veins. "What if they find out about the party?" he muttered to himself, his hands shaking as he wiped his own tears. "Mom and Logan would be furious... and the kennel—our only lifeline—might be lost forever."

Torn between the terror of losing his sister and the paralyzing fear of adult retribution, Oliver resolved to try and shock Elizabeth back to consciousness himself. "Maybe a cold shower will work," he murmured, his voice low and determined. With trembling resolution, he coaxed Elizabeth into the bathroom. "Just hold still, sis," he whispered as he turned on the tap and let icy water cascade over her limp form.

Elizabeth let out a faint groan as the freezing water hit her skin. Oliver's heart leapt when he thought he saw her eyelids flutter ever so slightly, but the moment passed, and she slumped once again. Desperate, he patted her gently. "Come on, Elizabeth... please wake up."

Frustration and terror warred within him as he tried every trick he'd heard of—dabbing her face with a cool, damp cloth, even splashing water on her arms. Each time, hope flickered only to be extinguished by her unyielding collapse. Finally, with no other choice, he laid her back in bed and covered her with a blanket, his own tears falling silently as he sat vigil beside her.

The next morning brought no improvement. Elizabeth lay motionless, her face slack and her skin clammy to the touch. Oliver, eyes red from sleepless worry, sat at her bedside and whispered, "I'm so scared, Elizabeth. Please come back." He tried coaxing her again, even lifting her gently into the bathtub to let steaming water run over her, hoping a change in temperature might shock her system into waking. For a brief moment, her head jerked upward and her lips parted in a low moan—then she sank back, her consciousness slipping away.

Hours later, in a final, desperate vigil, Oliver set up a small lamp beside Elizabeth's pallet. Every few minutes, he checked her pulse and forced a sip of water to her parched lips. "I'm here, Elizabeth," he whispered repeatedly as he cradled her hand. He would murmur, "You have to fight, sis. Please, just a little more..." His voice cracked with both hope and despair, echoing in the silent, cold house.

The nights dragged on in a haze of tension and fear. Each time Oliver left Elizabeth's room—even briefly to feed the dogs in the kennel—a wave of terror slammed into him. "What if I come back and you're gone?" he would worry aloud in a trembling whisper to himself. The dogs' distant barks were a constant reminder that life around him continued unabated, even as his sister's life hung precariously in the balance.

Finally, before dawn on the fourth day, Elizabeth stirred. Oliver, who had dozed off in a chair beside her pallet, jerked awake as he heard a faint cough. "Elizabeth?" he asked, his heart hammering. He leaned over, scanning her face. Her eyes fluttered open, bleary and confused. "Oh, I feel like crap," she croaked, her voice raw and her mouth parched.

"Three days," Oliver replied, tears glistening in his eyes. "You've been out for three days, Elizabeth." His voice was thick with a mix of relief and regret, his arms shaking as he reached for a cup of water and pressed it to her lips.

Elizabeth gulped, coughing as the water burned down her throat. Her head pounded with each movement—a brutal reminder of how close she had come to a fate far worse than a temporary blackout. After a few long, tense minutes, she slumped back against the pillows, her eyes searching the ceiling for answers.

Oliver sat back down, his voice soft and choked with emotion. "Elizabeth, I tried everything. I brought you water, gave you cold showers—please, you have to tell me what happened."

A fragile clarity began to return to Elizabeth's eyes. "I...I must have had alcohol poisoning, Oliver," she whispered, the words tumbling out as if set free by his concern. "I was drinking, and I—I don't remember much after that." Her voice was a broken mix of regret and gratitude. "You should have taken me to the hospital."

Oliver's eyes brimmed with tears as he reached out to squeeze her hand. "I was so scared. I didn't want to get you in trouble... I just—I didn't know what else to do."

Elizabeth's gaze softened, and despite the pain that throbbed in her body, she managed a small, grateful smile. "You did the best you could, Oliver. I'm alive; that's all that matters." She paused, her voice barely above a whisper, laden with guilt and sorrow. "But promise me, next time—no matter what—call for help."

Oliver nodded vigorously. "I promise, Elizabeth. I swear I'll never let this happen again."

The silence of the house was broken only by the low hum of the refrigerator in the kitchen and the distant rustling of the dogs in the kennel. As Elizabeth lay back, her eyes closing slowly, she thought of the stark reality of her ordeal—the nights of fear, the endless cycle of showers and desperate awakenings—and the immense weight of what might have been lost. Every pulse in her body was a reminder of the fragile line between life and death.

With a heavy heart, she whispered to herself, "I won't let this happen again." Her words were a soft vow to reclaim control over her life, to break free from the paralyzing grip of despair. Oliver sat beside her, his presence a silent promise that they would face whatever came next together.

As the first light of dawn crept into the room, casting a soft glow over Elizabeth's tired face, Oliver gently kissed her forehead. "You're okay now," he murmured, his voice thick with relief. "We're going to get through this together."

Elizabeth closed her eyes, letting the warmth of her brother's reassurance fill the cold spaces of her heart. In that quiet moment, with the world still in darkness but hope beginning to stir, she vowed that no matter how far she had fallen, she would rise again. The memory of the past few days would always be with her, a lesson in survival and the unyielding strength of family.

85

THE FINAL STRAW

Just days after the chaotic party, the tension at the kennel had reached its breaking point. Sophia and Logan were due to return from their supposed trip to California any day now, but the phone remained silent. In the meantime, Elizabeth and Oliver had decided —perhaps impulsively—to host a "small" get-together for a few friends. They had planned it as a brief respite from the endless responsibilities of running the kennel, a way to recapture a fleeting sense of normal teenage freedom.

That evening, the air was thick with the buzz of conversation and the soft clink of glasses. Elizabeth had spent hours cleaning the house after the last gathering, making sure there was no evidence on the walls, carpets, or furniture, and ensuring that the space looked inviting. When everyone arrived, Oliver found himself flitting about, laughing and teasing their few guests, while Elizabeth tried her best to smile through her anxiety.

In a quiet corner, a classmate named Lisa leaned in to Elizabeth. "Hey, are you sure you're okay with this? I mean, after all that happened..." she murmured, her voice laced with concern.

Elizabeth forced a laugh. "I'm fine, Lisa. We just needed a break." Yet inside, a nagging dread whispered that this break might be the final straw.

As the night deepened, Elizabeth noticed that Oliver, usually the life of the party, seemed distracted. He kept glancing at the door and murmuring to himself. When Elizabeth finally pulled him aside in a hushed tone, she asked, "Oliver, what's going on? You're not yourself tonight."

He sighed, lowering his eyes. "I just... I can't shake the feeling that we're in too deep. You know, every time something goes wrong, it's like we're getting one step closer to disaster."

Before Elizabeth could respond, the music grew louder, and a new, unexpected guest entered the fray—a tall, older boy named Jake, whose arrival was heralded by an enthusiastic shout from a group of peers. Jake's presence was magnetic, and he soon found himself surrounded by a few admiring classmates. Elizabeth felt a pang of conflicting emotions; part of her longed for the camaraderie, yet another part of her feared what reckless behavior might bring.

Things stayed pretty calm, and later that evening, as the party wound down, Elizabeth felt the weight of her decisions pressing in on her. She had decided, almost impulsively, to leave and visit Dale. "I need to see Dale," she announced quietly to Oliver as they helped clear the remnants of the party. "I won't be long, I promise."

Oliver frowned, worry creasing his brow. "Are you sure about that, Elizabeth? You know he didn't seem like he wanted to see you again after the last time."

Elizabeth managed a small, determined smile. "It's just a quick drive, Oliver. The truck still runs, and I need to see him." Her voice wavered with both excitement and fear.

Later, outside under the full moon, Elizabeth hopped into the battered yellow mini-truck—the one they had worked so hard to keep running despite its many faults. The truck sputtered to life under her cautious touch, its headlights long dead, leaving only the soft glow of the moon to guide her. As she drove along the quiet back roads, the thrill of independence mixed with a deep, gnawing anxiety. The engine's rattle echoed in the silence of the night.

After a few miles, the truck began to falter. "Come on, Old Yeller, don't fail me now," Elizabeth muttered, tapping the steering wheel anxiously. The truck's engine coughed and died just short of town. Elizabeth's heart sank. "No, no, no..." she whispered, trying the key again, but it was useless. Frustration mixed with panic. With a heavy sigh, she grabbed a beer from the passenger seat—one she'd stashed away as a last resort—and decided to walk.

The road was dark and deserted. Each step Elizabeth took on the uneven pavement echoed in the quiet night. Her mind raced with thoughts of what Sophia would say if she ever found out. As she walked, she took tentative swigs from the beer, but the buzz was unfulfilling.

Suddenly, the flash of blue and red lights startled her. A police cruiser pulled up alongside, its interior lights casting eerie shadows on the road. The window rolled down, revealing a stern-faced officer. "Miss, are you all right?" he asked, his voice cutting through the silence.

Elizabeth's pulse pounded. "I—I'm fine," she stammered, clutching the beer as if it were a lifeline. The officer eyed her suspiciously. "I'm going to need your ID. How old are you?"

Her throat tightened. "Sixteen," she managed, the truth hanging heavy in the air. Underage, out alone at night, caught drinking alcohol—it was a dangerous cocktail.

Within an hour, Elizabeth was processed at a local juvenile facility. The world around her blurred as she was placed in a cold, stark cell with a narrow bed and a metal sink. The days passed in a monotonous cycle of bleak meals and harsh fluorescent lights. Elizabeth's mind was a whirlwind of regret and fear—regret over her impulsive decision and fear of what consequences awaited her.

In the cell, she was assigned a roommate—a quiet girl whose haunted eyes spoke of her own battles. They exchanged few words, but the silence was a constant reminder that they were both paying the price for choices made in desperation.

At night, Elizabeth lay awake on the thin mattress, the cold from the concrete seeping through. She replayed the events of the past month over and over in her mind. "I shouldn't have done that," she whispered into the darkness, her voice trembling. "I just wanted to feel free."

On the fifteenth day, the cell door opened abruptly, and a guard ushered Elizabeth into a drab waiting room. There, at a metal table, sat Sophia. Her face was lined with anger, her eyes piercing Elizabeth with rage. Sophia's voice was low, but each word was weighted with disappointment. "Do you have any idea what you've put me through?" she demanded, her tone harsh.

Elizabeth's heart ached as she sank into the chair opposite her mother. "I'm sorry," she mumbled, barely audible. "I just... I wanted to see Dale. I didn't mean for it to go this far."

Sophia's eyes flashed with pain and fury. "You think a fleeting adventure justifies this behavior? You've jeopardized everything—your safety, our family's reputation, and the kennel's future. I'm not going to let you go on like this."

Tears welled in Elizabeth's eyes as she tried to explain, her voice choked with regret. "I didn't know what else to do, Mom. I felt trapped—like I couldn't breathe..."

Sophia's gaze softened slightly, but the hurt remained clear. "I will never forgive you, Elizabeth," she said in a voice that barely concealed her anguish. "This was the final straw. There will be consequences for your actions, and you must learn to think before you act."

Elizabeth nodded, her heart heavy. "I promise I'll do better."

Sophia exhaled sharply, her expression pained. "Let's go home."

The silence that followed was thick, filled with the unspoken truth that Elizabeth's life had veered dangerously close to unraveling completely. In that moment, Elizabeth realized that her impulsive choices had consequences far beyond a simple night out. They were a pattern—a pattern that, if not broken, could consume her entirely.

After what felt like an eternity, Elizabeth and Sophia finally arrived back at the kennel. When Elizabeth went inside, she noticed Oliver was already there. "When did she get him out?" Elizabeth wondered.

Elizabeth's eyes brimmed with tears, but she managed a quiet sob and then walked directly to her room to cry in the privacy of her pallet on the floor.

❧ 86 ❧

A NEAR MISS AT 100

The dark highway stretched out before Elizabeth like a gauntlet of fate. With trembling fingers, she gripped the steering wheel of Sophia's pristine sedan—a car she had borrowed in a moment of desperate rebellion. Tonight, that borrowed freedom came with a terrifying risk. Determined to escape the suffocating confines of her home, Elizabeth sped down the deserted rural road, her heart pounding with a cocktail of excitement and dread.

As the miles ticked by, Elizabeth's mind raced with thoughts both exhilarating and chilling. "I'm in control. I know these roads. I can do this," she reassured herself, even as her pulse hammered in her ears. But as the speedometer crept past ninety miles per hour and the night grew oppressively dark, an icy realization began to seep in: she might not make it home in time—and if Sophia found out, the consequences would be dire.

Elizabeth's focus was suddenly shattered as the car hit a rough patch of cracked asphalt. The sedan fishtailed violently, and in a heartbeat, the vehicle spun out of control. For an agonizing moment, time seemed to slow as she watched in horror; the headlights flickered off, and the steering wheel jerked violently in her hands. Then, emerging from the chaos, she saw it—a looming telephone pole, its metal frame nearly colliding with the driver's side door.

Her heart nearly stopped. Elizabeth sat there in stunned silence, the vehicle skidding to a halt just inches from the pole. She could see it clearly now: the pole was so close that if the car had continued its wild slide, it would have slammed into it—potentially crushing her. The shock was so overwhelming that she couldn't move; the thought that she might have died washed over her in a paralyzing wave.

"I could have been dead," she thought, her voice a mere whisper to herself. She sat frozen in the driver's seat, with no concept of time, the only sounds the eerie hum of the tires and the distant whisper of the wind. Every nerve in her body screamed in disbelief, and in that moment, all thoughts of Sophia's wrath vanished from her mind, replaced solely by the raw terror of what might have been.

It wasn't long before the sound of approaching sirens broke the silence. Police cars appeared, their flashing blue lights painting shifting shadows over the sedan. Two officers emerged and gently coaxed Elizabeth from the car. Her hands still shook as they guided her, checking to see if she was injured. An ambulance arrived moments later, and paramedics carefully examined Elizabeth, their faces serious but kind.

One paramedic said quietly, "You're lucky. That was a near miss, kid."

Elizabeth managed a weak nod, barely able to form words. "I... I'm okay," she whispered, though her voice trembled with the memory of the near crash.

As the ambulance assessed her condition and confirmed that no major injuries had been sustained, a tow truck rumbled up to the scene. The truck's driver climbed out, shaking his head as he surveyed the battered body of the sedan—its headlights shattered, the metal twisted, a grim testament to the chaos of moments ago. Elizabeth noticed all the damage as she watched the truck driver walk around the car. "How could it have sustained so much damage? I didn't hit anything?" she asked aloud.

The policeman approaching heard the question and answered, "It's wind damage because you were going so fast."

Before Elizabeth could process what was happening, Sophia arrived at the scene. Her eyes blazed with fury as she took in the sight of the damaged car and the disheveled figure of her daughter, still in the ambulance. "Elizabeth!" she barked, her voice echoing.

Elizabeth's stomach churned at the sound of her mother's anger. "Mom..." she began, but Sophia cut her off sharply. "Get out of the car. Now."

Elizabeth hesitated, knowing that any delay would only worsen the inevitable punishment, but she had no choice. She stepped out slowly, her legs unsteady and her heart pounding in terror of what Sophia would say. The police officers and paramedics exchanged tense glances as Sophia marched over to Elizabeth. "What the hell were you thinking?" she demanded, her voice low and seething.

"I—I just wanted to get home," Elizabeth stammered, tears welling in her eyes as the reality of her actions crashed over her. "I was in control."

Sophia's eyes narrowed dangerously. "Control? You nearly killed yourself, Elizabeth! And now look at this mess," she said, gesturing toward the crumpled car. "I can't believe you took my car without permission, and then you risked everything by driving like a maniac."

The paramedic interjected softly, "She's okay, ma'am. There are no serious injuries." But Sophia wasn't having it. "I don't want to hear excuses," she snapped, her tone icy.

Elizabeth's voice trembled as she tried to apologize. "I'm sorry, Mom... I didn't think—"

"Save it," Sophia cut her off, her eyes flashing with a mix of anger and disbelief. "You're coming home with me, and you're going to pay for this," she said, her voice rising. "You're grounded for the foreseeable future, and you'll be punished for your recklessness!"

The officers led Elizabeth toward the tow truck as Sophia continued to berate her, her words cutting deep. "You could have died, Elizabeth! Do you understand what you did? And now I have to deal with the fallout of your stupid decisions!"

Inside the house later that night, the atmosphere was as thick as the silence that followed Sophia's tirade. Elizabeth, still shaking and with tears drying on her cheeks, was led inside by Sophia. "Go to your room," Sophia commanded. "And you will not speak a word to anyone."

In the dim light of her room, Elizabeth sat on the edge of her bed, staring at the wall. The memory of the telephone pole, so ominously close, replayed over and over in her mind. She had narrowly escaped death, and yet her mother's wrath had been the least of her worries. For a long time, she couldn't even process the adrenaline that had surged through her—only the crushing weight of regret.

In the hallway, Sophia's voice echoed as she spoke on the phone with someone, her tone harsh and final. "I want a full report on this accident, and I expect the repairs to be done immediately," she hissed. The conversation ended abruptly, and she turned toward Elizabeth's door, her face set in stone.

"Elizabeth," she called out sharply. "You know the drill. No more sneaking around, no more foolish risks." There was a long pause, and then Sophia added, "And don't even think about trying to justify this. You're grounded. You'll stay in your room until I decide otherwise."

Elizabeth's eyes filled with tears, but she said nothing. The traditional punishment that had become a grim routine in their household loomed ahead. As she sank onto the cold floor of her room, she thought bitterly, "I nearly died, and this is how you repay me?" Her mind swirled with emotions—fear, anger, and a deep, paralyzing sense of failure.

Later, as the night deepened, Elizabeth lay on her makeshift bed, the silence around her oppressive. Every so often, she would open her eyes and stare at the ceiling, the memory of the near crash haunting her. The sound of distant sirens and the hum of the refrigerator seemed to echo the beating of her heart. "I have to change. I can't keep doing this," she thought, though the words felt hollow in the darkness.

The next morning, Sophia's punishment was carried out with cold precision. Elizabeth was forced to stand in the living room for what felt like an eternity, her eyes cast downward, as Sophia recited the litany of her failures. "You are reckless, Elizabeth," Sophia declared, her voice harsh. "Today, you will reflect on your actions, and tomorrow, you will start making better choices."

The words stung, and Elizabeth's tears fell silently as she endured the familiar punishment—a reminder of the unyielding cycle of anger, regret, and fear that had come to define her life. "Never again," she vowed silently, though the promise wavered with every strike from her mother.

As she was finally allowed into her room, Elizabeth curled up on the bed, her body aching from the physical punishment and her heart heavy with the knowledge that she had come dangerously close to losing everything. "I nearly died, and now I must pay for my mistakes," she whispered to herself. The memory of the telephone pole, the screech of the brakes, and the blinding fear of that near miss would haunt her for a long time.

In that bleak moment, Elizabeth resolved to change. The thrill of stolen freedom had nearly cost her life, and the weight of her mother's punishment was a harsh lesson. As the early morning light began to seep through the window, Elizabeth sat up and opened her sketchbook. With trembling hands, she sketched the scene as she remembered it.

Her hands, though shaky, carried a spark of determination. Elizabeth knew that the path ahead would be fraught with challenges, but she also realized that this near miss was the final straw—a moment that might finally force her to choose a different way of life. "I have to be better," she thought, her voice soft but resolute.

The chapter of that terrifying night had ended, but the road to true freedom was just beginning. Elizabeth promised herself that she would learn from her mistakes, that every near-death experience, every harsh punishment, would serve as a reminder of the value of her life. And as she stared out at the world waking up around her, she vowed, "Never again will I gamble with my life for a fleeting taste of rebellion."

TIPPING INTO EXHAUSTION

Elizabeth's late-night escapes had become a bittersweet routine. Every time she slipped out into the darkness, there was an undeniable thrill—a momentary burst of freedom that made her heart race. Yet, even as she savored those stolen minutes, a quiet worry gnawed at her: the fear that one misstep might shatter everything. Tonight, like many others before it, she crept out after the house had fallen silent. The cool night air brushed against her skin, and for a fleeting moment, she almost believed she had it all figured out.

She climbed into the driver's seat of Sophia's car—a car she never planned to drive, but one that now carried her away from the suffocating responsibilities of the day. As she started the engine, her mind danced between exhilaration and the nagging anxiety of what might happen if she were caught. "Just a few hours of freedom," she reassured herself silently, even though every beat of her heart reminded her of the risks.

For months, Elizabeth had balanced her responsibilities at the kennel with these midnight escapes. The work at the kennel was unrelenting: scrubbing pens until her arms ached, tending to the whelping of puppies, and handling every chore that seemed to pile up with each new day. The constant physical strain had begun to take its toll. To keep herself awake and alert during the long, weary mornings, Elizabeth had started taking NoDoz pills—three at a time—hoping to push through the exhaustion. The pills gave her a jittery energy that helped her manage her duties, but by mid-afternoon, her body felt like it was stretched too thin, and the relentless fatigue crept in like an unwelcome shadow.

One particularly draining afternoon, while scrubbing down a stubborn spot on a concrete floor in the kennel, Elizabeth felt her vision blur. The distant hum of the outside air mingled with the echo of her own labored breathing as she paused at a floor drain. "Not now..." she whispered to herself, swaying slightly. Before she could gather her strength, everything went dark.

The next thing Elizabeth recalled was the rough grip of Logan shaking her shoulder as he called her name. "You look wiped, Elizabeth," he said in a tone that was overly cheery, the forced concern making her skin crawl. "Do you want a massage? I'm pretty good at those."

She tried to protest, her voice barely rising above a whisper, "No, I'm—I'm okay." But her limbs felt heavy, and her thoughts swirled in a haze of exhaustion and uncertainty.

Logan's expression shifted as he stepped closer. "Come on," he said, slipping an arm under her elbow. "Let me help you up. You don't look so well."

Elizabeth attempted to stand, but her movements were sluggish. "I really am fine," she insisted, though her words were shaky. Logan's arm tightened around her, and before she could offer another protest, he maneuvered her toward a nearby table in the grooming area. His tone grew insistent. "You need to relax. Let me loosen those muscles. You'll feel so much better."

"Please... no," Elizabeth murmured, a knot of panic rising in her chest. In that moment, the warmth of the evening air and the adrenaline of her midnight escape were replaced by a stark realization: she was utterly vulnerable here, with someone whose intentions she couldn't quite read.

Logan's grip was firm as he pressed her shoulders against the table. "Don't make this difficult," he said in a low, steady voice. "I know you have been sneaking out at night, and I haven't said a word. You owe me."

Elizabeth's eyes darted around, searching for a way out, but the room was empty save for the soft hum of a distant radio and the muffled sounds of animals in the kennel. "Let me go," she tried again, her voice cracking with fear. But Logan's presence was overpowering, and her body, heavy with fatigue, refused to cooperate.

Time blurred, and all she could hear was the steady rhythm of her own breath mingling with Logan's murmurs. Every second stretched painfully long until, finally, he released her. Elizabeth slumped against the table, her body trembling with shock. "I... I'm sorry," Logan mumbled as if he'd completed a necessary task, leaving Elizabeth gasping for air, "but you left me no choice."

When she finally managed to pull herself away, Elizabeth stumbled toward the doorway. The cool night outside beckoned, a stark contrast to the stifling closeness of the grooming area. Her thoughts raced, not with defiance this time but with a raw fear of what might happen next—and a deep, painful relief that she was alone once more.

Alone in the quiet of the night, Elizabeth found herself on the cold concrete floor of the kennel, hugging herself tightly as she tried to make sense of what had just transpired. She could still feel the lingering pressure on her shoulders and the dull throb inside. "I almost couldn't fight back," she thought, a tear tracing a path down her cheek. Yet even as she sat there, a part of her steeled itself against the despair.

In the silent aftermath, Elizabeth made her way slowly out of the building. The cool air brushed over her face, and she looked up at the star-studded sky—a canopy of indifferent light that made her feel both small and strangely hopeful. She knew deep down that her nightly escapes had become more than just moments of freedom; they were her lifeline, however flawed.

Inside the kennel, the sounds of barking dogs and the rustle of cleaning supplies filled the air, a reminder that life continued relentlessly even after the darkness of the night. Elizabeth's mind wandered briefly to the promise she had made to meet her friends later—a brief respite from the crushing weight of her reality. Though her body ached and her limbs trembled, she had to hold onto the notion that even a short night away might bring her the solace she craved.

Elizabeth made her way back to her small, dimly lit room. She sat on her pallet, glancing at the thin blanket that offered little warmth. The only sounds were the faint hum of the refrigerator and her own labored breathing. She closed her eyes, attempting to steady her thoughts. "I'll be out in a little while," she reminded herself silently. "Just a quick escape, then I'll return. No one will know."

Her heart raced with a mix of fear and a reckless sort of hope—a conflict that she never spoke aloud but that pulsed through her veins with every beat. The idea of sneaking out again, even though she knew the risks, filled her with a dangerous excitement. Yet a voice inside cautioned her, reminding her of the near disaster just weeks before, the way the telephone pole had almost claimed her life. The memory was vivid—a scar etched in her mind that pulsed with each beat.

Elizabeth slept longer than she expected. She woke to an odd sensation. It was similar to the violations she had experienced in the past but somehow different. As she woke, she realized it was fingers moving slowly in and out. She startled, twisted, and sat up. It was Logan. "You won't be home later, so you better give it up now, or I will make sure you get caught," he threatened.

Afraid of getting in trouble with her mother, Elizabeth lay down and let Logan finish his task.

As the minutes passed, Elizabeth gathered herself enough to prepare for her midnight rendezvous with friends. In a low, determined tone, she whispered to herself, "I have to go out. I need to feel... normal, even if just for a little while." The words were soft, barely audible, but they carried a desperate longing for a taste of life beyond the relentless demands of Logan's thrusting.

When he was finished, he actually spoke, "Have fun tonight, sweetheart." Disgusted and a bit nauseated, she retrieved her small bag from under the bed, filled it with a change of clothes, and took one last look in the mirror. The reflection that stared back was tired, eyes rimmed with exhaustion and fear—but there was a glimmer of resolve there too, an unspoken promise to herself that she would manage to slip away without consequence and that Logan couldn't enter her again today. She paused for a moment, then decided to walk right out the front door. She was sure Logan wouldn't get up and confront her again tonight. There was no need to go out the window anymore.

Outside, it was completely silent, the only sound her own tentative steps on the gravel driveway. Each step was measured, and as she reached the ground, the weight of the world seemed to momentarily lift from her shoulders. Even though a part of her was terrified of what might happen if she were caught by her mother, she was confident that Logan had her back tonight. The thought of being free of responsibilities and Logan's prying eyes watching her every move was enough to make her want to stay gone forever. Though she knew she couldn't leave Oliver all alone.

As she moved into the dark embrace of the night, headed for the car, Elizabeth's thoughts shifted to the party that awaited her. The promise of laughing with friends filled her with a curious excitement, wondering what the night had in store. "I can do this," she whispered to herself, a fragile murmur that hung in the cold air.

At the corner of the block, the silence was broken only by the distant sounds of cars and the occasional murmur of voices. Elizabeth blended into the shadows, each step a delicate balance of caution and boldness. The memory of the near miss with the telephone pole had left a lasting impression—a reminder of just how close she had come to a tragic end. And yet, that very memory propelled her forward, urging her to grasp life, no matter how fleeting the moments might be.

A part of her hoped that tonight, everything would be different —tonight, she wouldn't feel the crushing weight of consequence. The fear of getting caught was ever-present, but it was buried beneath a steely determination. Elizabeth's heart throbbed with the uncertainty of what the night would bring.

Finally, as she approached the meeting spot—a small, inconspicuous café known only to a few trusted friends—Elizabeth slowed down, pausing to steady herself. The neon sign flickered softly above the door, its inviting glow a stark contrast to the dark thoughts that had accompanied her journey. With a deep, steadying breath, she pushed the door open, stepping into a world that promised laughter, music, and a temporary escape.

Inside, the murmur of conversation and the clinking of glasses provided a warm backdrop to her return to a semblance of normalcy. Elizabeth glanced around, trying to catch a glimpse of friendly faces, and for a brief moment, the heaviness in her chest eased. She spotted a familiar face—a friend from school—who waved her over with a smile that reached her eyes.

"Elizabeth! Over here!" Christy called.

"Hey," Elizabeth replied, a faint smile tugging at her lips despite the happenings of the evening. She slid into a booth, her heart still pounding with the rush of her secret escape. The conversation around her was lively, and for the next few hours, she allowed herself to be swept up in the moment.

In between laughs and shared stories, Elizabeth found herself letting go of the constant anxiety that had haunted her days. The thrill of being out with friends, of being part of something that wasn't defined by her oppressions at home, was intoxicating. Every laugh, every gentle touch on her arm from a friend reminded her that life was still full of moments worth living.

As the evening wore on and the party began to wind down, Elizabeth's thoughts turned inward. She knew that the brief reprieve from the relentless pressures of home was just that—a brief reprieve. Soon, she would have to return, and with it, the weight of home and the ever-looming possibility of punishment. But for now, under the soft glow of neon lights and surrounded by the comforting hum of friendly chatter, Elizabeth allowed herself to simply be.

In the quiet moments before she eventually slipped back out into the night to return home, Elizabeth sat for a moment alone at a corner table, her mind both racing and calm. "I'll be back soon," she whispered to herself, a promise that was both a comfort and a challenge. The mingling of fear and confidence was subtle, a quiet reminder that while the risks were real, so too was the fleeting taste of freedom. Though the sun would be up soon, she was sure everyone would be sleeping at that hour.

When the time came to leave, Elizabeth stepped out into the cool night air once more. She walked back along the dark streets, each step echoing with the memories of her journey—a journey of peril and small victories, of risk and reward. The café faded behind her as she retraced her steps toward home, her mind already racing with plans for tomorrow and the secret hope that one day she might find a way to balance the delicate scales of her chaotic world.

In that long, winding drive back, Elizabeth's heart pounded with a mixture of relief and lingering dread—a silent promise that even as she returned to a life filled with constraints, she would carry tonight's fleeting freedom like a hidden treasure. And though the night had been filled with both joy and terror, Elizabeth couldn't help but believe that somewhere, somehow, these stolen moments would add up to something more—a quiet rebellion that might one day pave the way to a life truly her own.

❧ 88 ❧

AN UNBELIEVED TRUTH

Sophia and Elizabeth faced each other in the cramped living room, the atmosphere heavy with unspoken pain. The air seemed to vibrate with tension as Elizabeth, her voice trembling and her eyes brimming with unshed tears, recounted what Logan had done—how he had forced himself on her in a cold, invasive manner. Her words, raw and desperate, filled the small space.

Sophia's eyes hardened as she listened. "You've lied about things before, Elizabeth," she said in a low, clipped tone, her voice laced with anger. "You're always looking for excuses. I'm not stupid. Logan's never been anything but good to us."

Elizabeth's heart sank as she searched her mother's face for a hint of compassion, but all she found was cold dismissal. "I... I'm telling the truth," Elizabeth managed to choke out, her voice quivering. "It wasn't like that—I didn't want him to..." She stopped, tears spilling silently as she tried to find the right words.

Sophia shook her head sharply. "Save it," she snapped. "I don't need you twisting the truth. You've made your bed, and now you must lie in it." With that, her mother stormed out of the room, leaving Elizabeth frozen in painful silence.

In the months to follow, the unspoken rift grew. Elizabeth found herself avoiding Logan whenever possible, yet his presence seemed to haunt every corner of the property. In quiet moments, when she was alone with her thoughts, the memory of his regular visits—of his unwanted touch—gnawed at her, even as Sophia's frosty treatment reinforced the notion that men are allowed to take what they want and that there is nothing you can do.

One evening, the tension finally reached a breaking point. A minor disagreement over dinner about the day's chores escalated quickly into shouting. Elizabeth sat at the table, head bowed, as her mother's voice trembled with fury. Suddenly, Logan's anger exploded. In a moment that seemed to stretch forever, he raised his hand and struck Sophia hard across the cheek. The sound of the slap echoed through the silent house. Sophia's hand flew to her face, and for a split second, the entire room fell silent as if time itself had frozen.

Elizabeth's eyes widened in shock. "Mom, no..." she whispered, her voice barely audible. Her heart pounded furiously as she watched her mother's expression change from fury to stunned silence. For the first time, the weight of the truth that Elizabeth had tried to reveal seemed to crack the dam of Sophia's denial.

Within hours, the atmosphere had shifted irreparably. Sophia, her eyes red with a mix of rage and sorrow, packed her bags hastily. "I can't live like this anymore," she said, her voice shaking as she spoke into the phone with Henry. "Logan hurt me—again. I'm taking Elizabeth and Oliver back to Arizona. We're leaving immediately."

Later that day, Sophia gathered Elizabeth and Oliver in the living room. "Pack whatever you can carry," she ordered, her tone a mixture of desperation and grim resolve. Logan's angry shouts echoed from somewhere behind her, but Sophia wouldn't let him be heard. Elizabeth's stomach churned as she clutched her few belongings, the gravity of her mother's decision lifting like a feather in her heart.

On the drive to Arizona, the car was filled with an oppressive silence. Elizabeth stared out the window, watching the familiar landscapes fade away, while her mind swirled with conflicted emotions. She recalled the incident—the slap, the raw pain on her mother's face, and the betrayal that had never been acknowledged. Her eyes welled with tears, but she blinked them away, determined not to let the emotion spill over.

Sophia bought a house; it was a small, worn building that offered little in the way of comfort but none of the terror that had haunted their previous home. Elizabeth felt a momentary release. Standing by the front door, she wrapped her arms around Oliver and whispered, "Whatever awaits us here, I hope it's better than what we left behind."

In the days that followed, the family began to rebuild their lives in Arizona. The small house, though dilapidated, felt like a fresh start. Sophia kept to herself, her eyes haunted by the events that had led them here, while Elizabeth and Oliver tried to adapt to the new routine. Elizabeth would often sit by the window, lost in thought, her mind replaying the moments of that fateful night, wondering if her mother would ever see the truth.

89

THE NIGHTMARE CONTINUES

The weeks in Arizona had passed in a blur of settling in, unpacking boxes, and trying to put some semblance of order into the new house. Sophia was determined that the upcoming housewarming party would be flawless—a fresh start in a home that promised to leave behind all the past conflicts. Nearly everyone in the family was invited: Henry, Margaret, Isabelle, Evelyn, James, Alice, Lacy, Mia—and, of course, Oliver. Even Julian, now a military police officer, had managed to arrange leave so he could attend.

Julian arrived in a brand-new truck, its tires crunching over the house's rugged desert gravel. Dressed smartly in his crisp uniform, he stepped out and offered Elizabeth a brief nod. Although it had been years since she'd seen him in person, his presence was both familiar and quietly imposing. Still, the family greeted him warmly, impressed by the calm confidence he exuded.

Inside the lively, sunlit living room, Sophia flitted about, organizing last-minute details. "We're short on napkins, ice, and a few folding chairs," she announced briskly as she spoke to a group of relatives gathered by the counter. "Henry, could you please help get these supplies? And Julian, would you mind taking Elizabeth to pick up a few things in town? I have a hundred other things to sort out?"

Julian replied without hesitation, his tone friendly yet

businesslike. "Sure thing, Sophia. Elizabeth, let's head out quickly, all right?"

Elizabeth followed him to the door, her eyes lingering on the familiar faces of family members before she climbed into the truck. As the vehicle rumbled away from the house, she tried not to look Julian in the eye. He tried to strike up a conversation, but Elizabeth would only respond in one- or two-word sentences. The ride was as uneventful as Elizabeth could make it.

When they reached her grandparents' modest single-story house—a relic with a wide, welcoming porch—Julian parked the truck and cut the engine. "Let's make this quick," he said, glancing at the bright midday sun. "Your mom sounded pretty stressed."

Elizabeth nodded. "Yeah, she wants everything perfect for the party." She stepped into the house and was immediately greeted by the gentle aroma of coffee mixed with the comforting scent of old wood. The supplies were piled neatly in one corner: napkins, paper plates, drinks, and a bundle of folding chairs.

Julian cracked a small smile. "I'll load these into the truck. Everything will be set in no time."

Elizabeth, feeling a bit dusty from the drive and the morning's chores, rubbed her arms. "I need to jump in the shower—I feel so gross."

"Go ahead," Julian said, already picking up a stack of chairs. "I'll be right here."

Leaving Julian to his task, Elizabeth hurried down the hall to the bathroom. As she closed the door behind her, she relished the brief privacy to wash away the grime of the day. The warm water cascaded over her shoulders, and she found herself thinking about the party. Would the family get along? Would old tensions rise again? A small hope fluttered inside her as she let the steam soften the harsh lines of the day.

Meanwhile, back in the living room, Julian finished loading the supplies. He paused, running a hand through his cropped hair, then glanced toward the hallway. "I wonder if Elizabeth needs company after a long day," he muttered to himself as he walked into the bathroom to enjoy his quiet time with Elizabeth.

After the second shower, Elizabeth dressed and rejoined the bustling preparations at Sophia's house. The house was alive with chatter and the clatter of dishes as relatives moved about, setting the stage for a promising evening.

Later that afternoon, as the party began in earnest, the atmosphere shifted from frenzied preparation to warm celebration. The once-quiet backyard had transformed into a vibrant gathering space. Strings of fairy lights draped over the patio, and a large bonfire crackled in a stone fire pit. Music played softly in the background, and laughter mingled with the gentle murmur of conversation.

Elizabeth watched as family members mingled—Henry and Margaret exchanged knowing glances, Isabelle and Evelyn laughed over shared stories, and James traded playful banter with Alice. Even Julian chatted amicably with a few of the older relatives.

Despite the merriment, Elizabeth couldn't help but notice how Sophia's gaze often drifted to her—an unspoken mix of disgust and something else she couldn't quite decipher. Elizabeth thought it might be rage. Did her mother think it was her fault they had to move?

As the evening deepened, the party began to wind down. Family members started to say their goodbyes, and the lively hum of conversation gradually softened.

Their conversation was interrupted by the soft chime of a doorbell. Sophia emerged from the house with a tired smile, calling out to the departing guests. "Alright, everyone, it's time to head home!" she announced, her tone a mix of finality and relief.

As the crowd dispersed, Elizabeth found herself walking back toward the house, her mind still lingering on how peaceful the evening was. For a change, everyone had gotten along, and there was no fighting at all.

Inside the house, the family gathered to tidy up. Oliver was busy stacking chairs, while Sophia surveyed the remnants of the party with a critical eye. Elizabeth hung back, lost in thought, when her mother approached her. "Elizabeth, did you enjoy tonight?" Sophia asked, her tone less harsh than before, almost curious.

Elizabeth hesitated, then nodded slowly. "It was nice, Mom. The party was... different. Calmer, I guess."

Sophia sighed, her eyes softening for a moment. "I just want things to change, Elizabeth. I want us to have a fresh start. I hope you can see that, too."

Elizabeth offered a small smile in return, though her mind still lingered on the thought of how her mother didn't believe her in regard to Logan. "I think I do, Mom," she replied quietly. "I think... maybe tonight helped me remember that even when everything feels broken, there can be moments of beauty."

Later that night, as the house grew quiet, Sophia retreated to her room and Oliver to his couch, while Elizabeth sat on the back porch. The cool night air caressed her face as she looked up at the starry sky. The events of the evening—joy, music, conversation—blended together into a mosaic of hope and uncertainty. She thought about how everyone got along and had a great time.

In a soft, reflective tone, Elizabeth murmured to herself, "Maybe tomorrow will bring more of that freedom—more music and laughter and moments when we can all just be." The gentle whisper of the wind seemed to echo her words, wrapping around her like a fragile promise.

Inside, Oliver slept soundlessly on the couch, and Sophia's light remained on in the hallway—a silent guardian over a house slowly learning to mend its broken pieces. Elizabeth closed her eyes, allowing herself a brief moment of peace. She knew that the road ahead was uncertain and that old tensions might resurface. Yet, for that one quiet moment beneath the stars, she dared to believe that change was possible—and that perhaps the seeds of newfound freedom planted tonight could one day grow into something lasting.

90

TRUST SHATTERED

That fateful afternoon, as the late Arizona sun slanted through the living room windows, Elizabeth knew she had to speak up. She had spent too many nights alone with the weight of Julian's abuse on her shoulders, too many days when the silence of her pain went unanswered. Today, the truth had to come out—even if it meant risking everything.

Elizabeth sat quietly at the kitchen table while Sophia busied herself with cooking dinner. The air was heavy with unspoken tension as Elizabeth fumbled with her courage. Finally, her voice trembled as she said, "Mom, I need to talk to you."

Sophia looked up sharply, her eyes narrowing. "What is it now, Elizabeth?" she asked, trying to sound neutral but betraying an undercurrent of irritation.

Elizabeth took a shaky breath. "It's... it's about Julian. About what he did to me." Her words faltered, and she swallowed hard, her cheeks flushing with tears. "He... he forced himself on me. In a way... I couldn't stop him."

For a long, agonizing moment, silence filled the room. Sophia's eyes widened in disbelief, then hardened with anger. "What are you talking about?" she demanded, her tone cold. "You're just making excuses. Julian has been nothing but good to us."

"Mom, please," Elizabeth pleaded, her voice rising with desperation. "I'm not lying. I've been so scared, and I didn't know how to tell you." She reached out, almost pleading, "I need you to believe me, to do something about him. I can't keep living like this."

Elizabeth, still bearing the weight of her secret, sat at the table with her arms wrapped tightly around herself. Her eyes, red and glassy, reflected the storm inside her as she listened to her mother's measured yet seething tone.

"How long, Elizabeth?" Sophia demanded, her voice low and trembling with anger and pain. "How long has this been going on?"

Elizabeth's throat constricted as she struggled to find the right words. The details of the abuse had been a lifetime of hidden torment, a collection of moments too numerous to count. "For... a long time," Elizabeth managed, her voice barely above a whisper, "it started when I was little." The confession, heavy with raw emotion, hung in the air like a curse.

Sophia's eyes blazed with fury and wounded pride. "You've always been so good at twisting things, haven't you?" she spat bitterly. "I know you've lied before, Elizabeth. I'm not blind to your drama. Julian's been nothing but good to us, and now you're telling me this?"

Elizabeth's heart sank as tears threatened to spill over. "But Mom, I'm not making it up! You have to believe me—what he did was horrible." Her voice cracked with anguish as she pleaded, "I needed help—I never wanted any of this."

Before Sophia could respond, the door creaked open, and the sound of muffled voices from the hallway signaled the arrival of the grandparents. Henry and Margaret stepped into the living room, their expressions a mixture of disbelief and concern when they heard the conversation taking place. Margaret's eyes narrowed as she took in Elizabeth's tear-streaked face and Sophia's tense posture.

"Elizabeth," Margaret said coolly, "explain yourself. What is it you're saying?"

Henry's gaze remained fixed on the floor, his silence louder than any words could be. Elizabeth hesitated, then blurted out the painful details of Julian's violation. "He... forced himself on me. I—I couldn't stop him," she admitted, her voice trembling with shame and sorrow.

Margaret's face contorted into a look of cold disbelief. "That's a ridiculous story, Elizabeth," she said sharply. "You've always had a wild imagination. You need to stop these fabrications, or you'll cause more harm than good."

Henry cleared his throat but said nothing as Margaret's disapproval filled the room. Elizabeth's eyes burned with unshed tears as she looked from her grandparents to her mother. "I'm telling the truth," she whispered desperately. "I'm hurting, and no one believes me."

Sophia's voice rose suddenly. "Enough, Elizabeth! I won't have these baseless accusations ruin what we've built. You're a compulsive liar—always making excuses." Her tone was harsh, leaving Elizabeth feeling more isolated than ever.

Silence fell over the room. Henry and Margaret exchanged glances before slowly exiting the living room, leaving Sophia and Elizabeth alone. The silence was oppressive—a crushing void where understanding should have been.

Elizabeth's breathing grew shallow, and she slid away from her mother's accusing gaze. "Why won't anyone listen?" she murmured, her voice barely audible. "I'm trying to tell you something important... something I've suffered in silence for so long."

Sophia's expression softened for just a split second, as if the weight of her own guilt flickered behind her eyes, but then hardened once more. "I'm done with your lies, Elizabeth," she said coldly. "If you keep this up, you'll lose everything—and I mean that."

Unable to bear the tension, Elizabeth escaped to the porch. The cool evening air brushed against her tear-stained cheeks as she stared at the streetlights flickering in the distance. "I just want someone to believe me," she whispered to the night, her voice raw with despair. In that moment, she vowed that one day she would break free from the chains of disbelief and betrayal that had defined her life.

Later that day, Sophia insisted that Elizabeth must recount everything in front of her parents again. Reluctantly, Elizabeth sat at the dining table with Henry and Margaret, her heart pounding so hard she was sure they could hear it. "Tell us the truth, Elizabeth," Margaret demanded, her voice icy as she crossed her arms. "We deserve to know what's been happening."

Elizabeth took a deep breath, her hands trembling as she began, "Julian... he... he forced himself on me a long time ago. I—" She broke off, tears streaming silently down her cheeks as she tried to articulate the unbearable pain.

Henry's face darkened, but he said nothing. Margaret's eyes, however, were filled with disdain. "That's enough," Margaret said sharply. "You're just going to cause more problems for the family with these stories."

Elizabeth's voice dropped to a choked whisper. "But I'm not lying... I'm hurting so much."

Sophia's glare turned icy. "Your words have consequences, Elizabeth. I'm not going to have our family's reputation ruined by your fantasies." She gestured dismissively toward Henry and Margaret.

In the ensuing silence, Elizabeth's soul shattered. The trust she'd desperately sought was now broken, not just by Julian's vile act but by the betrayal of those who were supposed to protect her. "I'm all alone," she thought bitterly, her eyes filling with hopelessness. Then she realized that her grandparents didn't come back to comfort her; they came back to silence her.

"Elizabeth, if you keep telling these lies, then neither Grandpa nor I will ever talk to you again. Do you want that?" Margaret asked cautiously.

"No. But..." Elizabeth started.

"No buts. This is the end of it, or you can leave this house right now," Sophia added forcefully, letting Elizabeth know she was very serious.

After what seemed like an eternity of discussion, everyone finally came to the agreement that Elizabeth wouldn't say anything again and that everyone else would pretend she had never said anything to begin with.

That night, as darkness blanketed the house, Elizabeth sat on the living room floor, Oliver snoring on the couch behind her. The sound of her own sobs filled the space while Sophia paced in the background, her footsteps heavy with regret and anger. "You've done this to yourself, Elizabeth," Sophia muttered to no one in particular, her voice muffled by the storm of emotions inside her.

Unable to contain herself any longer, Elizabeth whispered, "Why can't anyone believe me?" Her plea echoed off the walls, unanswered, as she clutched her arms around herself.

Days later, when Henry and Margaret returned briefly to collect a few items from the house, their eyes avoided meeting Elizabeth's. As they drove away, the car's taillights blurred into the night, leaving Elizabeth with a lingering ache of betrayal. Sophia's silence and cold dismissals had severed any hope Elizabeth might have had for familial support.

Alone in her room, Elizabeth stared at the cracked mirror, trying to piece together the shattered fragments of her trust. "One day, I'll make them see," she vowed, though her voice trembled with uncertainty. She wished for a world where her pain wouldn't be dismissed—a place where her truth would be honored, not ridiculed.

As the days turned into weeks, Elizabeth's inner turmoil deepened. The memory of that night—the humiliation, the rejection, the betrayal—haunted her every moment. In quiet moments, she recalled her mother's harsh words and her grandparents' cold dismissal. Each recollection was a blow, another shard of trust that had been scattered and lost.

In the dim light of dawn, as Elizabeth's tired eyes finally fluttered open, she realized that broken trust is not easily mended. And though her heart ached with betrayal, she clung to the hope that one day, the weight of her truth would be lifted, and the world would see the real Elizabeth—a girl who was not a compulsive liar but someone who had suffered in silence for far too long.

91

SILENCED RESENTMENT

Elizabeth hadn't spoken a word about what Julian had done to her in weeks. Every time she tried to bury the memory of his cold, invasive touch, it resurfaced with a vengeance. Lately, though, another twist of fate had ignited feelings she hadn't expected—jealousy. Julian was now dating Jenny, a bright and outgoing girl who laughed easily and held his hand in public, as if nothing could ever go wrong. And though Elizabeth wasn't entirely sure why, seeing them together stoked an anger in her that she fought hard to keep hidden.

It started subtly at first. Whenever Julian drove his pickup truck around town, Jenny would ride shotgun. Elizabeth began to position herself in the vehicle—squeezing into the middle seat before Jenny could claim it. One afternoon, as they set off from the ranch for an errand, the tension in the truck was almost tangible.

"Good morning," Julian said with a casual nod as he started the engine, his eyes briefly meeting Elizabeth's before flicking to the rearview mirror.

Jenny offered a small smile, but Elizabeth, already feeling a mix of hurt and determination, shot a quick, tight-lipped glance in response. "Is everything all right?" Jenny asked softly, as if trying to smooth over an awkward moment.

"Yeah, fine," Elizabeth replied, her voice clipped. Internally, she raged silently—this wasn't just about the truck seats; it was about the feeling of being excluded from something that she believed should have been hers.

As the drive continued, Elizabeth peppered Julian with small quips about their shared memories. "Remember when we used to sneak out for ice cream after school?" she said, half-teasing. Julian chuckled, nodding. "Yeah, those were the days." He glanced at Jenny, then back at Elizabeth, and the air grew heavy with unspoken competition.

At one point, Jenny began to speak about her own experiences— stories of fun parties, of nights out with friends—but Elizabeth interjected with a memory of her own: a childhood prank that only she and Julian seemed to share. "Oh, come on, Jenny," Elizabeth said with a forced laugh, "you wouldn't understand the genius of our old pranks." Her tone was light, but her eyes betrayed a flicker of pain. Jenny's smile faltered for just a moment before she recovered, nodding politely.

The conversation continued, each remark from Elizabeth laced with a subtle undercurrent of possessiveness—a need to remind everyone that she and Julian shared something special. At times, when Jenny tried to contribute to the conversation, Elizabeth would cut her off with a dismissive, "Oh, that's nothing compared to what we did back then," her voice low and firm. It was a game for Elizabeth—a way to assert a connection she desperately craved, even if it was built on twisted feelings.

As days turned into weeks, the dynamic grew increasingly tense. Elizabeth found herself spending every moment she could with Julian on rides around town, her efforts to monopolize his attention becoming more blatant. "Julian, remember that time at the lake?" she would say, leaning in close. "It was the best day ever." Her voice carried a note of nostalgia, but also a hint of something darker—an expectation that Julian's memories should match hers.

Julian's responses were measured. "Yeah, Elizabeth," he would say, his tone casual but his eyes darkening whenever she spoke of their past. The tension between them was nearly palpable, and while Elizabeth's heart pounded with both excitement and dread, she maintained her composure outwardly.

One evening, as they rode home from a late afternoon errand, the atmosphere in the truck grew thick with unspoken words. The radio played a familiar tune, and Jenny sat silently by the window, watching them with cautious eyes. Finally, Jenny spoke up, "Elizabeth, why do you always insist on riding with Julian? I mean, aren't you... tired of being the 'third wheel'?" Her tone was curious but laced with a hint of challenge.

Elizabeth turned to Jenny, her eyes narrowing slightly. "I'm just... used to it," she replied coolly, her voice barely above a whisper. Internally, she thought, "Maybe it's not comfortable, but it feels like where I belong."

Jenny frowned and leaned forward. "But you're not a kid anymore, Elizabeth. You can decide where you want to be. You shouldn't have to follow him everywhere." Her words struck a nerve, and Elizabeth's pulse quickened.

Before Elizabeth could respond, Julian interjected, "Alright, let's focus on the road, okay?" His tone was even, and he avoided the brewing conflict. The rest of the ride passed in strained silence.

Later that night, after the ride had ended, Elizabeth sat alone in her room, the echo of the day's tension reverberating in her thoughts. She stared at the ceiling, lost in conflicting emotions— part of her craved the closeness that came from being around Julian, while another part resented the very idea of him sharing his life with someone else.

Unable to sleep, she whispered to herself, "Maybe I'm just confused... maybe I need to figure out what I really want." But the more she thought, the more the complexity of her feelings swirled inside her like a storm.

The next day at school, Elizabeth tried to focus on her classes, but the memory of the pickup truck ride, Jenny's questions, and Julian's quiet detachment haunted her. In a whispered conversation with her friend Tina during lunch, she confided, "I'm not sure why I get so worked up about him. It's like... every time he looks my way, something inside me just breaks open, and then I feel this mix of anger and longing."

Tina's eyes widened in concern. "Elizabeth, maybe you need to sort through your feelings. It's not healthy to feel this way; it's tearing you apart."

Elizabeth shrugged, pushing away the uncomfortable truth. "I don't know what's wrong with me," she admitted softly. "I just feel like I'm the only one who really understands him. And when Jenny is around, it's like everything falls apart."

Tina reached across the table, placing a comforting hand on Elizabeth's arm. "Maybe you should talk to someone—a counselor or someone who can help you make sense of it all."

Elizabeth forced a small smile. "I'll think about it," she said, but deep down, she wasn't sure she wanted to confront the tangled mess of emotions inside her.

That night, as she lay in bed, Elizabeth replayed the day's events over and over. Her thoughts were a mix of whispered conversations, fleeting touches, and the stark reality of the relationships that now defined her life. In the quiet of her room, she resolved, "I need to figure this out for my own sake." Yet, the solution remained elusive —a shifting mirage of emotions that left her simultaneously hopeful and terrified.

In the days that followed, Elizabeth's internal struggle deepened. She became increasingly aware of the subtle ways in which she tried to keep Julian's attention on her. At school, she would linger near his classes, catch glimpses of him laughing with friends, and then retreat into herself when he wasn't looking. The more she tried to ignore it, the stronger the feelings grew, festering into a complicated mix of jealousy, love, and self-loathing.

One afternoon, after a particularly grueling day, Elizabeth found herself alone in the library. She sat at a secluded table, books open before her, but her mind wandered instead to Julian. The quiet hum of the fluorescent lights seemed to echo the persistent beat of her heart. She pulled out a notebook and began writing down her thoughts—secret confessions about her own feelings, a desperate attempt to unravel the knot inside her.

"Why do I care so much?" she scribbled, the ink smudging slightly as tears blurred her vision. "I shouldn't—no, I can't keep doing this." Her handwriting wavered as she poured out every ounce of frustration and longing onto the paper.

A classmate, noticing her distressed state, approached cautiously. "Hey, Elizabeth, are you okay? You look really upset."

Elizabeth blinked back tears, hastily covering her notebook. "I'm fine," she murmured, forcing a smile that didn't reach her eyes. The classmate nodded sympathetically but didn't press further.

That small encounter left Elizabeth feeling both exposed and oddly comforted. Perhaps, she thought, it was time to stop pretending that everything was just fine. Maybe she needed to seek help, to finally speak to someone who could help her navigate these turbulent emotions. But the fear of judgment and the potential fallout from confronting the truth kept her silent—for now.

As the semester wore on, Elizabeth's inner turmoil remained largely hidden behind a mask of nonchalance. Yet, every time she saw Jenny laughing with Julian or noticed how easily he interacted with other people, a pang of jealousy and heartbreak surged within her. Late at night, when she lay awake in her room, she would stare at the ceiling and wonder if she'd ever be free from the web of these complicated feelings.

In one quiet moment, Elizabeth resolved to speak up about her emotions, to at least acknowledge them to someone who might understand. But when she finally gathered the courage to approach her school counselor, Mrs. Stone, her words faltered. "I—I just feel so confused about everything," Elizabeth managed, her voice barely above a whisper. Mrs. Stone's kind eyes met hers. "It's okay to feel that way, Elizabeth. Sometimes our hearts lead us down unexpected paths. After everything that has happened to you, it's normal for your emotions to get twisted and wrong. You do need to talk to someone, but I am not qualified for this much work. I am going to refer you to a professional."

Elizabeth nodded, the weight of her secret finally starting to lift. "Thank you," she said softly. "I just didn't know where to start."

Mrs. Stone offered a gentle smile. "Start by writing it down, if that helps. And remember, you're not alone in this. I'm here to listen whenever you're ready, and this doctor will help a lot."

That conversation marked a tentative turning point for Elizabeth. She began to keep a journal, pouring out her conflicted emotions—her fierce longing for Julian, her deep-seated jealousy when Jenny was near, and the crushing sadness of feeling unheard. In those pages, she found a fragile outlet for her pain, a way to articulate the tumult inside her without fear of immediate repercussions.

Though the feelings didn't vanish overnight, Elizabeth started to notice subtle shifts. At school, she still lingered near Julian's classes, but now she also began spending time with Tina and a few other friends who listened without judgment. Slowly, she learned that sharing her thoughts—even in fragments—could bring a measure of relief. She never really told any of her classmates the whole story.

Still, every time she encountered the sight of Julian and Jenny together, she felt a raw stab in her chest. One evening, as she walked home alone, she paused and looked up at the starry sky. "Maybe someday," she whispered to herself, "I'll be able to let go of this pain."

The road ahead was uncertain, and Elizabeth's journey was far from over. But in those moments of quiet reflection, she clung to the hope that speaking her truth—even if just on paper—might eventually help her heal. For now, she continued to navigate the treacherous waters of her emotions, trying to find balance between longing and loss, between love and hate, and the bitter taste of jealousy.

In the stillness of the night, as the lights of the school faded in the distance, Elizabeth realized that the path to healing was long and winding. Yet, each small step—each conversation with a friend, every note in her journal—was a victory over the silenced resentment that had plagued her for so long. And maybe, just maybe, one day she'd look back and see that the pain was a necessary part of growing up, a dark chapter that ultimately led her to a brighter future.

❦ 92 ❦

A NEW REALITY

Elizabeth stared at the small white stick in her trembling hand, her heart pounding so fiercely she could barely register the details around her. Two unmistakable pink lines glowed in the dim bathroom light. She rubbed her eyes hard, as if trying to erase the vision, but the lines remained. The truth—unavoidable and raw—settled over her like a heavy shroud. She was pregnant.

In the cold silence of that small bathroom, the tile floor sending shivers up her bare feet, a torrent of emotions surged within Elizabeth: fear, uncertainty, and even a flicker of hope. Every hardship of her past—every bruise, every betrayal—seemed to converge into this single moment. The new life hinted at possibilities that both terrified and enticed her.

For a long, agonizing minute, Elizabeth just stood there, grappling with the implications. Then, a quiet determination stirred inside her. "I need help," she whispered to herself. "I have to talk to someone who cares." Her thoughts drifted to Sebastian, an old friend from junior high with whom she had once shared quiet moments during horseback rides. Sebastian was the only man she had ever known who treated her with gentle respect—a stark contrast to the men who had hurt her in the past.

Gathering her courage, Elizabeth stepped out of the bathroom and made her way to the phone, her hands shaking as she dialed Sebastian's number. Each ring felt like an eternity. When his warm, familiar voice finally answered, a small measure of her fear began to ebb.

"Sebastian, it's Elizabeth," she said, her voice soft and tentative. "I... I need to see you. Can we meet?"

There was a pause on the other end—a quiet moment where time seemed to slow—then Sebastian replied, "Of course, Elizabeth. I'm here for you. Where do you want to meet?"

Elizabeth's voice faltered as she suggested, "Maybe... the coffee shop?" She wasn't sure how to explain the urgency without sounding desperate, so she kept her words minimal, hoping that Sebastian's concern would fill the gaps.

Later that afternoon, the coffee shop was a haven of low murmur and the comforting hiss of the espresso machine. Elizabeth found a secluded booth in the back, away from prying eyes, and sat waiting. The soft jazz playing in the background provided a fragile sense of normalcy. When Sebastian arrived, his presence filled the small space with gentle warmth. He wore a slightly rumpled shirt, and his eyes, though shadowed with worry, lit up the moment he saw her.

"Elizabeth," Sebastian said, settling into the booth opposite her, "I've been worried. You sounded upset on the phone. Are you okay?"

Elizabeth's throat tightened. "No, I'm not," she admitted, the words tumbling out in a rush. "I... I took a test this morning. I'm pregnant, Sebastian."

Silence reigned between them for a moment as Sebastian absorbed her words. His brow furrowed, and he reached out, covering her trembling hands with his. "Elizabeth, that's... that's a lot to take in," he said softly, his voice thick with emotion. "I'm surprised, yes, but I'm here for you—no matter what."

She searched his eyes for a sign of judgment or pity and found only genuine concern. "I... I didn't expect this," she confessed, her voice barely above a whisper. "I'm scared, Sebastian. I don't know what to do."

Sebastian squeezed her hand gently. "We'll figure it out together," he assured her. "I know this isn't what you planned, but I want you to know that I'm not going anywhere. I care about you, Elizabeth." His words, though simple, wrapped around her like a lifeline.

They talked for over an hour, their conversation moving slowly from shock and uncertainty to tentative plans for the future. Elizabeth told him everything, even who the father is. Sebastian asked softly, "Have you thought about what you want to do next?"

Elizabeth looked down, her fingers nervously tracing the rim of her coffee cup. "I... I don't really know. Everything feels so overwhelming right now," she admitted. "I always thought I'd have a plan, but I don't."

Sebastian's eyes softened with empathy. "It's okay not to have all the answers right now. Sometimes, life throws us a curveball, and we just have to take it one day at a time. I promise I'll help you, whether that means supporting you through a decision to keep the baby or whatever you choose."

His calm, assuring tone allowed a spark of hope to ignite in Elizabeth—a glimmer that maybe this wasn't the end of her world after all. "Sebastian, I... I never thought I'd be in this position," she confessed, her voice quivering. "I'm scared of what might happen, but... hearing you say that... it makes me feel less alone."

They continued to talk about practical steps: consulting a doctor, discussing her options, and even considering counseling to help navigate her feelings. Sebastian's gentle insistence that she take care of herself resonated deeply with her. "I really need to get help, Sebastian," she said, her eyes welling up. "I can't do this on my own."

Sebastian nodded. "And you won't. I'll be by your side, every step of the way. You deserve to feel safe and supported, Elizabeth. I believe in you."

At one point, Sebastian leaned in closer, his voice dropping to a hushed tone. "I want to marry you," he said, surprising her. "I know it's a lot to ask, especially now, but I can't imagine facing this future without you. I want us to build something together—even if it's not perfect, it'll be ours."

Elizabeth's heart pounded, her breath catching in her chest. The idea was overwhelming—marriage, commitment, building a life together. It was a promise of stability in a world that had been so unstable for her. "Sebastian, I—" she began, but the flood of emotions left her momentarily speechless.

After a long pause, she finally whispered, "If you're sure, then... I'd like that."

The words hung in the air, fragile and tentative, like a newly planted seed. Sebastian smiled, a mixture of relief and determination lighting up his face. "I'm more sure than I've ever been," he said softly, taking her hand in his. "We'll figure it out, one step at a time."

They left the coffee shop under a dusky sky, their hands still intertwined as they walked slowly toward the parking lot. The evening air was cool and gentle, and Elizabeth felt a strange calm settle over her. Despite the chaos of the past few hours, the simple connection with Sebastian made the world seem a little less dark.

That night, as Elizabeth returned home, she felt a conflicted blend of emotions. On one hand, the warmth of Sebastian's promise still lingered, but on the other, the weight of her new reality pressed heavily on her heart. In her room, as she lay on her bed, Elizabeth clutched her journal and thought about what she was going to write that night. She knew that the road ahead would be fraught with challenges and that her relationship with Sebastian would be just the beginning of a new chapter in her life. But in that quiet moment, she allowed herself to believe that maybe, just maybe, this time things could be different.

Elizabeth's thoughts wandered to her past—a collage of pain, betrayal, and loneliness—and then shifted to the tender memory of Sebastian's words. "I'm not going anywhere," he had said. And somehow, that promise felt like a fragile lifeline. She closed her eyes, and as she drifted off to sleep, she whispered a silent vow: to embrace this new reality, to face the future with hope and courage, and to take one day at a time, no matter how uncertain it might be.

In the stillness of the night, Elizabeth clung to that promise as her last thought before sleep claimed her—a small, determined seed of a future in which she might finally feel whole.

ENGAGEMENT

Because Elizabeth was only seventeen, marrying Sebastian without parental consent was legally impossible. Even though she had long felt more like an adult than a child, the law required her mother's signature on any marriage papers. The reality sent a shiver of anxiety through her, and the thought of confronting Sophia—whose relationship with Elizabeth had always been fraught with tension and unspoken pain—made her stomach churn. Yet, despite the many unresolved issues between them, Elizabeth and Sebastian had agreed that time was of the essence.

One crisp autumn afternoon, Sebastian and Elizabeth drove to Sophia's modest home. The car ride was quiet except for the occasional soft reassurance Sebastian offered by gently squeezing her hand. Elizabeth's grip tightened as the car rolled slowly along the paved driveway. Each mile deepened her mix of fear and anticipation, a cocktail of emotions she could barely keep in balance.

When the car pulled up, Sophia opened the door almost before they had even arrived. Her eyes flicked first to Sebastian and then to Elizabeth, as if silently assessing the gravity of their visit. "You two look serious," she remarked in a tone that managed to be both curt and curious. "Come on in."

Inside, Elizabeth perched on the edge of a battered couch, while Sebastian settled beside her, keeping her hand in his. Sophia took her usual seat in a worn armchair across from them, her arms crossed over her chest as if to shield herself from the oncoming storm.

After a long, heavy pause, Elizabeth spoke up. "Mom," she began, her voice barely above a whisper, "I—I have something important to tell you."

Sophia's eyes narrowed slightly as she leaned forward, her voice low and edged with expectation. "Go on," she said. There was a brief silence as the weight of the moment pressed in.

Taking a deep, shaky breath, Elizabeth glanced over at Sebastian, who nodded encouragingly. "I'm pregnant," she said, the words sounding louder than she had intended. For a long moment, the room fell into a stunned silence, as if the very air had been sucked out.

Sophia's expression hardened; her eyes shifted from Elizabeth to Sebastian and back again. "Pregnant," she repeated slowly, as though tasting the word. "And you want to get married, too?"

Elizabeth's heart pounded in her ears. "Yes," she whispered. "I know I'm seventeen, but Sebastian and I—we want to get married. We want to start building a life together."

At that, Sophia's face contorted with conflicting emotions. Her jaw tightened, and she stared at the floor for several agonizing seconds before looking up again. "You can't marry without my permission," she stated flatly. The room felt thick with tension.

Sebastian cleared his throat, his voice steady. "I understand that, ma'am," he said, glancing at Sophia with respectful earnestness. "That's why we're here, asking for your consent. I promise you, I'll take care of Elizabeth and the baby. I won't let anything happen to her."

For a moment, the air was heavy with silence as Sophia studied Sebastian. Finally, she exhaled, her voice softening just a touch. "If you're truly committed—and if you can prove that you're willing to do what it takes to raise my daughter and this child—then... I'll sign the papers."

Relief surged in Elizabeth, and tears glistened in her eyes. "Thank you, Mom," she managed, her voice thick with emotion. "I know this isn't easy for you, but we'll make it work. We promise."

Sophia's gaze, now less hostile and more resigned, softened ever so slightly. "I'm not doing this because I'm happy," she said quietly.

"I'm doing it because I'm ready for you to move out, and I am not taking care of this child too." She paused, the silence filled with unspoken pain and years of disappointments. "But don't you dare make me regret this decision. You're going to face real consequences for raising a child at your age."

Sebastian reached over and squeezed Elizabeth's hand. "We will," he said firmly. "We'll do everything right."

Elizabeth's eyes flickered with a mix of fear, hope, and longing as she met her mother's gaze. In that brief moment, she saw a glimpse of relief in her mother's eyes. "Thank you for doing this for us," Elizabeth added.

Sophia's expression was unreadable for a moment before she nodded slowly. "Elizabeth, I... I'll support you, but you must understand: this isn't a solution to all our problems. It's a new beginning—one that will demand hard work and sacrifice from both of you."

Elizabeth wiped her tears, mustering a small smile. "I know," she said softly. "I'm ready to try."

Sebastian added, "We're in this together. I won't let anything happen to Elizabeth."

Sophia's eyes, filled with a mixture of relief and cautious hope, lingered on Sebastian for a moment longer. "Then prove it," she said, her tone more measured now. "Prove that you're ready to take on this responsibility. I'll help you get started on the paperwork and set up some appointments for you two to see a counselor. I want you both to understand the challenges ahead."

Elizabeth nodded, feeling a weight lift off her chest. "Thank you, Mom," she murmured. "I promise we'll do our best."

The conversation drew to a close as Sophia stood up, her posture stiff but her expression softening ever so slightly. "I'll be in the office later to sign the papers," she said. "For now, I suggest you both get some rest. There's a lot ahead of you, and you need to be ready."

Sebastian and Elizabeth exchanged a glance—an unspoken promise that they would face whatever came next together. As they stepped out of the living room, the warm autumn air brushed against Elizabeth's cheeks, mingling with the bittersweet taste of hope and apprehension.

Later that evening, as she prepared for bed, Elizabeth found herself reflecting on the day's events. In the quiet of her room, she pulled out her journal and scribbled down her thoughts, trying to make sense of the tumultuous emotions swirling inside her. "Today changed everything," she wrote. "I'm scared, but I feel like there's a way forward—a chance to rebuild, to be heard, to be loved. A chance to leave this family forever."

As midnight approached, Elizabeth lay in bed, the soft hum of the air conditioner a constant reminder of the fragile peace that had been brokered that afternoon. She closed her eyes, imagining a future where the promise of a new life—one built on love, sacrifice, and shared dreams—could finally eclipse the shadows of their past.

For the first time in what felt like an eternity, the future seemed to hold a real glimmer of light. In that quiet moment, Elizabeth whispered to herself, "Tomorrow, we begin again." And with that, she drifted off into a sleep filled with both hope and the lingering ache of uncertainty, ready to face whatever challenges awaited her in this new chapter of her life.

❧ 94 ❧

A CHOICE DEFENDED

The house was alive with activity in the days following Elizabeth's engagement. Invitations were being sorted, venues discussed, and every detail of the impending wedding meticulously planned—at least by those who still dared to dream of a future together. Amidst the bustle, Sophia moved through the rooms with practiced efficiency, her smile tight and her eyes narrowing whenever the word "wedding" was mentioned. Elizabeth, however, could sense a storm beneath that thin veneer of control.

One quiet afternoon, while Elizabeth sat at the kitchen table reviewing the guest list, Sophia stepped into the room and picked up the phone. The sound of dialing echoed briefly before Elizabeth heard her mother's measured tone shift to something softer yet resolute. Elizabeth's curiosity mixed with apprehension as Sophia murmured into the phone, "Yes, Caleb, I remember... I understand." Elizabeth recognized the familiar warmth in the voice on the other end—Caleb, her mother's old boyfriend who had once been a steady presence during tougher times.

After a few moments, Sophia ended the call and set the phone aside. Then, turning toward Elizabeth with eyes that flickered with both determination and vulnerability, she said, "Elizabeth, I need to talk to you about something important."

Elizabeth's heart raced, and she set aside her paperwork. "Okay,

Mom," she replied softly, her voice betraying a tremor of uncertainty.

Sophia took a deep breath and, in a measured tone, began, "I know we haven't always seen eye to eye, and I know our family has been through more than its fair share of turmoil. But I've come to realize that there are decisions in life you must make—and sometimes, those choices come with consequences we have to accept." She paused, searching Elizabeth's eyes for a reaction.

Elizabeth's gaze fell to her lap. "What do you mean?" she asked, her voice barely above a whisper.

Sophia continued, "Your engagement with Sebastian, your decision to marry despite everything... It's a big step, Elizabeth. And I understand that you believe this is the right path for you. I want you to know that I may not always agree, but I'm willing to support you—if you're sure this is what you want." Her voice wavered, betraying the pain of past disappointments.

Before Elizabeth could answer, the phone rang again. Sophia glanced at it, then at Elizabeth. "It's Caleb," she said. "You need to speak with him."

Reluctantly, Elizabeth listened: "Elizabeth, I'm calling because I want you to know that marriage isn't the only path forward, especially when you're facing such life-changing circumstances. I care about you, and I believe you deserve the chance to explore every option."

Elizabeth's eyes widened, and she swallowed hard. "But... I want to marry Sebastian. I want to build a life with him," she managed, her tone a mix of defiance and pleading hope.

Caleb's voice softened. "I know you do, sweetheart, and that's why I'm not trying to take that away from you. But promise me you'll consider every possibility before you make a final decision. Your future is important, and I just don't want you to rush into something that might not be best for you."

Sophia looked at Elizabeth, her expression torn. "I'm not saying you have to change your mind," she said slowly. "But I want you to be sure you're ready for all the challenges ahead—raising a child, building a home, and facing the world on your own terms. I want you to have our support, but you need to understand what you're committing to."

Elizabeth's mind raced. The weight of Sophia's words, combined with Caleb's caution, stirred up conflicting emotions. She had always prided herself on her independence, yet here she was, on the brink of a life-altering decision that felt both empowering and terrifying. "I... I appreciate your concern," Elizabeth said, her voice trembling with restrained emotion. "But Sebastian and I have talked about it. We're ready to take this step together."

There was a long pause as Sophia's eyes searched Elizabeth's face. Finally, she sighed and said, "Then I will support your choice. But understand this: if you decide to go through with the wedding, you must be prepared for all that comes with it. And if things don't work out, you'll have to face the consequences of that choice."

Elizabeth nodded, tears glistening in her eyes. "I know, Mom. I'm ready," she replied, her voice firmer now, laced with fragile determination.

As the conversation ended, Sophia stood and moved toward the window, watching the late afternoon sun cast long shadows across the yard. Elizabeth sat quietly, processing the gravity of the discussion. She felt a strange mix of relief and sorrow—relief that her choice was finally acknowledged, but sorrow that it came with such painful reminders of past failures and betrayals.

Later that evening, Sebastian joined them in the living room. His presence brought a subtle shift to the atmosphere, softening Sophia's stern demeanor. "Hey, Elizabeth," Sebastian said gently as he approached her. "Are you okay? I heard what happened today."

Elizabeth looked up at him, and for a moment, their eyes met. "I'm okay," she said softly, managing a small smile. "I just... I had to make sure you knew how serious this is for me."

Sebastian nodded, reaching out to take her hand. "I know, and I promise you, I'm in this for the long haul," he said, his voice warm and sincere. "We'll get through whatever comes our way—together." Sebastian didn't tell Elizabeth about his conversation with Caleb earlier in the day; that was a secret to keep.

Sophia interjected, her tone firm yet not unkind. "I expect you both to be responsible from now on. This isn't just about a wedding —it's about building a life, and that means making tough decisions and facing them head-on."

Sebastian squeezed Elizabeth's hand reassuringly. "We will. We're not going to let you down."

The conversation shifted to practical matters as the family

began to discuss the upcoming wedding plans. Sophia produced a stack of wedding invitation drafts and a calendar marked with potential dates. "We need to finalize these details," she said. "I want everything perfect for the day."

Elizabeth listened, her thoughts a whirlwind of emotions. Amid the tension, she caught fragments of Sophia's voice—statements about tradition, responsibility, and family honor. It all seemed so heavy, yet somehow necessary. "Mom," Elizabeth ventured, "do you really believe this is the best way for me to move forward?"

Sophia's eyes softened briefly, revealing a glimpse of the pain beneath her stern facade. "I don't have all the answers, Elizabeth. But I do know that you deserve to make your own choices. I just want to protect you from making mistakes that will hurt you later."

Elizabeth's heart pounded as she replied, "I understand, but I need to follow my own path. Sebastian and I have a plan, and we're ready to face the challenges together."

A long silence followed before Sophia spoke again. "Then I will do my best to support you. But remember, if you ever need help or if things don't turn out the way you expect, you are on your own. You will be considered adults in the eyes of the law."

Elizabeth's eyes filled with tears, and she nodded. "I promise," she whispered. In that moment, she realized that her mother was serious about this being the last help she would give them.

That night, as Elizabeth lay in her room, the weight of the day's conversations pressed upon her. The quiet hum of the air conditioner and the soft rustle of leaves outside her window were a stark contrast to the turmoil of her thoughts. She thought of Sebastian's gentle promise, of Sophia's reluctant support, and of the uncertain future ahead. There was pain in her heart, a lingering fear of making the wrong choice, but there was also a spark of hope—a fragile belief that maybe, just maybe, this time she could shape her own destiny.

The next morning, the family gathered for a modest brunch before the wedding preparations truly began. Sophia had prepared a spread of fresh fruit, toast, and coffee, all arranged neatly on the dining table. Sebastian sat next to Elizabeth, his hand covering hers gently as they exchanged silent smiles. Sophia watched them, her expression unreadable, then finally spoke up.

"Today is about moving forward," she said, her voice firm yet carrying a note of wistful resignation. "We're not just planning a wedding; you're starting a new chapter in your lives. And I expect you to pull your weight."

Sebastian leaned in, whispering to Elizabeth, "We'll get through this. I believe in us."

Elizabeth nodded, a small smile tugging at her lips despite the lingering uncertainty. "I know," she murmured.

Their conversation continued over brunch, with Sophia occasionally interjecting reminders about the importance of responsibility and tradition. Elizabeth listened quietly, absorbing the words like a reluctant sponge. Deep down, she knew that this path would be fraught with challenges and sacrifices—but she was determined to face them.

As the day wore on, preparations for the wedding moved forward. Elizabeth found herself assigned small tasks like sorting invitations and managing the guest list, while Sebastian handled more substantial details. The couple's determination was evident, and despite the storm of emotions swirling beneath the surface, there was a sense of unity between them that gave Elizabeth a glimmer of hope.

Later that afternoon, Elizabeth sat on the back porch with Sebastian, watching the sun set over the horizon. The sky was a canvas of fiery oranges and deep purples, and for a moment, everything seemed possible. Sebastian broke the silence, his voice gentle.

"Elizabeth, do you ever wonder what life will be like after the wedding?" he asked, his gaze fixed on the fading light.

She turned to him, her eyes reflecting a mix of resolve and uncertainty. "I do," she admitted softly. "I wonder if all of this— everything we're doing—is really going to make things better. Sometimes I'm scared of what might come next."

Sebastian reached out, taking her hand in his. "I'm scared too," he said. "But I believe that together, we can handle whatever comes our way. We've made our choice, and I'm with you every step of the way."

Elizabeth squeezed his hand, the simple gesture grounding her. "Thank you," she whispered, feeling the warmth of his support soothe some of her lingering doubts.

Their conversation continued as twilight deepened, and the

promise of a future—though uncertain—shone softly between them. Elizabeth's thoughts drifted to the wedding, to the life she was choosing, and to the hope that maybe her family could mend its fractured bonds. In that moment, she resolved to embrace the journey ahead, to trust in the choices she had made, even if the path was strewn with thorns.

Inside the house, Sophia retreated to her bedroom, her face shadowed with a mixture of regret and determination. Though she had expressed her support, her eyes betrayed a lingering conflict—a worry that this new chapter might bring more pain than healing. She knew all too well the stakes of every decision, and as she gazed at the family photos on her dresser, a solitary tear traced down her cheek before she wiped it away.

The day ended with a quiet dinner, the family coming together in a tentative display of unity. Elizabeth felt both the weight and the promise of what lay ahead. In the soft glow of the evening lights, amid the clinking of cutlery and the low hum of conversation, she sensed that their lives were about to change irrevocably. There would be challenges, heartbreaks, and hard choices—yet, for the first time, Elizabeth felt a spark of possibility.

As she lay in bed that night, Sebastian's whispered "goodnight" still echoing in her ear and the weight of Sophia's expectations pressing down on her, Elizabeth made a silent vow. No matter how difficult the journey, she would face the future head-on. She would honor her choice, hold onto the support of those who truly cared, and carve out a life that was her own—even if it meant defying the past.

And as the darkness deepened outside her window, Elizabeth closed her eyes, allowing herself to believe that, somehow, this new chapter would bring them closer to the life they all desperately sought—a life where love, hope, and resilience would triumph over fear and doubt.

95

SECOND THOUGHTS ACROSS THE STREET

The morning after her confrontation with Sophia, Elizabeth awoke to a heavy silence that pressed down on her. As she lay on her thin, rumpled blanket, she stared at the ceiling and replayed every harsh word from her mother, every accusation, and every moment of anger. In that quiet darkness, a knot of uncertainty twisted in her stomach—a reminder of the weight of the choices looming over her.

Instead of sinking back into her bed, Elizabeth decided to step out. She needed the familiarity of a place where she could hear friendly voices instead of the echo of her own doubts. Across the street from Henry and Margaret lived Dave and Josh, childhood friends who had always been there to offer her a comforting beer, a shoulder, and a listening ear. Clad in a worn pair of jeans and a hoodie, Elizabeth slipped out the front door before Sophia could notice her absence.

The early morning air was cool, and long shadows stretched across the pavement as Elizabeth made her way through the quiet streets. She hesitated for a moment at the door of Dave and Josh's small, weathered house, then knocked lightly.

Dave opened the door, his eyes still puffy from sleep but softening when he saw Elizabeth. "Morning, kid. You look like you could use a pick-me-up," he said, stepping aside with a gentle smile.

Inside, Josh was sprawled on their battered couch, a half-empty coffee cup clutched in his hand. When Elizabeth entered, he quickly set aside the cup and motioned for her to sit. "Hey, Elizabeth. Everything okay?" he asked in a quiet, concerned tone.

Elizabeth managed a shaky laugh. "I'm... I'm alright. I just needed to get out for a bit. Got a beer?" she asked, trying to sound casual.

Without a word, Dave rummaged in the fridge and returned with a cold can of beer, handing it to her as he plopped down beside her. Elizabeth cracked open the can and took a small sip—not so much for the alcohol, but for the familiar routine that momentarily eased her troubled mind.

They sat in companionable silence for a few minutes, the only sound the soft hum of the refrigerator and the distant creaks of the old house. Finally, Elizabeth cleared her throat. "I have something I need to tell you," she began hesitantly, her voice barely above a whisper.

Josh leaned forward, his eyes searching hers. "What is it, Elizabeth?" he asked gently.

Her hands trembled as she took a deep breath. "I'm... I'm getting married. And I'm pregnant. But I'm not sure I'm doing the right thing." The words trembled out of her, heavy with fear and uncertainty.

Dave exchanged a glance with Josh before speaking softly, "Elizabeth, this is big. Do you want to talk about it?" His tone was earnest, inviting her to share more without judgment.

Elizabeth's eyes filled with tears as she sank into the couch. "I feel torn," she confessed. "On one hand, Sebastian's been good to me—he makes me feel safe, like I'm finally being treated like an adult. But on the other, I'm scared. I'm only seventeen, and I don't know if I'm ready for a marriage that feels more like an escape than a promise of love."

Josh nodded slowly, offering his support. "It's okay to be scared," he said softly. "Decisions like these aren't easy, especially when you're young. What matters is that you decide what you truly want for yourself."

Elizabeth sniffled. "I know, but every time I try to think about the future, all I see is chaos. I remember the fights at home, the fear, and now this... It's overwhelming."

Dave placed a reassuring hand on her arm. "You're not alone, Elizabeth. We're here for you, and you deserve to have your voice heard. Whatever you decide, it has to be what feels right for you— not what others expect."

They fell into a thoughtful silence, the weight of the conversation settling over them. Elizabeth sipped her beer, her mind swirling with memories of her mother's harsh words and the painful moments when her fears were dismissed.

After a long pause, Elizabeth spoke again, her voice steadier. "Sebastian... he's been there for me, always so gentle. I know there's a lot of uncertainty, but I think I want to marry him. I want to believe that we can build a life together—even if it's going to be hard."

Josh's eyes softened. "If you truly feel that way, then that's what you have to follow through with. Don't let anyone tell you otherwise."

Dave added, "Just promise us that you'll be careful, that you won't rush into anything you're not ready for. It's okay to have second thoughts."

Elizabeth nodded, wiping away a tear. "I promise," she said, though her voice trembled with a mixture of fear and hope.

The conversation continued for nearly an hour, with Dave and Josh offering gentle advice and sharing memories of their own youthful dilemmas. They didn't push her to change her mind; instead, they helped her explore her feelings, providing a small haven where her thoughts could unravel in a supportive atmosphere.

By the time the sun was fully up, Elizabeth felt a cautious sense of relief. Though the future remained uncertain, the kindness and understanding of her old friends had given her the strength to face what lay ahead. She wasn't entirely sure if marrying Sebastian was the right choice, but she knew that, whatever happened, she would have to live with that decision.

Dave looked at Elizabeth and smiled. "You know, Elizabeth, sometimes the hardest choices are the ones that define us. Just remember, you deserve to be happy." He placed a reassuring hand on her knee.

Elizabeth managed a small smile. "Thanks, Dave. I... I really appreciate both of you."

"You know," he continued, "I know how to determine if you wanna marry him," Dave said gently, giving her a nudge with his shoulder. He then pulled the hand on her knee up her thigh and between her legs and ran it up to her crotch. "Josh, lay her down," he continued, but his tone had changed from caring to determined.

Josh pulled Elizabeth down onto his lap and held her shoulders firm. Elizabeth knew she had to just give in, but in but in this moment she realized that Dave and Josh weren't really her friends. In that moment she knew she was going to marry Sebastian because he never forced himself on her, ever.

96

LIES

Elizabeth's heart pounded as she quietly stepped into Henry and Margaret's house—a modest sanctuary nestled across the street from Dave and Josh's. The early morning light had long faded, leaving her alone with the heavy burden of what had happened earlier at Dave and Josh's. She decided she wasn't going to tell anyone about the assault that morning, and every step she took was measured, each one an effort to keep her secret locked away. The only sound in the empty house was her own tentative breathing and the soft creak of the floor beneath her feet.

She made her way to the spare bedroom, where she planned to isolate herself, trying to steady her emotions. The events of the morning replayed in her mind in disjointed fragments—a touch here, a shove there—until she finally sank onto the bed, her heart heavy with unspoken pain. Before she could allow herself a moment of solace, the door to the room opened slowly. In the doorway stood Julian, his silhouette betrayed by the light from the bedroom window.

Julian's eyes, dark and unwavering, fixed on Elizabeth. "Elizabeth," he said in a low, measured tone that carried both authority and something like fervor, "we need to talk."

Elizabeth's pulse quickened. She hesitated, then sat up as he stepped forward. The room felt smaller, the air heavier with his presence. Julian closed the door behind him, ensuring their conversation would remain private.

"Do you remember the scriptures?" he asked, his voice soft yet insistent. He moved closer until he was standing right beside the bed. "You know, the Bible tells us that suffering refines us, that our trials are not without purpose. It is written that our hardships are part of God's plan for us."

Elizabeth's eyes watered. Every word of his sounded rehearsed—a mantra she had heard countless times in sermons, twisted now into something personal and invasive. "Julian... I'm not sure I understand," she replied cautiously, her voice trembling slightly as she tried to keep her tone neutral.

He reached out and gently took her hand in his, his grip firm and unyielding. "Elizabeth, listen," he murmured. "I have always tried to protect you. Everything I did—everything I said—was to show you that our union is preordained. God has laid it out for us. You are meant to be mine, in every way." His eyes bore into hers as he continued, "Marriage is not a mere formality; it is a sacred covenant. And you, my dear, are chosen by God to be my wife."

A shudder ran through Elizabeth. She pulled her hand back instinctively. "Julian, I... I can't. I'm still trying to make sense of everything that happened this morning. I'm not ready—"

He cut her off, his voice rising with a passion that bordered on desperation. "You're not ready because you haven't seen the truth yet. The pain you feel, the fear that clutches your heart—it's not punishment, Elizabeth. It's a sign, a call from God. He is telling you that we are bound together. Don't you want to be free from the fear you've carried for so long? Don't you want to be protected?"

Elizabeth's mind raced. Part of her—buried deep under layers of exhaustion and hurt—craved relief, a way to make sense of the chaos that had defined her life. Yet, the idea of binding herself to Julian with all his controlling justifications filled her with dread. "Julian, I... I don't know if this is what I want," she whispered. "Everything's so confusing. I'm scared."

Julian's expression softened, though the intensity in his eyes remained. "I know you're scared, Elizabeth," he said gently. "But think about it—when you were out this morning, when you came home looking like you had been defeated, didn't you wish that someone would make it all right? I want to be that someone for you. I want to be your shelter, your salvation."

Her breath hitched as she looked down and noticed a ring in Julian's hand—a token he'd purchased as a symbol of their covenant. "This is not just a ring," he explained, almost reverently. "It represents the promise God made, the assurance that our lives are intertwined. I have seen the signs, Elizabeth. I have seen them clearly. You are meant to be my wife."

Elizabeth's heart pounded erratically. Every fiber of her being screamed to run away from the oppressive weight of his words, yet there was a part of her that, in its weakened state, longed for any escape from the pain and isolation that had defined her recent days. "I... I'm so confused," she admitted, her voice breaking with a mix of defiance and sorrow. "How can I be sure that this—us—is what God truly wants?"

Julian stepped closer, lowering his voice so that only she could hear. "Because I have always been here for you, Elizabeth. Remember all those nights when you felt alone? I was there, even when you didn't notice. I know the Scriptures, and I know that God's plan for us is perfect. We are meant to heal together, to create a life that is sanctified by His love. I promise you, if you give me this chance, I will never let anything harm you again."

Tears welled in Elizabeth's eyes, blurring her vision. "But what about everything that happened tonight? What about the hurt I felt, the way I've been treated?" she pleaded, her voice barely audible. "How is that all part of God's plan?"

Julian's jaw tightened as he listened. "That pain—your suffering —it was not in vain. It was a trial meant to prepare you for what is to come. I know it sounds hard to accept, but you must trust that every hardship is a stepping stone toward a greater future. I am that future, Elizabeth. I can make you whole."

The room was silent except for the sound of their breathing, a deafening sound that haunted her. Elizabeth's mind swirled with a torrent of emotions—fear, anger, and a gnawing sense of betrayal. Yet, as she looked into Julian's unwavering gaze, she felt a small, bitter flicker of something like understanding. "I don't want to be hurt again," she murmured. "I want to be safe."

Julian reached out, his hand brushing against her cheek gently. "I will protect you, Elizabeth. I swear it. Our love is divinely ordained.

Don't you see? We are destined to be together, and by accepting this covenant, you will find the strength to overcome every trial."

Elizabeth pulled her hand away, shaking her head as if to clear it. "I can't... I can't accept this," she said, her voice trembling with a mixture of resolve and uncertainty. "I need time. I need to figure out what's right for me."

Julian's face contorted with a mix of frustration and hurt. "Time will only leave you wandering in the darkness," he retorted sharply. "Every minute you delay is another minute of pain. You owe it to yourself—and to the promise of salvation—to commit to what God has shown you."

Elizabeth's eyes filled with tears. "I—I'm not ready to decide my fate based on your interpretation of scripture," she whispered, her tone soft yet defiant. "I need to decide for myself what's right."

For a long, agonizing moment, Julian and Elizabeth stood locked in a silent battle of wills. The air between them felt charged, a fragile equilibrium teetering on the edge of collapse. Finally, Julian's expression softened into one of resigned sorrow. "If that is truly your choice, then I cannot force you," he murmured, his voice barely audible. "But know this, Elizabeth—I will not let you walk this path alone. I still care, even if you reject God's Word."

Elizabeth felt a lump rise in her throat as she stared at him. "I don't know what I want, Julian," she admitted, her voice quivering. "I'm tired, and everything is so confusing."

He stepped closer, his tone gentler. "I'm sorry for all the pain I've caused, for twisting everything into something unrecognizable," he said, his eyes glistening with unshed tears. "I only want you to be safe, to be loved. If you choose to leave me, you will rip my heart apart."

Elizabeth's mind raced as she tried to reconcile the person before her with the memories of abuse and the promises of protection. "I can't... I can't let you decide my fate for me," she whispered firmly, though her heart ached under the weight of his words.

Julian's eyes dropped as he reached out to slip his hands into Elizabeth's pants. "Feel my love for you. Do you feel that, right there?" He slid his fingers into her. "Do you feel God, right there?" Julian then continued to pull her pants off with his other hand and laid her down on the bed to show her God's love and reassure her of His plan for her.

As his thrusts became more fervent, he proclaimed more determinedly, "Feel God's love for us; can you feel it swell up in me as I give you His love?" Then, as he came inside her, he grunted, "There, we are married." He then slid the ring onto her finger and leaned down to kiss her vagina in a very unusual fashion for him. "I love you," he whispered between her legs, "I love us." He then rubbed himself once more. Elizabeth thought he was going to enter her again, but he didn't; he just got up and walked out of the room without another word. Pride was in his step, as if he had won a prize.

Elizabeth rolled over in the bed, her tears falling silently onto the worn sheets.

For what felt like an eternity, she sat there, processing every word, every promise, and every lie. The echoes of Julian's fervent declarations mingled with the pain she was feeling. "I am not yours," she whispered to herself, though the words felt empty against the backdrop of her turmoil.

In the stillness of the room, Elizabeth swore to herself, "Today, I learned that I must choose my own path," she whispered to the air. "I will no longer be bound by someone else's twisted interpretation of love or destiny. I am in charge of my own life, and I will decide what is right for me."

The tears flowed over the pillow, a testament to her struggle and her slowly emerging resolve. She vowed silently that, despite the chaos of the past and the tangled web of promises that had been made, she would find a way to rebuild herself. She would seek help, confide in someone who truly cared, and find the strength to break free from the shadows of the past.

With a final, resolute sigh, Elizabeth whispered into the quiet, "I will choose my own destiny." And though the road ahead was uncertain, in that moment, she felt a flicker of hope—a fragile spark of the freedom to decide her own future.

97

HONEST CONFESSIONS

Elizabeth woke the next day with her heart still heavy from the events of the previous morning. The cool Arizona morning light filtered through the window of her small room, casting long shadows over scattered textbooks and notebooks. Today was meant to be a turning point—a day for clarity before the future could unfold. Though she had already spoken to Sebastian about many difficult truths in the past, she knew that what had happened the previous morning with Dave, Josh, and Julian needed another airing. It was a confession she had been dreading yet felt compelled to share if their life together was ever to be truly honest.

After a hurried breakfast, Elizabeth arranged to meet Sebastian at the local park—a quiet, open space framed by clusters of juniper trees swaying gently in the early breeze. She chose a secluded bench beneath a large juniper, its gnarled branches providing an almost protective canopy. The park, with its muted sounds of rustling leaves and the distant laughter of children at play, offered the privacy Elizabeth craved.

When Sebastian arrived, he stepped out of his car with a tentative smile that warmed her despite the storm in her heart. "Hey, Elizabeth," he greeted softly, settling beside her. His eyes, earnest and kind, searched hers for a sign of her state.

Elizabeth took a deep breath and reached for his hand. "Sebastian, I need to talk to you about yesterday," she began, her voice quivering but determined. "Something happened, and I need you to know the truth."

Sebastian's expression shifted from curiosity to concern as he gently squeezed her hand. "I'm listening," he said. "Tell me everything."

For a few long moments, Elizabeth stared out at the horizon, gathering her thoughts. She explained what happened with Dave and Josh, "After I left Dave and Josh's place, I ended up alone," she said softly. "I felt so lost and scared, and then Julian—" Her voice faltered as her memories swirled painfully. "Julian did something terrible. He... he forced himself on me." The words broke free, raw and unfiltered. "I felt trapped and powerless. I didn't know how to say no, and I—I ended up feeling ashamed and confused."

Sebastian's eyes darkened with pain and anger. "Elizabeth, I'm so sorry," he murmured, his voice low. "No one should ever make you feel that way. I wish I could have been there to stop it."

She nodded, tears welling in her eyes. "I know you would, Sebastian. I know you care about me. But it happened, and I'm scared—scared that if I ever let it go unspoken, it will keep haunting me. I need to get it off my chest, even if it means reliving the pain."

Sebastian leaned forward, his voice gentle yet firm. "Elizabeth, your past doesn't define you. You are so much more than what happened. I want us to move forward together, but only if you're ready to heal and to get help. I promise I'm not going anywhere, and I'll do everything in my power to support you."

Elizabeth's eyes glistened with unshed tears as she replied, "I— I'm terrified, Sebastian. Every time I think about it, I feel this knot in my stomach. I was alone, and I felt so violated. And then, after all that, I was so ashamed. I'm worried that I'll never be free of it, that I'll always feel unworthy of love."

He reached out and gently brushed away a tear that had escaped. "Listen to me," he said, his tone soothing. "You deserve every bit of love and happiness. I want to help you find your strength again. We can get counseling together if that will help. I promise to be there for you, no matter what."

A small smile flickered on Elizabeth's face as she absorbed his words. "Thank you," she whispered. "I—I really need that help. I don't want to live in fear anymore. I want to move on from this nightmare."

Sebastian nodded, his eyes never leaving hers. "We'll take it one step at a time. I know you're only seventeen, and there's so much pressure on you, especially with everything happening so fast. But I'm here, and I believe in you."

The silence stretched between them, filled with the gentle rustle of leaves and the distant hum of the railroad tracks beyond the park. Finally, Elizabeth broke the quiet. "Sebastian, do you think... do you think it's possible for me to truly heal? To forget that night, to not feel like I'm always under threat?"

He squeezed her hand reassuringly. "I believe healing is possible, Elizabeth. It won't happen overnight, and there will be tough days. But I promise to walk every step of the way with you. You're not alone in this."

Elizabeth took a deep, steadying breath. "I want to believe that," she said. "I want to start over with you, without that constant terror. I'm tired of feeling like I have to hide everything."

Sebastian's expression softened further, and he offered a slight smile. "Then let's make a pact, here and now. We'll face our challenges together, share our burdens, and build a future where you can finally feel safe. I love you, Elizabeth, and I want to support you in every way."

Her heart swelled at his words, and she nodded, her voice barely audible. "I love you too, Sebastian. And I want us to have a future together—a real, honest future where I can finally be free."

They sat in silence for a while, the weight of the conversation mingling with the gentle warmth of the sun. The park around them, framed by the stately juniper trees, seemed to hold the promise of new beginnings. Sebastian broke the silence with a light-hearted remark. "You know, maybe we should get a little celebration going for this new start—something small, just us, maybe with a few close friends."

Elizabeth managed a small laugh. "I'd like that," she said. "But let's not plan anything huge right now. I need time to process everything."

"Of course," Sebastian replied, nodding in understanding. "We'll keep it simple—a quiet dinner with a couple of close friends. Something that reminds you that life can be gentle."

Elizabeth looked into his eyes, the sincerity in his gaze easing some of the turmoil inside her. "It sounds perfect," she murmured.

Their conversation continued, touching on practical matters. Sebastian asked, "Have you thought about the wedding today? Did you sort out the bridesmaids and their dresses yet?"

Elizabeth hesitated, then admitted softly, "I've been thinking about the wedding a lot. I was worried you wouldn't want to get married, so I kind of put it out of my mind for a bit."

Sebastian's grip on her hand tightened. "We can do all that together. Let's sit down today and hash out the rest of the details. The big day will be here sooner than you think. It's just a couple of days away."

Elizabeth felt a tear roll down her cheek, but she smiled. "Thank you, Sebastian, for everything."

He leaned in and kissed her gently on the forehead. "We've got this."

They spent the next hour walking slowly through the park, discussing plans and sharing hopes. The gentle breeze rustled through the juniper trees, carrying away some of the heavy doubts that had clung to Elizabeth the night before. Sebastian's quiet assurances mingled with the natural calm around them, forging a bond that felt both tender and unbreakable.

As the afternoon waned into early evening, Elizabeth and Sebastian returned to the park bench where they had started their conversation. The quiet murmur of other park-goers provided a comforting background, and the setting sun cast a warm glow over everything. Elizabeth felt the heaviness in her heart lighten just a bit, replaced by the promise of a new beginning.

Before they parted ways, Sebastian took one last look at Elizabeth, his eyes soft and earnest. "I love you, Elizabeth. I believe in you—and I believe in us."

Elizabeth's response was a whisper, yet it carried the weight of her hope and determination. "I love you too, Sebastian. And I'm so excited to be marrying you."

They embraced briefly before Sebastian walked away, leaving Elizabeth with a renewed sense of purpose and a promise of support. In that moment, Elizabeth realized that while the road ahead would be fraught with challenges, the truth she had shared was a necessary step toward healing. With Sebastian's unwavering support, she felt a spark of hope—a possibility of a life where she was no longer defined by her past but empowered by the choices she made for her future.

Elizabeth returned home with a lighter heart, each step echoing the gentle promise of new beginnings. The weight of her secrets was slowly lifting, replaced by the resolve to move forward, one honest confession at a time. And as she drifted to sleep that night, the murmur of the juniper trees outside her window whispered softly of the future—a future built on trust, healing, and love.

98

WHITE WEDDING

The little church sat on the edge of a sunlit field, its whitewashed walls and modest stained-glass windows glowing softly under the clear Arizona sky. Today was a simple wedding—a quiet gathering of family and friends, each face filled with tender hope for Elizabeth's new beginning.

Inside the church, rows of wooden pews were arranged neatly, the faint scent of fresh lilies mingling with the dusty aroma of old wood. At the front of the sanctuary, a small altar was adorned with pink roses and delicate ribbons that echoed the gentle hues of the day. The air was calm, the quiet punctuated only by the soft hum of the air conditioner and the rustle of fabric as guests shifted in their seats.

Elizabeth stood in the anteroom, her heart fluttering with anticipation and quiet resolve. She wore a pristine white wedding dress that cascaded gracefully to the floor, its lace and chiffon shimmering with every movement. Delicate pink roses were woven through her hair, a nod to the vibrant energy of the day. Though she had faced storms in her past, today was a promise—a promise of something new.

Across the room, three bridesmaids in mismatched pink dresses gathered in a loose semicircle. Each dress was unique—a splash of dusty rose, a vibrant fuchsia, and a soft blush—yet together they created a collage of joyful imperfection. They whispered words of encouragement to Elizabeth, their voices a soothing murmur amid the quiet excitement.

At the other end of the church, the groom and his groomsmen made their entrance. Clad in immaculate army uniforms that gleamed with discipline and honor, they marched in with measured steps. The groom's uniform, crisp and adorned with medals, contrasted sharply with the informal air of the celebration—a proud reminder of his service and the life he hoped to build. Their disciplined presence brought a sense of solemnity to the moment.

Henry, Elizabeth's beloved grandfather, waited by the entrance of the church. His eyes were warm behind thick glasses, and his weathered hands trembled slightly as he held a single white rose. Henry had always been her steady anchor, and today he had the honor of walking her down the aisle.

As the ceremony was about to begin, the chatter hushed, and a soft instrumental hymn began to play from the small sound system near the altar. Henry stepped forward, his voice gentle yet strong. "Elizabeth, my dear, come with me," he said warmly.

Elizabeth's heart swelled as she took his arm. "Grandpa," she whispered, her voice thick with emotion. Together, they began their walk down the aisle. The procession was slow and measured, every step echoing in the hushed church. Along the aisle, family members and close friends smiled softly at Elizabeth, their expressions a mix of pride and hope. Each step felt like a step away from the past and toward a future she was only beginning to imagine.

When they reached the altar, the minister—a kindly older man with kind eyes—welcomed everyone. "Today, we gather not just to witness a union, but to celebrate new beginnings, resilience, and love that endures despite the storms of life." His words floated over the congregation, soft and comforting.

Sebastian, Elizabeth's fiancé, stood tall beside the altar, his eyes never leaving hers. His expression was a portrait of quiet determination and gentle adoration. As Elizabeth approached, Sebastian's smile widened, and for a brief moment, all the weight of her past faded away in the brightness of his gaze.

The ceremony unfolded in a series of heartfelt exchanges and simple vows. Sebastian reached for Elizabeth's hand, his voice steady as he spoke. "Elizabeth, I promise to stand by you, to honor you, and to help build a future where your dreams take flight. I may not have all the answers, but I promise you this: I am here, and I will always be here for you."

Elizabeth's eyes glistened with unshed tears as she replied, "Sebastian, you give me the courage to face every day, even when the night is darkest. I trust you, and I trust that together we can create something beautiful."

Their hands intertwined, and the minister pronounced them husband and wife. A soft murmur of approval rippled through the gathered crowd. The bridesmaids clapped, and the groomsmen exchanged nods of respect. Sebastian leaned in and kissed Elizabeth gently—a tender promise of the life they would build together.

After the ceremony, the celebration moved to a small reception hall adjacent to the church. The hall was decorated with simple white and pink accents, echoing the theme of the day. Close friends and family mingled, sharing soft laughter and gentle conversation. The joyous atmosphere was palpable—a stark contrast to the hardships that had preceded this moment.

As the afternoon wore on, Elizabeth found herself speaking quietly with her grandmother, who had always been a source of comfort. "You look radiant, dear," her grandmother said softly, patting Elizabeth's hand. "Today, you are a vision of strength and grace."

Elizabeth smiled, though a shadow of uncertainty flickered behind her eyes. "Thank you, Grandma," she replied, her voice barely above a whisper. "It feels like... a new start."

Later, Sebastian joined them, his face alight with hope. "I can't wait to see what tomorrow brings," he said, his hand warm around Elizabeth's. "Together, we'll face whatever comes our way."

A few moments later, gentle laughter echoed from the corner where the bridesmaids were reminiscing about their childhood antics. One of them, a friend from high school, teased, "I remember when Elizabeth used to be so quiet. Now look at her—she's got a whole wedding's worth of wisdom in those eyes!"

The room burst into soft laughter, and Elizabeth felt a warmth spread through her—a sense that, despite everything, she was finally seen for who she truly was. The evening wore on with shared toasts, soft music, and a quiet promise that the future, while uncertain, held the potential for healing and love.

As night descended, the reception slowly came to an end.

Sebastian walked Elizabeth back to the car under a sky awash with stars. The gentle desert night was cool, and the juniper trees swayed softly in the breeze, framing the path ahead. They paused at the car, where Sebastian looked down at her with a gaze that blended tenderness and resolve.

"Elizabeth," he said quietly, "today was perfect, but this is just the beginning. I promise to always stand by you, no matter what. We have our whole future ahead of us."

Elizabeth's heart beat a little faster at his words, and she reached up to squeeze his hand. "I believe you, Sebastian. I truly do."

They drove off into the night, leaving behind the familiar church grounds and the echoes of their heartfelt vows. In that quiet car ride, with the stars above and the soft hum of the engine, Elizabeth allowed herself to hope for a future where the pain of the past would no longer hold her captive. Though the road ahead might be uncertain, she knew that with Sebastian by her side, every challenge would be met with love and determination.

As the car turned onto the main road, Elizabeth glanced at the dark silhouettes of the juniper trees lining the path, their branches swaying gently. They whispered of promises and new beginnings—a reminder that every end was a prelude to a fresh start. Elizabeth closed her eyes for a moment, feeling the comforting presence of Sebastian, and let herself imagine a life filled with quiet joys and lasting peace.

In that moment, as the night wrapped around them like a soft blanket, Elizabeth felt her heart lighten. The wedding, the vows, the simple, raw emotions of the day had carved a path forward—a path where every step was a testament to the strength it took to embrace love, to trust, and to move forward despite the scars of yesterday.

After several hours on the road, Elizabeth and Sebastian finally arrived at the hotel designated for their honeymoon. The atmosphere was light and joyful as they prepared for bed, both visibly exhausted after a long day's travel. Elizabeth excused herself to the bathroom, where she changed into a white satin nightgown that her mother had thoughtfully helped her select.

Upon returning to the bedroom, Elizabeth paused in surprise to find Sebastian already in bed. Uncertain of his intentions, she hesitated before reluctantly climbing in beside him. As she shifted to settle in for the night, a subtle unease stirred within her—she was not entirely sure what to expect.

Without a word, Sebastian moved closer, gently lifting the hem of her nightgown. In that quiet moment, Sebastian consummated the union of their marriage.

Elizabeth, in shock, never would have thought Sebastian would take from her, too...